Economic Survey of the Baltic States

The Reform Process in Estonia, Latvia and Lithuania

Brian Van Arkadie
and Mats Karlsson

This study was initiated by the Swedish Ministry for Foreign Affairs and undertaken by an independent team of experts in collaboration with the government authorities of Estonia, Latvia and Lithuania

Pinter Publishers
London

First published in Great Britain in 1992 by
Pinter Publishers Limited
25 Floral Street, London WC2E 9DS

British Library Cataloguing in Publication Data

A CIP catalogue record for this book is available from the
British Library

ISBN 1 85567 032 1

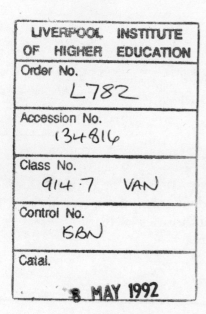
Typeset by Mayhew Typesetting, Rhayader, Powys
Printed and bound in Great Britain by Biddles Ltd, Guildford and King's Lynn

Contents

I Introduction

II An economic profile of the Baltic states

The Baltic region

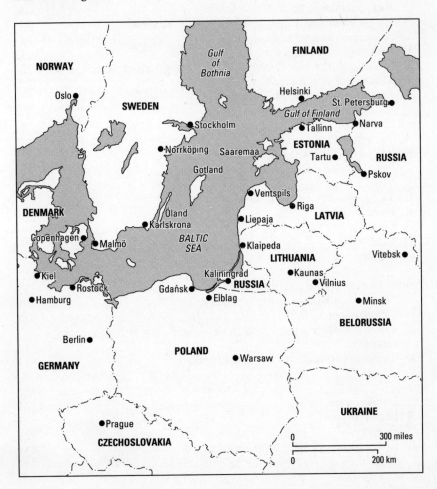

The Baltic states

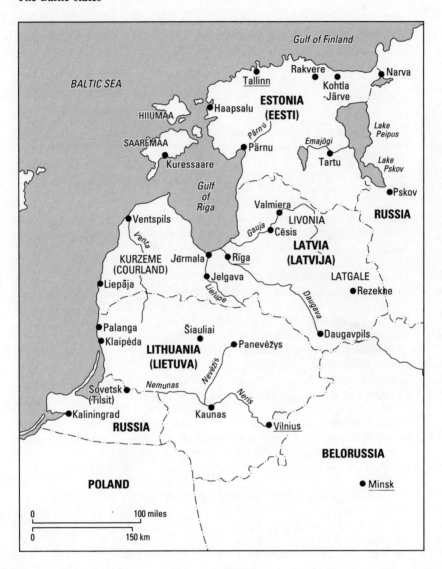

BALTIC SEA

Gulf of Finland

ESTONIA (EESTI)

Tallinn · Rakvere · Kohtla-Järve · Narva

Haapsalu

HIIUMAA

SAAREMAA

Kuressaare

Pärnu

Pärnu

Emajõgi

Tartu

Lake Peipus

Lake Pskov

Pskov

Gulf of Riga

Valmiera

LIVONIA

Gauja

Cēsis

RUSSIA

Ventspils

Venta

KURZEME (COURLAND)

Jūrmala

Rīga

LATVIA (LATVIJA)

LATGALE

Rezekne

Liepāja

Jelgava

Lielupe

Daugava

Palanga

Klaipėda

Šiauliai

Panevėžys

Daugavpils

LITHUANIA (LIETUVA)

Nevėžis

Sovetsk (Tilsit)

Nemunas

Neris

Kaliningrad

Kaunas

Vilnius

RUSSIA

BELORUSSIA

POLAND

Minsk

0   100 miles

0   150 km

List of tables

List of figures

List of boxes

Members of the team

Note: subject area of member's main contribution is in parenthesis.

Brian Van Arkadie (team leader)
Economist. A graduate of London School of Economics and Berkeley, California, he has taught economics at Yale, IDS Sussex, Cambridge (where he was a fellow of Queen's College and director of the Latin American Centre), ISS The Hague and Dar es Salaam. He has worked as an economist for the British government, for the OECD and for a number of African governments. His most recent publication is an economic survey of Vietnam for the United Nations Development Programme.

Mats Karlsson (deputy team leader)
Chief Economist at the Swedish Ministry for Foreign Affairs, Department for International Development Cooperation. He has worked on economic and political transformation in developing countries and in East and Central Europe. He studied economics and humanities at the University of Stockholm and at academic institutions in Vienna and Prague.

Ilze Brands (Latvia)
Ph.D. candidate at the Department of Political Science, Columbia University, New York. She is a junior fellow at the Harriman Institute for the advanced study of the Soviet Union, Columbia University.

Peter Broch (transport)
Transport economist with a Danish consultancy firm. He has been project manager and economist at a number of infrastructural and industrial projects in the Middle East, Africa and South-East Asia.

Stuart Brown (external economic relations)
Assistant Professor of Economics, Georgetown University, Washington D.C. An expert on the Soviet economy, he has among other things specialised in intra-republican trade. He received his Ph.D. at Columbia University.

Philip Hanson (external economic relations)
Professor of Soviet Economics, Centre for Russian and East European Studies, University of Birmingham. He is the author of numerous books and articles on the Soviet economy, East–West trade and comparative economic systems. He is one of the few international economists with an extensive knowledge of the Baltic states. He is at present working with the United Nations Economic Commission for Europe.

xiv   *Members of the team*

Ardo Hansson (macroeconomic policy, Estonia)
Research Fellow at the World Institute for Development Economics
Research, Helsinki. He is Assistant Professor of Economics at the University
of British Columbia, Canada. His research has focused on the transformation of Central and East European countries and the Soviet Union. He has
previously written on the economies of the Asia–Pacific region.

Rudolf Jalakas (finance, Estonia)
Bank economist. Previously Chief Economist at the Svenska Handelsbanken,
he is now retired and acts as advisor to the Estonian government and banking sector. Mr Jalakas fled Estonia in 1944. He studied economics in Tartu
and Stockholm.

Anders Kreuger (Lithuania)
Head of the information office of the Nordic Council of Ministers in Vilnius,
on leave from the Swedish Ministry for Foreign Affairs. A specialist in Baltic
linguistics from the University of Stockholm, he has worked as interpreter
and translator in the Lithuanian language and acquired extensive knowledge
about Lithuania.

Bo Libert (agriculture)
Research Fellow at the Swedish University of Agricultural Sciences, Uppsala.
Previously agricultural counsellor at the Swedish Embassy in Moscow. He is
Doctor of Agronomy.

Alec Nove (history and institutional setting, agriculture)
Professor emeritus and former Director of the Institute of Soviet and East
European Studies, University of Glasgow. One of the foremost experts on
Soviet economy and history, he is the author of numerous books, among
others *The Economic History of the USSR*, *The Soviet Economic System*,
The Economics of Feasible Socialism and *Stalinism and After*. Nove is a
Fellow of the British Academy.

Susanne Oxenstierna (labour market)
Research Fellow at the Swedish Institute for Social Research, University of
Stockholm. She specialises in labour economics, specifically in relation to the
transformation of the East European countries.

Sirje Pädam (Estonia)
Graduate student at the University of Stockholm. At present living in
Tallinn, she has made several studies on energy, environment and geology
in Estonia.

Jürgen Salay (energy and environment)
Researcher at the Department of East European Studies, Uppsala University.
His research is focused on energy policy and environmental management.
His publications include a recent book on the environmental problems of
Eastern Europe.

Peter Semneby (Estonia)
First Secretary at the Trade Department of the Swedish Ministry for Foreign Affairs. He specialises in the economy of the Soviet Union and the Baltic states. He studied at the Stockholm School of Economics and at Harvard University.

Andrew Vickerman (Lithuania)
Economist. As a consultant to the World Bank and the UNDP he has written studies on the economic transformation of developing countries. He has served as Senior Economic Advisor to the Prime Minister of Papua New Guinea. He is a graduate of Queen's College, Cambridge.

Contributing experts from Estonia, Latvia and Lithuania

Ivi Proos
Adviser to the Estonian Council of Ministers on matters of economic reform. She has for several years worked closely with Prime Minister Edgar Savisaar. She is a Member of the Board of the Central Bank of Estonia and Assistant Professor at the Estonian Management Institute. She studied economics and sociology at Tartu University.

Aare Purga
Deputy Chairman of the Estonian Governmental Commission for Foreign Assistance. Previously economic advisor to the Ministry of Economy and a member of the 'IME project' (Economic Independence for Estonia). He graduated from Tartu University and received a Ph.D. in theoretical physics.

Uldis Osis
Deputy Director-General of the Latvian Department for Foreign Economic Relations. Previously economic advisor in the Council of Ministers. He has worked as a business consultant in the area of commercialising state enter-prises and establishing private firms. He studied in Leningrad and Moscow and received the degree of Candidate of Economy (Ph.D.).

Dalia Grybauskaite
Programme director in the office for economics and foreign relations in the Lithuanian Council of Ministers. Previously at the Institute of Economics (Ministry of Economics), she specialises in foreign trade, the creation of a stock market and privatisation. She studied in Leningrad and Moscow, where she received the degree of Candidate of Economy (Ph.D.).

Kestutis Zaborskas
Director of a 'Business Incubation Centre' in Vilnius and senior secretary of the Lithuanian Management Association. He was previously Director of the Institute of Economics (Ministry of Economy) and manager in several industrial enterprises. He studied engineering economy at Kaunas Technological University.

Acknowledgements

Many people, in the Baltic states and outside, contributed to make the survey possible. We are, of course, first of all indebted to a great many people in Estonia, Latvia and Lithuania. We thank the members of government, the government officials, experts and other people with whom we met. Without the time and information they so generously shared with us this study would not have been possible.

We wish to extend particular thanks to Gun-Britt Andersson, Assistant Under-Secretary in the Swedish Ministry for Foreign Affairs, who initiated the survey and whose ideas have been an important inspiration to us. We also wish to thank Dag Sebastian Ahlander, Swedish Consul General in St. Petersburg, and Lars Fredén, at the time Swedish Consul in Riga, whose knowledge, good contacts and support were indispensible during the work.

Particular thanks further go to Professor Michael Ellman of the University of Amsterdam and Per Sandström, formerly of the Stockholm Institute of Soviet and East European Economics, whose comments on the first draft were very valuable.

Preface

Estonia, Latvia and Lithuania have again achieved their independence. After half a century under Soviet rule, the three Baltic nations have restored their independent statehood. They now face the task of carrying out a profound transformation of their societies, establishing working democracies and opening up to the rest of the world. In particular, they face the formidable task of transforming their economies and integrating into European and world markets as three productive trading nations on the shore of the Baltic Sea.

This book surveys the economic situation and the reform process of Estonia, Latvia and Lithuania. Work on the study began when the team travelled to the Baltic republics in January 1991 when the political situation was extremely tense. The study was finished by mid-year, when independence was still highly uncertain. However, the study was written from the outset on the assumption that sovereignty would be restored to the three republics. Although the fast-moving events of recent months have changed the political context much faster than any of us really dared expect, the perspective we adopted now takes on more realism and, we hope, relevance.

The failed coup attempt in Moscow of August 1991 provided an opportunity for the re-establishment of the independence of the three Baltic states. During the uncertain coup days, Estonia and Latvia declared their full independence, Lithuania having done so at an earlier stage. Within days of the collapse of the coup, Baltic independence was recognised the world over, including by Russia and, later, by the Soviet Union.

The outcome of the coup not only secured Baltic political independence, but radically improved the possibilities of economic sovereignty as well. There are three main reasons for this. First, the Baltic states will now be able to establish the instruments crucial to economic sovereignty, for example an autonomous monetary system and their own trade regime, thus enabling the countries to pursue independent macroeconomic policies. Second, negotiations with authorities in Moscow on many issues, such as ownership of assets, access to infrastructure and transitional trade arrangements, should now be possible, though not necessarily easy. Third, real economic reform in Russia, Belorussia, the Ukraine — whatever political bodies will come out of the demise of the present Soviet Union — is now more likely and would in turn increase the economic options open to the Baltic states.

Whatever the longer term gains to be achieved from greater economic autonomy and reform, the short-term prospects are daunting. The economies will have to shift to a world market price footing. With the present composition of trade, this will lead to a very strained balance-of-payments situation. Oil and fuels, now received at very low prices, will become more expensive, without there being very obvious short-term prospects in raising export revenues. Estonia, Latvia and Lithuania have few natural resources; initial foreign exchange reserves are minimal; and growth of new exports will depend on structural change in the economies.

Assuming the Baltic states will be granted a short-term respite through foreign assistance and favourable agreements with the former Soviet Union, what are the medium-term prospects for Baltic industry and trade? The Baltic states do possess quite diverse economies — agriculture, food industry, forestry and wood industry, textiles and clothing industry, chemicals, manufacturing and electronics industry and an extensive transport infrastructure. However, the existing structure is adapted to the past requirements of the Soviet planned economy more than the future needs of trading in the world market. It is not easy to predict how the Baltic states will earn their way.

This is partly in the nature of things — market success is unlikely to be predictable in such a profound process of transformation. The difficulties of entering the world market are obvious. Will the countries of the European Community, already overproducers of agricultural goods, accept imports of butter and bacon again, like they did during the inter-war independence period? Will the Baltic states be able to compete in textiles, manufacturing and electronics with Korea and Thailand? Will they attract the extra dollar, mark or krona of foreign investment that would otherwise go to Mexico or Brazil or to the other Eastern European countries which have had a head start in reform? It will not be easy. However, they are small economies. If they can produce efficiently their exports could be readily accommodated in world markets. Ultimately, the economic fate of the Baltic states will depend on human ingenuity in response to the challenges and opportunities facing them.

Judging by the determination of the people we met in our work and the evidence of a small group of emerging Baltic entrepreneurs, we concluded that the Baltic states will find prosperous niches in the world economy. They will both be exporters and trading and service intermediaries across the Baltic Sea and between the vast Russian hinterland and the rest of the world. They would thus regain a thousand-year-old economic role in this northern part of Europe.

We concluded our study, therefore, with a belief in our minds that Estonia, Latvia and Lithuania will make it. The first task is for the government to put in place a new policy and institutional framework. This includes creating appropriate macroeconomic policy instruments, providing a relevant market-economic legal framework, and implementing the very difficult tasks of enterprise reform and privatisation.

After 50 years of Soviet domination, there is widespread support for economic change. However, that process of change will be difficult and much is uncertain, including the future of Russia and the other republics that previously made up the Soviet Union. The Baltic states will themselves have to resolve their own potentially divisive nationality and ethnic issues. And while there are widespread expectations regarding the eventual benefits of the market economy and integration into Western markets, there is little experience of the problems to be overcome in managing a market system.

Estonia, Latvia and Lithuania are today set on integration with the Nordic countries, the rest of Europe and the world. Membership of the United Nations and the international financial institutions, as well as direct links to the European Community, other international organisations and individual countries, will facilitate this process.

Technical assistance and, once fully-fledged economic reform programmes are in place, official financial assistance in various forms, will be forthcoming. However, the main impetus for change must come from the multitude of potential actors in the Baltic states and outside, who can create a new pattern of relationships with the rest of the world. Such a process could be impeded by the sad lack of knowledge about the Baltic nations elsewhere in the world.

This economic survey of the Baltic states aims to reduce that information gap. The survey is intended to give an overview for a broad audience of interested partners — governments, international organisations, businesses, non-governmental organisations and interested individuals. It reviews the economic structure of the three countries, past developments, present reform and future potential.

Initiative to undertake the study was taken by the Swedish Ministry for Foreign Affairs in the autumn of 1990. The initiative was welcomed by the Baltic republics, which agreed to give the study their support. A team, listed above, worked closely with Baltic officials and economic experts from 24 January to 22 March 1991. Five weeks were spent in the region, mainly in Riga, Vilnius and Tallinn. Three weeks were then spent in Stockholm writing the first draft.

Final editing was completed with significant contributions from Ardo Hansson and Philip Hanson. The survey was presented in Stockholm at a conference in June. Only minor editing has been made since the August 1991 events.

In undertaking its task the mission was confronted with a lack of reliable statistics and written documentation. On the other hand, the team benefited from informative discussions and close cooperation with a great number of individuals in the Baltic republics: to all of these the team wishes to express its deeply felt gratitude. It is our hope that the survey will contribute to a better understanding of the challenges of economic transformation that face Estonia, Latvia and Lithuania.

Responsibility for the content of the survey rests solely with the team leaders and the team members. Of course, views developed should not be taken to imply any particular view of the Swedish government, nor of the governments of Estonia, Latvia and Lithuania.

Stockholm and Dar es Salaam,
October 1991

Brian Van Arkadie
Mats Karlsson

I Introduction

1 The transformation of the Baltic economies

A. The forces for change

The Baltic states are on the verge of a profound economic transformation. The impetus to transform their economies comes from two sources: the drive for independence from the Soviet Union and the crisis in the Soviet economic system itself. The Baltic states have achieved their political independence half a century after their annexation by the Soviet Union under the provision of the infamous Molotov–Ribbentrop pact.

Political independence has economic implications. Political sovereignty is only meaningful if a minimum set of national economic institutions are created and the national government has control over sufficient economic policy instruments to pursue a national economic policy.

Independent Baltic governments might well, as a matter of national policy under normal conditions, choose to continue a high degree of economic cooperation with the Soviet Union. Also, of course, national policy-making will be constrained by the underlying economic realities. It has been noted that the Baltic economies have benefited from access to Soviet fuel at below world market prices. In turn, access to fuel has to be balanced against all the other factors which link the Baltic economies to the Soviet Union when assessing the costs and benefits of the existing situation and of possible changes. Nevertheless, it is inevitable that political independence will result in national governments taking the opportunities to change many aspects of the economy and, in particular, of external economic relations.

By the same logic, the Soviet Union, or its constituent republics, can be expected to pursue their own policies in relation to newly independent Baltic states, in light of their perceptions of their own economic and political interest. The consequences for the Baltic states of such changes in policy on part of its Soviet trading partners remain uncertain. For example, all analysis of the relationship with the Soviet Union is complicated by the extended crisis in the Soviet economy. The Soviet economic crisis and the attempts of authorities to reform the economic system have created pressures for change throughout the Soviet Union. As reform measures have met with little success, the Soviet economic crisis has deepened. As the system breaks down, the actors in the economy — households, firms and public authorities — increasingly pursue strategies at variance with official policies.

The dynamics of movement towards a more market oriented economy thus involve both the results of conscious policy choices by the authorities in command of the decision structure and the decisions of the actors in the economy, partly in response to the new opportunities created by reform and partly through spontaneous reactions to the breakdown of the old system such as through the growth of the parallel market and of barter trade. In a successful reform process, the actors in the economy are likely to be ahead of the official process of reform, accelerating the breakdown of the old system by circumventing its rules. The task of policy-makers is as much to accommodate spontaneous change as to initiate new activities. Moreover, increasing conflict between republic and union laws means that it is often far from clear what is the law. In the current reality of the Soviet Union, it is therefore of great interest to identify how the system really works for consumers, workers and the enterprise and to identify how it is changing in practice, whether in conformity with existing laws and official procedures or not.

Although the drive for economic reform in the Baltic states takes on urgency because it is associated with the political ambition to break with the Soviet system, the issues to be confronted in the reform process are in many respects no different than those arising in the Soviet Union or other centralised economies in need of reform. However, the options open to the Baltic states in seeking a more autonomous and liberal economic system will be affected by the pace and nature of the reform process in the Soviet economy.

B. National economic sovereignty

In considering the prospects for the Baltic states, one set of issues relates to the economic plausibility of the three republics operating as independent states, a basic objective of the process of economic transformation now under way.

Together the three republics have a total population of only 7.99 million people (1989), accounting for 2.8 per cent of the total population of the Soviet Union. As independent states they will be small, particularly in comparison to their eastern neighbour. However, in terms of population and income they are no smaller than a large number of countries that the world is used to accepting as nation-states. And, indeed, all three enjoyed a good degree of economic success in their period of independence between the two world wars, as described in Chapters 2–5.

It is, of course, a vitally important political fact that the three republics were independent states from 1918–20 to 1939–40. Lithuania had at one time been a sizeable power in its own right, until its union with Poland in the 16th century. Estonia and Latvia have no such traditions of statehood, having at various times been occupied by the German 'crusading' knights and the Swedes, before being incorporated, as was Lithuania, in the Russian Empire in the 18th century. The collapse of the Empire in 1917 was followed by the defeat of the Bolsheviks' attempt to take over the area — though at least in Latvia they did for a time have significant local support. Lithuania was in dispute with Poland, and the Poles took over Vilnius (the capital between the wars being in Kaunas). In fact, Lithuania had at that time no common border with the Soviet Union.

The three republics were economically cut off from their Russian hinterland: trade remained at a low level. However, in the 1920s all three were able to build up a sizeable trade with Western countries, exports being predominantly foodstuffs and raw materials. The three republics traded little with each other, and this still remains true today: they have followed a broadly similar path of development and their economies are not complementary.

Like the rest of the world, they were badly hit by the Great Depression but had largely recovered by 1938. While of course these were small and semi-developed countries, they were able to enter with fair success into world markets; Estonia and Latvia, for example, achieved living standards comparable to Finland's at that time. It is certainly the case that Soviet soldiers and officials who entered these republics in 1939–40 were astonished at the apparent abundance of goods and the living conditions of the peasantry.

While there is no evidence that the size of countries has an influence on prosperity, size does influence the appropriateness of choices of economic strategy. The smaller an economy, the more the need to trade. However, in the current world economy even nations the size of Britain or France find it efficient to maintain a high degree of openness to international trade. For nations the size of the Baltic republics, economic sovereignty will only be sustainable on the basis of an efficient integration into the international economy, implying a quite different set of strategies than the autarkic approach associated with Soviet central planning. Similarly, the high degree of openness necessary for economic efficiency is likely to constrain options in relation to fiscal policy, suggesting caution in the use of deficit finance and monetary expansion.

Some Western commentators addressing issues of reform in the Soviet Union have tended to emphasise the economic virtues of maintaining Union institutions, feeling that at a time in which Western Europe is moving further down the path to economic integration, splintering the Soviet economy into small units would be economically retrogressive.

However, politically and economically, integration between nations must arise from a perception of shared interest, involving not only an agreement about divisions of cost and benefits, but also a common acceptance that the larger unit has an economic dynamism to provide an attractive context in which to participate.

The national aspirations of Estonia, Latvia and Lithuania demand political independence; the degree to which political independence is followed by a commitment to a continuing high degree of interdependence with what remains of the Soviet Union will depend on the perceptions of the success of the reform process in the Soviet Union and the future of the Soviet economy. At the moment, the republics seem more concerned to guard against the consequences of policy failure and economic crisis in the Soviet Union than to reap future benefits relating to a successful, expanding Soviet economy.

Another issue addressed in this volume concerns the prospects for future cooperation among the Baltic states. Outsiders tend to perceive the Baltic republics as a unit and, indeed, there has been in the West a widespread lack of knowledge in distinguishing among the three countries (even in Sweden, one Swedish–Estonian member of this team has been asked at a public meeting whether he speaks Baltic!).

It is true that the Baltic states, sharing borders, have a shared historical experience largely because of their geographical location as a result of which they have been subjected to the same external influences. In the past two centuries they have shared the experience of subjection first to Imperial Russia and then, following the inter-war period of independence, to the Soviet Union. To varying degrees in earlier times they have been affected by German and Scandinavian political and economic expansion.

In terms of recent history in particular, they have shared the experience of being battered by international forces over which they had no control. Subjected to the Soviet Union as an outcome of the Molotov–Ribbentrop pact, they were then occupied by the advancing German army when war broke out between Germany and the Soviet Union, only to fall again into Soviet control as the Red Army repelled the Nazi invasion. And now geopolitics and the events in the Soviet Union have given the three republics the possibility of once again asserting their independence. How far does this shared fate provide a basis for future cooperation?

The immediate situation has certainly demonstrated the need for coordination and cooperation at the political level. Moreover, in future, geographical location is as likely to result in shared experiences as in the past. The position of the three republics might be seen as similar to that of the Benelux countries, relatively small neighbouring economies, whose fate is strongly influenced by the opportunities and pressures arising from a much more powerful neighbour.

However, while continuing cooperation between the republics would be desirable and can be expected, certain basic limits on the common nature of their interest should also be recognised.

While the concept of the 'Baltic States' is politically useful, particularly at this time, this should not lead to an unrealistic assumption of homogeneity. The national languages are not at all similar. Estonian (which is close to Finnish) belongs to a quite different family of languages than Latvian and Lithuanian. Estonia and most of Latvia share a Lutheran religious heritage, while Lithuania is predominantly Catholic in religion.

The balance between the majority national groups and minorities varies: ethnic Lithuanians account for 79 per cent, Estonians for 61 per cent and Latvians for only 52 per cent of their respective republic's populations. The natural growth rate of the Lithuanian population was historically more rapid than that of Latvia and Estonia.

The difference in the national composition of the population is reflected in the employment structure, particularly in industry. In 1987, 71 per cent of employees in Lithuanian industry were Lithuanian nationals, while comparable figures for Estonia and Latvia were 43 and 38 per cent respectively.

The existing economic linkages between the three republics are insignificant. As data in Chapter 7 indicate, there is little commodity trade between the three. In terms of external connections, physical proximity and linguistic compatibility has meant that the link with Finland has been particularly important for Estonia. The shared border with Poland may take on increasing economic significance for Lithuania in the future. Nor is it evident that the structure of the three economies is such that the growth of trade among the republics would be a salient feature of any spontaneous development under free-market trading arrangements.

The fate of the Baltic republics is currently linked by virtue of their common dependence on political developments in Moscow. In many respects they will face similar problems and options in the reform process. Therefore, it is appropriate to consider prospects for the three in one study. But they are also different from each other: their histories and their current reform processes have to be considered separately and any future economic cooperation will not spring spontaneously from existing economic links.

C. Transforming the structure of production

The period of Soviet rule had a profound effect on the structure of the Baltic economies. The Soviet occupation proceeded by stages following the Molotov–Ribbentrop pact. A start was made with sovietisation, including mass deportations of socially 'unreliable' elements, but the process was interrupted by the German invasion. German troops very rapidly overran the Baltic states and were not completeley defeated until capitulation came in 1945. The war did much damage to the economy, many were killed in massacres and fighting, and fear of the return of Soviet rule led to the emigration of large numbers of citizens.

The return of the Soviets was at first accompanied by promises of less severe policies (for example the peasants were to keep their land if this did not exceed 30 hectares), but soon there were still more deportations, nationalisation of virtually all private enterprise and forcible collectivisation of agriculture. Resistance lasted longest in Lithuania. Severe damage was done to national culture and traditions. The republics were in effect cut off from the rest of the world, and had to follow Moscow's bidding in all matters. Their institutions were altered to fit the Soviet pattern, and the Communist party, fully subordinate to the Central Committee in Moscow, was the only permitted political organisation. Key positions in party and state were held by Baltic nationals who had lived long in Russia.

The economic results were grim at first, especially in agriculture, and this in the context of generalised poverty in the early postwar years in the Soviet Union. In particular, Lithuanian and Latvian farming was severely damaged, not least by the deportation of most of the efficient farmers in order to break the opposition to collectivisation. Even in 1955 farm output in all three republics was well below prewar levels. However, the situation improved in subsequent years and the three republics achieved levels of productivity above the all-union average. At the same time, Soviet centralised investments in Baltic industry rose substantially, especially in Estonia and Latvia. Partly this was due to the comparatively well developed infrastructure (including hard-surface roads), partly to the availability of a skilled workforce, and partly as a means of russification: large-scale industry required an influx of workers from outside the republics. Industrial output rose rapidly; the following figures give a picture of rapid growth. For reasons familiar to

Table 1.1 Industrial production (1940 = 1)

	Estonia	Latvia	Lithuania
1950	1.4	1.3	0.8
1960	4.8	4.6	4.3
1970	11.6	11.4	13.0
1980	20.1	19.0	24.0

Source: Misiunas and Taagepera, 1983.

students of Soviet statistics, they must be regarded as exaggerated, but even allowing for overstatement the record is impressive, and compares well with that of other Union republics.

Many of the large heavy industry plants derived their materials from distant parts of the Soviet Union, producing specialised equipment (for example electric motors, diesel engines) which was delivered to other republics. Some small-scale workshops which existed in the inter-war years (for instance to make tools for agriculture) were closed. Consequently the republics' industries, and also their agriculture, were heavily dependent on intra-union deliveries which were administered by the central planning agencies.

As for trade with countries outside the Soviet Union, this was until recently a matter decided in Moscow, by the central planning organs, while the (all-union) Ministry of Foreign Trade and its trading corporations handled negotiations and signed contracts. Direct contacts with the West were next to impossible.

In examining the need for structural change, and the constraints on its achievement, two characteristics of the economies, inherited as a legacy of the Soviet planning system, stand out: the high degree of integration into the Soviet economy and the unbalanced industrial structure.

Soviet planning created an industrial structure characterised by large-scale production, dependent on inputs delivered from other large-scale enterprises, often over great distances from other parts of the Soviet Union and, in turn, supplying markets throughout the Soviet Union. This sometimes involved transactions between virtual monopolists and monopsonists, delivering and receiving in quantities and on terms determined by the command system of central planning.

The result is an industrial structure in each republic with a high degree of dependence on links with other Soviet republics for both supplies of inputs and markets for outputs. This means that dislocation in one part of the Soviet system quickly translates into production problems elsewhere — for many specialised intermediate goods the narrow range of producers (sometimes only one) means that there is little choice when an existing source of supply dries up. In a supply-constrained economy, it is shortage of inputs which acts as the constraint on production rather than insufficient demand.

In the short term, this degree of dependence will constrain the options open to the Baltic economies — it would be difficult to replace quickly Soviet sources of supply or to create alternative markets. By the same token parts of the Soviet economy are dependent on the Baltic republics, providing a basis for negotiating continuing trade. In the longer term, however, many of the inherited patterns of exchange will prove disadvantageous to one or the other side, as the economies face the opportunities and pressures of increasingly market-based transactions. In the longer term, how is the structure of industrial production likely to adjust?

Decisions about the location of production under central planning no doubt to some degree reflected planners' assessments of comparative advantage — the location of high-tech industries in the Baltic republics responded to the high educational and skill levels of the Baltic populations. However, other factors at play in the planning process meant that only to a very limited degree did the Soviet geographical pattern of production reflect efficient choices of location. After an extended period of adjustment to the market, the existing geographical pattern of production will be transformed and much industrial capacity is likely to become redundant.

In contrast to, and partly as a corollary to, the high degree of interdependence with the Soviet economy, the Baltic economies only have a very limited direct trading connection with the rest of the world. This results both from the autarkic ambitions of Soviet planning and the degree to which external trade has been centrally controlled through Moscow.

A critical task for the Baltic states will be the promotion of foreign trade. Not only are export earnings required to cover the cost of obvious 'essentials' such as fuel supplies and other basic intermediate goods but also to facilitate greater openness of domestic markets to imports. Increasing openness of the economy to imports would provide one stimulus to increasing the efficiency of domestic production.

The underlying potential for successful industrial transformation derives from the technical competence of the workforces of the Baltic economies. The relative sophistication of the Baltic economies in the Soviet context, as evidenced by the development of high-tech industries, could provide the necessary flexibility to adjust to the requirements of international trade. However, the relatively sophisticated nature of Baltic production also places it in a directly competitive relationship to international imports in the Soviet market.

The aggressive promotion of new patterns of international trade would require that the Baltic states control their external economic borders. At the moment they do not, and the possibilities for international trade are still limited by Soviet trade and foreign-exchange policy.

Another characteristic of the Baltic economies is the relatively high level of development of agriculture, in particular dairy and meat production. This could provide one basis for continuing trade with the Soviet Union, particularly if the implementation of agricultural reforms generates a further growth in productivity.

The weak development of the service sector and of small and medium-sized firms, characteristic of the Soviet economy, is carried over into the Baltic economies. While this is being corrected with the growth of new businesses, economic activity is still heavily biased towards large-scale industrial activity. This is unfortunate in a period in which the economies will need, above all, to respond swiftly to market opportunities.

On a more positive note, a shift from large-scale to small-scale industry and to service activities by and large involves movement into relatively less capital-intensive activities. Also, the existence of a substantial cadre of engineers and scientists may support fast expansion of some segments of the smaller-scale sector.

D. Enterprise reform

In the unreformed Soviet economy the dominant economic form is the state-owned industrial enterprise. Most of the more important enterprises have been controlled by an all-union ministry, some light industry has been under the control of the republic ministries and still other sectors fell under the joint jurisdiction of union and republic authorities. The agricultural sector has been dominated by collective farms and state farms.

In the Baltic republics as elsewhere in the Soviet Union, an important part of the industrial economy has been devoted to military production. This sector is of considerable potential economic significance, not only because of its size (which is a matter of dispute) but also because of the concentration of high-tech resources devoted to its activities.

Under the classic Soviet planning system, production was coordinated through a centralised command structure, emphasising quantity targets for output and input supply. Unlike a Western enterprise, financial constraint has not been critical in determining economic activity, nor has profit been a business objective.

The command economy worked inefficiently, but it could be argued that it worked and even, at enormous cost, delivered what was intended — military power and capital accumulation. The system has now collapsed. This has left enterprises like battalions in a defeated army, after the disappearance of its high command. The organisation within the enterprise remains intact. The informal web of contacts between enterprises, always more important for the operation of the planned system than its formal logic suggests, becomes even more important. But the high command is no longer there to issue instructions, to allocate key resources and to demand — albeit always with limited success — compliance with the plan. It is therefore not surprising that the boss of one large all-union enterprise in Tallinn, when asked who was *his* boss, answered that for the past two years he had had none!

Transformation will require a totally new institutional context which does not yet exist. In the Baltic republics, the creation of a new institutional environment has so far tended to be conceptualised very much in terms of the creation of new legal forms of ownership and control. Given the vacuum created by the collapse of the old system, this is of unquestionable importance. The need to specify a new system of ownership not only reflects a political or ideological choice but represents a practical necessity.

Ownership of the property located in the three Baltic republics involves two related, and difficult, sets of issues:

(i) What is to be done with the 'all-union' enterprises in the republics? They form the major share of the industrial and transport sectors and have, in the past, been 'owned' by parent ministries in Moscow.
(ii) What is to be done with publicly owned property under the control of the republics? How much is to be privatised, by what mechanisms and when? Even apart from the all-union enterprises, public (or collective) ownership in the republics accounts for a significant number of industrial enterprises, most agricultural land and most urban real property.

Thus, one important part of the creation of a new economic environment is through legal development of new forms of ownership to define a new pattern of property rights, including the disposal of some public and collective property and the legal reconstruction of the remaining public sector. However, legal rules are only one part of the 'rules of the game' which make up the necessary conditions for an operating market. Equally important are the economic conventions and sanctions which constrain enterprise behaviour. An autonomous public enterprise, faced with a real budget constraint, competition and market clearing prices, may take on many characteristics of a private business.

Similarly, a private business, enjoying a monopolistic position, with access to soft credit, faced with bureaucratic controls and a supply-constrained market may well behave like the worst sort of public enterprise.

Problems to be faced in creating 'market conditions' as a means of coordinating, stimulating and constraining enterprise behaviour in the Baltic republics include:

(i) the widespread lack of understanding of 'markets' as a market-clearing, price-determining mechanism;
(ii) the risks involved in freeing markets in the face of the monopolistic positions of many industrial enterprises; and
(iii) the difficulties to be overcome in creating market conditions for Baltic enterprises which do such a high proportion of their business within the Soviet economy.

Changing the behaviour of enterprises involves both a transformation of the external factors conditioning enterprise behaviour and a response from the organisation itself. How far can innovative, entrepreneurial responses be expected? Change in legal ownership and forms of control may in themselves stimulate new behaviour. Many of the Baltic intelligentsia see themselves as more 'Western', or even 'European', than the rest of the Soviet Union and therefore as more receptive to market-oriented business methods.

The specific competence of enterprise managers tends to be located in engineering or production skills. Knowledge often includes a sophisticated understanding of the gap between their own capacity and 'state of the art' Western technology. Also, it should be noted that such technical know-how has been supplemented by the experience of keeping enterprises in production under conditions of scarcity and systemic confusion, involving a high level of ingenuity and 'technical know-who' in relating to Soviet conditions.

However, despite the pool of management talent, the past environment has meant that the growth of some skills required for survival in a market economy has been stunted. There has been little need for the financial management expertise which will be required when enterprises have to work to tight budget constraints, for high ownership expectations for returns to equity and on credit markets with positive real interest rates and realistic collateral requirements. The conditions of a supply-constrained economy tend to lead to hoarding of input supplies rather than economising on inventories. A scarcity economy breeds little consciousness of marketing requirements, and concern for quality in design arises more from professional commitment than sensitivity to customers' requirements in a competitive market. Perhaps most dangerous is that the security provided by the planned economy environment can lead to inertia, resulting in slowness to adjust to new market conditions — which can and does prove fatal to businesses operating in a fast-changing market environment. In a broad sense, what will be required is a radical change in the business culture of the enterprise if the Baltic economies are to adjust to the sharp changes of conditions which are inevitable in the next few years.

The creation of new enterprises will be at least as important as changing the performance of existing bodies. The lop-sided structure of industry will need to be corrected. This has already begun, since 1988, through the creation of large numbers of new cooperative enterprises and is now proceeding with registration of new joint-stock companies as new legislation comes into force in the three republics. There will be a need for many small- and medium-scale firms to produce a wider range of commodities for the consumer, to seek out opportunities in external markets and to provide services and intermediate goods for the larger enterprises that currently undertake many activities in-house which might better be sub-contracted to outside suppliers. A large population of small firms will also provide a breeding ground for entrepreneurs, some of whom could be the large-scale producers of the future.

In the early stages of adjustment, businessmen are likely to find the greatest opportunities arising from the extreme disequilibrium of the economy, often by shifting commodities and assets from one use to another. In the current situation, such activity is often criticised — at worst it may appear as no more than an example of socially questionable 'black market' activities. At best trading is still accorded a low social status by the managerial and bureaucratic elite, encapsulated in the critical comment by one large enterprise manager that 'all that many cooperatives (that is, new businesses) do is buy cheap and sell dear' (presumably the reverse would be more socially desirable, if hardly a recipe for business survival). This sort of attitude is shared by those who accept the need for administratively established 'market prices' as an accounting device for orderly transactions between established enterprises but have no affection for the realities of market-clearing economic activity and no appreciation for the essential role in that process of the trader.

A fundamental difficulty for the creation of small enterprises is that access to inputs is still largely through the large-scale enterprises. In practice, many new firms are being formed by cannibalising disused equipment of state enterprises and acquiring by one means or another materials from the state sector. Not surprisingly, the mechanisms at work are often far from transparent and are open to the suspicion that at least some new businesses have symbiotic, if not parasitic, relationships to the state sector.

A robust interpretation of the realities of transition from a centralised command economy must recognise that at the early stages the dominant state-enterprise sector must be the main source of the resources needed for the development of new business. It is the repository of a pool of labour, not used to its full capacity as a result of disguised unemployment; it has an excess stock of equipment and underutilised buildings and receives the lion's share of available materials. The new sector must grow through the transfer of resources from the state sector, either by formal transfers of property, as provided for under the various privatisation processes, or by more informal mechanisms.

Given the past atrophy of the small-scale sector and suspicion of private business, its fast development will require a strong initial boost. A minimum requirement, not yet implemented by the Baltic authorities, would be an unequivocal commitment that new business is welcome in all lines of economic activity except for those which have been specifically excluded.

The requirements for enterprise reform are explored at greater length in Chapters 8 and 11.

E. Impact on the household

Transformation of the Baltic economies will have a deep impact on the economic life of individuals and households. The underlying objective of economic reform is to increase household incomes, widen the range of consumer choice and improve the quality of life. However, while economic reform will bring eventual economic benefits, currently, and to an increasing extent in the immediate future, the costs of economic crisis and transition to a new economic system are being borne by the household. Moreover, individual workers and households will have to adjust to new rules of the economic game just as much as enterprises. There will be losers as well as winners, and while a market economy can be expected to bring widespread benefits, it also carries costs when compared to the old economy, particularly in terms of job security.

Available measures of income suggest that the population of the Baltic republics receives income significantly higher than the Soviet average. By the middle 1980s, the three republics were above the general all-union level in consumption and in national income per capita, with Latvia and Estonia occupying the top two places. International comparisons of living standards are notoriously difficult, even between nations sharing similar economic

Table 1.2 Per capita national income (net material product, Soviet average = 100)

	1985	1989
Latvia	127	121
Estonia	121	119
Lithuania	103	110

Source: Goskomstat, Moscow; World Bank, 1990.

systems. Comparison over time is also tricky since salaries are not a very good indicator of real income levels — even the popular journalistic assess-ment based on 'the lack of goods in the shops' is not particularly revealing in a system in which a relatively low proportion of sought-after goods ever reaches the shelves of the shops.

However, the inhabitants of the Baltic republics do not compare themselves with Azerbaijan or Kazakhstan or with provincial Russia. Their point of comparison is Baltic: Helsinki, Stockholm, Copenhagen. By such standards not only are they very far behind, but they have lost ground in recent decades. It is not possible to give any precise estimate of how far behind they are. This is, primarily, a result of the artificial prices and frequent shortages encountered in the Soviet republics and also the generally much lower quality of goods as well as restricted choice. It is not appropriate to compare, say, the pay of a Finnish worker in Finnmarks and the Estonian worker in roubles and then to compare the prices in the respective countries. Purchasing power parity only has meaning if there is a real power to purchase. Now, with so few goods available, with a growing disequilibrium between demand and supply, the gap has widened.

Observation of the existing economic system suggests that one sense in which a movement towards a 'market economy' might dramatically change the nature of Baltic life is in relation to the means whereby households meet their consumption requirements. Currently, cash salaries do not play the same role as the basic determinant of real budget constraint and actual consumption levels as is typically the case for a household in a market economy.

The real income of a household is, of course, influenced by the level of cash income. However, a number of other factors compete for importance as determinants of household welfare. In a supply-constrained, price-controlled economy, cash does not necessarily result in command over goods; it is likely to be queuing (and contacts) plus cash that enables the household to acquire goods. Furthermore in much of the Soviet Union, including the Baltic republics, one form or another of rationing system controls allocation of some essential commodities. But there is also an array of other factors which determine the real consumption of a Baltic family which should be considered qualitatively at the outset even if the data is not available to make a quantitative assessment.

Housing rents and utility costs claim a much lower percentage of cash incomes than is typically the case in a market economy. Official access to housing does not depend on cash payments but on allocation based on queuing, the application of 'norms' for space and the patronage of the employer. Renting space unofficially can, on the other hand, be very expensive, while those owning (mainly rural) dwellings may find repair costs much higher than rents.

Scarce commodities are often distributed at the workplace. Access to sought after luxuries may be used as an incentive by the enterprise. Some things (for example entertainment and sports facilities) which are typically consumed individually or through the household in a market economy may be consumed socially through the enterprise or local community. This is not to say that non-market distribution of goods has been particularly fair or equal — the privileged access of the *nomenklatura* to scarce commodities is by now a well-known scandal of inequality. It does, however, indicate that wages cannot be used as a very revealing indicator of income levels or differentials.

Alongside the access to commodities deriving from position in relation to the formal organisational structure, informal networks remain important. One advantage indigenous urban dwellers have over immigrant populations is that relatives in the countryside may supply food. Likewise, in a supply-constrained economy, scarce goods may be allocated among friends and relatives before reaching the shop counter. Scarcity of goods in the shop is a source of difficulty and inconvenience for all, and may be a source of deprivation for some, but cannot, in itself, be taken as a straightforward index of lack of access to goods by the household.

Real income arising from employment thus derives as much from direct access to the goods produced by the enterprise, or goods procured by the enterprise for its workers, as from the formal cash income.

One consequence of the resulting lack of transparency of the system of distribution and entitlement is the great difficulty in analysing the incidence of any costs and benefits resulting from reform. An apparent inconsistency is often encountered between a spoken commitment to a movement towards the market in principle but an objection to market clearing prices and growth of open market transactions in practice. This derives from the fact that the existing system, for all its agreed weaknesses, nevertheless did provide access to benefits through well-understood mechanisms. Diversion of goods from the official allocation system to an open market must, in the short term, be at the cost of those who currently benefit from the system.

F. Macroeconomic issues

In so far as the planned economy has been typically supply constrained, and resources allocated by physical targeting, the instruments of macroeconomic demand management have not been part of the arsenal of government policy-makers. Demand has not determined prices or supply; excess monetary demand resulted in rationing or queuing rather than supply or price adjustments.

Moreover, the Baltic republics have been managed as a relatively minor part of the Soviet economy as a whole. Even those instruments of potential macroeconomic demand management which have existed — the banks and the planning agencies — have been centralised in Moscow. Republic institutions are, by and large, creatures of the union organisations, with only limited powers, acting more as a transmission belt for instructions from the centre than as loci for autonomous decision-making. As a result there is an absence of experience of macroeconomic management and little understanding of the principles and issues which will have to be faced in the formulation and implementation of autonomous macroeconomic policy.

In 1990–1, the macroeconomic issue coming most publicly into focus is the money supply. The excessive availability of roubles, an endemic feature of the Soviet system, reached crisis proportions. As the system of planning collapsed, the Union government expanded the money supply in an indiscriminate fashion, leading in January 1991 to an ineffectual effort at monetary reform and to the Soviet Prime Minister seeking scapegoats through either cynical or paranoic accusations that the Soviet system was flooded with roubles in a shadowy conspiracy by Western banks!

The overhang of roubles, churned out by the Union authorities, has posed a problem for the republics, including the Baltic republics. The rouble is not internationally convertible. Under conditions of repressed inflation, the excess liquidity flows about the system in search of scarce goods, such that ordinary consumers travel great distances in search of scarce items. In order not to supply scarce commodities to non-residents for increasingly worthless roubles, all manner of restraints have been introduced, including policing of internal borders to restrict the outflow of commodities, rationing of goods to the benefit of residents in particular republics and restriction of sales to non-residents. In other words, the rouble is increasingly losing usability internally and as such increasingly lacks the characteristics of a real currency.

Apart from any longer-term desires to create independent currencies as one of the usual attributes of sovereignty, there is an immediate need to create some form of monetary autonomy to protect the local market from the inflationary pressures emanating from the excess supply of roubles at the union level. That is, monetary autonomy is required not so much to provide national governments with opportunities to finance their activites through fiduciary money issue but to protect the national economy from pressures resulting from excess monetary expansion at the union level.

The options open to the Baltic republics in developing instruments of monetary policy are explored in Chapter 6. The monetary issue in turn relates to the government budget. All three governments are in the process of developing increasingly autonomous fiscal arrangements, involving the creation of new tax systems and the negotiation of fiscal agreements with the union authorities.

As they move towards economic sovereignty, the Baltic governments will also increasingly have to turn their attention to the management of their external accounts. As long as the economies have been integrated into the Soviet system, concern about external payments is limited and the instruments for influencing foreign exchange transactions have not been available. Without national currencies it is not possible to define an exchange rate for the rouble. Consequently trade and payments with the rest of the world have been controlled at the Union level.

In the recent past, external transactions have attracted the attention of a number of the union republics. There has, for example, been a concern to stem the outflow of scarce commodities in exchange for roubles. As there is no exchange mechanism to adjust the value of the rouble, control has been exercised by direct constraints on the cross-border flow of commodities.

The availability of convertible foreign exchange is crucial for many activities. Until now, foreign exchange has been obtained either by external transactions which by-pass the official centralised foreign-exchange mechanism or from allocations by Soviet foreign and banking institutions. In some circumstances the official regulations allowed enterprises to retain a percentage of the foreign exchange earned for their own use. Soviet allocation was made through decisions related to particular transactions rather than through a global allocation at republic level.

The governments of the Baltic states will seek to disentangle their own external accounts from the Soviet payments system. As the three governments have opted for the creation of national currencies, they will be faced with the task of managing the exchange rate between the new currencies, the rouble and the currencies of the rest of the world.

Management of the external account will not be easy. At the outset, the allocation of the stock of outstanding external obligations (the Soviet external debt) and reserves will have to be negotiated. The Baltic governments would expect to acquire control over the gold reserves of the predecessor independent governments held in Western Europe. The outcome of such negotiations will contribute to the determination of the initial reserve position.

Initially, management of the current-account situation will be dominated by transactions with the Soviet Union. In Chapter 7 the starting conditions for that trading relationship are explored in some detail. If the rouble were convertible internationally at a single exchange rate, the task of managing the foreign-exchange account would, in principle, be straightforward. An exchange rate would be set for the rouble in line with rates set for all other currencies. However, the rouble is not convertible and is at present subject to a multiple exchange-rate regime. Policy in relation to rouble transactions will therefore have to address two main questions: the rate (or rates) of exchange with the rouble and the degree of convertibility (on both sides) of the currencies acquired in transactions.

In relation to transactions with the rest of the world the three governments will be faced with a difficult dilemma. Given the initial weakness of the trading position and limited reserves, there will be good reasons to exercise controls over foreign-exchange transactions, as did most Western European countries in the aftermath of World War II and as do many developing countries today. Controls might be necessary because the governments might not be willing to accept the consequences of a free-market rate, particularly the inflationary pressures in the initial period when the instruments of domestic monetary and fiscal policy have not yet been developed.

However, there are many difficulties with maintaining exchange controls.

If the rate is set well below a market clearing rate there will be considerable excess demand for foreign exchange. Moreover, access to foreign exchange is likely to be a crucial constraint on implementing enterprise adjustment programmes in the transition period, while those who gain access to foreign exchange at the official rate are likely to reap rich rents under conditions of extreme disequilibrium.

Under such conditions, to place the allocation of the critically scarce resource under bureaucratic control is likely to be a serious impediment to the process of reform and liberalisation. It would, in fact, mean that one of the most crucial allocation decisions was not handled through the market, while the power of a key part of the government bureaucracy would be reinforced.

One powerful potential stimulus to the transformation of the structure of the Baltic economies and to improvement in enterprise performance could be exposure to foreign trade — the market opportunities on the export side and improved inputs and competition in product markets on the import side. Having that trade take place in a relatively free fashion at exchange rates which reflect the low supply and high demand for foreign exchange would both powerfully promote the nascent export sector and provide a degree of protection in the domestic market in the difficult transition period.

Therefore in exploring options for future foreign-exchange management, one objective should be that a significant, and growing segment of trade should take place under free-market conditions.

G. Pointers to the future

To conclude this introduction, a few points about the current situation should be emphasised. The Baltic states are at the beginning of a process. Economic reform is only just getting under way. Even as the three republics acquire their political sovereignty, there is great uncertainty as to how economic sovereignty will develop. Given the high degree of integration with the 'east', a great deal depends on what happens in Moscow, on the consequences of disruption (or recovery) of the Soviet economy. Meanwhile, the governments of the three republics have inevitably adopted an interventionist stance: on prices, on production and delivery obligations, on the movement of goods in and out of the republics even while the reform programmes emphasise the need to shift to a market economy with very much less state intervention. Control over money and credit is complicated by having to use the rouble, in the absence of any short-term alternative, when the rouble is not able to serve as a multilateral means of payment even within the Soviet borders, and all sorts of bilateral barter deals replace normal trade relations. A market requires an acceptable and accepted monetary unit which does not at the moment exist within the Soviet system.

The short-term uncertainties facing the Baltic states are enormous, both because of the unknowns regarding the political evolution of the Soviet Union and the disordered economic policy environment. However, in the longer run, economic prospects could be bright. In a worst-case scenario, in which independence was associated with maximum economic sanctions, prospects could be very grim indeed.

The very inefficiency of the existing economic system and past investment decisions, while posing a heavy burden for those now managing the economy, also leaves a great margin for improved performance if a more effective economic system is put in place. And while current economic relations with the Soviet Union are a source of tension and debate, a positive economic relationship can be envisaged for the future, in which the Baltic republics' geographical location and undoubted potential as a source of high-tech services and industry could provide a niche for the Baltic economies as an entrepôt, acting as an intermediary between the Soviet Union and the rest of the world, to the mutual benefit of the Baltic states and the Soviet Union.

From the point of view of the West, the economies of Estonia, Latvia and Lithuania could also serve a useful function as a gateway to the Soviet economy, given the knowledge of the Soviet economy in the Baltic republics, the relatively higher level of development of services and the geographical location.

Table 1.3 Basic figures for Estonia, Latvia and Lithuania, 1989

	Area (km^2)	Population (000s)	Density per sq. km.	Share of titular nationality (%)	Share of national minorities (%)	
Estonia	45,100	1,583	35.1	61.5	Russians	30.3
					Ukrainians	3.1
					Belorussians	1.8
Latvia	63,700	2,687	41.7	52.0	Russians	34.0
					Belorussians	4.5
					Ukrainians	3.5
Lithuania	65,200	3,723	57.1	79.6	Russians	9.4
					Poles	7.0
					Belorussians	1.7
Soviet Union	22,403,000	288,624	12.9	–		–

Source: A Study of the Soviet Economy, IMF et al., 1991.

Table 1.4 Soviet Union: population, national income and share of trade, by republic

	Population (% of total in 1989)	National income (net material product, NMP) (current prices, % of total in 1988)			NMP per capita (roubles, 1989)	% of average	Deliveries to other republics (% of republican NMP in current domestic prices)	Exports abroad (% of republican NMP in current domestic prices)
		Total	Industry	Agriculture				
Estonia	0.5	0.6	0.6	0.7	2,780	119	66.5	7.4
Latvia	0.9	1.1	1.1	1.2	2,844	121	64.1	5.7
Lithuania	1.3	1.4	1.1	1.9	2,584	110	60.9	5.9
Armenia	1.1	0.9	1.2	0.7	2,102	90	63.7	1.4
Azerbaijan	2.5	1.7	1.7	2.2	1,621	69	58.7	3.7
Belorussia	3.6	4.2	4.0	4.9	2,764	118	69.6	6.5
Georgia	1.9	1.6	1.4	2.1	1,861	79	53.7	3.9
Kazakhstan	5.8	4.3	2.5	6.1	1,713	73	30.9	3.0
Kirghizia	1.5	0.8	0.6	1.3	1,297	55	50.2	1.2
Moldavia	1.5	1.2	1.0	1.8	1,968	84	62.1	3.4
Russia	51.4	61.1	61.9	18.0	2,794	119	18.0	8.6
Tadjikistan	1.8	0.8	0.5	1.2	917	39	41.8	6.9
Turkmenistan	1.2	0.7	0.4	1.2	1,363	58	50.7	4.2
Ukraine	18.0	16.3	16.7	17.1	2,104	90	39.1	6.7
Uzbekistan	6.9	3.3	2.3	5.2	1,069	46	43.2	7.4
Residual	–	–	3.0	4.4	–	–	–	–
Total	100.0	100.0	100.0	100.0	–	–	–	–

Source: The Economy of the USSR, The World Bank, December 1990; *Ekonomicheskoye i sotsialnoye razvitiye soyuznych respublik*, Goskomstat, 1990.

II An economic profile of the Baltic states

2 Lithuania

A. The origins of Lithuania

For Lithuanians, interpretations of their national history are an important input into contemporary national consciousness. Therefore an interpretation of the current political and economic situation of Lithuania should start with a brief account of its history.

Paradoxically, Lithuania, at the very crossroads between East and West, close to the great historical waterways that connect northern and southern Europe, has throughout its history been characterised by a certain isolation and even backwardness. Since the middle ages, Lithuania has continuously been striving to be a part of Western culture but it has always been lagging behind. The Lithuanians, a small but ethnically and culturally distinct people, are in the uncomfortable and often dangerous position of being surrounded by powerful and expansive neighbours — Russia, Germany and Poland.

It is believed that Baltic tribes, the ancestors of the Lithuanians and Latvians of our days, first settled in the swampy, forested region east of the Baltic Sea in the third millenium BC, replacing or assimilating an earlier population, probably of Finno–Ugric origins. Before the great eastward expansion of the Slavs, in the sixth, seventh and eighth centuries, Baltic tribes had long inhabited, admittedly rather sparsely, a vast territory best defined by drawing an imaginary line from Riga via Moscow, Kiev and Warsaw to Gdansk at the lower Vistula River. We have to rely on archeological and linguistic evidence to reconstruct this period, which saw the last flourishing of the ancient amber trade route between the southeast corner of the Baltic Sea and Mediterranean Europe, along with the emergence of a new powerful nation in the east, as Slavic, Baltic, Finno–Ugric and eventually also Scandinavian peoples mixed to form Kievan Russia in the ninth century.

To linguists, Lithuanian is known as the most archaic Indo-European language still in everyday use. It belongs to the Baltic language group along with Latvian and a few other languages now extinct, like Old Prussian, Curonian and Yatvingian. Grammatically, Lithuanian is similar to Sanskrit and Homeric Greek, and consequently it has been of great importance to the comparative historical study of the Indo-European languages.

The Baltic peoples definitely entered written history at the beginning of the thirteenth century, as they were confronted with German eastward expansion, camouflaged as religious fervour to baptise the last pagans of Eastern Europe. Despite several attempts to rise against the German knights, the peoples of Estonia, Livonia (more or less comprising the territory of present-day Latvia) and Prussia were definitely subjugated by the end of the thirteenth century.

In the southeastern parts of the Baltic lands, however, local chieftains united in the mid-1230s to fight against the intruding crusaders. This was the rise of Lithuania as a state under its first and only king, Mindaugas, who was baptised and crowned in 1253 with the recognition of the Pope. Christianity, prematurely introduced in a warrior society constantly in conflict with a more sophisticated enemy, was soon abandoned, and the king was deposed.

Throughout the fourteenth century, Lithuania was continuously at war with the Germans, and young knights from all over Europe were invited to participate in the so-called *Litauerreisen*, looting and burning of Lithuanian settlements and fortresses. The Lithuanians, of course, also made incursions on Prussian and Livonian territory. Towards the end of the fourteenth century, the Lithuanian 'warrior democracy', in which every man was both peasant and soldier, developed into a feudal structure as the warriors had to become more specialised and were allotted land and peasants to support them.

The Lithuanians' wish to liberate fellow Baltic peoples under German rule never succeeded; instead the Lithuanian leaders, the Grand Dukes, in the thirteenth century started expanding their territories to the east. Kievan Russia had been overrun by the Mongols by 1240, and the Slavic principalities chose to pay tribute to the Lithuanians rather than to the Golden Horde.

Lithuania, still officially pagan and still fighting the Germans along the lower Nemunas River, was gradually becoming a European power of some importance. The capital was moved to Vilnius in 1323, during the reign of Grand Duke Gediminas who also invited foreign traders and craftsmen, including Jews, to come and settle in Lithuania.

The Lithuanian Grand Dukes, looking for a way out of the perpetual struggle against the Germans, already seriously considered baptism but were long manoeuvring between orthodoxy and catholicism. Muscovy, after defeating the Mongols in 1380, became as much a threat as the Teutonic knights. To avoid a devastating war on two fronts, Lithuania chose to turn to Poland for support at the end of the fourteenth century.

In 1387, Grand Duke Jogaila (Jagiello in Polish) married the Polish crown princess. Lithuania entered a personal union with Poland and officially adopted Roman Catholicism. Jogaila's cousin Vytautas, who was in charge of the Grand Duchy of Lithuania, opposed the coalition. Under the name of Vytautas the Great he has become the national hero of the Lithuanians, first during the national revival in the late nineteenth century, then as part of the state ideology of independent Lithuania in the 1930s and now, once again, as a symbol of the Lithuanian struggle for independence from the Soviet Union. (Sometimes, his portrait hangs on the same nails that carried pictures of Lenin a year ago.)

The united Lithuanian and Polish armies virtually stopped the German eastward drive, the *Drang nach Osten*, in the battle at Grunwald-Tannenberg in 1410, and the crusaders never recovered from this defeat. Vytautas centralised the multi-national Grand Duchy of Lithuania and successfully waged war against Muscovy. At his death in 1430, Lithuania had reached the height of its power and stretched from the Baltics to the Black Sea.

The somewhat ambiguous personal union of Poland and Lithuania under kings of Lithuanian origins gradually developed into a real coalition between the two countries, dominated by the more Westernised but politically weaker Poland. In 1569, when the Jagiello dynasty was becoming extinct, a definite Polish–Lithuanian Union was signed in the town of Lublin.

Although according to the Lublin treaty, Lithuania and Poland had separate parliaments, governments and separate armies and were administrated separately and thus never become a fully centralised state, Lithuania was gradually polonised in the seventeenth and particularly in the eighteenth century. In this period, the word 'Lithuanian' meant a citizen of the Grand Duchy of Lithuania rather than an ethnic Lithuanian. In fact, the Lithuanian-speaking inhabitants of Lithuania proper, a territory roughly equivalent to the post-war Soviet republic in our century, were a minority in the Grand Duchy. By the early nineteenth century, only peasants and some of the smaller gentry of this region still spoke Lithuanian.

After the Lublin Union, the Lithuanian gentry was guaranteed the same privileges as their Polish counterparts. The extensive political rights of the nobility and the smaller gentry would eventually lead to the downfall of the union. After continuous wars against Russia over Belorussia and Ukranian territories and against Sweden over Livonia and the control of trade in the Baltic Sea, Poland–Lithuania finally became the victim of a coalition between Russia, Prussia and Austria at the end of the eighteenth century when its main long-time ally, France, was occupied with a revolution of its own.

The three partitions of Poland in 1772, 1793 and 1795 left the Grand Duchy of Lithuania largely within the Russian Empire. In the first decades of Russian rule, the situation for the Lithuanian peasants worsened. The social and economic differences between Lithuania and the Baltic provinces, which Russia had conquered from Sweden in the Great Northern War of the early eighteenth century, were accentuated when serfdom was abolished in Estonia, Livonia and Courland in 1817, helping to create an Estonian and Latvian petty bourgeoisie, engaged in trade and handicraft. There were practically no indigenous townspeople in Lithuania which explains the traditional dominance of Jews in most branches of trade. The fact that the ethnic Lithuanians almost exclusively engaged in agriculture may explain the origin of some of the negative attitudes towards business and trade that still prevail.

In 1863, the Polish uprising spread to Lithuania, but it was badly organised, and the Russians had no real problems in dealing with the insurgents. Although serfdom had officially been abolished in the whole of the Russian Empire in 1861, the implementation of this reform in Lithuania was not seriously begun until after the uprising in 1864. However, that same year also saw a ban on printing any texts in Lithuanian with latin characters, intended as a means of limiting the influence of the Roman Catholic church in the 'Northwestern Territory', as the former Grand Duchy was now called.

In the latter part of the nineteenth century, as the right to national self-determination was asserted throughout Europe, Russia was widely known as 'the prison of nations' and the Lithuanian 'national awakening' in the decades before and after the turn of the century is just one example of a national movement within the Russian Empire.

The development of nationalism was, in Lithuania and elsewhere, closely tied to the social changes taking place after the abolition of serfdom, as the Lithuanian peasants were given agricultural land and an economic differentiation among the peasantry became noticeable. The more well-to-do farmers sent their children to school, thus laying the foundations for a national intelligentsia. However, the ban on printing and primary education in Lithuanian, which was not lifted until 1904, made the consolidation of national culture considerably more difficult in Lithuania than in Poland, Latvia, Estonia or Finland.

In books and magazines printed on the Prussian side of the border and smuggled into Lithuania, the foundations of a national ideology, notably an ethnocentric interpretation of history, were propagated. Parents secretly taught their children to read and write in Lithuanian. National culture was also supported by the Lithuanian diaspora, which had emerged after the 1863 uprising, as deportations to Siberia were carried through and a massive emigration of Lithuanians to America began.

To achieve their goals, the Lithuanians created political parties, notably the Social Democratic Party in 1896. The Russo–Japanese war and the revolution of 1905 helped accelerate events throughout the Russian Empire, and in the periphery there was a pronounced shift in favour of self-government, from which the Lithuanians also benefited. In 1905 a 'Lithuanian Popular Parliament' convened in Vilnius to demand Lithuanian autonomy and free elections to a legislative body. The creation of an independent, ethnically Lithuanian state was not, however, an uncontested political objective. Among the Polish-speaking population, the generally supported idea was rather to restore the multi-national, though preferably Polish-dominated, Grand Duchy of Lithuania.

The decade following the first Russian revolution was marked by considerable economic and cultural dynamism in Lithuania, as the reforms put forward by the Russian Head of Cabinet, Pyotr Stolypin, favourably affected the economic activity of the peasantry. Moreover, the first Russian attempt at creating a parliament, the 'National Duma', brought about some political activity among the national minorities of the Empire, including the Lithuanians.

In the first months of the Great War, Lithuanian territory was affected by military action as part of the eastern front between Germany and Russia. In 1915, almost all of Lithuania was occupied by the Germans. Consequently, the struggle to achieve political independence had to be fought not against the Russian Tsar, but against the German Kaiser.

During the German occupation, the diaspora, both in Russia and in the West, actively propagated the idea of Lithuanian independence. After the Russian February Revolution, in the autumn of 1917 a Lithuanian Conference convened to elect an Executive Council, with the permission of the Germans. When the Bolsheviks had seized power in Petrograd in November, and peace negotiations with Germany in the city of Brest-Litovsk were being prepared, the Germans made an agreement with the Lithuanian Council to guarantee the independence of a Lithuanian state, closely tied to the Reich both militarily and economically.

However, as nothing much came out of the Brest–Litovsk negotiations, as far as the Lithuanian issue was concerned, on 16 February 1918 the Lithuanian Council unilaterally declared Lithuania an independent state. To make their intentions more palatable to the Kaiser, the Council chose the German Prince Urach of Württemberg to be King Mindaugas II, but this was soon revoked as the situation in Germany changed.

Although the Germans had capitulated on the western front, their occupational forces were not immediately withdrawn from the east. Indeed, the German military nurtured plans, which never materialised, for creating a German Baltic state stretching from Estonia to East Prussia.

The continued German military presence, as well as German help to the embryonic Lithuanian voluntary army, were instrumental in countering the invasion by the Bolshevik Red Army, early in 1919, to support a 'Soviet' government set up in December 1918 by Lithuanian communists operating on Moscow's orders. In January 1919, the 'Lit-Bel' Soviet republic of the reunified Lithuania and Belorussia was proclaimed, but by August the Red Army had been driven out of Lithuania, except for the Vilnius region.

The Poles, who had also regained independence in 1918, intended to restore the Polish–Lithuanian–Belorussian Union, a project which brought them into war with the Bolsheviks. During this war, on 12 July 1920, a peace treaty was signed between Lithuania and Soviet Russia, including Soviet promises to refrain eternally from any claims on Lithuanian territory and to acknowledge Vilnius as the capital of Lithuania. The Poles, however, regarded Vilnius as a Polish city and brought up the question of its status in the newly founded League of Nations.

In the town of Suwalki, a treaty was signed on 7 October 1920 according to which Vilnius was to be transferred to Lithuania. Two days later the Poles violated the treaty and seized Vilnius. After a short war between Poland and Lithuania, a cease-fire and a provisional line of demarcation were agreed upon after the League of Nations had intervened. This became the most well-guarded European border in the inter-war period, and the Lithuanian government refused to establish diplomatic relations with Warsaw until it was presented with a Polish ultimatum in 1938. Owing to the seizure of Vilnius by the Poles, Kaunas was made the capital of Lithuania.

The period of parliamentary democracy in the early 1920s was politically confused, and the party system insufficiently developed to be able to produce stable governments; still it was the years preceding the military coup of 1926 that saw the introduction of substantial economic reforms, notably the land reform of 1922 and the introduction of the Lithuanian national currency, the litas, that same year. Also, in 1923 the port of Klaipeda was transferred to Lithuania, after a coup had been organised against the French troops who were stationed there in accordance with the Versailles treaty.

After a military coup in December 1926, staged by army officers critical of the new moderately left-wing government, the leader of a small nationalist party, Antonas Smetona, became president. Smetona was the first Baltic leader to introduce an authoritarian regime, which lasted until the Soviet occupation of 1940. The nationalist party rule, supported by the paramilitary 'Iron Wolf' organisation, could certainly be characterised as a 'bourgeois party dictatorship', but except for the harsh crackdown on a strike by western Lithuanian peasants in 1935 and executions of communist activists, the Smetona regime never attained a level of brutality that would justify the accusations of 'Baltic fascism' put forward by the Soviets.

Despite the fact that independent Lithuania was one of the less-developed countries in Europe, considerable economic progress was made in the inter-war period. Under tsarist rule, Lithuania was an under-developed agrarian society dominated by large rural estates, and although agriculture still employed some 77 per cent of the population in 1939, most of the land had been redistributed to private farms specialising in the production of high-quality animal foodstuffs, particularly butter and bacon, for export to Western Europe. The economic policy of the Smetona regime encouraged the development of dairy farming and the raising of pigs, and great efforts were also taken to maintain a stable national currency sometimes necessitating compensation to farmers.

Although Lithuania was basically a free-market economy, a significant role was played by the government in partnership with powerful agricultural cooperative marketing companies. Until 1933, Germany was the main trading partner, but in the 1930s Lithuania reorientated itself towards the British market. With the exception of the food-processing industries, the level of industrialisation remained considerably lower in Lithuania than in Latvia and Estonia, and in early 1939 there were only about 40,000 industrial workers.

Throughout the 1930s, there had been some tension between Lithuania and Nazi Germany over the Baltic port of Klaipeda and its surroundings (in German, the *Memelgebiet*). After Austria and parts of Czechoslovakia had been added to the Third Reich in 1938, Lithuania was forced to transfer its only port to Germany on 22 March 1939. The Soviet Union had recognised Lithuania in 1920, since it did not wish Poland to become too strong. In 1926, a Soviet–Lithuanian non-aggression pact was signed. It was valid until the Molotov–Ribbentrop pact between the Soviet Union and Nazi Germany was signed on 23 August 1939. This marked the beginning of World War II since in a secret additional protocol Eastern Europe was divided into spheres of interest. Thus the Soviet Union became free to intervene in Finland, the Baltic states, eastern Poland and Moldavia.

After the joint German–Soviet attack on Poland in September 1939, Lithuania was forced to accept Soviet military bases on its territory on 10 October, and as compensation, Vilnius was returned to the Lithuanians by the Soviets, who had just seized it from the Poles.

On 25 May 1940, however, the Soviets accused the Lithuanian government of having kidnapped and molested Soviet soldiers, and on 14 June, as the Germans were launching their final attack on Paris, the Soviets presented Lithuania with a final ultimatum to dismiss the government and allow an unspecified number of Soviet soldiers to enter its territory. On the next day, 15 June, the Soviet occupation was effectuated. President Smetona escaped abroad and later died in the United States.

All power now lay in the hands of the Soviet special emissary to Lithuania,

Dekanozov, who set up a puppet regime and organised Soviet-style elections to a so-called 'People's Parliament', which declared Lithuania a Soviet republic on 21 July. On 3 August 1940, the Moscow Supreme Soviet approved the incorporation of Lithuania into the Soviet Union.

The Soviets immediately imposed their ideology on Lithuanian society, nationalising all industrial property and real estate, limiting private farm holdings and introducing socialist propaganda against the national bourgeoisie. Their 'destruction by the proletariat' meant the deportation to Siberia in June 1941 of some 34,000 of the political, administrative and cultural elite.

Violating the Molotov–Ribbentrop pact, the Germans attacked the Soviet Union on 22 June 1941. The Lithuanian resistance movement, which had been secretly operating during the Soviet occupation, set up a temporary government the next day, but the Germans, who entered Kaunas on 25 June, made no attempts to cooperate with it. Although at first the Germans were greeted with relief, almost as liberators, it soon became clear that they regarded the conquered Eastern territories only as a resource for labour and material supplies, and had no intention of restoring the independence of the Baltic states. Moreover, the Gestapo and the SS effectuated, during three years of occupation, the massacre of about 250,000 Lithuanian Jews, some 95 per cent of the influential pre-war Jewish community. The participation of some Lithuanians in these activities is one of the darker pages of Lithuanian history. However, the Lithuanians refused to set up a national SS legion. Only when the Soviets were approaching the Baltics once again, in 1944, did the Lithuanians agree to form military units, allegedly for self-defence, but when they were summoned to protect Germany they dissolved, retaining all their equipment. These armed groups of men, hiding in the forests, would later serve as the basis for resistance to the Soviets.

During the war against Germany, the Soviet Union never renounced its claims on the Baltics. Marching towards Berlin, the Soviet Army reoccupied Lithuania, entering Vilnius on 13 July 1944 and finally defeating German resistance in Klaipeda on 28 January 1945. An estimated 50,000 Lithuanians fled to the West at the end of the German occupation. When Soviet control in the Baltics was re-established, the structures of the first occupation were revived, and society sovietised. The post-war Soviet regime was for an exceptionally long period dominated by Antanas Snieckus, who was the leader of the Lithuanian communists from 1936 until his death in 1974.

There was strong resistance to the Soviets throughout the Stalinist period. Guerrilla warfare in Lithuania, involving a total of some 100,000 partisans, was, at least initially, more effective than in Latvia and Estonia.

In the first post-war years, there were attempts at achieving 'voluntary' collectivisation of agriculture by gradually pauperising private farmers. The next stage, which had had to wait because of the need for economic recovery after the war, was the forced collectivisation by means of mass deportations of peasants to Siberia. Seventy thousand people were deported in 1947 and another 70,000 in 1948, 80,000 joined the earlier groups in 1949. The remaining peasants, for fear of being deported, joined collective farms. Since this process was delayed by guerrilla activities, the collectivisation of

Lithuanian agriculture was completed only in 1952. It has been estimated that Lithuania lost more than 300,000 people in the first post-war decade as a result of deportations and armed resistance to the Soviets.

The reasons for collectivising agriculture, which brought about a disastrous decline in production and miserable conditions for the farmers, and for rapidly developing heavy industry, for which there was no material or human basis in Lithuania, were of course political, not economic.

In Lithuania there was a surplus of labour in the countryside to be employed in the new industries, and guerrilla activities deterred immigration. This is mainly why the Lithuanians are still in such a strong majority in their own republic, around 80 per cent of the population.

The Khrushchev era, and particularly the system of regional planning councils, which was created in 1957 and lasted until 1965, brought some economic benefits, and many of the comparative advantages in the standard of living Lithuania still enjoys are the results of local planning policies in the early 1960s.

From the late 1960s to the early 1980s, under Brezhnev's rule, Lithuania experienced the so-called 'period of stagnation' along with the rest of the Soviet Union, as the whole system was re-centralised and gradually wore down, held upright by an official ideology increasingly devoid of content.

Contemporary Lithuania is thus strongly influenced by its consciousness of national history, going back to its mediaeval glories and by the impact of the Roman Catholic church, which has survived the half-century of Soviet rule. Lithuanians also stress the interwar independence period and the degree of economic success then achieved. A half-century of Soviet rule and the economic system to which Lithuanians had to adjust in their day-to-day lives is, of course, also part of the historical heritage, leaving an imprint in terms of popular attitudes towards economic life.

B. Towards renewed independence

There is a primacy of politics over economics in Lithuania today. The Lithuanians have been more inclined to make bold political moves than to deal pragmatically with economic and other everyday matters.

On 11 March 1990, they confronted Moscow by declaring the restoration of the independent Republic of Lithuania, occupied by the Soviets fifty years earlier, omitting mention of any 'period of transition' for negotiations with the Soviet Union. A conflict between Moscow and Vilnius ensued, including the 'war of nerves' and the economic blockade of spring and early summer 1990, culminating with the violent events of January 1991. Violent confrontations continued up until the coup days of August, after which Russian recognition paved the way for worldwide recognition of the restored Lithuanian independence.

A brief look at the political development in Lithuania from the earlier years of *perestroika* until now, a period of rapid and thorough change, provides a background to the present situation.

In the first years after Gorbachev's entering office in 1985, the nationalities' issue received only limited attention in the Soviet Union. In the Baltics, protests against ecologically threatening industrial projects were among the first hints of the emergence of new attitudes towards the centre, and, in 1986 one of the earliest signs of *perestroika* in Lithuania was a campaign of protest against oil-drilling off the Baltic coast. The local communist leadership, however, remained solidly conservative.

Although the general political trends in the Soviet Union had some impact on Lithuanian society in 1987, in April 1988 Lithuania was still described as 'the last bastion of Stalinism in the Baltics'. Change was, however, under way among the intellectuals.

Perhaps their most important inspiration was the events in Estonia, where economic reform, aiming at self-sufficiency, had already been initiated and the 'Popular Front' was allowed to establish itself in mid-April. The visit to Vilnius by a group of Estonian economists at the end of May, along with the Communist Party's attempts at manipulating the Lithuanian elections to the 19th Party Conference in Moscow, was instrumental in the establishment of a group of reform-minded intellectuals. The Movement for Perestroika in Lithuania (in Lithuanian — Lietuvos Persitvarkymo Sajudis, or just Sajudis) was set up during a meeting at the Academy of Sciences on 3 June. Among its members, about half of which belonged to the Communist Party, were the musicologist Vytautas Landsbergis and the economist Kazimiera Prunskiene. In this initial stage, Sajudis was careful not to raise openly political questions, and instead, preliminary commissions were set up to address social, cultural, economic, legal and ecological problems.

Along with Sajudis, two other organisations emerged as politically important in 1988. The Catholic Church, which had been the major institutional alternative to Soviet rule in the 1970s, entered a more active phase. The Lithuanian Freedom League appeared in May, claiming to have been operative since 1978. The Freedom League was supported by some Lithuanian *emigré* circles initially suspicious of Sajudis because of its affiliations with the Communist Party.

Sajudis gained popular support during the summer of 1988, when a series of mass rallies was staged. At a meeting with the delegates to the party conference, the Communist Party Central Committee Secretary Algirdas Brazauskas addressed a crowd of some 20,000 people and was thus launched into a new political career. When the delegates returned from Moscow the 'Lithuanian national awakening' continued with another meeting attended by some 100,000 people. Brazauskas declared, on his own initiative, that the national flag would soon be legalised. The Lithuanians had now definitely entered the first phase towards ultimate independence from the Soviet Union, the revival of national symbolism on a massive scale. About 200,000 people demonstrated, waving the tricolor, in commemoration of the Molotov–Ribbentrop pact on 23 August.

By late August, Sajudis was already acting as a parallel power to the Communist Party. A wave of discussion on previously taboo subjects, such as the period of independence, the Molotov–Ribbentrop pact and the deportations, was unleashed. Among the questions raised was the concept of 'economic self-sufficiency' including republican control of resources and

taxes within the Lithuanian borders, recognition of private property, orientation towards the market and a stable, convertible currency.

The first violent conflict between demonstrators and militiamen at a
demonstration on 28 September proved that the authorities were unable to
re-establish their own order, and a joint Party–Sajudis commission was set
up to investigate the event.

In October, Sajudis was already enjoying massive popular support, despite
the fact that it, as it stated, was 'not a party, not an organisation, not an
opposition'. There was an increasing pressure on the Communist Party
leaders to resign, and on 19 October, First Secretary Songaila was replaced
by Brazauskas. The first Sajudis Congress on 22–24 October saw a virtual
explosion of national euphoria and the final establishment of Sajudis as a
mass movement, the equivalent of the Popular Fronts of Estonia and Latvia.

Although the Lithuanians are in a comfortable majority in their own
republic, they still have important ethnic minorities' issues to address,
particularly in and around the capital Vilnius, where only about 50 per cent
of the population is Lithuanian, about 22 per cent Russian and 18 per cent
Polish. Local Russians soon claimed to be frightened by the Lithuanian
'nationalism'. This called for a careful response from Sajudis, but the Polish
minority proved to be the more difficult problem. The relations between
Lithuanians and Poles had been tense since the discord over Vilnius in the
pre-war period. The Lithuanians generally resented the special treatment the
Soviets accorded the Poles in the early post-war period, and the Poles in the
Vilnius region, nowadays mostly collective farm-workers, resent attempts by
Lithuanian intellectuals to call them polonised Lithuanians.

Despite efforts to reconcile the minorities with the national movement, the
decidedly pro-Soviet *Yedinstvo* (Unity) organisation was established in
November 1988. Most Lithuanians saw it as entirely controlled by Moscow
and the armed forces, and it has failed to attract a majority of the non-
Lithuanian population.

Towards the end of October, Moscow signalled a tougher stand on the
Baltic issue. A proposal for changes in the Soviet constitution was put
forward to restrain the rights of separate republics and to make secession
from the Union virtually impossible. The Popular Front started collecting
signatures against the proposal, and in Lithuania some 1.5 million people
signed.

In this period of tension between Moscow and the Baltics, the Estonian
Parliament declared its republic sovereign *vis-à-vis* the all-union legislation,
with the right to nullify laws emanating from the centre. Lithuania, however,
lacked the political unity and preparation of Estonia on this issue.

After Brazauskas rejected the proclamation of Lithuanian sovereignty on
17–18 November, Sajudis took a more radical attitude to the Party, and
elected Vytautas Landsbergis as its president. He had originally taken a
moderate centre position on most issues, but, now just like the whole of
Sajudis, he became more radical.

On 16 February 1989, the Lithuanian national independence holiday was
officially celebrated for the first time since 1940. An obvious sign of
radicalisation in Lithuanian politics was Sajudis's public announcement of

complete political independence as the ultimate goal — with reference to the right of secession guaranteed by the Soviet constitution.

The elections to the new Soviet Parliament, the Congress of People's Deputies, that took place on 26 March 1989 were, in the spirit of *perestroika*, partially free, as some of the seats were contested by several candidates. In Lithuania Sajudis enjoyed an overwhelming victory. These elections were not only an obvious defeat for the Communist Party (two Sajudis candidates even stepped down to guarantee the First and Second Party Secretaries their seats), but also marginalised the Freedom League, which had opposed participating in any elections arranged by the 'occupiers'.

After the elections, the cooperation between the Party under Brazauskas and Sajudis intensified. The Lithuanian Supreme Soviet adopted a law on economic autonomy on 18 May 1989, along with an Estonian-inspired declaration of sovereignty.

In May–June, during the first session of the Congress of People's Deputies in Moscow, the Lithuanian delegates were among the most active, propagating liberal and national views. There were also notable instances of political coordination with the other Baltic republics. In July, the Baltic republics jointly managed to get Moscow's approval for economic autonomy, and on 23 August, on the fiftieth anniversary of the Molotov–Ribbentrop pact, some 1.7 million inhabitants of the three countries formed a human chain from Tallinn to Vilnius. There was a sharp reaction to this demonstration from the Moscow leadership, who drew a firm line at secession from the Soviet Union.

After negotiations during the summer and autumn of 1989, the Congress of People's Deputies finally adopted the necessary legislation on Baltic economic sovereignty on 27 November. The resulting law was a compromise, designed to allow republican control over the agricultural sector, most of the industrial sector, the state budget and the banking system, whereas the defence industry, the chemical industry, the energy supplies, inter-republican transport etc. were to remain under centralised Soviet jurisdiction.

In late autumn, the political interest of the Lithuanians was focused on the Lithuanian Communists' attempts to secede from the CPSU. The absolute indivisibility and unity of the Soviet Communist Party were stressed by Gorbachev on several occasions. This did not, however, stop the Lithuanian Supreme Soviet from abolishing the 6th article of the Soviet Lithuanian constitution which had institutionalised the power monopoly of the Communist Party.

The break between Brazauskas's party and the CPSU became definite on 19–20 December 1989, when the 20th Congress of the Lithuanian Communists voted for the establishment of an independent party. A small minority of delegates formed 'an autonomous LCP within the structures of CPSU' still loyal to Moscow. Brazauskas was re-elected as the First Secretary of the independent LCP. A new party programme was adopted, stressing Lithuanian independence and democratic values.

For the first time, a republican branch organisation had dared to break its ties with the indivisible CPSU. In Moscow, an emergency plenary session of the CPSU Central Committee proved incapable of deciding what measures the centre should take. The Soviet President then chose to visit Vilnius personally, and the whole style of his visit, on 11–13 January 1990, was curiously similar to an official trip abroad. In televised spontaneous conversations with ordinary people in the streets and factories Gorbachev argued against Lithuanian independence. Obviously, he had not fully understood the seriousness of the Baltic drive for independence, since he rhetorically asked an auditorium of intellectuals whether they truly intended to leave the Soviet Union. The resounding answer was, of course, 'yes'.

The first free multi-party elections in the Soviet Union were held on 24 February 1990 to replace entirely the Lithuanian Supreme Soviet. Since political parties were still very undeveloped, with the exception of LCP, and since Sajudis did not consider itself a party, people were supposed to vote for the political outlook of separate candidates. There was some confusion in the pre-election campaign, since both major political forces in Lithuania, Sajudis and the LCP, adopted political independence as the basis for their programme.

The candidates backed by Sajudis won an overwhelming victory, and soon adopted the strategy of declaring Lithuanian independence before 12 March, when the Congress of People's Deputies was scheduled to gather in Moscow and grant extended presidential powers to Gorbachev, as well as adopting a legal mechanism for secession from the Soviet Union. The Lithuanian attitude was that since Lithuania never joined the Soviet Union in any legal way, it need not follow the rules of secession from it but should instead restore its independence and statehood by a unilateral declaration.

Working around the clock, the election winners prepared for the first session of the new Supreme Soviet in less than a week, virtually ignoring the popular Brazauskas. On the eve of the first session of the new Lithuanian Supreme Soviet, Moscow demanded that the Lithuanians, if they were to secede, pay for all further deliveries of Soviet goods in hard currency. Claims were also made respecting border regions in southeast Lithuania and the port of Klaipeda.

On 11 March, at the first session of the new Supreme Soviet, Vytautas Landsbergis was elected its president, replacing his main opponent Brazauskas. The session went on to debate three documents re-establishing the pre-war independent Republic of Lithuania. In the first, the deputies were empowered to vote on independence, in the second, the name and coat of arms of the Republic of Lithuania were restored and the third document restored the independent state. The 1938 Lithuanian Constitution was declared still valid but was suspended and replaced by a hastily drafted interim basic law. With the abstention of six CPSU deputies, the Supreme Soviet of the Lithuanian SSR, henceforth the Supreme Council of the Republic of Lithuania, unanimously declared the restoration of the independent Republic of Lithuania.

From the very beginning the Lithuanian Parliament explicitly called for negotiations with the Soviet Union. On 15 March, Gorbachev declared the activities of the Lithuanian Parliament illegal and invalid, and he gave the Lithuanians three days to inform him how they planned to guarantee the rights and interests of the Soviet Union and of Soviet citizens in Lithuania.

On 17 March, the first unusual Soviet army activities were reported near the border between Lithuania and Belorussia. Both Belorussia and the Kaliningrad region of the RSFSR would later make claims regarding certain Lithuanian territories, but these were never enforced. Soviet military helicopters began hovering over Vilnius. The 'war of nerves' between Moscow and Vilnius had started, a conflict in which the Lithuanians had virtually no other means of defending themselves other than to be decisive and appeal to the world's, including the Soviet Union's, conscience.

Landsbergis replied in a telegram to 'His Excellency the President of the Soviet Union' that Gorbachev's assessments had 'no legal foundation' and that human rights in Lithuania were guaranteed by Lithuanian laws. Moscow answered by introducing restrictions on foreigners travelling to Lithuania and forcing the Lithuanians to suspend the setting up of an internal border and security force.

On 23 March, as the Parliament was holding an emergency all-night session, Soviet tank divisions entered Vilnius and drove past the Parliament building. Despite attempts in the last of March by the Lithuanian leadership to negotiate with the armed forces, Soviet troops and Lithuanian pro-Moscow Communists occupied a number of buildings in Vilnius, claimed by both the CPSU (Moscow) and the independent LCP.

The difficult conditions for Baltic conscripts in the Soviet army had long been a topic of heated discussion in Lithuania. After the Declaration of Independence, several hundred Lithuanian soldiers deserted the army and set off to hide in Lithuania. Some were caught and forcibly brought back to their barracks.

These first weeks of tension between the Soviets and 'independent' Lithuania helped to unify the Lithuanian people, and secured popular support for the newly elected Parliament. Many had initially been critical of the way independence was quickly declared and would have preferred a more cautious attitude. People also resented the way their popular Communist leader had to step down in favour of 'the musician', the victorious Sajudis president, and petitions were circulated in support of Brazauskas.

Although it was still too early to speak of a well-defined parliamentary opposition, there was considerable tension between the winners and losers of the elections, Sajudis and the LCP, in the days following the Declaration of Independence. Inexperience and hurt feelings were about to cause a major split, but the pressure put on the Lithuanians by Moscow reunited the Parliament, where democracy was still only in its infancy.

On 17 March, Kazimiera Prunskiene was elected prime minister. Brazauskas became deputy prime minister having earlier refused to become vice-president under Landsbergis. The number of ministries in Lithuania was reduced and by early April a new government had been formed. After a few weeks of uncertainty, on 13 April, President Gorbachev and Prime Minister Ryzhkov issued an ultimatum to the Lithuanian Parliament, threatening to suspend deliveries of goods that could be sold on the foreign market for hard currency if the Lithuanians did not, within two days, revoke all decisions adopted after 11 March, including the Declaration of Independence itself. Landsbergis maintained that all questions were negotiable except the Declaration of Independence.

The economic and political blockade of Lithuania began on 18 April, when the supply of crude oil to the refinery at Mažeikiai was completely cut off, and the next day natural gas supplies to Lithuania were sharply reduced. The rationing of fuel and energy was immediately announced. In addition to the energy blockade, railway transport to Lithuania of certain goods was also blocked, although this was never officially acknowledged by the Soviets. Unemployment and a decrease in production were already noticeable in the first weeks of the blockade.

A political debate started after Landsbergis received a letter, jointly written by French President Mitterrand and West German Chancellor Kohl in which they suggested 'a temporary suspension of the effects' of the 11 March declaration to facilitate the beginning of negotiations with Moscow, particularly when Gorbachev declared that the 'freezing' of the implementation of the 11 March declaration, rather than its revocation, would be a sufficient pre-condition to a dialogue with the Lithuanians.

After heated discussions in Parliament, the Lithuanians passed a resolution to freeze certain laws adopted after 11 March if negotiations with the Soviets were to begin, but it did not go far enough and was rejected by Gorbachev. Meanwhile, the economic effects of the blockade on neighbouring republics and territories were considerable, owing to the extreme interdependence of the Soviet system. The deadlock was finally resolved, after several rounds of talks between Moscow and Vilnius and after lengthy parliamentary debates, when on 29 June a decision was taken to introduce a 100-day moratorium on the Declaration of Independence from the start of bilateral negotiations. This symbolic step was obviously what Moscow needed to lift the blockade. On 30 June, crude oil supplies to Lithuania were restarted.

Estimates suggest a total loss of production by some 15 per cent as a result of the blockade. Still, the effects, however noticeable, were not as disastrous as might have been expected. Only about ten industrial enterprises had to be completely shut down, along with the natural gas-fired power plants. Of course, many enterprises had to reduce their production, but unemployment never exceeded roughly 3 per cent of the total workforce — or 58,000 people.

While reminded of their economic vulnerability, the Lithuanians were united in their support for independence, despite fiery debates on the moratorium and the beginning of political conflict between Parliament and the government. The blockade of Lithuania also worked as a catalyst for a shift to a market-orientated economy, although some critics now regret that more decisive measures towards economic deregulation, privatisation and price liberalisation were not taken during this period, when readiness to adapt to economic changes was obviously greater than under normal everyday Soviet conditions.

Along with the rationing, private trade in fuel from neighbouring republics and even from army supplies was thriving. The attempts to establish 'horizontal' trade and barter relations with sympathetic partners such as the

Leningrad and Moscow city administrations and the oil-producing region of Tyumen in Siberia later resulted in a series of bilateral treaties with different Soviet republics, towns and regions.

The Council of the Baltic states, a pre-war policy coordinating organisation established in 1934, was revived on 12 May. The Estonians had declared their independence on 30 March and the Latvians on 4 May, both including the notion of a transitional period for negotiations with Moscow to take place.

During the blockade, the new Lithuanian leadership called for, and got, massive popular support for the idea of independence. At the same time, there were obvious signs of discord within the leadership. The radical, Sajudis-backed deputies in Parliament launched continuous attacks on more moderate LCP deputies, particularly on Brazauskas, accusing them of treachery regarding the 11 March declaration. There was, however, a marked lack of political experience and administrative competence among these radical parliamentarians. This very soon also led to a conflict between Parliament and the government of Kazimiera Prunskiene, who accused the deputies of being incompetent and of meddling with the government's business. The government, consequently, was seen by many parliamentarians as a stronghold of Communist Party administrators, unwilling to implement any real change.

The conflict between Prunskiene and Parliament was highlighted by the discussions on the moratorium, during which Prunskiene repeatedly called for a Lithuanian *Realpolitik*, while being accused by some for betraying Lithuania in her dealings with Moscow. The Freedom League in particular staged a campaign against Prunskiene in the last days of the moratorium debate.

The difference in political style between Prunskiene and Landsbergis, as it emerged during the spring and summer, could be observed in their attitudes towards the West. Landsbergis on several occasions stressed the West's moral responsibility to stand by the Baltic countries and actively maintain their non-recognition of the Soviet annexation. Prunskiene advocated broader perspectives in foreign policy, as the one who had done the first round of travel abroad in early May to meet with Western political leaders. She called for more moderate expectations of support from the West.

The issue that dominated the autumn of 1990 was of course the attempts at negotiations between Lithuania and the Soviet Union. The Soviet delegation for negotiations with Lithuania was appointed in early July. It was to be headed by Prime Minister Ryzhkov. The Lithuanian leadership, inexperienced in the art of dealing with Moscow and not trusting its predecessors with negotiating the question of independence, delayed appointing an official delegation of negotiators. Instead, a preparatory committee was set up to create working groups of specialists in various fields.

The period of 'talks about talks' had begun. One reason high-level negotiations with the Soviets were not immediately started seems to have been the Lithuanian desire to make deals with the Russian Federation and to develop the 'horizontal' ties established during the blockade. A main political issue in the Soviet Union during the summer was the controversy between

Gorbachev and the newly elected Russian President, Boris Yeltsin. Yeltsin's readiness to begin talks with the Baltic republics on economic assistance and diplomatic recognition may have led the Soviet Union to soften its position on Lithuania, but it also possibly made the Lithuanian leadership, some say Landsbergis in particular, adopt a wait-and-see attitude.

In August, representatives from the Baltic, Russian, Belorussian and Moldavian governments, as well as the Leningrad and Moscow city councils, convened in Tallinn to investigate the possibilities of direct inter-regional economic cooperation. A Russian–Lithuanian agreement on economic cooperation for 1991 was signed. At this stage, there was even talk of the Russian Federation seceding from the Soviet Union.

Since the Lithuanian economy had been deteriorating after the blockade, the government introduced temporary measures to protect the inner market of Lithuania, providing for better economic safeguards at the Lithuanian borders to prevent basic commodities being taken out of the republic. A special buyer's card was to be issued to every resident of Lithuania.

Although the Lithuanians appointed a delegation for negotiations with the Soviets in late August, Moscow seemed to have lost interest in these talks, since the differences between Gorbachev and Yeltsin had temporarily been settled and the Gulf Crisis attracted the world's attention. Landsbergis also tied the beginning of negotiations to the signing of an initial protocol as a test of both parties' intentions. Still, two consultative meetings on future negotiations were held by the two delegations, headed by Ryzhkov and Landsbergis, in October. Negotiations were scheduled to begin at the end of November, and a joint group was set up to work out an initial protocol. However, Ryzhkov accused Lithuania of deliberately delaying the beginning of talks and of neglecting economic problems.

Heated debates on privatisation of property started in the Lithuanian Parliament. Opinions were divided as to whether all property should be returned to the former holders, but in the end this was the decision taken, on 15 November. The Prunskiene government, which recently had been accused of incompetence, corruption and inappropriate links with Moscow by right-wing politicians, presented an economic reform programme, but it was rejected in Parliament by a single vote on 22 November.

As the negotiations on the reunification of Germany were being concluded, the Balts stressed that the consequences of World War II would not be finally eliminated as long as the Baltic problem remained unsolved. A major objective in Baltic foreign policy during the autumn had therefore been to raise this question at the CSCE conference in Paris on 19 November. The foreign ministers of Lithuania, Latvia and Estonia were initially granted guest-participating status, but following a protest by the Soviets who threatened to walk out of the meeting if the Balts were allowed in, the three ministers were not readmitted.

The ousting of the Balts in Paris, without any substantial protest or action from the Western powers, has by many observers been considered a turning point in Moscow's attitude towards the Baltics. In late autumn, the relations between the Soviets and the Baltic republics gradually deteriorated. Gorbachev's new Union Treaty was conceived by the Lithuanians as an attempt to re-establish central control over the peripheral republics, and the Council of the Baltic States stated the firm resolve of its members not to sign it.

Despite the increased tension between Moscow and Vilnius over the Soviet military presence in Lithuania, the joint Soviet–Lithuanian working group met in the Kremlin on 30 November to discuss a protocol for negotiations. The Lithuanians insisted on defining future official talks as inter-state negotiations. No agreement was reached.

The next consultative meeting between the Soviets and the Lithuanians was scheduled to take place in mid-December, but it was put off until the Congress of People's Deputies had ended its session. At that session, Foreign Minister Shevardnadze announced his resignation, protesting against an anticipated military coup in the Soviet Union, and Prime Minister Ryzhkov was dismissed after he had had a heart attack. Many of Gorbachev's advisers, identified with *perestroika*, left office and were replaced by a new leadership.

Food prices had recently been increased in Latvia and Estonia but so far remained unchanged in Lithuania. Nevertheless, tension was building up in Vilnius during the events in Riga, where in the first week of the new year several buildings, including the Latvian Press Centre, had been occupied by Soviet armed forces, seemingly at the request of local Communists, loyal to Moscow. In this context, Prunskiene suddenly announced, on 6 January, a 320 per cent price increase for basic foodstuffs and a system of compensation that only covered half of the population. Landsbergis was notified that additional paratroopers were moving into Lithuania to enforce the military draft, since nearly 10,000 Lithuanian youths were avoiding conscription. These troops started arriving on 7 January.

Early on 8 January, a large crowd gathered outside Parliament to protest against the price increase and demand the resignation of Parliament in a manifestation arranged by the *Yedinstvo*. After Landsbergis had appealed on radio and television for people to come and protect their legal authorities, the pro-Soviet demonstrators were pushed away, but more than thirty *Yedinstvo* supporters had already made their way through the broken doors and had to be forced out.

At half-past ten in the morning, Parliament voted to suspend the price increases. Harsh criticism of the timing of this reform was delivered by many of the deputies. At one o'clock, Prunskiene left for Moscow to discuss the activities of the paratroopers with Gorbachev. Back in Vilnius in the evening, Prunskiene resigned with all her cabinet ministers.

Gorbachev issued an appeal to the Lithuanian Parliament, much in the style of an ultimatum, on 10 January. He required that all acts enforcing Lithuanian independence be revoked. Albertas Šimenas, an economist and Parliament deputy, was appointed new Prime Minister in the evening. Large crowds of Lithuanians were by now gathering to keep an all-night vigil outside Parliament.

The attempted Soviet military takeover in Lithuania began on 11 January. The Lithuanian Press Centre, with the only newspaper printing works in Vilnius, was stormed and occupied. Soviet military activity was also reported in other Lithuanian cities. In the afternoon, the pro-Moscow Communists announced, without disclosing any concrete names, that a 'National Salvation Committee' had been set up 'to take care of Lithuania's future'.

Thousands of people from all over Lithuania were now hastening to Vilnius to help guard the Parliament building, the radio and TV centre, the TV tower and the telephone station. Gorbachev promised not to use force, and the Soviet Federal Council, strongly against military intervention in Lithuania, decided to send a delegation to Vilnius the next day.

However, on the night of 13 January, later to be called 'Bloody Sunday', Soviet tanks and paratroopers attacked and occupied the Vilnius TV tower. Thirteen people were killed, several crushed by tanks swirling in the crowd protecting the tower, others shot by paratroopers. As the radio and television centre was stormed, the events were reported directly from the studio. At around two o'clock, the TV screens went blank, but the radio and television in Kaunas soon managed to get on the air, picked up by satellite and transferred to the world.

Paratroopers dressed in civilian clothes were expected to storm the Parliament building in the morning. The protecting crowd was growing by the minute as people rushed to 'Independence Square' outside the Supreme Council. Lithuanian Foreign Minister Saudargas, on a visit to Poland at the time, was charged with forming an exile government, if Parliament was overtaken by Soviet troops, but for some reason Parliament was never stormed. Later in the morning, the anonymous National Salvation Committee announced that a curfew had been imposed in Lithuania which the military would later deny.

On Saturday night, Prime Minister Šimenas had disappeared and therefore Gediminas Vagnorius was appointed instead of him in the morning. Most of Prunskiene's ministers had been reinstated. Simenas then reappeared at noon, claiming to have been detained by strange men while attending to the safety of his family.

Strong reactions to the violent events in Vilnius were already being expressed in the West, despite the fact that the main focus of attention was on the escalating Gulf crisis. Boris Yeltsin, the parliamentary president of the Russian Federation, also expressed his support for the Lithuanian leadership. Visiting Tallinn, he appealed to soldiers drafted from the Russian Federation not to participate in anti-constitutional activities against the legal Baltic authorities.

The parliamentary delegation from the Soviet Federal Council arrived on the 13th for talks with the Lithuanian leadership and representatives of the Soviet Armed Forces, who promised that military actions would be called off in the night if the protecting crowds withdrew from Parliament. Gorbachev and Soviet Defence Minister Yazov claimed, on Soviet TV, that they did not authorise the shooting in Vilnius, but that the decision had been taken by the commander of the Vilnius garrison.

The victims of the attack on the TV tower were laid out in the Vilnius Sports Palace. Enormous queues of people waited to honour the dead, and the funeral procession on 16 January became a massive demonstration of national determination. In the following week, the focus of attention in the

Baltics shifted to the tense situation in Riga and particularly the shooting that took place at the Latvian Ministry of the Interior on 20 January. Gradually, life in Lithuania returned to normal, although military patrols continued in the outskirts of Vilnius and the Vilnius–Kaunas motorway at night, killing a young man who did not stop his car at a roadside control.

In anticipation of the all-union referendum to help guarantee the signing of Gorbachev's new Union Treaty, Lithuania arranged a separate 'opinion poll' on 9 February, calling for the population to answer by yes or no the question: 'Are you in favour of an independent and democratic Republic of Lithuania?'

The results could only be described as a very convincing support of independence. Of all people entitled to vote 84.43 per cent actually made use of their right (roughly 2.2 million out of 2.6 million) and 90.47 per cent of these were in favour of Lithuanian independence from the Soviet Union. These figures indicate considerable support for Lithuanian independence even among the non-Lithuanian national minorities. Similar polls held in Latvia and Estonia on 3 March also resulted in substantial support for independence from the entire population.

The Vilnius shootings marked the failure of Soviet tactics to achieve a 'clean' military takeover by relying on the support of local Moscow loyalists and anonymous 'salvation committees'. The outcome of the Baltic opinion polls, although officially outlawed by Gorbachev, also indicated a shift in the attitudes of the non-Baltic population. It was no longer possible to claim that only a handful of 'separatists' were striving for Baltic independence.

C. Population, geography and natural resources

Lithuania has an area of 65,200 square kilometres. The republic borders Latvia to the north, the Baltic Sea and the region of Kaliningrad (formerly East Prussia) in the Russian Federation to the west, Poland to the south and Belorussia to the east and south-east. The total length of Lithuania's borders is 1,846 kilometres, of which 1,027 are with either the Russian Federation or Belorussia. The country is predominantly flat, part of the north-European plain, with the highest hill under 300 metres. The lakes in the north-east of Lithuania occupy 880 square kilometres. A temperate climate is typical of the region with a January average of one or two degrees and a July average of around 20 degrees; average rainfall is around 60 millimetres per month.

Lithuania's population was 3.72 million in 1990, with a population density of 57 per square kilometre. A major shift of population from the rural to urban areas occurred after the end of World War II. In 1939, 78 per cent of the population was rural; this proportion had fallen to 61 per cent in 1959 and 39 per cent in 1979; in 1990 only 31 per cent of the population lived in the rural areas. There are five cities with populations of over 100,000. The capital, Vilnius, had a population of 593,000 in 1990, followed by Kaunas (the capital in the inter-war period) with 430,000, Klaipėda (the main port in Lithuania and one of the largest ice-free ports in the Baltic) with 206,000, Šiauliai with 148,000 and Panevėžys with

129,000. The female proportion of the population rose significantly during and after World War II as a consequence of war deaths and deportations; 54.1 per cent of the population was female in 1959. This had fallen to 52.6 per cent by 1990. Compared to Latvia and Estonia, Lithuania is ethnically relatively homogeneous; 80 per cent of the population are Lithuanian, 9 per cent are Russian and 7 per cent Polish.

The natural population growth rate has fallen continuously in the last three decades and was 4.8 per thousand (0.48 per cent) in 1989; with a birth rate of 15 per thousand and death rate of 10.3 per thousand. Infant mortality was 10.7 per thousand in 1989, although the methodology used to calculate infant mortality differs from that of the World Health Organisation (WHO) and the reported figure will rise a little now that the authorities have adopted the standard methodology. The average age of the population has remained around 34 years of age during the last decade and life expectancy was 72.4 in 1988–9. The overall population growth rate has been boosted by a positive migration balance of around 20,000 people per year in the 1980s, mainly from the Russian Federation.

Like Estonia and Latvia, Lithuania has very few natural resources other than agricultural land and forests. The total land area is 6.52 million hectares, of which 4.63 million hectares are used for agriculture, 1.45 million hectares are forested and 444,000 hectares are used for other purposes. Small volumes of oil and gas have been discovered in Lithuania, and there are also limited reserves of peat and certain building materials: lime, sand, gravels and clays. There are no economically significant metal deposits in Lithuania. The virtual absence of substantial primary resource inputs make Lithuania's industrial sector heavily dependent upon other parts of the Soviet Union.

D. Structure of the economy

a. Structure of production

The net material product (NMP), or national income, of Lithuania in 1989 was reported as 2,478 roubles per capita. This is about 10 per cent above that of the average for the Soviet Union and somewhat below that of its Baltic neighbours, Latvia and Estonia. Lithuania's population was 1.3 per cent of that of the whole Soviet Union while its NMP in current prices in 1988 was 1.4 per cent of Soviet NMP. Estimate GNP figures for 1989 give a per capita GNP of 3,185 roubles. In dollar terms Lithuania's GNP per capita can be estimated to be a little higher than the Soviet average of $1,780 in 1989, but significantly lower than the World Bank estimate of Czechoslovakia's GNP per capita at $3,460 in 1989. However, these dollar GNP measures depend crucially on exchange-rate assumptions. Other social indicators show Lithuania to have higher life expectancy, lower infant mortality and a higher proportion of the labour force with higher education than the average for the whole Soviet Union.

The Lithuanian economic system is characteristic of a traditional Soviet-style centrally planned economy and its economic structure was developed as a component of the Soviet economy, particularly the north-western region of the Soviet Union with which it is fully integrated in terms of transportation and energy. In common with the rest of the Soviet Union, the Lithuanian economy is more socialised than other Eastern European economies. In 1988, according to one official data source, only 0.9 per cent of production was from the private economy. Official data underestimate the size of the private economy by including private agricultural production from private plots with the collective farm sector when this actually accounts for around 30 per cent of agricultural production or approximately 6 per cent of total output. However, the private sector is clearly much smaller than in Poland where, owing to its predominance in agriculture, the private economy accounted for some 30 per cent of GDP. The virtual non-existence of the private sector outside of agriculture has important implications for the process of economic liberalisation in both its economic and social aspects. A visitor to Vilnius was still in early 1991 immediately struck by the almost total absence of informal market activity and of private trading; even the number of private restaurants and cafés was still extremely limited.

According to official statistics, NMP increased by around 5 per cent per year during the 1980s in current prices and probably at around half this rate in constant price terms. If allowance is made for the underestimation of inflation in the official statistics then there may have been little or no growth in national income in the last decade. The growth rate declined in 1989 and, while comprehensive national income statistics are as yet unavailable, it appears to have fallen further in 1990 as a consequence of continuing uncertainty and the partial economic blockade of Lithuania by the Soviet Union following its declaration of independence in March 1990. Industrial production fell 3.2 per cent in 1990, while some other indicators show even greater reductions in the same year; for example, the volume of freight transported fell by 15 per cent. One senior official reported that national income may have fallen by as much as 10 per cent in 1990. Agriculture production reportedly fell by more than industrial production, and livestock numbers were reduced as a consequence of the shortage of feedgrain caused by the blockade and the problems of the Soviet supply system. Investment expenditure is also believed to have fallen sharply. Further falls in economic activity reportedly occurred in early 1991 in both agriculture and industry.

Table 2.1, which presents some summary economic data for the economy in the 1980s, shows that average salaries have been increasing faster than the growth of real output. This has been apparent throughout the Soviet Union in recent years and has been a major contributing factor to the creation of considerable excess purchasing power, or monetary overhang, in the economy as the availability of goods lags behind income growth. In 1990, despite the fall in industrial production and economic activity, incomes rose by 7 per cent resulting in a further accumulation of excess or involuntary savings. Household savings as a proportion of income almost doubled in the 1980s to 8.5 per cent in 1989 and reportedly rose further in 1990. Lithuanian household deposits are estimated to exceed 7 billion roubles; it is claimed that 5 per cent of the population hold approximately half of this amount.

Table 2.1 Lithuania: general economic data, 1980–9

	1980	1985	1986	1987	1988	1989
National income (m roubles)	5,867	7,514	7,922	8,280	8,913	9,145
(% change)			5.4	4.5	7.6	2.6
National income per capita (roubles)	1,717	2,116	2,212	2,289	2,439	2,478
Employment (thousands)	1,461	1,563	1,580	1,600	1,591	1,567
Average monthly salary (roubles)	166	190	195	204	223	241

Source: Lithuanian Statistical Yearbook, 1989.

The Soviet economy is characterised by a relatively small service sector, and data is not comprehensive for this sector, considered non-productive and is largely excluded from the calculation of NMP. To date there has been only very limited development of new private-sector activity in Lithuania, and in this respect it is lagging behind both its Baltic neighbours and parts of the Russian Federation.

Table 2.2 presents summary data on the composition of production in Lithuania between 1980 and 1989. The parameters of the economy were set prior to 1980 with little change having taken place since then. The major transformation of Lithuania's industrial structure occurred from the mid-fifties. The country was less industrialised than its Baltic neighbours in the inter-war period and, partly owing to the ongoing guerrilla struggle in the immediate post-war period, it did not really commence industrial restructuring, utilising the surplus labour force from agriculture, until the Khrushchev era. Industry currently accounts for a little less than three-fifths of total production with agriculture's share rising from one-fifth to a quarter over the past decade. These figures are in current prices, and the increased share of agriculture resulted partly from a shift in relative prices in favour of agriculture over the second half of the decade.

As shown in Table 2.3, the majority of industrial enterprises are in machinery, light industry and food processing. These also account for the bulk of industrial production; in 1989 the machinery sub-sector contributed 25.7 per cent of industrial production, light industry 20.8 per cent and food processing 21.9 per cent. The 12 per cent share of industrial production accounted for by the electricity, fuel and chemical sub-sectors reflects, in part, oil imports from Siberia to produce electricity, some of which is in turn supplied to other republics.

Labour productivity is higher in the Baltic republics and unit labour costs are lower than in the other republics of the Soviet Union according to calculations based on official statistics. This is seen as one reason for the relatively high levels of past investment by Moscow in the Baltics and the development of high-technology industries. This is an important basis for future development in Lithuania if industry can also show sufficient ability to adapt to the pressures of competition and the requirements of the world market.

Table 2.2 Lithuania: composition of gross production, 1980–9 (current prices, million roubles)

	1980	1985	1989
Industry	9,335.5	11,074.3	13,663.9
share %	60.0	54.9	56.3
Agriculture	3,039.9	4,775.1	5,565.3
share %	19.5	23.7	22.9
Construction	1,449.7	2,065.6	2,422.6
share %	9.3	10.2	10.0
Transport, communication	506.0	715.9	869.3
share %	3.3	3.5	3.6
Trade, other	1,233.6	1,538.2	1,740.6
share %	7.9	7.6	7.2
Total	15,564.7	20,169.1	24,261.7

Source: Lithuanian Statistical Yearbook, 1989.

Table 2.3 Lithuania: industrial structure, 1989

	% of industrial production	no. of enterprises	employees 000's	average no. of employees	average wage/ month (roubles)
Electricity	4.6	20	16.2	810	275.8
Fuel	4.0	12	5.0	417	264.6
Chemicals	3.8	15	18.2	1,213	265.4
Machinery	25.7	139	193.2	1,390	271.8
Timber, pulp, etc.	5.3	59	41.4	702	263.3
Building materials	5.0	64	38.8	606	275.0
Light industry	20.8	106	97.4	919	242.4
Food processing	21.9	122	61.7	506	259.7
Flour, cereals	4.2	20	4.3	215	251.2
Others	4.7	47	33.0	702	—
All enterprises	100	604	509.2	843	262.9

Source: Lithuanian Statistical Yearbook, 1989.

Table 2.4 presents summary data on the agriculture sector during the 1980s which show distinctly slower growth from 1986 than in the first half of the decade. Crop production grew by 55 per cent in the first six years of the decade, while animal husbandry grew much more slowly at less than half this rate. Animal husbandry continued to show only minimal growth since 1986 and its share in total agricultural production fell significantly over the decade, from 71 per cent in 1980 to 66 per cent in 1989, and fell further in 1990 and early 1991 as a consequence of the blockade and the disruption

Table 2.4 Lithuania: agricultural production, 1980–9 (1983 prices, million roubles)

	1980	1985	1986	1987	1988	1989
Total	3,559.0	4,564.3	4,772.5	4,774.7	4,890.5	4,978.3
growth %			4.6	0.0	2.4	1.8
State & collectives			3,275.8	3,392.1	3,456.1	3,453.9
share %			68.6	71.0	70.7	69.4
Private			1,496.7	1,382.6	1,434.4	1,524.4
share %			31.4	29.0	29.3	30.6
Crops	1,046.9	1,511.4	1,623.7	1,586.2	1,639.9	1,706.4
share %	29.4	33.1	34.0	33.2	33.5	34.3
growth %			7.4	– 2.3	3.4	4.1
State & collectives			1,119.7	1,139.9	1,147.1	1,181.4
share %			69.0	71.9	69.9	69.2
Private			504.0	446.3	492.8	525.0
share %			31.0	28.1	30.1	30.8
Animal husbandry	2,512.1	3,052.9	3,148.8	3,188.5	3,250.6	3,271.9
share %	70.6	66.9	66.0	66.8	66.5	65.7
growth %			3.1	1.3	1.9	0.7
State & collectives			2,156.1	2,252.2	2,309.0	2,272.5
share %			68.5	70.6	71.0	69.5
Private			992.7	936.3	941.6	999.4
share %			31.5	29.4	29.0	30.5

Source: Lithuanian Statistical Yearbook, 1989.

to feedgrain supplies caused by the breakdown of the supply system. Lithuania is unable to meet its commitments to supply meat products and is engaging in direct barter of meat for feedgrain.

The shares of the state, collective and private sectors have remained constant over the decade, although this began to change in 1990 as collective land was made available to private farmers. Previously, private agricultural production had come from the small family gardens of collective farmers or state farm workers. The data underestimated the share of private agriculture in the past and especially its importance to the cash incomes of rural families. Further substantial shifts in agriculture are largely related to policy decisions on the privatisation of land and other state assets which will be discussed elsewhere. The Department of Statistics estimates that there are currently 20,000 private farmers as compared to 300,000 in the inter-war period.

In 1989, 40 per cent of the enterprises were all-union enterprises responsible to ministries or branch-ministries in Moscow; 50 per cent were so-called union-republic enterprises while 10 per cent of the enterprises were responsible only to the republic administration. This pattern of ownership and control of enterprises changed during 1989 and 1990 with some all-union and practically all union–republic enterprises being transferred to republic control and the development of some private firms, although these remain few in number and small in size. There were in early 1991 reportedly around 2,000 new firms in Lithuania with 80,000 workers (or 2 per cent of the workforce) engaged in the private sector.

b. Trade and external relations

As a consequence of the total integration with the economy of the Soviet Union, trade with other republics accounts for a relatively high proportion of national income and production, while trade with the rest of the world is relatively limited. It has been estimated that deliveries to other republics account for 61 per cent of Lithuania's NMP, while exports to the rest of the world account for only 6 per cent; imports from the rest of the world were 14 per cent of NMP in 1989. The main imports are fuel, intermediate industrial goods, final consumer goods and food. However, in the last three of these categories, Lithuania has a positive trade balance. Lithuania is particularly dependent upon imports for the supply of raw materials and intermediate goods (all metals originate in other parts of the Soviet Union) while being a major supplier of consumer goods to the rest of the Soviet Union. Table 2.5 gives the Lithuanian authorities' statistics for the trade balance of the industrial sector.

Table 2.5 Lithuania: sources and use of industrial production, 1987

	Sources			Use			External
	Lith. %	USSR %	O'seas %	Lith. %	USSR %	O'seas %	balance (million roubles)
All industry	69.8	25.9	4.4	74.2	23.7	2.2	− 984.1
Electricity	84.9	15.2	—	77.3	22.7	—	49.5
Oil & gas	48.0	52.0	—	75.3	13.6	11.1	− 534.0
Coal	9.9	27.6	62.5	100.0	—	—	− 51.6
Other fuels	81.3	18.7	—	93.1	—	6.8	− 2.8
Ferrous metals	30.2	64.4	5.3	94.0	5.2	0.6	− 342.5
Non-ferr. metals	7.5	88.3	4.2	95.3	4.7	0.1	− 151.5
Chem. & oil ref.	44.4	50.0	5.6	74.0	25.2	0.8	− 408.0
Machinery	59.5	35.4	5.2	67.9	30.1	2.0	− 486.2
Timber etc.	77.9	20.6	1.6	74.4	23.0	2.7	36.0
Construction mat.	88.9	10.2	0.9	90.7	8.7	0.6	− 15.1
Light industry	77.9	15.4	6.7	68.0	31.5	0.5	440.0
Food industry	87.7	7.7	4.6	75.7	22.4	1.7	525.2
Others	91.2	8.2	0.6	95.4	4.4	0.2	− 43.1

Note: The last column gives the balance of all imports and exports, both to the Soviet Union and the rest of the world.

Source: Lithuanian authorities.

In 1991, on the basis of the prices ruling on 1 January, the Lithuanian authorities believe that they will be in trade balance with the Soviet Union and the rest of the world combined and will have surpluses with many republics, noticeably Russia, but a deficit in overseas trade. This analysis takes into account the various inter-republic agreements as well as the wholesale price increases effective throughout the Soviet Union in January 1991. The Lithuanian calculations attempt to approximate the trade balance of a fully independent Lithuania by only accounting for that trade which takes place through Lithuanian economic agents and it does not take into account certain 'imports' which the authorities would not willingly choose to import such as military supplies.

For an independent Lithuania, it will be the overall balance of payments which will be of interest rather than the trade account alone. Lithuania has a potential for considerable service income from the Soviet Union or other republics, given the size and importance of the port at Klaipeda. It is too early to speculate on the composition of a Lithuanian capital account.

The current inability of the central Soviet system to guarantee supplies is resulting in the development of new horizontal relationships at republic levels. Lithuania currently has fifty-eight agreements with other republics or regions or enterprise groupings signed between June and December 1990 and at least twelve more are in preparation. Many of these agreements reconfirm the allocations of inputs and outputs laid down in the central plan but claim to offer an inter-republic guarantee that the transfers will be made: for example the agreement between the Lithuanian Ministry of Resources and the Stavropol Supply Board. Agreements also cover continuing cooperation between relevant ministries: for example an agreement between the Lithuanian Transport Ministry and the Russian Transport Ministry.

Enterprises are also dealing directly with one another to ensure supplies of essential inputs with barter playing an increasing role in these exchanges. Some enterprises are also beginning to utilise the commodity exchanges which have developed in Moscow and St Petersburg as a means of mediating the often bizarre transhipment of goods across the Soviet Union; for example, one industrial enterprise in Lithuania sent four tons of butter, which had been obtained by means of a separate transaction, a considerable distance in order to receive vehicle spare parts. The current economic disruption within the Soviet Union, along with the impact of the short blockade of Lithuania in 1990, led to a reduction in both trade and economic activity in Lithuania. Transport indicators for Lithuania for 1990 show at least a 15 per cent fall in activity.

There is very limited development of private trade in Lithuania at present and it is believed to represent not more than 2 per cent of retail and wholesale trade. Cooperative and private economic activity have been relatively slow to develop in Lithuania. They can play a particularly important role in trading activities by mediating the various exchanges, increasing competition as well as widening consumer choice. It will be important for the authorities to ensure the removal of bureaucratic impediments to the establishment of new trading activities and help ensure adequate credit for such services.

One trade issue of particular concern is the growing protectionism evident in the introduction of trade barriers and border controls as well as the narrow bilateralism of many trade activities and agreements. There are clearly many motivations for the trade restrictions, including differences over the pace and nature of reform, the absence of coordination of reform measures, as well as cruder manifestations of nationalism. As temporary restrictions they may have some justification, but there is a danger that temporary measures will become permanent. Lithuania, as a small economy, will need to ensure a very open trade regime in order to maintain competitive pressures and maximise its own trading opportunities.

Direct export and import to countries outside of the Soviet Union has been very limited and up until the present Lithuania's external trading relationships with the rest of the world were still mediated through authorities in Moscow. However, Lithuania had an extensive pattern of trading relationships in the inter-war period and should be able to find a number of opportunities if it pursues an open trade stance. Foreign exchange and investment policies, considered in more detail elsewhere, will be important determinants of Lithuania's eventual trading pattern.

E. Economic reform

a. The economic impetus to introduce reform

Given the problems and inefficiencies of the Soviet system, which have worsened in recent years as the command economy has begun to disintegrate, support within Lithuania for the transition to a market economy has gathered strength. However, there are also concerns about both the economic and social problems which will arise in the process of transition. The Lithuanian draft economic programme states that: 'The essence of the economic reform being conducted in Lithuania consists of transforming the Soviet model of the economy into a moderately state-regulated socially-oriented market economy.'

There is a widespread desire to achieve a transformation to a society and economy similar to that of the economies of Scandinavia; Finland and Sweden have been seen as particular models. However, there is not an equally clear understanding of the means by which such a transformation can be achieved or of the degree of social and economic dislocation involved, and perhaps there is some misunderstanding about the degree to which the state regulates the economy in Sweden and Finland.

There is some ambivalence in relation to the 'market' and capitalism. One senior adviser commented that 'Bolshevik thinking' was still prevalent; for example, there was a reluctance to sell assets to those who have money because of doubt where the money came from and because it meant that some people would have more than others.

There is a widespread perception that the performance of the Lithuanian economy has been disappointing since 1940, when it was incorporated into the Soviet Union. Comparisons are frequently made with Finland implying that Lithuania, along with Estonia and Latvia, was at a similar level of development to Finland in the inter-war period. Available data only partly bears out this perception. While there are some notable similarities between the three Baltic economies and Finland in the late inter-war period, there are also a number of differences, particularly between Lithuania and Finland. Industry and construction accounted for 21 per cent of employment in Finland as against around 16 per cent in Estonia and Latvia and only 10 per cent in Lithuania. Agricultural yields, life expectancy and literacy and the availability of modern consumer goods such as cars, radios and telephones were all higher in Finland. For example, Finland had 708 cars and 4,441 telephones per 100,000 population in 1939 compared with 89 and 885 respectively for Lithuania. Moreover, recent comparisons show that disparities have increased.

While Lithuania lagged behind its Baltic neighbours in industrialisation and urbanisation in the inter-war period, it was industrialised relatively rapidly in the 1960s and 1970s and appears to have narrowed the gap with its neighbours. Lithuania's 'later' development also appears to have produced both a more 'modern' industrial structure as well as a better level of basic infrastructure, especially in transportation. It has other advantages over its Baltic neighbours: a greater degree of ethnic homogeneity, a larger workforce and labour resources in agriculture still to draw upon and a number of industrial centres outside of the capital. In contrast, Lithuania's disadvantages include its relative lack of contact with and access to overseas countries and an apparently greater ambivalence in the perception of the benefits of a market economy.

Lithuania's economic performance in recent years cannot be separated from that of the Soviet economy. Even official data, which typically overstate growth, show the Soviet economy to have stagnated. Available data, circumstantial evidence and popular perception indicate that per capita incomes have been stagnant at best in recent years. The availability of goods and services is increasingly limited, as is their quality and variety. In short, Lithuania's economic performance, social development and international competitiveness have continued to lag behind that of Europe in general since the 1940s. Lithuania has also seen its performance falter compared to its growth in earlier years, which had exceeded the average for the Soviet Union, as well as that of its neighbours Latvia and Estonia.

In early 1991, the economic situation in Lithuania could only be characterised as one of confusion. The economy remains an integrated part of the Soviet economy, which is itself in a state of almost total confusion as its formal structures collapse and insufficient consensus exists for the establishment of new ones. Because of the stalemate at the political level, discussions of economic matters had not proceeded far. Lithuania asserted that the Soviet Union owes it 300 billion roubles. The Soviet Union claimed that Lithuania should pay $33 billion for its freedom. The Lithuanian Parliament passed legislation, the impact of which is limited owing to technical difficulties, ambiguity over its application and most importantly because legislation is only one of the necessary steps towards a market economy. Despite the general breakdown in normal economic relationships, enterprises and households somehow struggle to make ends meet through a combination of past relationships, flexibility and guile. A visitor to Lithuania was struck by the fact that the economy functions at all in the face of so much formal disintegration and confusion.

b. Prices and consumption

In the case of Lithuania, the problems arising in the transitional period can be clearly illustrated in relation to price reform, which is among the most fundamental problems currently facing the Soviet Union and all of the republics. Official prices have been infrequently adjusted and the retail price index, which measured the movement of official prices, had limited meaning as an indication of inflation; prices in Lithuania, according to the official retail price index, rose by only 13 per cent between 1980 and 1989. In reality the divergence between supply and demand manifested itself as increases in 'free' or 'black' market prices and in formal rationing or queuing. Various attempts have been made to incorporate both the 'free'-market prices and an allowance for rationing/queuing as suppressed inflation in order to derive an overall index of inflation.

Lithuania has now adopted standard methodology of price index formation and is collecting data on a large number of commodities in a number of centres in order to compile an official consumer price index. This has only been fully operational since the beginning of 1991 but recent calculations show an increase in the prices of non-food commodities of 9.6 per cent in 1990. Most commodities rose by around 10 per cent, with some items (medicine and soap) falling in price and tobacco doubling in price in 1990. Inflation will be considerably higher in 1991 as a result of the forthcoming price reform.

Official statistics on free- or black-market prices are also now becoming available as a result of the changes in the methods of collection and calculation of price data. Free-market clothing prices are between two and five times official prices; footwear is five to seven times official prices; electric commodities are two to five times more expensive; cosmetics two to seven times; and cars are around four to five times more expensive. The considerable divergence in price is not purely a result of scarcity but is also due to quality differences in some cases; better clothing is available outside of the rather drab, limited choice available in official stores. The various price reform proposals are intended to narrow these price differentials between free and official prices before removing the distinction completely.

The Lithuanian government had originally intended to implement a price reform in late 1990. It was to give priority to the liberalisation of prices along with privatisation as steps towards the full determination of prices solely by supply and demand. In the interim, it was accepted that some state regulation in price formation would be necessary in order to lessen the shock impact of reform and to protect consumers in the case of monopoly producers. Regulated prices would be based on costs of production, sales margins and a 'fair' profit of 15 per cent. Price reform was also seen as essential in order to remove the burden of subsidies from the budget. For a large range of commodities prices were to be completely deregulated, while for other commodities the state would set maximum prices. The reform was to be accompanied by the replacement of turnover taxes by excise duties and taxation of profits. The first setback faced by the government of Prime Minister Prunskiene was the rejection by the Supreme Council of the overall economic reform programme, of which price reform was a critical component, in October 1990. The government then moved to implement different elements of the reform programme individually. Price reform became more urgent at the beginning of 1991 with the increase of wholesale prices throughout the Soviet Union and the increasing burden of paying subsidies to producers of final goods and agricultural produce which this imposed on the republic budgets. The attempt by the Prunskiene government to introduce price reform in January 1991 failed (as described in section B of this chapter).

The January price reform and compensation package had involved overall food price increases of 430 per cent. The compensation payments were to be related to household income. The package approved by the government in February 1991 for implementation in March or April involved overall food price increases of approximately 300 per cent, with meat products increasing 420 per cent and milk and dairy products 330 per cent. Consumer goods prices rose by approximately 250 per cent, largely as a result of the flow-on impact of higher energy prices. Prices were to be freely determined for most non-food items, except for certain goods such as children's shoes and clothes, schoolbooks etc. Prices for most personal services and transportation were also increased. Railway fares rose by up to 200 per cent, which still leaves them very low by international comparison. Housing rents, which had been only notional, were not increased. The intention is to eventually sell off a large part of the housing stock.

It has been estimated that the overall impact of all the price adjustments would be an increase of between 300 per cent and 350 per cent. The shape of the final package to be introduced in Lithuania will depend on the nature and timing of price reform in the Soviet Union and especially in Russia. Coordination is important in order to avoid aggravating the current protectionist tendencies in the various republics, and even within republics, of the Soviet Union. In Lithuania many goods could only be bought with coupons issued at the workplace and a Lithuanian identity card to ensure that non-Lithuanian residents did not take advantage of the current prices and the marginally better availability of goods. Unfortunately, even the three Baltic republics failed to coordinate their price reforms.

A considerable amount of work has been done on alternative compensation packages to cushion the impact of the price increases. One comprehensive proposal was based on the per capita consumption of basic foodstuffs by an adult with an income of 100 roubles per month and an amount of compensation to maintain an adequate intake of these commodities to ensure consumption of 2,160 calories per day. The package actually approved by the government in February along with the price reform consists of payments of 105 roubles per month to workers and 85 roubles to non-workers (students, pensioners etc.). Payments for children are made if the worker's salary is less than 180 roubles per month and are paid from the social insurance fund. Workers in enterprises receive the extra payments with their salaries from enterprise funds while recipients of income from the state are paid from the budget. Only the cost of the compensation payments to direct government employees and some of the pension and other payments appear in the budget projections.

The cost of the compensation payments to direct government employees is estimated at 560 million roubles for 1991. The total cost of the compensation and subsidy package will exceed earlier forecasts and it is likely that revenue increases and expenditure reductions will be required to balance the budget. Incomes will subsequently be partially indexed to prices and adjusted in accordance with a law protecting the incomes of the population.

It is assumed that enterprises will be able to pay the additional amounts of compensation to their employees since they will be free to raise the prices of their output. This may not be true in all cases and largely ignores the impact of the price increases on the structure and level of consumer demand; some senior officials appeared to believe that an increase in non-food consumer goods prices by 2.5 times would automatically increase expenditure on these goods by the same amount. While demand may be largely price inelastic for many goods in short supply, there will undoubtedly be some adjustment and some producers may be unable to realise sales and pay their employees. Lithuania has not yet approved a draft law on bankruptcy and may not be sufficiently prepared for the employment and social consequences of some aspects of adjustment.

The price increases will have a severe impact on consumers even with the compensation payments. In 1989, the average household income per family member was 199 roubles per month, of which 29 per cent was spent on food, 35 per cent on non-food consumer goods, 4 per cent on alcohol, 9 per cent on services and 9 per cent was saved. Unfortunately, without comprehensive household survey data it is very difficult to generalise about consumption levels. Households consume from a number of sources and may also have a number of sources of income, including more than one job and income from other activities.

It is virtually impossible to evaluate the magnitude of these other income and consumption flows, but they should not be overestimated. Communal facilities vary in both quality and availability, participation in free-market activities as either buyer or seller is still limited, and it seems that the majority of the population lives solely on their official income which they spend on the limited range of goods intermittently available in official stores. Queues are a fact of everyday life. A senior government economic adviser asserted that 65 per cent of household members subsist on less than 200 roubles per month. The very high free-market prices are thus accessible only to a few and it is a minority who benefit from the higher-quality collective consumption facilities and the restricted access to scarce goods and services, including housing and travel. Income distribution data is not available, and neither is consumption distribution data which would be more illuminating in showing the extent of the relative inequality. As one observer remarked: 'the problem with socialism is that it produces so much inequality.'

c. Money and banking

Since Lithuania's declaration of independence from the Soviet Union in March 1990, it has attempted to establish an independent monetary and banking system. As is the case for Estonia and Latvia, an independent currency is seen as a fundamental characteristic of an independent state and is thus important for political reasons. The authorities in Lithuania also see a separate currency as a means of addressing the problem of the excess volume of roubles.

The Bank of Lithuania which was established by a Law of the Lithuanian Supreme Council of 13 February 1990 as the embryonic Central Bank has been limited in its range of functions by the absence of border control by the Lithuanian government. The Bank has taken over the local activities of the Moscow-based all-union banks. It is currently attempting to: establish an internal payments and clearing system; encourage the formation of private banks; develop supervision and regulatory procedures; and to attempt to engage in other activities characteristic of a central bank. There is considerable confusion in banking with policies being developed and implemented by both the Soviet Union and Lithuania. So far, enterprises and the individual banks appear to have been adept at adapting to the situation and the various sets of laws, but it raises concerns over the state of financial supervision and regulation.

Foreign-exchange dealings have continued to be done through the Soviet Bank for Foreign Trade in Moscow (Vneshekonombank), although the Bank of Lithuania is attempting to develop correspondent banking relationships directly with other overseas banks. While Lithuania no longer formally participates in the all-union foreign-exchange banking system, participation is a practical necessity for individual enterprises since the allocation of a part of foreign exchange earnings is done through the Moscow Bank for Foreign Trade. There are still Lithuanian overseas gold holdings, dating from the pre-1940 period, in France and Switzerland, and the authorities are hopeful of securing the return of these holdings once they are in a position to establish their own foreign-exchange and gold reserves. Gold belonging to the pre-war government and held in Sweden was turned over to the Soviet Union during World War II. Gold held in Great Britain was turned over in the mid-sixties as part of a political deal.

Six private commercial banks have been established in Lithuania. One of these, the Lithuanian Joint-Stock Innovation Bank, which was first registered with the all-union authorities in December 1988, has more than sixty shareholders consisting primarily of state enterprises and scientific organisations. Its share capital is currently fifteen million roubles compared to five million at the time of formation and it has offices in Vilnius and Kaunas. The bank focuses on the provision of banking services to enterprises and organisations engaged in the development and commercialisation of innovations and has close links with research institutes within Lithuania and overseas. It provides loans for periods up to three years and relies on term deposits from enterprises and individuals for its funds. As of March 1991 it had a loan portfolio of forty-five million roubles, approximately 70 per cent of which is to state enterprises. The bank is currently registered under both Lithuanian and Soviet law, and its clearing and accounting systems operate through Moscow. The regulatory requirements of both authorities are similar and there is no conflict. Lithuanian law is in some respects stricter, most noticeably in its prohibition on banks taking equity positions in companies. This is seen as a constraint on the activities of the Innovation Bank as shortage of capital is a particular problem for emerging entrepreneurs.

F. The social situation

Lithuania, along with Estonia and Latvia, has consistently had higher standards of health care and education than other parts of the Soviet Union. This is a legacy of the pre-war period. The deteriorating economic situation and the current political and economic upheavals inevitably have an adverse effect on the social situation and the provision of social services to the population. In the process of transformation to a market economy, there will be changes in the way in which many social services are provided. The market economy will have different social consequences compared to the old system. While the Soviet economy guaranteed employment, in a market economy unemployment is an inevitable consequence of the process of competition, which forces the closure of factories that are no longer able to operate profitably. Eventually a well-run mixed economy will generate new job opportunities for those thrown out of work and a welfare system will provide financial support. However, in the early period there are likely to be high levels of transitional unemployment with attendant social consequences.

The Lithuanian authorities have already prepared a number of measures to cope with some of the transitional difficulties. As detailed earlier, households will receive compensation payments to ease the impact of the higher prices for most consumer goods. Laws have been passed by the Supreme Council to ensure that income recipients are partially indexed against the anticipated higher inflation in the coming period and to improve the pensions system. A law has also been passed on employment, including the establishment of labour exchanges to play an active role in helping those made unemployed to be retrained and find new jobs. The administrative competence to administer the new systems is yet to be established.

The main challenge for the education system in the coming period is to maintain the level of provision of all levels of education, in the face of budgetary restraint and declining economic activity, and to adjust syllabuses to the new economic and political situation. The quality of basic education is good and the main requirements are: to increase the range of foreign-language teaching, to change the social studies syllabus and to prepare more textbooks in the Lithuanian language.

At the higher levels of education there is an even more urgent need to produce relevant texts in Lithuanian; for example, the first Lithuanian textbook on standard Western economics has just appeared. There is also a need to develop adult education, which is almost totally absent.

The funding of education is also under review. With pressure on the overall budget, educational spending will also be under pressure. However, the spending requirements are considerable. Teachers' salaries, around 250 roubles per month, have always been low and the status of education workers, from teachers to university professors, in a society which elevated the industrial worker, is also low. The government intends to improve teacher in-service training and relate salaries to ability and performance and also to take advantage of increasing opportunities for overseas scholarships and training. Equipment and textbooks will be expensive to provide; there are currently almost no computers in the schools. Some consideration has been given to introducing fees for some parts of the education system, but currently very few people have money to pay for education. A senior education official commented that those who do have the money are the 'wrong' sort of people with the 'wrong' source of money.

The level of spending on health care has remained at around 3.5 per cent of national income in recent years and, as with education, cannot be expected to increase. While health care provision has been generally good in Lithuania and standard indicators are comparable to countries with higher income levels, the authorities have a number of concerns and wish to adjust the focus of health care. In 1989 Lithuania had 46 doctors per 10,000 inhabitants, one of the highest levels in the world; the United States had 27 doctors per 10,000 inhabitants in 1985, Finland 32 and Sweden 37. The number of hospital beds per 10,000 inhabitants is also among the highest in the world. With its emphasis on curative medicine, senior officials at the Ministry of Health joked that it was previously the Ministry of Diseases! The new focus will be to reorient the available resources and place much greater emphasis on preventative primary health care. Lithuania currently has no family doctor system and inadequate health education, and health officials believe that a reallocation of resources towards these areas will provide a more cost effective health care system.

Infant mortality has fallen rapidly in the last four decades, but the authorities are concerned over shortages of equipment to deal with premature births and are also concerned by an increase in children with birth defects from 21 per 1000 in 1987, to 25 in 1988 and 26 in 1989. The reasons for the increase have yet to be identified, and the health authorities intend to improve pre-natal screening to identify problems at an earlier stage.

The major cause of death in Lithuania is diseases of the circulatory system which accounts for 57 per cent of deaths followed by neoplasm, 17 per cent, and injury and poisoning, 11 per cent. Some major causes of morbidity are seen as smoking, poor diet, lack of exercise and environmental pollution. Lithuania reportedly has one of the highest levels of obesity in Europe, and smoking is on the increase among women and the young. All of these are 'preventable' and the Health Ministry is preparing an extensive health education campaign, integrated with the education system to inculcate better attitudes towards health care, including improved diet and healthier living. Popular literature on health care was unavailable until very recently.

The relative absence of family-planning services and extremely limited availability of contraceptives have resulted in a high level of abortions in Lithuania: 55.6 abortions per 100 live births and 33.4 per 10,000 fertile women are officially recorded, but the authorities believe that up to half as many again are carried out outside the official system. Family-planning centres are now being organised, but the problem of contraceptive availability remains as they are produced elsewhere in the Soviet Union and are in short supply. Partly owing to the unavailability of contraceptives and partly owing to the influence of resurgent Roman Catholicism in Lithuania, the authorities are encouraging natural birth-control methods. Sex education literature is in preparation as existing literature was aimed only at doctors and sex education was taught only in science classes to the extent that it was taught at all. A well-produced Lithuanian version of a 'Where Do I Come From?' book (which would be readily available for young children in Western Europe) has apparently produced criticism and opposition in Lithuania.

The health authorities believe that a refocusing on preventative care and health education can be made without additional resources. The availability of medication, drugs and hospital equipment may, however, become a serious problem as dislocation increases throughout the Soviet economy. The authorities intend to introduce private medicine alongside the official system, through the privatisation of some health institutions. The status and pay of doctors will also be raised and their remuneration linked to their numbers of patients. It is expected that enterprise-level health care will diminish as enterprises have to control their costs and aim to maximise profits. A broad state preventative health care system, retaining many of the strengths of the existing system and functioning alongside a mixed and private system is the current objective.

Box 2.1 Note on statistics in Lithuania

The Department of Statistics in Lithuania has 136 employees with offices in each town and district and its headquarters in Vilnius with modern computer technology and publishing equipment. It is the main official provider of statistics, although it is dependent upon individual ministries for some of the operational data. The Ministries of Agriculture, Health and Justice also produce some of their own statistics.

The collection, analysis and publication of statistics is currently undergoing considerable change in Lithuania. Formerly, a vast quantity of data on physical quantities was collected by enterprises and all sections of government as part of the system of preparing, compiling, implementing and assessing the overall production plan. Information on values and financial parameters was collected but had limited meaning and was little used. Data collection methods were based on collection of as much data as possible from all enterprises, ministries, departments and other instrumentalities of government with little concern as to its accuracy, validity or usefulness. Data analysis was limited and much of the considerable quantity of data collected was not made available and certainly was not widely published. Some statistical data was completely concealed. This attitude has not completely disappeared and this group had some difficulty persuading Soviet authorities at Riga airport to allow them to leave the country with such subversive material as public, official statistics!

The department is now adjusting its methods of collection, analysis and presentation and attempting to come into line with standard international conventions. The majority of the staff are trained in mathematics, although they do have some economists and are developing educational and training courses for the staff, utilising material from the United Nations and other sources.

The department is attempting to present Lithuania's national income accounts in the Standard National Accounts (SNA) methodology. Initial estimates for the Soviet Union have indicated that gross national product (GNP), on standard international definitions, would be 37 per cent higher than net material product (NMP), which excludes most services and depreciation. NMP is also collected only from the production side unlike GNP/GDP statistics which are normally calculated from both income and expenditure perspectives. The first estimate for Lithuania shows GNP to be about 25 per cent higher than NMP in 1989.

The department has also changed its methodology with respect to another major economic indicator, the inflation rate. Previously it merely computed the retail price index from the officially determined prices, which were infrequently adjusted. The department is now utilising a standard sampling approach and is surveying prices in the five largest cities and eight centres. It now incorporates all prices: state, cooperative, collective-farm markets and free-market prices. The index includes 300 basic foodstuffs, 650 other consumer goods and fifty services. The new system has been in operation since January 1991 and the department intends to publish monthly inflation rates by the 20th of the following month. The new methodology faces some problems as a result of an unwillingness to reveal prices in some cases and of the actual unavailability of numerous goods which are included in the index.

Sampling and survey techniques are also being introduced in other fields. Formerly, with only one form of ownership, the department relied on data supplied by enterprises and had no means of verification. Enterprises frequently reported that they had exceeded their plan by 0.1 per cent, which was ideal in ensuring that they were not penalised and also did not face a more arduous target in the following period. With more differentiated forms of enterprise, there is no longer the obligation to fulfil plans or quotas or to report upwards to branch ministries. The department currently utilises the tax declarations of producers to ensure comprehensive coverage of the new forms of ownership and is developing sampling and surveying techniques: for example, it questions 400 of the 2,000 private farms. As more private economic activity develops and the state sector diminishes, these new techniques will be introduced into all areas of the department's work. Questionnaires issued to respondents at the end of 1991 will be very different from previous ones.

The department feels it will have little difficulty obtaining the necessary raw data, but requires assistance in analytical and presentational techniques. In the area of national income accounts, it is seeking additional assistance in the form of experts and training. New styles and methods of presentation are necessary for the new market conditions and the differing requirements which now exist. Other areas of development are foreign trade and external relations, using world market prices, and analysis of inter-enterprise linkages.

3 Latvia

A. History

The history of Latvia includes only a brief period of independence, from 1918 to 1940. Despite this, Latvians have a keen sense of national identity. The awareness stretches beyond culture and language into the political consciousness of today and the demands for renewed independence.

The lack of a historical state does not, however, imply a lack of national history. Since prehistoric times Finno–Ugric and Baltic tribes have inhabited the territory of present-day Latvia. From the twelfth century onwards they were under foreign rule. From the fourteenth to the sixteenth century the area was under the control of Teutonic Orders, who established a Livonian state, covering the territory of Latvia and parts of present-day Estonia. Then southern Livonia and Courland (west Latvia) came under Polish–Lithuanian rule, until 1621, when Sweden took over Livonia. One century later, in 1721, Livonia was incorporated into Russia, as was Courland in 1795, to become Russian Baltic provinces until independence was achieved in 1918.

As elsewhere in Europe, nationalism emerged and developed in Latvia during the nineteenth century. Its sources are connected to the German Enlightenment leader J. G. Herder who worked as a pastor in Riga in the 1760s where he became interested in and collected Baltic folklore. The agrarian reforms in the nineteenth century (particularly the abolition of serfdom, 1816–19) provided additional possibilities for the development of national consciousness. The movement attracted increasing numbers of activists, and by the second half of the century the idea of a separate national identity with an independent culture spread widely. In 1873 the first song festival was held, initiating a strong tradition that has played an important role in the present rebirth (*atmoda*) of national consciousness. Political movements combined social ideas from Russia and Western Europe with nationalism, and radical nationalist organisations were very active in the beginning of the twentieth century. For the Russian Baltic Provinces 1905 was a violent year, and Latvians were active in the 1917 Russian revolution.

Economic life during the period before Latvia's political independence was characterised by relatively undynamic agriculture and a rapidly emerging industry. Despite the agricultural reforms of the first half of the nineteenth century — a generation before serfdom was abolished in Russia — peasants were still largely dependent on the Baltic German nobility, which had little inclination to modernise its big landed estates. The region's historical role as a trade link between Russia and the other countries of the Baltic region and beyond had become more important as industrialisation transformed Europe. Riga, founded in 1201 and soon a key Hanseatic city, grew to become one of the most dynamic and cosmopolitan cities of the Russian empire, in the Baltic area certainly the most important after St Petersburg.

Riga's population had reached half a million before World War I.

During World War I, Latvia's territory became a battleground for Germans and Russians causing considerable destruction. The collapse of the two powers at the end of the war allowed Latvian independence to be proclaimed on 18 November 1918. There was an active Latvian communist movement, which gave significant support to the Russian revolution and the creation of the Red Army. An independent Soviet Republic of Latvia existed briefly during 1918–19. After renewed battles, the end of the summer of 1920 finally brought peace for Latvia with Germany as well as Soviet Russia.

The independent Latvian Republic established a single-chamber parliamentary system. The president was elected by Parliament. A constitution modelled on the Weimar Constitution was adopted in 1922. Small parties proliferated until 1934, when Prime Minister Karlis Ulmanis established an authoritarian regime, concentrating power politically as well as economically in the state. He himself became both prime minister and president.

The population of Latvia in 1914 was 2.5 million, of which around 60 per cent were Latvians. Deaths, deportations and emigration drastically reduced the population during the war and the revolution. Even by 1935, it had only reached 1,950,000, of which 75.5 per cent were ethnically Latvian. The main minorities were 10.6 per cent Russian, 4.8 per cent Jewish, 3.2 per cent German, 2.5 per cent Polish, 1.4 per cent Belorussian and 1.2 per cent Lithuanian.

Despite the destruction caused by the war and the disruption of the traditional East–West trade, rapid economic recovery and growth took place. At independence, the agrarian sector employed 66 per cent of the population. Radical agrarian reforms in 1920 broke up large holdings of land. After the redistribution of land, the average size of a farm was 16.3 hectares.

During the interwar period cultivated land expanded and agricultural production increased as did its productivity. The number of cattle increased from 912,000 in 1913 to 1,278,000 in 1939, while the butter yield per cow went from 108 kilograms in 1913 to 130 kilograms in 1939. Grain production (rye, wheat, barley and oats) increased, but the average yield remained low, less than half that of the most efficient producers at the time (for example Denmark) but well ahead of Russia. The production of potatoes almost tripled from 1913 to 1937, and wheat production more than quadrupled.

Dairy farming assumed an increasingly important role in agriculture. Processed milk production increased from 35,600 tons in 1914 to 273,700 in 1927 and 542,590 in 1937. In 1914 Latvia produced 1,500 tons of butter. By 1937 this production had increased to 21,855 tons. Butter, together with meat production, provided the basis for export, especially to Great Britain and Germany.

Latvia had started to industrialise at the end of the nineteenth century, but the war had drastically reduced industrial production and employment. After independence industry was restructured to adjust to the loss of the Russian market, and by 1930, only 13.5 per cent of the workforce was employed in the industrial sector. The largest employer of industrial labour was the manufacturing industry, followed by the woodworking, food-processing and textile industries. Latvia successfully produced certain high-technology goods such as radios and cameras.

The government pursued monetary and fiscal policies that stabilised the economy and enabled the introduction and support of a convertible currency, the lat (for an account of this successful reform, see Box 6.2). Export consisted first and foremost of agrarian products, followed by timber and wood. Trade grew steadily, except for a slump in 1929–30. As with Estonia, Latvia's main trading partners were Great Britain and Germany. Trade with the Soviet Union was very limited, and in 1938 the Soviet Union accounted for only 3 per cent of Latvian exports and 3.5 per cent of imports.

Latvia on the eve of World War II was that of a small, primarily agrarian nation, whose per capita industrial production lagged behind not only the most advanced European nations, but also for example Finland, though incomes were higher than in neighbouring Lithuania. Latvia was oriented to the West through trade as well as culturally and had a reasonably high standard of living. Meat and milk per capita consumption was high in comparison to other European nations. Improvements had taken place in all social spheres. Illiteracy levels and education levels ranked Latvia in the middle range of European nations. In terms of numbers of students Latvia ranked very high in the 1930s, apparently holding the first place in Europe in numbers of university students as a share of all inhabitants. Only Denmark published more books proportionally to population.

On 17 June 1940 the Soviet Red Army marched into Latvia. A new government was formed and elections were staged for a People's Assembly, which applied for membership into the Soviet Union. In August, Latvia became part of the Soviet Union.

Deportation started in 1940, and there were massive deportations on 13–14 June 1941. Estimates of population loss during the first year of Soviet rule range around 35,000, that is 1.5–2 per cent of the prewar population. The outbreak of war interrupted the deportations and the Soviets retreated in front of the Germans to return only in the summer of 1944. The losses in population and property during the war years were enormous. It has been estimated that 30 per cent of Latvia's prewar population were lost in deportations, executions, emigration, territorial changes, evacuations and mobilisation.

Sovietisation of all aspects of life started immediately and included an integration of Latvia into the Soviet political and economic spheres as well as cultural and linguistic russification.

The administrative structures created mirrored those in Moscow to which they were subordinated: a Latvian Communist Party with a First Secretary, a Council of Ministers with a Chairman and a Supreme Soviet, whose Presidium was headed by a chairman in a largely ceremonial post. In 1950, Soviet administrative units (*raiony*) were adopted.

Nationalisation started in July 1940. In industry, all factories with twenty workers or more were affected; commercial enterprises and banks were expropriated. Housing above certain limits was also nationalised. Fifteen per cent of farms were nationalised (those exceeding 30 hectares) and land redistributed to smallholders.

Non-Latvians started to arrive in large numbers — first as administrators and soldiers, later as labourers. The non-Baltic immigration during the first decade of Soviet rule (1945–55) has been estimated at 535,000. Over the years, the ethnic composition of Latvia has dramatically changed, and the perception of a threat to national survival was a major factor in the recent national consciousness revival and the independence movement.

Production in both agriculture and industry fell significantly from prewar levels. Industrial output only recovered to 1940 levels in 1950. In agriculture, grain production had fallen to 732,000 tons in 1950, from 1,372,000 tons in 1940 and continued to decline in the first half of the 1950s. The 1940 level had not yet been reached in 1960. The area of land under cultivation, yield per unit of land and number and live weight of farm animals all continued to decline during the 1950s.

Agriculture was collectivised by force. Massive deportations in March 1949 assured speedy compliance, and by December 1951 98 per cent of Latvian farms were collectivised. State farms were also created. Agricultural policies like the reorganisation of kolkhozes into larger units in 1950, compulsory deliveries of produce and the centralised control over technical equipment through the Machine Tractor Stations all contributed to subsequent problems in agriculture. After policies were liberalised, especially with the 1957 so-called *sovnarkhozy* reforms that allowed for greater local control, agriculture started to improve, and by the mid-1960s production had increased. The living standard of Latvian farmers was improving with a significant share of income on collective farms coming from the small private plots.

Agriculture has increasingly focused on animal husbandry. Many crops have declined in volume since the 1930s, as Latvia has imported increasingly large shares of the grain feed from the rest of the Soviet Union, while exporting meat and dairy products.

Industry and infrastructure developed according to central directives integrating Latvia fully into the Soviet economy. While accounting for little more than a percentage of Soviet output, the Latvian economy acquired significant importance to the Union, in particular because of the presence of some high-tech enterprises and because of the harbours and railways. Though a significant part of Soviet foreign trade passed through Latvia, the country as a Soviet republic was effectively cut off from other contacts with its neighbours across the Baltic Sea and the rest of Europe and the world. Instead, Sovietisation and russification continued. A considerable military presence further underlined Latvia's Soviet integration. Liepaja became an important naval base, harbouring Soviet submarines and other war ships, while Riga housed the headquarters of the Soviet Baltic military region.

B. Population, geography and natural resources

Latvia is historically divided into three regions: Courland (*Kurzeme*), south and west of Riga, on the Baltic Sea; Livonia (*Vidzeme*), the centre of the country including Riga, and to the north, bordering Estonia; and Latgale to the east, bordering Belorussia. In addition there is a stretch of land south and east of Courland bordering Lithuania, Zemgale, sometimes considered part of Courland. Thus, the Latvian national symbol consisting of three stars stands for Courland, Livonia and Latgale.

The regions have considerable historical and cultural significance while at present having no administrative role. Livonia historically often refers to an area roughly covering *Vidzeme* and southern Estonia. The Livonian Confederation that existed from the thirteenth to the end of the sixteenth century included an even greater region. During Swedish and Russian rule, Livonia was an administrative area on both sides of the present day Estonian–Latvian border. Courland and Zemgale, an independent duchy in the seventeenth and eighteenth centuries, have, together with Latgale a history that is more linked to Polish–Lithuanian developments. While most of Latvia has a Nordic and Protestant cultural character, in the south and east, particularly in Latgale, there is a strong Catholic influence.

During the time of the Russian Empire, present-day Latvia was part of four *gubernia*, Livonia, Courland, Pskov (in Russia) and Vitebsk (in Belorussia). At present, there is discussion about what administrative system to adopt. The soviet system of *raiony* will likely be replaced with a system giving cities and local councils a stronger role, including that of handling their own economic affairs.

Finally, a small remnant of a once-important people deserves mention. They are the *livs*, a Finno–Ugic people that traditionally inhabited the peninsula between the Baltic Sea and the Bay of Riga. Today numbering perhaps no more than a thousand, they still have their place in Latvian culture.

Presently, the territory of Latvia covers 64,589 square kilometres (slightly less than the prewar figure of 65,791) which makes it larger than such other small European nations as Denmark, Switzerland and Belgium.

Latvia has a 500-kilometre long coastline on the Baltic Sea. The western-most point is a mere 145 kilometres from the eastern coast of Gotland off the Swedish coast. To the north and south it borders on Estonia and Lithuania, respectively. To the west it borders on Russia and Belorussia. The distance from Riga, the Latvian capital, to Helsinki is 360 kilometres and to Stockholm 440 kilometres, while Moscow is 850 kilometres away.

The country is flat — the highest 'mountain' is 312 metres — and 40 per cent of the land is covered by forest, while approximately 45 per cent is cultivated. The climate is temperate. The landscape is marked by numerous small rivers and lakes. There are 777 rivers longer than 10 kilometres, their cumulative length is 37,500 kilometres. The largest river is the Daugava (*Düna* in German, *Dvina* in Russian): of its 1,020 kilometres, 357 flow through Latvia. The Gauja is 460 kilometres long. There are sixteen lakes with a surface exceeding 10 square kilometres. The largest lake is Lake Razna, 53.5 square kilometres.

Like both other Baltic republics, Latvia is poor in natural resources. They consist mainly of forest, peat and raw materials for construction such as clay, dolomite, limestone, sand and granite. An abundance of amber provides the basis for jewellery handicraft.

The population of Latvia was 2,686,000 as of 1 January 1991, a density of 42.6 inhabitants per square kilometre. In 1989, 71 per cent of the population lived in urban areas and 29 per cent in rural areas. The population of Rīga was 915,200. The seven most important cities are Daugavpils, Liepāja, Jelgava, Jūrmala, Rēzekne, Valmiera and Ventspils. The ethnic composition of Latvia's population is 52 per cent Latvian and 34 per cent Russian. Other minorities are Belorussians (4.5 per cent), Ukrainians (3.4 per cent), Poles (2.3 per cent), Lithuanians (1.3 per cent) and Jews (0.9 per cent).

The legacy of war and deportation deaths can still be seen in the gender statistics: men make up 46 per cent of the population and women 54 per cent. In 1990, 56 per cent of the population was of working age (16–59 for men and 16–54 for women), down from 58 per cent in 1980, while the older share of the population had increased in the period from 19 per cent to 21 per cent. The urban pensioner group has grown from 17 per cent in the beginning of the 1970s to almost 20 per cent in 1988. The natural growth rate of the population was 2.4 per thousand inhabitants in 1989 which is significantly lower than the Soviet average of 7.6 per thousand. The relative share of immigration in overall population growth was high; until it suddenly dropped in 1989 it represented between half and two-thirds of the total growth. The birth rate is low at 14.5 per thousand in 1989.

C. Recent political developments

Political repression under Soviet rule effectively contained all attempts at political and nationalist opposition. However, many Latvians did rise to positions of power. As in Estonia and Lithuania, many of these became leaders in the movement for political independence and total reform of the communist system, once Soviet *glasnost* and *perestroika* had opened the lid. The Latvian reawakening, the *atmoda*, has its roots in an opposition and consciousness that, of course, did exist throughout the period of Soviet rule. It first came out strongly in 1987, after which events moved very rapidly.

In June 1987, the dissident Human Rights' Group Helsinki 76 put forth a demand for Latvian political independence, and the gradual development of popular action was initiated. In June 1988, the Latvian National Independence Movement (LNNK) was formed. In June 1988 the Writers' Union made demands for democratisation and national sovereignty. Boris Pugo, first secretary of the Communist Party and Anatolijs Gorbunovs, CP secretary of ideology, participated. After some political discord, seventeen intellectuals headed by Writers' Union chairman Janis Peters signed a proposal for the formation of a Popular Front. Political disagreements threatened to split the movement, but finally the Popular Front was established as an umbrella organisation. At the congress in October 1988 the Popular Front demanded sovereignty and democracy. A language law making Latvian the official state language and the legalisation of the flag from independent Latvia were signs of the growing popular support for nationalism. In reaction to these developments Interfront was formed in October 1988 with the declared aim of protecting the rights of the 'Russian-speaking' population.

As these events were taking place during 1988, conflict with Moscow was growing. In October the proposal for a new Soviet constitution, threatening to limit the rights of the republics, including the right to secede, sparked large protests by the Popular Front. Soviet Politburo members Chebrikov, Medvedev and Slyunkov travelled to the Baltics, ostensibly in an attempt at dialogue, while also indicating the gravity with which the Kremlin viewed the situation.

The intensification of conflict with Moscow only served to fuel popular support for the independence movement. During 1989 the Citizenship Committee, introduced by the LNNK, the environmental group VAK and Helsinki '76 group, started to register Latvian 'nationals' as citizens. The popular support expressed for the idea served to radicalise the Popular Front which shifted from the demand for autonomy to the outright aim of restoring independence. In the relatively free March 1989 elections to the People's Congress, the Popular Front won 32 out of 40 seats. In its second congress in October 1989, the Popular Front adopted a new programme, which stated independence as the goal of the movement.

On 23 August 1989, the anniversary of the Molotov–Ribbentrop Pact, a human chain demonstration through the three Baltic republics was organised as a protest against Soviet occupation. A few days later the Soviet Central Committee passed a resolution condemning it. Meetings and warning signals from the Kremlin during the autumn failed to stop the independence movement's development. Pro-independence and reform-minded Communist Party members formed a new independent party, splitting the Latvian Communist Party in April 1990.

In the free parliamentary elections held on 18 March 1990 the Popular Front won 66 per cent of the seats, while 29 per cent went to the Communist Party led by the very conservative Alfreds Rubiks. The remaining 5 per cent are held by independent deputies.

In order to pre-empt the new Soviet law on the secession of republics introduced in the spring of 1990, ostensibly clearing the way for secession but in fact setting up very demanding conditions, Lithuania declared its independence on 11 March 1990. On 4 May 1990 the turn came for Latvia to declare its independence, albeit with somewhat more caution, allowing for a transitional time period, during which the Soviet constitution was still valid, except for where it contradicted republican laws.

The momentum of the independence movement had arguably been unstoppable from even earlier in the process when national emotions pent-up for decades were allowed to resurface, but Moscow's hardening attitudes only increased it. The bloody January 1991 events in Vilnius and Riga rallied ethnic Latvians and non-Latvians alike around the 2 March poll on a democratic and independent Latvian republic. In the poll 87.6 per cent of the registered electorate voted, of whom 73.7 per cent supported independence.

From that time it was clear that Latvia, like Estonia and Lithuania, could be retained in the Soviet Union only by the use of military force. The Soviet Interior Ministry special OMON forces tried to spread fear through attacks in Riga and on newly erected Latvian border posts. The crumbling of centralised Soviet power accelerated, however. When the August coup attempt took place in Moscow, the Latvian Parliament immediately, on 21 August, suspended the period of transition provided for in the independence declaration of 4th May 1990 and proclaimed the country's fully restored independence. Within days of the collapsed coup (one of the coup participants having been the Latvian Boris Pugo, Soviet Interior Minister, later to commit suicide) Russia recognised the right of Baltic republics to full statehood. World-wide recognition followed. In September, the General Assembly of the United Nations voted to include Estonia, Latvia and Lithuania as three new member countries.

D. Structure of the economy

Wholly integrated in the Soviet economy since about 1950, Latvia has come to possess a quite diverse economy, though beset by all the problems characteristic of command economies. Income and productivity levels are considered high in relation to other parts of the (former) Soviet Union, but low in relation to Western Europe or even to the former East European countries. Latvia's agriculture and food industry is an important asset, which together with the forestry and wood industry, could become valuable components of independent Latvia's future exports. Manufacturing and electronics have made Latvia an important supplier of both consumer and capital goods to the Soviet market, for example, textiles, consumer durables, telecommunication equipment and heavy machinery. This industry is also likely to hold future potential but is in need of restructuring and substantial foreign investment. Transport infrastructure has made Latvia crucial to Soviet trade — Riga and Ventspils being two of the most important Soviet harbours, and Liepaja an important naval base. Transport and other trades services also hold potential to boost the country's future current account. Developing export earnings is crucial, dependent as the country is on imports of raw materials, energy and other inputs. The present structure of the economy links Latvia's economic future to the fate of the Soviet economy.

This reality has been an important factor in determining the pragmatic approach adopted by the Latvian authorities, as they seek to implement reform and regain the nation's economic sovereignty.

The paucity of Soviet economic statistics marks Latvia as well. According to official statistics, national income as measured by the net material product (NMP) was 7,301 million roubles in 1989. Per capita NMP was 2,722 roubles (compared with Estonian and Lithuanian averages in the same year of about 2,850 and 2,480, respectively). Neither being a measure of total output nor readily translatable into Western terms, this tells us very little about the standard of living. Based on the IMF estimate of a Soviet GNP of around US$ 1,750 in 1989 and on the assumption that Latvia has an income roughly 20 per cent above the Soviet average, Latvia might be said to have a GNP of around US$ 2,100. Translating NMP by using current exchange rates (in the region of 30 roubles to the dollar in mid-1991) would give a much lower figure, on the level of the poorest countries of the world.

Table 3.1 Latvia: composition of national income, 1980–9 (net material product, current prices, million roubles)

	1980	1985	1989	Sectoral share in 1989 %
Industry	3,254	2,855	3,301	45
Agriculture	697	1,629	1,822	25
Construction	412	548	645	8
Transport and communication	321	459	532	8
Trade, other	1,106	859	1,001	14
Total	5,790	6,350	7,301	100

Source: Latvian Statistical Yearbook, 1989.

However, purchasing power comparisons would probably have raised the figure. In comparison with other East European countries, the figure of US$ 2,100 per capita puts Latvia slightly ahead of Poland, but significantly behind Hungary and Czechoslovakia, a not altogether unreasonable conclusion.

As elsewhere in the Soviet Union, growth rates have steadily declined over time, especially since the late 1960s. In the early 1970s the official average yearly growth rate in Latvia was about 7–8 per cent (current prices). In the mid-1970s it was 6 per cent. In the 1980s, the yearly growth rates hovered around 3–4 per cent. Given the existence of some open inflation and weaknesses in the Soviet statistical system, these figures do not reflect actual growth. In fact, stagnation is likely to have set in already in the 1970s and Latvian economists estimate that in the late 1980s stagnation may well have turned into an actual decline in real output.

Preliminary figures for 1990 provided by the Latvian Statistical Committee indicate that official estimates of national income fell in 1990 by 3 per cent, compared to 1989, and there is an absolute decline in 82 out of the 108 'most important production means'. This includes a 1.3 per cent decline in industrial output and a 10 per cent decline in agriculture and transport volume. These figures were the basis for Prime Minister Godmanis' characterisation of the present situation in Latvia as one of 'economic crisis'.

The structure of the economy has changed significantly since the prewar period. In 1930 the relative weight of industry and agriculture in terms of employment shares were 13 per cent in industry and 66 per cent in agriculture, while in 1987 40 per cent of employment was in industry and 16 per cent in agriculture.

After the major changes in the 1950s and 1960s, the structure has remained relatively stable. Table 3.1 shows the various sectoral shares of national income in current prices from 1980 to 1989. These figures suggest the sectoral contributions to national income. Determined as they are by the peculiarities of the Soviet pricing system, too much cannot be made of them. Even over time, interpretation is fraught with fallacies. For example, the increase in the share of agriculture in 1985, as compared to 1980, is partially

Table 3.2 Latvia: industrial structure, 1980–9 (1982 prices, in per cent)

	1980	1985	1989
Heavy industry:	49.3	53.7	54.9
Electroenergy	1.4	1.4	1.4
Fuel	0.5	0.5	0.4
Metallurgy	1.9	1.8	1.6
Chemical	6.2	7.2	7.6
Machine building and metalworking	23.4	26.6	27.6
Woodworking, cellulose and paper	5.4	5.9	5.7
Construction material	3.5	3.2	3.2
Glass and porcelain	0.7	0.6	0.6
Light industry	23.4	20.5	19.0
Food industry	26.7	25.3	25.4
Total	100	100	100

Note: Classifications as between 'heavy' and 'light' industry are as shown in the original source and are somewhat different from that used in Chapter 11.

Source: Latvian Statistical Yearbook, 1989.

explained by price restructuring in the early 1980s.

Table 3.2 shows the various industrial branches as shares of total industrial production. Despite the lack of raw materials, a sizeable heavy industry has developed, the largest share of which is represented by machine building and metalworking (including the electrical and electronics industries) but also including the chemical, wood and construction material industries. Light industry (textiles, shoes, leather etc.) represents about one-fifth and food industry about one-fourth of industrial production.

Heavy industry includes essentially all large industrial enterprises, mainly producing electronic goods like radios and telecommunication equipment or machinery like engines or minibuses. Some of these have a near-monopoly on production within the Soviet Union, and many of them produce goods partly for the military. Almost all enterprises in this category have been subordinated to all-union ministries. They are completely integrated into the Soviet economy with vast interchange networks of goods and services throughout the Union.

The food industry and the light industry, representing 25.4 per cent and 19 per cent of industrial production in 1989, have remained under republic control.

Latvia's pattern of industrial development has made it very dependent on the import of raw materials, energy and labour from the Soviet Union. This is particularly true of the heavy-industrial sector, since Latvia has no metals and few indigenous energy resources. One of the most important factors of integration into the Soviet Union has been the extreme dependence on imported energy — mainly oil and gas from Siberia. In 1990, 90 per cent of heating fuel, 100 per cent of oil and 50 per cent of electricity used was imported. The food industry uses domestic raw materials (even though

Latvia imports feed and fertilisers for its agriculture), but light industry relies on raw material imports, mostly cotton and wool from Uzbekistan, Kazakhstan and Georgia.

The chain of command over at least the 'non-essential' enterprises has gone through various changes, notably with the Khrushchev and Kosygin reforms. Following the July 1987 session of the Central Committee of the CPSU, the control structure for industry started to change significantly in some respects. In 1987, 50 per cent of industrial production came from union–republic enterprises (that is controlled by both republican and all-union branch ministries). In the following years most of union–republican enterprises have come under republican control. The all-union enterprise share of industrial output decreased only marginally from 40 per cent in 1987 to 37 per cent of industrial output in 1990.

In 1989, there were 403 industrial enterprises and production complexes, of which 237 were in heavy industry, 73 in light industry and 89 in food industry; 29.8 per cent of all enterprises were under all-union subordination in 1990. Latvia claims ownership to all assets on Latvian soil. However, even with independence this issue may not be finally settled.

The consumer goods' share of industrial production is large in comparison to over-all Soviet industrial structure and has increased slightly over the 1980s to 45 per cent in 1989. The per capita production of consumer goods measured in retail prices in 1988 was 2,555 roubles, higher than in any other Soviet republic. (The average for the Soviet Union was 1,224; Estonia was second with 2,504 and Lithuania third with 2,090.) Nevertheless, capital and intermediate goods still accounted for 55 per cent in 1989.

In 1989, 373,700 workers were employed in the industrial sector, 259,900 of whom were employed in heavy industry. Numbers employed in industry grew until 1984, since when there has been a decline. In 1989 there were 43,500 fewer employees in industry than in 1984. This may reflect three developments: a downturn in output, a burgeoning net emigration and, possibly, incipient restructuring away from heavy industry.

Latvian agriculture's focus on animal husbandry has been strengthened during the Soviet period. Meat, poultry and dairy products are delivered to the Soviet Union. Animal husbandry production has increased to almost twice the level of 1938 and now represents more than two-thirds of agricultural production. The volume of crop production has grown slowly, being only 14 per cent higher in 1989 than in 1938. The area of land used for agricultural purposes has declined from 3.8 million hectares in 1935 to 2.6 million hectares at the end of 1989.

In 1989 there were 363 kolkhozes in Latvia, with an average size of 5,980 hectares, using 53.3 per cent of agricultural land. The 199 state farms, with an even larger average size of 7,295 hectares, used 38.4 per cent. The average size can be compared to the 1935 Latvian farm average size of 16.3 hectares. After years of official support for the supposed technological and economy-of-scale advantages of very large agricultural complexes, the recognition of the inefficiency of the giant farms has in recent years led to their division into smaller units, and some sovkhozes have been transformed into kolkhozes.

The 1988 Council of Ministers' resolution on farms paved the way for the establishment of private farms. Their number grew from 900 in the spring of 1989 to almost 4,000 at the end of 1989. At that time they used 49,000 hectares, or 2 per cent, of all agricultural land. Although the number of private farms continued to grow in 1990, their average size is small — 17 hectares in 1989. However, significant change will come only after new privatisation legislation is adopted.

The government envisages land to be fully privatised over the next twelve to fifteen years, and it is envisaged that 75 per cent of agricultural land will then be privately owned. The lack of available and appropriate machinery, inputs and credit still makes the prospect of private land less attractive in practice than in theory. Cases have been reported of voluntary collectives forming after it was found that the individual farms were not viable. Some rural areas (for example Bauska) have been so depopulated in the general urbanisation process that it is hard to find willing takers who know the area and farming. Nevertheless, as government privatisation plans and intentions to return nationalised property to its former owners proceed, the private farm share of agriculture should increase.

Although the share of transport in national income is significantly smaller than industry's or agriculture's, it is a traditionally important branch of the Latvian economy. Rail and ocean transport are used for external trans-actions, while trucking is mainly used for domestic cargo transport. In 1990, the ice-free ports of Riga and Ventspils had cargo traffic of 7 and 35.7 million tons, respectively. Ventspils had thus been one of the Soviet Union's main harbours, with very important shares of, among other things, oil exports and grain imports. Practically all Soviet oil exports to the Rotterdam market is said to pass through Ventspils.

Railway, shipping and air transport are subordinated to all-union ministries, but the Latvian government expects these branches to become major sources for foreign-exchange earnings when transferred to republican control or privatised. Though independence has radically improved the prospects for such a transfer, large-scale Union investments and the military significance of this branch may still make aspects of this issue subject to difficult negotiation.

The trade pattern with the Soviet Union has been relatively simple. Latvia has exported processed food stuff and manufactures and imported energy, agricultural and industrial inputs, testifying to the large degree of integration into the Soviet economy. As examined in Chapter 7, Latvia's trade balance has been negative in recent years. Foreign trade in convertible currencies and foreign-exchange transactions has also been of only marginal importance to Latvia. This is likely to change with independence and represents an impor-tant aspect of current reform discussions.

E. The government structure and the reform process

a. Forces for and against reform

Fundamental changes are taking place in all spheres of life in Latvia. The pace of transformation in the last years is such that it is difficult to recall the consensus before 1987 in the world at large as well as within the country on the prospects for Latvian sovereignty. Soviet *glasnost* allowed the emergence of social and political beliefs in 1987 that had previously existed as undercurrents in Latvian society. Rallying around cultural preservation and environmental issues, a popular movement emerged that increasingly focused on national revival and sovereignty.

There has been alongside the goal of independence a strong impetus for fundamental economic change. The goal of transition to a market economy is unquestioned, and strategies and programmes for it are constantly being reworked as experience accumulates. The government is attempting to change the institutional and personnel structure of government itself and the legal framework for social and economic activity. A factor contributing to the forces for change is the popular perception of belonging to the West and unambivalent positive attitudes toward it. A complete rejection of the former system is easier than in other parts of the Soviet Union since it is perceived as imposed from the outside. It is often argued that cultural values such as the Protestant work ethic and individualism contribute to the adaptability of Latvia to Western-style economic functioning. The rapid development of the cooperative and self-employed sectors since 1987 lends support to this argument. Nevertheless, there is a series of factors that impedes radical change. Latvia is still very much part of the Soviet Union in reality if not in spirit, particularly in terms of economic dependence.

Institutional resistance to change goes beyond ordinary bureaucratic resistance. New institutions are only now being created and therefore the old ones cannot be discarded. There is often confusion about the new policy-making role of government: the creation of an environment and incentives for individual actors rather than directing the economy through plans and administrative orders. Beyond bureaucratic inertia, the vested interests of the previous *nomenklatura*, whose main asset was the access to goods and privileges, are cited by Popular Front leaders as a factor blocking certain initiative even within the front. Yet, some of today's most active and respected leaders also held important positions before 1987, indicating that generalisations are not easily made. The centralised and administrative system also has exhibited predictable bureaucratic resistance to change: such as the view that decentralisation in principle is good but that lower or local level institutions are neither capable nor 'ready' to handle such responsibility.

The heritage from the postwar years obviously includes popular values shaped by experience of the centrally planned system. These attitudes affect the development of a market economy rather directly by influencing popular attitudes towards the new economic actors. The attitude to markets is verbally positive but in reality ambivalent. The perception that high incomes are often connected to criminal activity remains strong. High profit rates are often seen as unjust, and there is tension between wanting free prices but socially appropriate and 'just' prices. Another consequence of the centralised system is the suspicion of decentralisation. It was illustrated by the fears of a dynamic and inventive cooperative leader, who for all his support for new style economic activity was dismayed at the news that a near-by huge kolkhoz would be divided up into several farms. He took it to mean that it was 'falling apart', in his eyes as a consequence of bad economic times.

The desire for political democracy and a market economy presupposes a transition on the part of the ministries to a more Western-oriented policy-setting role. The bureaucracies are not only structurally the same as they have been for years, but also contain much the same personnel with the same tasks and rules. Though many struggle to lead the reform process, government authorities acutely feel a need for young and educated personnel. When the new government was formed in May 1990 there were simply not enough highly qualified people to fill more than the most essential positions, and as a result it is often only the minister and perhaps one or two others who are new. In some cases new ministers had no support staff of their own and consequently are virtually captives of the old structures. For all the 'new thinking', work descriptions and habits are much the same and often include a deeply rooted suspicion of non-administrative methods of economic decision-making.

Resistance comes not only from 'above', from people who have administrative positions to defend. An example of resistance 'from below' is provided by the Trade Ministry, which concerns itself with the internal distribution of goods in the republic. When the new minister assumed his position in May 1990, he set out to reform his ministry to reduce direction of enterprises, encouraging the establishment of more horizontal, freer ties between them, especially for the supply networks. Free pricing was encouraged (except for certain basic goods where state prices were retained). But before long firms which had difficulties agreeing turned to the ministry to resolve their disputes and tell them what to do. The minister drew the analogy of a teenager fighting to be independent from his or her parents, but, when freedom is gained, comes running back for support and guidance.

The formal structure of the Latvian government has not yet changed much, except for the role of the Communist Party, as illustrated by its exclusion from the government telephone book. The Communist Party was subsequently suspended and its assets confiscated as a result of its support for the Moscow coup attempt in August 1991. The governing organs remain the Council of Ministers, chaired by Ivars Godmanis and the Supreme Council (Parliament) with its chairman, Anatolijs Gorbunovs. On a fundamental level, however, the administrative links to Moscow have been severed, which is especially important for the ministries. The Latvian government now is supposed to function as a separate, self-contained unit.

A government structural reform has been planned for 1991, but not worked out as of this writing. Meanwhile, the ministries and departments have remained more or less the same, with a few new ones, such as the Department of Nationalities Questions, added as the need is perceived. There is a lot of overlap in responsibilities among the ministries and a lot of room for improved coordination, for instance, between the Ministry of Economy and the Ministry of Finance.

This can at least partly be explained by the role traditionally played by the ministries in the centrally planned system: they were organs charged with the implementation of specific policies set from above rather than policy-making bodies. This is especially true for the ministries responsible for economic branches, such as the Forestry Ministry, the Industry Ministry, the Agriculture Ministry etc.

Economic decisions are coordinated in the Council of Ministers, the Ministry of Economy and the Ministry of Finance. There are also two important departments that are placed directly under the Council of Ministers: one for foreign economic relations and one for privatisation.

In the Council of Ministers, Vice-Premier Arnis Kalnins has a group of economic advisers. Kalnins is also the chairman of the Council of Ministers' commission on economic reforms, also called the 'little Council of Ministers', which includes the ministers of economics, finance, agriculture, industry and justice and directors of departments under the Ministry of Economics and the Council of Ministers.

The Ministry of Economy was formed in the summer of 1990 on the basis of the State Planning Committee (the republican branch of the old Union Gosplan), while certain committees, which had had more or less the status of ministries, such as the price committee, became departments under this ministry.

The Council of Ministers' commission on economic reform deals with main questions of economic reform and structural change, while the ministry and its departments work out more specific programmes, draft economic law proposals etc. There is a shortage of qualified specialists in specific economic areas.

The Ministry of Finance, formerly only an accounting appendage to the central planning, distributional and financial authorities of the Soviet Union, is being pressured to play a new economically important role as Latvia is gaining fiscal and eventually also monetary independence.

In addition to these institutions there is also the year-old Department of Foreign Economic Relations directly under the Council of Ministers. The department is actively promoting joint ventures and other business relations with hard-currency partners and, for example, led the negotiation on Latvia's share of Soviet debt.

To deal with the politically very important issues of privatisation and property, the relevant department in the Ministry of Economy was turned into a Department of the Conversion of Property Relations directly under the Council of Ministers in May 1991.

b. Parliament and the legislative process

The Supreme Council has 201 deputies, who were elected for five years on 18 March 1990. Approximately two-thirds of the deputies belong to the Popular Front fraction. The rest represented the Ravnopravie (equal rights) grouping, including the Interfront and Communist Party deputies until their support for the Moscow coup attempt in August 1991 forced some of the grouping's members to resign and the pro-Soviet factions to be dissolved. New parliamentary elections are foreseen, for the near future, though the present Parliament is elected for a five-year period. The political process in the near future, however, is highly dependent on the resolution of the difficult citizenship issue (see separate section): who is a citizen of Latvia and who has the right to vote?

Fifteen permanent parliamentary commissions have been formed, the largest of which is the Economics Commission with seventeen members. It deals with all economic issues, and has sub-committees on budgets, price reform and other issues. Privatisation has become such a pervasive issue within the Economics Commission that there is a proposal to create a new privatisation commission.

The relation between the administration and the Parliament is close, since the Godmanis cabinet was selected from within the Popular Front, who have the overwhelming majority in the Supreme Council. However, the general view is that the qualifications of the deputies are very uneven, and there is no staff to support them. It is not uncommon to hear expressions of government frustration at parliamentary opposition to government policy proposals. At the same time, some Popular Front leaders are starting to voice concern over the government leaders' apparent bureaucratisation and administrative orientation. In reality, the government has not had much trouble getting its proposals through Parliament, and even the opposition has in many cases voted in favour of proposals presented by the government such as the tax and enterprise laws. Certain issues, like privatisation, are more complicated, however, and for a long time there were three rivals to the government plan circulating in Parliament: one from the Popular Front and two from the opposition. The passage of the government proposal was by no means assured, but a compromise between the Popular Front version and the government proposal was finally accepted in order to initiate the process.

c. The economic reform process

The first major step towards economic transformation was Parliament's adoption on 27 July 1989 of a law on economic sovereignty. Similar to the laws of Estonia and Lithuania, it makes far-reaching claims regarding economic resources and enterprises on republican territory, and stipulates the aim of replacing the Soviet central planning system with a regulated market economy. Private property is permitted and put on equal footing with other forms of property. The right and intention to institute a national currency and financial institutions and to conduct and control the republic's foreign trade is proclaimed. The Supreme Soviet in Moscow did not reject this law, but rather adopted proclamations (*ukaz*) that in principle gave republics the go-ahead to enact economic legislation. However, negotiation with Moscow followed on more precise division of authority. On 27 November 1989, the Supreme Soviet adopted a 'Law on the Economic Sovereignty of Estonia, Latvia and Lithuania'. The law was vague on all crucial issues, and provided no basis for further negotiations and agreements between the union and the republics. However, it enabled work to proceed on a new legal framework.

Two months after the May 1990 independence proclamation the government presented its first economic reform programme. The 'overriding goal' is said to be a smooth transition to a market economy while 'at the same time recreating the integrity of the Latvian economy as a separate unit'. The long-term goals are summarised in seven points: to guarantee stable socioeconomic development while securing domestic consumption and social needs; to make a transition to a market economy; to establish stable, treaty-based relations with the Soviet Union and other republics and states on a fair and equal trade basis and to develop foreign trade; to protect the domestic market through trade quotas, own money and customs; to develop a unified Baltic market and close ties to the Scandinavian and other West European nations; to prevent further degradation of the environment and to initiate its clean-up, and; to guarantee property and individual rights. The document then goes through major issues such as privatisation, prices and taxes, and the major sectors of the economy. The document, albeit long, is rather vague and while the long-term goals have not changed much, the Latvian government is discussing the neccessity to work out a new and more specific economic reform programme during 1991.

Underlying and occasionally dominating the economic reform process has been the political search for independence. The transformation of the economy and the effective use as a sovereign state of macroeconomic instruments can only take place if territory and borders can be controlled. The Latvian government has seen negotiated agreement with Moscow as the only realistic path to follow, and even while a general settlement did not seem near, progress, albeit limited, was made in negotiations on certain specific economic issues. This was the case, for instance, with the question of the lump sum to be paid to Moscow from the Latvian budget, where agreement was reached. Of course, independence has now radically changed the situation and opened new opportunities for economic reform and sovereignty.

It is the declared intention of the Latvian Parliament to establish its own currency and economic borders. As during the pre-war period of independence, the currency's name will be the lat. So far however, Parliament has not yet approved the actual printing of bank-notes and minting of coins. There has in the government and among the government's experts been a great deal of hesitancy at introducing the currency too early before the Latvian government really is in control of the necessary instruments. A currency which could not retain its value might compromise the idea of economic reform as a whole. With independence at hand, there is now the ambition to introduce the lat as soon as possible. Barring economic breakdown and hyper-inflation in the Soviet Union, or its successor, which may be a too heroic assumption, the introduction of the lat is not likely to come before the second half of 1992. That would give Latvia the time to become a member of the International Monetary Fund and muster the necessary stabilisation loans that will be necessary.

To protect against high Soviet inflation, various alternatives to a full-fledged new currency have been considered. One idea was 'white money', essentially a system by which wage earners in Latvia would get a certain part of their rouble wages coupled to divisible certificates. The 'white money' would be required for the purchase of designated consumer goods. Another system discussed is the 'debit card', essentially the same system, but with an electronic card replacing the paper certificates and enabling better monitoring of money flows and prices. With independence, these ideas can now happily be discarded. Instead, alternative currency regimes need to be considered, in particular the relations to the other two Baltic states, which will also be introducing ther own currencies. Some of the options are explored in Chapter 6.

Equally important for a functioning independent monetary system is, of course, the existence of an adequate financial system. This process has already come some way. In 1989 new cooperative banks started to form. Today, there are nine commercial banks in Latvia. They are overseen by the Bank of Latvia, which was founded in July 1990 but which so far has not developed many central bank functions. The new banks exist parallel to the old system, with a Latvian branch of Gosbank and the specialised banks for industry, agriculture and housing. The nine new commercial banks do business through Gosbank branches, in Latvia and elsewhere, and remain largely dependent on the Soviet system to carry out trade outside Latvia. It is proposed that the Bank of Latvia will merge with the Latvian Gosbank branch during 1991. Such a change would be significant since it would give the Latvians control over the important Gosbank branch and create the basis for the development of a real Latvian central bank.

Vneshekonombank, the Soviet foreign-trade bank, was until independence still officially the main handler of foreign exchange. In practice, it has been avoided as much as possible. Interlatvia, the Latvian Foreign Trade Association, arranges import and export deals and has considerable autonomy. It has so-called border trade rights which exempt it from having to deal with Vneshekonombank and surrender foreign exchange to Soviet reserves.

During 1990, the number of actors dealing with foreign exchange increased. Four of the new cooperative commercial banks were given the right to engage in foreign trade. These banks, like their counterparts in Estonia, engaged in the auctioning of or trade in foreign exchange, despite the apparent illegality of such activity according to Soviet law. Direct barter deals with foreign companies are also made on an increasing scale. Riga is apparently a centre for such deals, many of them far outside Latvia, in the Caucasus for example. In practice, many companies keep most of their foreign-exchange holdings abroad. Svenska Handelsbanken is one such bank, through which trade payments have been made.

Obviously, it has been a main policy goal for the Latvian authorities to gain control over the handling of foreign exchange. In pursuit of this goal the Latvian government negotiated with the Soviet authorities to take over a part of the Soviet foreign debt. Latvia's potential access to shares of new Western credits to the Soviet Union was seen as an additional reason for Latvia to accept this burden. This obviously is a charged political issue, related as it is to the whole issue of claims and counter-claims between Latvia and the Soviet Union, resulting from the fifty years as part of the Soviet Union. In choosing to negotiate the assumption of part of the Soviet debt, Latvia furthermore chose a different strategy from both Estonia and Lithuania. Apparently, a preliminary agreement was at one point reached on Latvia's share, corresponding to its relative size by population, 0.9 per cent. The value and repayment terms of the debt have not been disclosed. The order of magnitude discussed seems to be around US$ 400 million, to be repaid over a period of three to four years. Annual payments would likely have been high in relation to present foreign-exchange earning capacity. With independence, this whole issue must, however, again be considered as undecided.

Budgetary sovereignty was proclaimed at an early stage, abrogating all Soviet taxes (except import and export duties). A new set of taxes has been legislated and are being implemented. A major price reform has been undertaken, changing the expenditure side of the budget by a switch from price subsidies to income transfers. The first independent budget has been adopted. Finally, negotiations led to an agreement in June 1991 on how and what Latvia should contribute to the Soviet budget.

During 1990, following the proclamation of independence, the payment of taxes to Soviet authorities practically ceased. Preparations for a number of new tax laws were made. So far nine laws have passed Parliament, to be implemented from 1 January 1991. Turnover and excise taxes are meant to cover almost two-thirds of expenditure. The intention is to replace the turnover tax with sales tax and eventually with a value-added tax. The three other most important taxes are the profit tax, the income tax and the road tax (actually a fuel and motor tax tied to expenditure on road maintenance etc.). There is also a payroll or social tax of 37 per cent of the wage bill, paid by employers into a special pension and social security fund. The new taxes, especially the latter one, have raised an outcry among firms, state and cooperative alike, for being much too high. It seems a review is under way.

With one major exception, the expenditure side of the budget does not look much different from earlier years. The exception is the substantial price reform undertaken 3 January 1991. By the reform, prices on meat, milk and bread were raised by as much as two to three times. A large part of the subsidies thus saved was used for compensation, generally to all wage earners and specifically for child allowances and pensions.

It is difficult to assess the new budget. On the income side, the taxes are new, and projected yields are not much more than conjectures. There is uncertainty whether all-union firms will respect Latvian laws and pay taxes to Latvia. In fact, the uncertainties were so great that just a few months after a balanced budget was adopted, the Government stated that a deficit of 400 million roubles could be expected in 1991. A revised version of the budget is under preparation.

Latvia has made progress in the negotiations with the Soviet Union on budgetary matters. The Soviet authorities initially demanded that a percentage of collected turnover tax be sent directly to Moscow, while Latvia insisted that all tax revenue should remain in Latvian hands, but a single payment to Moscow could be made for specific purposes. The Latvian demand was accepted during the negotiations. Initial Soviet claims on the order of three billion roubles came down to an agreed payment of 350 million roubles for 1991. The use is later to be specified. The import and export taxes, presently under Soviet authority, remain an unresolved issue.

F. The social situation

a. The nationality issue

There is one aspect of Latvian society that pervades all social questions: the issue of nationalities. In 1935, 77 per cent of the 1,905,400 inhabitants of the Latvian republic were ethnically Latvian, while 8.8 per cent were Russian and 4.9 per cent were Jews, the other nationalities representing fewer than three percentage points each. In 1989, there were 52 per cent Latvians, 34 per cent Russians, 4.5 per cent Belorussians and 3.4 per cent Ukrainians. In rural areas, 71.5 per cent of the inhabitants are Latvian, but only 44 per cent of the urban population is Latvian. For Riga, the numbers are very dramatic: 36.5 per cent Latvian and 47.3 per cent Russian. And in southeastern Latvia, Daugavpils has a 58.3 per cent Russian majority, while Latvians there represent only 13.0 per cent. That a majority in this city also voted for independence in the March 1991 referendum therefore carries great political significance.

The speed and volume of Russian immigration, together with low rates of assimilation to the local culture measured by such indicators as knowledge of the local language, has led to a widespread popular Latvian perception of threat to their national survival. In the 1989 census 66 per cent of Latvians reported mastery of Russian as a second language, while only 21 per cent of Russians reported mastery of Latvian.

Immigration to a large extent has consisted of blue-collar workers, so that only 36 per cent of industrial labour is Latvian. In railway transport and waterway transport the figures are even lower: 26 per cent and 11 per cent respectively. Meanwhile, the administrative apparatus was 56 per cent Latvian-manned in 1987 and the cultural and art field had 75 per cent Latvians. Thus the nationalities question is interwoven with socio-economic factors. The large all-union enterprises have a particularly high concentration of Russian workers, and ethnic tensions could easily intensify as a result of conflicts with Moscow or simply economic problems such as unemployment in specific sectors.

If Latvian popular nationalism is resentful about recent history, the Russian-speaking population often expresses fears about their future rights in an independent Latvia. Myths and prejudices exist on both sides, but apart from a few incidents in 1989, the level of ethnic tension in society has been low.

Some measures affecting the Russian-speaking part of the population have already been taken by the Latvian government. This includes the 1990 language law, according to which all workers in the administrative, service and health fields will have to know sufficient Latvian for their professional purposes by 1 January 1992. (The implementation of this plan has run into problems, however, owing to lack of qualified teachers, textbooks etc., and few people seem to believe that the law can be implemented on time without exceptions.) Through penalties and restrictions, the government cut immigration to the point where in 1990 for the first time in the postwar years there was negative migration. A law on migration is in the process of being adopted. A new programme of education is being worked out which includes certain provisions giving preference for Latvian for higher education for the future as well as making Latvian mandatory from first grade even in Russian-language schools.

The big unresolved question is that of citizenship in an independent Latvian republic. Although Latvian government leaders and officials have indicated their preference for the so-called 0-variant (that is citizenship to all presently residing in the republic) or the modified 0-minus-5-variant (those who have lived there a minimum of five years), some of the more outspoken nationalists and Parliament deputies call for other options, the most extreme being that citizenship should be granted only to those who held Latvian citizenship in 1940 and their descendants. The question is far from being resolved. The general Latvian population may be more radical in its views on this question than the present Latvian government.

Awareness of potential problems has led to the creation within the new government of an infrastructure to deal with these issues. Members of the Supreme Council's Commission on Human Rights and National Questions have participated in international conferences recently in Oslo and Tallinn on issues of the rights of nationalities. On 6 February 1991 a Department of Nationalities with ministerial status was created by a resolution of the Council of Ministers whose task it will be to study the nationalities' situation and work out proposals such as a potential addition to the language law, if it is found that it cannot function as intended. There will be a law on national minorities, concerning culture and education, and the national minorities will receive government funds for their activities in these fields.

b. Health

Average life expectancy in 1989 was 71 years — 66 years for men and 75 years for women. This is 3–7 years lower than in the majority of European nations. Infant mortality has declined from 17.9 in 1970 to 11.0 per thousand births in 1988, which is low in comparison to the aggregate Soviet Union figure of 24.7. Birth defects have been increasing. The leading causes of death are circulatory system disease, cancer and accidents.

In 1989, there were 50 physicians (including all specialties) and 147 hospital beds per 10,000 inhabitants. In 1989 51,500 abortions were performed, that is 79 per 1,000 women between the ages of 15 and 49.

Health care has been provided by the state for free, except for certain services like dentistry. Care is accessible in polyclinics or hospitals, the location being determined by place of residence. As in all of the Soviet Union, there has been a shortage of advanced technology and medication. Medical workers including doctors have had extremely poor official salaries (the beginning monthly salary for a physician is 120 roubles). These factors have led to a general perception of poor health care, even if above the Soviet average.

A transition to a payment and insurance health system is planned and the specifics are being worked out by the republican Physicians' Society. Part of the cost will be provided for from the 37 per cent social insurance tax, but part will be paid by individuals. There are already some doctors' cooperatives, who receive patients for payment outside of their official practices. This kind of care is expected to expand.

c. Education

Of 1,000 inhabitants 15 years or older, 115 had completed higher education in 1989 (that is 241,200 people), 23 had started but not completed higher education, 168 had special middle (352,400) and 298 had general middle education (623,900 individuals). In 1989–90 there were 933 general education high schools with 351,900 students, 44 per cent in Latvian-language schools, 40 per cent in Russian-language and 16 per cent in the mixed schools. There are ten higher education institutions with 45,600 students. Every year, 20,000 students study in vocational schools. For people over the age of fifteen with high school education or more, Latvia is only in tenth place among the Soviet republics.

There is a general recognition that education needs to be improved and indeed transformed in several spheres. A new Law on Education has been drafted but not yet passed. The proposed education reform attempts to give increased autonomy to the schools, with centralised final exams rather than tightly controlled curricula. Russian-language education will be expanded to twelve years (from eleven). Higher education will continue in two groups, one for Latvian and one for Russian (but hoping for one integrated group in three to four years).

It is recognised that a major effort will have to be put into preparing new textbooks and courses, particularly in the social sciences and humanities, and to create new specialties.

d. Housing

The average living space per person in urban areas was 17.5 square metres in 1989 and 24.5 square metres for rural inhabitants. The urban average, which has increased from 15.7 in 1980, is now approaching the prewar urban average of 17.8 square metres. Urban housing in 1989 consisted of 28 million square metres in the state and social sectors and 5 million square metres privately owned living space. Living space in the countryside is privately owned.

Provision of services varies considerably between urban and rural areas. In the cities, 93 per cent of living units have running water and sewerage systems, 77 per cent have hot water and 80 per cent have central heating. In the countryside, only 67 per cent of homes have running water, 45 per cent have hot water, 65 per cent have sewerage systems and 54 per cent have central heating.

The quality of housing is visibly low by Western standards. Poor post-war construction and lack of maintenance materials and effort make for rundown old and new houses. Repair and touch-up efforts were made in Riga in the 1980s, so parts of the city like the old town appear to be in reasonable shape. Other parts of Riga are literally crumbling, while massive low-quality housing was thrown up in ugly clusters around the previous outskirts of town.

Housing has been a problem throughout the postwar period. Immigration to the republic and increasing urbanisation have meant that new construction has not taken care of the problem. In the last couple of years construction has all but stopped, particularly because of the shortage of construction materials.

In 1989 there were some 165,000 on housing waiting lists. To get on to the waiting list, one needs to fulfil certain criteria such as having less than five square metres of dwelling space per person. There are obviously no shortages of people with abysmal living conditions. Multi-family (so called communal) apartments, with sometimes as many as five families sharing bathroom and kitchen, abound in the centre of Riga. In the capital 3,000 houses have been classified as *avarijas*, that is should be torn down.

Once on the list for housing, the waiting period for an apartment is hopelessly long: in 1990 persons in the queue from 1974–5 were receiving living space. At the same time, certain companies build their own housing for their employees and so does the army. This has in many cases increased discontent, since it often meant that the migrating labour received new apartments after only two or three years' waiting.

A government commission on housing is being formed. The leader of the commission has indicated three main directions in which to search for housing solutions: the normalisation of rents, that is major increases and greater differentiation depending on type and size of housing; privatisation, including the return of nationalised property and consequently the repair and maintenance of buildings; and government credits for construction.

e. Consumption standards

According to statistics, the annual per capita consumption of meat products in 1989 was 85 kilos (the same as in 1935), milk products 457 kilos (566 in 1935), 286 eggs (76 in 1935), 102 kilos of grain products, 47 kilos of sugar, 76 kilos of vegetables and 42 kilos of fruit. In addition, the per capita consumption of alcohol was 5.6 litres of absolute alcohol in 1989 (down from 11.3 litres in 1980).

Per every thousand inhabitants there were 411 televisions, 439 radios, 397 refrigerators and 289 washing machines. There were twenty-six cars per hundred families in the same year, or ninety-four cars per thousand inhabitants.

Basic food products are accessible in stores and at markets, and since the price increases in January 1991 the difference in prices between state stores and the free kolkhoz markets has decreased. Another effect of the price increases that is very much part of lifestyle evaluation is that the queues have diminished — and hence also innumerable hours of women's wasted time. Meat costs 7–15 roubles per kilo, butter 10 roubles/kilo, cheese 7–10 roubles/kilo, milk 65 kopeks/litre and a loaf of bread less than a rouble. The quality of the foodstuff is not only lower than in Western Europe but also lower than in prewar Latvia say some who remember. Other goods are available on ration coupons: namely flour, noodles, sugar (one kilo per month), coffee (one jar per month), alcohol (0.5 litres per month) and cigarettes (five packs per month). Ration coupons are provided for all individuals, including children, and the alcohol coupons can also be used for alternative goods such as socks, chocolate, sweets and children's clothes. Although basic foodstuffs are widely available, choice is limited, and there is a lack of fresh fruits and vegetables in the winter. At those times queues continue to signal the arrival of scarce goods.

The fulfilment of consumption desires is obviously dependent on two factors: the availability and the affordability of goods. There are seeming paradoxes in both of these dimensions for the unknowing observer in Latvia: average wages are too low to explain levels of consumption, and people in the streets of Riga are dressed far more elegantly than the not very inspiring stores would seem to allow. There are many factors that explain this real consumption.

Non-food consumption, especially clothing, illustrates both problems of unaffordable prices and availability of goods. Goods are sold in state stores, where shipments of good quality are quickly sold out, and commission stores, where more goods are available but for a higher price and often of a different quality, home-made or small producer-made. Prices are so high in the commission stores that it is simply not possible to clothe a family on an average salary. Many women sew their family clothes (fabric was until recently relatively easily available) and have over the years devoted considerable energy to copying Western fashion.

There are many ways of acquiring quality goods other than the ubiquitous queues. For people with money, there are high-priced black markets. More importantly, there are networks of mutual services: employees reserve goods at their work place or otherwise for their friends, who in turn do the same in return. Stealing from state companies and shipments is pervasive as is putting goods under the counter. An example was given of men's suits shipped to a state retail store. One man had agreed to provide professional legal advice to a distributor, and as part of his payment he was promised a new suit for the official (low) state price. The distributor still had to go through the motion of shipping the goods, and therefore agreed with the retailer to provide an extra suit for the retailer if he would 'sell' the legal adviser his reserved suit. It obviously takes some time to develop supply networks; newcomers to the region may have only two options: be poorly dressed or make large amounts of money.

Goods like televisions, electronics and household appliances are presently difficult to get, except at very high prices. A television set in a commission store costs 3,000 roubles, that is almost a full year's salary. The view is widespread that people live off what they had accumulated before the last couple of years of *perestroika*. Some scarce goods, especially but not exclusively those produced by the company itself, may be distributed by firms to their workers.

What emerges is an image of a vast system of consumption relations based on personal or professional supply networks. Many prices paid are higher than official prices in the stores. Some goods are marketed at very high, free prices. In fact there are large differences in income. It was pointed out by more than one person that many people have legal incomes above 1,000 roubles a month. Taking into account also the substantial incomes of black marketeers, it is easy to understand the frequently expressed view that this society consists of socio-economic extremes. Experience of differentiation may thus be higher than is sometimes assumed. However, there is a widespread assumption that high incomes are associated with illegal or at least questionable activities, an attitude that adversely influences perceptions of money-making, influencing policies in relation to the development of market relations.

4 Estonia

A. History

Estonia, the smallest of the Baltic republics in population and area, shares certain historical experiences with Lithuania and Latvia, while also having a quite distinct culture and history in many important respects.

Estonia was under Russian Imperial rule from 1721 until 1918 and, like the other Baltic republics, enjoyed a period of independence between the world wars. As in Latvia, the dominant Christian church is Lutheran, but the Estonian language belongs to the Finno–Ugric language family, like Finnish and Hungarian, and is therefore unrelated to Latvian, Lithuanian or other Indo-European languages.

It is believed that precursors of modern-day Estonians settled in the Baltic region some five thousand years ago. Estonian history since the middle ages is a chronicle of foreign conquests. The Danes ruled northern Estonia from the early thirteenth century. They were challenged by German military orders, who gradually conquered Estonian territory, forcibly baptising the population and imposing serfdom under a foreign nobility, the 'Baltic barons'. In 1346, Denmark sold its remaining Estonian territory to the Teutonic Order. Tallinn was, however, controlled by the Hanseatic League.

As Ivan IV, 'The Terrible', of Russia began to threaten Estonian territory in the mid-sixteenth century, northern Estonia submitted to Swedish rule in 1561. In the early seventeenth century, the whole of Estonia was conquered by the Swedes. Estonians subsequently characterised the seventeenth century as the period of 'the good Swedish rule'. Rule of law was introduced, education was promoted and a university formed, and serfdom was alien to the Swedish tradition.

Russia conquered the Swedish Baltic provinces during the Great Northern War in the early eighteenth century and gained possession of present-day Estonia in 1721. The Baltic barons' extensive rights over the peasantry were restored, and the Estonian peasantry had to endure the severe conditions of serfdom until achieving personal emancipation in 1816–19. A middle class of Estonian townspeople and craftsmen emerged, since the freed peasants had few possibilities of acquiring agricultural land.

In the mid-nineteenth century, an Estonian national consciousness emerged. There was increasing confrontation between the Estonians and the German gentry, along with intensified attempts at russification of Estonian society. Nevertheless, basic education in Estonian was introduced, resulting in almost complete literacy among the peasants.

In the early twentieth century, as regional and local administration was reformed throughout the Russian empire, nationally minded representative bodies came to power in Estonia. The Russian revolution of 1905 brought demands for national autonomy, along with an uprising against the Baltic barons which was brutally crushed. Still, the subsequent fifteen years saw a steady rise in national awareness.

In 1918, as the Russian and German empires simultaneously collapsed, the Estonians managed, for the first time, to achieve formal statehood. On 24 February 1918 the autonomous Estonian government issued a Declaration of Independence, which was followed by a costly but eventually successful war of independence against Bolshevik and German troops. In the Peace Treaty of Tartu, in February 1920, Soviet Russia forever renounced all claims of sovereignty over Estonia.

The 1920s were, generally speaking, a period of national consolidation, despite a parliamentary system incapable of producing stable governments. The economy, still predominantly based on agriculture, experienced steady growth. However, the world-wide economic depression, culminating in 1932–3, brought about a political crisis that ended liberal democracy in Estonia. The right-wing 'League of Veterans of the Independence War' emerged as a political power, launching populist attacks on Parliament. General opinion was in favour of a strong executive power, and eventually the leader of the Agrarian Party, Konstantin Päts, staged a *coup d'état* in March 1934. Allegedly, this was to eliminate the threat from the increasingly aggressive league, which was soon outlawed along with all the political parties. Päts' authoritarian regime was one of the mildest in Eastern Europe and nobody was executed for political reasons. Termed 'the era of silence', it lasted throughout the 1930s with a limited shift towards democracy in 1937–8.

In the inter-war period, Estonia was ethnically fairly homogeneous. In 1934, the Estonians accounted for 88.2 per cent of the population, the most important ethnic minorities being Russians, Germans, Swedes and Jews.

As a result of the Molotov–Ribbentrop pact, Estonia was placed in the Soviet sphere of influence. A Soviet–Estonian assistance pact was signed on 28 September 1939, forcing Estonia to accommodate Soviet troops on its territory. During the Soviet Winter War with Finland, the Soviets launched bombing raids on Finland from Estonian air-force bases. Also as a result of the Nazi–Soviet pact, the Baltic Germans emigrated to the Reich in October 1939.

As the Germans were invading France, Estonia was occupied by the Soviet Union on 17 June 1940, two days after a similar fate befell Lithuania. A puppet government was set up, and to give an air of legality to the annexation, 'elections' were staged to a new Chamber of Deputies. At its request Estonia was incorporated by the Supreme Soviet of the Soviet Union as a Soviet republic on 6 August 1940. In Estonia, just as in the other Baltic states, the Soviets rapidly imposed their order during the first year of occupation. The urban economy was nationalised, although agriculture was treated with more caution. In mid-June 1941, some 9,000 people were deported, including a sizeable part of the national elite.

After the Germans attacked the Soviet Union in late June 1941, they soon reached Estonia, and by October the whole country, including the islands, was under their control. The Germans let Estonian pro-independence partisans do much of the fighting against the retreating Soviets, but they had no intention of restoring independence, although the Estonians were regarded as racially superior to the Slavs. A programme was adopted to entirely germanise Estonia entirely within twenty years. The small Jewish community was virtually extinguished. As the Germans were facing difficulties on the eastern Front, a general mobilisation of Estonians was imposed in February 1944. Still, the Soviet offensive in the summer of 1944 could not be fought back. Before the Soviets had reoccupied Estonia, by October 1944, some 70,000 Estonians fled to the West, most of them to Sweden or Germany.

As in Latvia and Lithuania, there was armed resistance to the Soviets throughout the 1940s, involving an estimated 5,000 'forest brothers', as the partisans were called in Estonia. Despite resistance to the intensive collec-tivisation campaign, guerrilla warfare ceased in the early 1950s as hope of restoring Estonian independence, with help from the West, gradually vanished.

The economic development in Estonia after the war echoes that of the other Baltic republics. There was a marked shift towards heavy industry, which involved a massive influx of labour recruited from Russia. Estonian agriculture was rapidly collectivised in the spring of 1949, after an estimated 60,000 peasants had been deported.

Native Estonians were purged from the Communist leadership in the early 1950s, since Stalin only trusted the 'Russian Estonians', Communists of Estonian descent who had grown up in the Soviet Union. They would continue to dominate the Estonian party administration until the late 1980s.

In the mid-1950s, however, conditions began to improve. Some progress was made in agriculture, and Estonia was slowly opening up to the outside world, as contacts with Finland were re-established. The system of regional planning under Khrushchev benefited smaller republics, and in the 1960s living standards rose. Still, the immigration of labour from other Soviet republics was a cause for concern, and the ethnic Estonians' share of the population decreased from 75 per cent in 1959 to 65 per cent in 1979. A general russification was also noticeable in administration and culture during the 1970s.

During the 1970s and 1980s, the economic administration of Estonia was relatively innovative, a number of institutional reforms and experiments being tried out in Estonia for the first time in the Soviet Union (see the discussion of reform in the later part of this chapter) and in the process, Estonian enterprises achieved a degree of autonomy from Moscow control which was unusual in the Soviet Union.

B. Population, geography and natural resources

a. Geography and natural resources

Estonia has a surface area of 45,200 square kilometres, making it smaller than Latvia or Lithuania but larger than Denmark. The country is characteristically flat; the highest point is Suur Munamägi, 318 metres above sea level. While lower Estonia is mostly flat and marshy, the landscape of upper Estonia is more varied and, as a result of glacial deposits, has more fertile soils.

The coastline of Estonia is approximately 3,800 kilometres long, with a total of over 1,500 islands, of which Saaremaa and Hiiumaa are the largest. Lake Peipsi towards the Russian border and Lake Vortsjärv in the south are the two largest lakes. The most important ports are Tallinn (including Muuga) and Loksa on the north shore and Pärnu on the west coast.

The population of the capital Tallinn is 500,000. Other major cities are: the university town Tartu with 110,000 residents, Narva with 82,000 and Kohtla-Järve with 77,000 inhabitants. The population density is 34.9 persons per square kilometre, not including Soviet troops on Estonian territory.

Unlike Lithuania and Latvia, Estonia possesses important mineral resources. Deposits of oil shale and phosphorite ore are situated in the northern parts of the country and stretch from Tallinn eastward. The shale is combusted in two large power stations in Narva, but it is also refined in the chemical industry to produce oils, sulphur, phenols and other products. Phosphorite ore is used in the production of fertiliser.

Approximately 25 million tons of oil-shale has been mined annually since the mid-1970s. For 1991, there are plans of reducing the production to twenty million tons. At this rate of depletion, the deposits should last for another forty years.

While not mined directly, large amounts of oil-shale of a low quality are dug out from the phosphorite quarries in Maardu, near Tallinn. Like Swedish alum-shale, it disintegrates easily because it contains pyrite, releasing vanadium and radioactivity, sometimes leading to fires that are difficult to extinguish.

It is assumed that Estonian oil shale has been used to produce uranium. The uranium content is low. In Sillamäe, close to Narva, a plant probably based on oil-shale processed uranium ore between 1949–89. Today, Sillamäe processes another radioactive mineral, loparite, which is brought in from the Kola peninsula. Extracted materials include niobium and tantalum (used in steel processing) and rare earths such as neodynium (used in magnets).

The large reserves of phosphorites in Estonia are estimated to total fourteen billion tons. Four deposits have been identified, with the largest and richest one located near Rakvere in the north-central region (eight billion tons). Today, phosphorites are mined only in Maardu. The quarries are almost exhausted, and mining will end in 1993. A chemical plant in Maardu produces fertilisers as well as gravel from the limestone layer that covers the findings.

Deposits of magnetite (iron ore) east of Johvi were discovered during the time of independence. The iron content is low (25–28 per cent) and the magnitude of deposits is still undefined.

The bedrock of the islands and of northern and central Estonia is rich in limestone and dolomite. Limestone is mined for production of lime, cement and building materials from a total of seventeen quarries. Dolomite is mined at Kaarma quarry on Saaremaa and at six other quarries.

Commercially useful sands, clay and mud of different qualities are found all over Estonia. These are mainly used in the building materials industry. Glass sand, for instance, is mined in southern Estonia. Diatomite from Narva is extracted to produce insulation. Blue clay, which is suitable for ceramics, and cambrian mud are utilised in the production of heat-resistant bricks.

Roughly 40 per cent of Estonia is covered with forests. The northern forests are mainly coniferous, while those in the south are mixed or deciduous. After World War II, former pasture lands became forested. These new forests are now ready to be cut and the timber could be used in pulp production. Two pulp and paper mills are in operation today, in Tallinn and Kehra, each with a capacity of about 40–50,000 tons of cellulose per year.

About 20 per cent of Estonia's surface area is covered by marshlands. The layer of peat in the marshes and fens is an average of three metres thick. In 1989, total peat production was 3.6 million tons, of which one million came from state and collective farms. Peat is used as fuel and in the agricultural sector as bedding and fertiliser. It was traditionally a main source of energy until the extensive investments in district heating in 1965. Today, peat accounts for 2 per cent of the Estonian energy supply. Estonia's environmental programme now stipulates that peat harvesting should not exceed regrowth capacity as extensive use endangers the marshes.

b. Demography and the nationalities issue

The demographic evolution of Estonia after incorporation into the Soviet Union has been marked by two processes with far-reaching consequences: first, the losses due to World War II and Soviet repression in the first few years after annexation and, second, the massive influx of mainly Russian workers in the post-war years.

In 1939, that is before the exodus of the Baltic Germans, the population of Estonia was 1,333,917, of which 88.2 per cent (1,000,360) were Estonians. According to the latest census of 1989, the population was 1,565,662, of which only 61.5 per cent (963,281) were Estonians. Thus, in 1989 there were fewer Estonians living in Estonia than fifty years before.

From October 1939 to January 1945, Estonia lost about 25 per cent of its entire population through flight to other countries, repressions, war casualties and loss of territory. About 60,000 people are thought to have perished by repression during the first year of Soviet rule in 1940–1, and 50,000–60,000 in the immediate post-war years. In the largest deportation of March 1949, more than 20,000 people were forced to leave. In addition, an estimated 72,000 people became permanent refugees during the 1940s. An important consequence of these events was deformation of the age and sex structure of the population.

The second important development was the massive immigration of labour from Russia and other parts of the Soviet Union. This was triggered by a Soviet decision in 1945 to develop the oil-shale industry in northeastern Estonia and adjacent parts of the Leningrad region in order to provide Leningrad with gaseous fuel. A concentration of new industries in Tallinn also led to a large influx of Russian-speaking workers. It has been estimated that, during the period 1945–58, the net increase of population by migration was 283,500. Thereafter, the net inflow averaged about 7,000 per year until 1987. Since virtually all immigrants were non-Estonians, there has been a drastic change in the nationality composition of the population. In 1989, ethnic Estonians constituted 61.5 per cent of the population, Russians 30.3 per cent, Ukrainians and Belorussians 4.9 per cent and other nationalities 3.3 per cent. Of the non-Estonians, over 85 per cent live in towns, whereas the countryside continues to be fairly homogeneously Estonian.

Large concentrations of non-Estonians live in Tallinn and the northeastern part of Estonia. In Tallinn, only 47 per cent of the population is Estonian, while the largest northeastern cities (Narva, Sillamäe, and Kohtla-Järve) have only very small Estonian populations (4, 3 and 21 per cent, respectively). As these are among the most important industrial centres of Estonia, non-Estonians dominate the industrial sector.

These developments have been perceived as a threat to the survival of the Estonian nation. The possibility of a further massive influx of migrants was one of the main sources of opposition to the 1987 plans to exploit phosphorite deposits outside Rakvere. Because of strong public pressure, this project was eventually cancelled. In that year, the Estonian government also took measures to prevent a further influx of immigrants. For example, enterprises were charged a substantial fee for each new worker employed from outside Estonia. While overtly designed to cover the cost of social services, the clear purpose was to discourage the hiring of new workers from elsewhere in the Soviet Union. However, as enterprises faced ambitious targets under soft budget constraints, monetary incentives proved ineffectual. Therefore, a law on immigration was passed by the Supreme Council in 1990, establishing a quota for immigration to Estonia, along with large fines for municipalities registering immigrants above the quota (100,000 roubles per person). The total immigration quota for 1991 was set at 2,290 people. The quota is distributed by cities and regions, primarily to prevent a further concentration of Russian-speakers in Tallinn and the North-East. The large northeastern cities are even obliged to ensure a negative net balance of migration.

Already in 1990, however, there was a negative net migration balance of 4,021 persons, probably owing both to the stagnation of the large-scale industrial sector and to the declining attractiveness of the Baltic republics for Russian migrant workers as a result of the political situation. The net outflow from Estonia to the Soviet Union was 3,181 (7,554 arrivals and 10,735 departures). A more recent development is the growing tendency towards emigration to the West, especially among better educated Estonians. In 1990, the net emigration to other countries was 840 (827 arrivals, 1,667 departures). The population statistics omit most of the Soviet military personnel in Estonia and only count a relatively small number of officers with Estonian residence permits.

Extensive immigration has caused several problems. First, many of the immigrants are transient workers who stay for only a few years before moving elsewhere. It has thus proved difficult to integrate these people into

Estonian society, and they have formed the backbone of the militant anti-reform Intermovement.

Concern over the ethnic composition of the population is exacerbated by other factors. The birth rate among Estonians, which has always been low relative to other nationalities in Estonia, has declined. In the early 1980s, this even caused the Estonian population to decrease in absolute terms. While the birth rate subsequently increased a little, preliminary figures for 1990 again indicate a sharp drop, possibly owing to economic instability and declining living standards. The Estonian population is ageing rapidly, particularly in rural southern Estonia, where in some areas pensioners make up one-third of the population. The predominance of young families among immigrants further raises the natural growth of the non-indigenous population.

The policy of reversing the migration pattern has achieved some success. Other developments that have caused concern (falling birth rates and an ageing rural population) may be more difficult to influence and are, in fact, similar to changes that have already taken place in Sweden, Finland and other European countries.

C. Recent political developments

Before 1987, there was only very little open political activity in support of democracy and Estonian independence. Those that overtly expressed their 'dissident' views would face surveillance and almost certain arrest. In that year, two developments signalled the beginnings of open protest and the gradual process of restoring a democratic, civil society. The first was the wave of opposition to the plans of the all-union mineral fertilisers ministry to establish a huge, potentially environmentally disastrous phosphorite mine in northeast Estonia. The second was a rally organised by former political prisoners in Tallinn on 23 August, the anniversary of the Molotov–Ribbentrop Pact, demanding the publication of the pact and its secret protocols.

The early initiative was almost fully carried out by true dissidents. The resulting polarisation with the ruling Communists left room in the centre for a 'loyal opposition' which would seek change from within the system. This emerged in April 1988, when the Estonian Popular Front was organised at the initiative of the current prime minister, Edgar Savisaar. This movement mobilised a great number of people with its initial rhetoric stressing the need to achieve greater autonomy within the Soviet Union.

On 16 November 1988, the Estonian Supreme Soviet adopted a declaration of sovereignty of the Estonian SSR which meant that Estonian laws would take precedence over Soviet laws on Estonian territory. Despite a harsh initial response, Moscow quietly accepted Estonia's position and confirmed negotiations on devolution of economic power. However, by the time Moscow's response had been prepared and the Law on Economic Independence had been adopted, Estonia went through a series of extraordinary political manifestations, culminating in the Baltic Way demonstration of 23 August 1989, which prompted Moscow to react in a highly threatening way. This reaction galvanised public opinion, and by the year's end confederation and economic independence were being replaced on the Estonian political agenda by complete political independence. The election on 18 March 1990 led to an independence-minded Supreme Council, the first act of which was to declare a transitional period for restoring the independent Republic of Estonia, during which the necessary institutions of an independent state would be created and the necessary settlements with Moscow and the other republics negotiated. In reaction, Moscow halted further discussion on sovereignty within the federation. A frantic legislative campaign began with the purpose of establishing the legal framework for creating all institutions of an independent state based on a market economy.

The March elections for the Supreme Council were contested by a wide range of parties, while others boycotted the vote on the ground that a Soviet-established body elected under Soviet rules was not a legitimate representative of the Estonian nation. As the democratisation was still at an early stage, and true parties had not yet formed, most of the groupings were 'fronts' or 'movements'. As their platforms were vague, the voters focused on personalities more than ideologies.

Among the groups contesting the vote was the Popular Front, which continues to exist while its members also join new parties. Popular Front activists play a key role in the Social Democratic Party and Liberal Democratic Party, both formed in 1990.

A second grouping called itself 'Free Estonia' (Vaba Eesti) and claimed national independence among its most prominent goals. Much of its leadership consists of high and medium-level officials from the previous administrations, including enterprise managers and previous ECP leaders, many of whom had left the ECP by this time. It is led by former Prime Minister Toome. According to opinion polls, Free Estonia seems to receive strong support from non-Estonians, despite the dominating position that Estonians have among the leaders.

A third contingent which contested the election is a group of so-called 'national radicals' with links to the earlier dissident movement. These deputies form the core of the right-of-centre legislators. Prominent members include the conservative leader, Kaido Kama, and the Christian Democrats, Mart Laar and the Reverend Illar Hallaste. This group has no representative in the government and only reluctantly participates in the work of the Supreme Council since it questions the legitimacy of this body. Instead, its members have largely chosen to work through the Congress of Estonia, a non-Soviet Parliament built up from the grass-roots in 1989–90. This was elected by citizens of the Republic of Estonia at the time of the Soviet occupation and their descendants. Gradually, however, national radicals have been forced to take a more pragmatic line, supporting the March 1991 referendum on independence despite initial misgivings.

The last significant group to contest the Supreme Council election is the Russian-dominated Intermovement, which has been opposed not only to

Estonian independence but to far-reaching reform in general. It has staged some spectacular actions of protest, the most infamous being the attack on the Parliament building on 15 May 1990. Most of its representatives are members of that part of the Communist Party that remained faithful to Moscow after the split in 1990. The four deputies holding seats reserved for the Soviet military also vote with the Intermovement.

The independent Communist Party is largely without significance, since it has virtually no electorate left. None the less, about three-quarters of Supreme Council members are or have been Party members.

The distribution of votes to the 105-member Supreme Council was roughly the following: Free Estonia 28 per cent, Intermovement and allied groups 26 per cent, Popular Front 24 per cent, and national radicals 22 per cent. Since that time, allegiances have shifted and the establishment of a true multi-party system has progressed. In mid-1991, at least twelve 'fractions' have been registered in the Supreme Council. This makes impossible a very clear characterisation of the balance of power. Since the Popular Front dominated government neither has a majority nor formal coalition partners, decisions have sometimes been difficult to carry through Parliament.

D. Structure of the economy

a. National income

During the inter-war period, Estonia underwent rapid economic develop-ment. Living standards increased, and by the late 1930s per capita income was close to that of Finland. During and immediately after World War II, the destruction and disorganisation resulting from successive Soviet and German occupations contributed to a severe decline in incomes. Eventually, performance began to improve, and in the 1960–85 period, national income measured by 'net material product' grew at a nominal annual rate of about 6–7 per cent. Within this time span, the 1960s and early 1970s were a period of considerable economic growth. In contrast, the 1980s were a difficult period with slow or even negative real growth.

Material living standards in Estonia have remained above the Soviet average as was the case during independence. In 1989, officially reported 'net material product' was 4.5 billion roubles, or about 2,850 roubles per head (compared to 2,342 roubles in the Soviet Union as a whole). The average salary in the state sector was about 270 roubles/month, or 3,240 roubles/year. (By April 1991, the average salary was reported to be around 500 roubles/month.) As indicated in Table 4.1, nominal wages in agriculture have tended to be above salaries in industry, an opposite pattern to that prevailing in the Soviet Union as a whole.

A precise breakdown of the sources of growth is not possible. However, gross material product (the sum of output at all stages of production, not only value added: about 11.5 billion roubles in 1989) grew more rapidly than net material product over the last twenty years, indicating that the relative cost of material inputs has increased and that efficiency of resource use has declined.

Table 4.1 Estonia: general economic data, 1980–9

	1980	1985	1988	1989
National income	3,222	3,605	4,062	4,478
(current prices, million roubles)				
National income per capita	2,183	2,358	2,602	2,847
Capital stock (1973 prices)	8,465	10,920	12,542	12,952
(million roubles)				
Employees (thousands)	762.7	786.8	770.3	761.2
Average monthly non-agricultural wage	188.7	215.1	249.2	—
(roubles)				
(Soviet average)	168.9	190.1	219.8	—
Average monthly collective farm wage	206.6	272.7	304.9	—
(roubles)				
(Soviet average)	118.5	153.4	181.8	—

Source: Estonian Statistical Yearbook, 1990.

b. Broad structural changes

Before its incorporation into the Soviet Union, Estonia was a farming country with a rapidly developing industrial sector. The latter almost doubled its production between 1929 and 1939. The economy was based on small production units in agriculture, industry and trade.

There was considerable entrepreneurial activity with only about 30 per cent of the active population being wage-earners. This enabled Estonia to respond in a flexible way to developments on internal and external markets and simplified adjustments in the labour market.

A sectoral breakdown of employment in 1934 shows that, in spite of industrialisation, independent Estonia remained an overwhelmingly agrarian society (see Table 4.2).

Independent Estonia interacted with the rest of the world mainly by exporting agricultural products (especially butter and meat) and importing manufactured goods. After the monetary reform in 1924, which ended a period of rapid inflation (see Chapter 6), Estonia's new currency, the kroon, achieved convertibility and a high degree of stability. The exchange rate fluctuated only between 3.67 and 3.81 kroons/dollar during the decade 1925–34. From 1925 onwards, the external trade accounts were always near balance.

There was a significant cooperative movement. In 1939, about 3,000 consumer and producer cooperatives in banking, insurance and trade had a total membership of 270,000 and a total turnover that exceeded the state budget by half.

The government budget stayed close to balance. The social welfare system, including social insurance and labour protection laws, was advanced in comparison to other developed countries.

During the war, there was much plundering and destruction of industrial capacity. Subsequent Soviet rule brought near-total state ownership and central planning, with rapid nationalisation in 1945 being followed by

Table 4.2 The sectoral division of Estonian employment in 1934 and 1989 (%)

Sector	1934	1989
Industry	18	32
Agriculture and forestry	45	13
Education and culture	12	12
Construction	4	10
Trade	6	9
Transport and communication	3	18
Other	12	16
Total	100	100

Source: Horm (1990); *Estonian Statistical Yearbook*, 1990.

concentration into fewer and larger firms.

While the high reported growth rates of Soviet industry should not be fully believed, the Estonian economy did undergo a notable structural transformation, changing from a predominantly agrarian economy to one of the most urbanised and industrial regions in the Soviet Union. Total industrial employment overtook agricultural employment around 1960.

While the direction of change was to be expected at that stage of Estonian development, the fast pace was dictated by a policy of 'forced industrialisation'. This reflected a Soviet desire to exploit the relatively good infrastructure of post-war Estonia, with the additional political motivation of fostering assimilation and russification in the borderlands of the empire.

Agriculture based on small farms was replaced by collective and state farms. In 1989, Estonia had 200 collective farms and 126 state farms, with heavy dependence on inputs from monopolistic organisations in the Soviet Union. The industrial structure (284 enterprises in 1989) has been shaped largely according to the plans and priorities of around twenty all-union ministries and departments with little, if any, account being taken of the local market, labour force and natural environment. Exports to the West were curtailed and replaced by centrally planned exchange of goods with the Soviet Union at arbitrarily fixed prices.

Table 4.3 presents the recent evolution of national output and its composition. Net material product (NMP) attempts to subtract inputs used at each stage, coming closer to international accounting methods than gross material product, the other measure sometimes used. The latter totals production at each stage, resulting in some double counting.

Agriculture accounted for about 25 per cent of NMP on average during the last five years, industry for about 45 per cent, with the remainder accounted for by trade, construction, transportation and other activities.

Over time, concentration of state-owned industrial firms increased, and by 1980, 21 per cent of them employed over 1,000 persons. By 1989, there were only around 300 such concerns, together employing about 220,000 persons, or an average of around 780 workers each (see Table 4.5). These coexisted with smaller enterprises, for example state agricultural enterprises, cooperatives, municipal authorities and construction organisations, which

Table 4.3 Estonia: composition of national income, 1980–90 (net material income, current prices, million roubles)

	1980	1985	1989	1990
Industry	1,605	1,592	1,957	2,021
per cent share	49.8	44.2	43.7	44.5
Agriculture	531	893	1,132	1,140
per cent share	16.4	24.8	25.3	25.1
Construction	302	389	488	516
per cent share	3.4	10.8	10.9	11.4
Transport communication	159	210	278	273
per cent share	4.9	5.8	6.2	6.0
Trade, other	625	522	621	593
per cent share	19.4	14.5	13.9	13.0
Total net material product	3,322	3,605	4,478	4,543
Total gross material product	8,277	9,886	11,503	

Source: Estonian Statistical Yearbook, 1990.

together employed around 65,000 persons. Today, state-owned industry accounts for 80–90 per cent of industrial employment, production and fixed assets, a level which has begun to marginally recede only in the last year.

The late 1950s saw a shift in the Soviet Union from sectoral control by central ministries to local control over industry by fifty regional economic councils, or sovnarkhozy (see Chapter 5). Estonia, like some other small republics, became a single sovnarkhoz. This period also saw a shift in emphasis from producer to consumer goods and a further concentration of industry.

These developments were reversed with the 'Kosygin reforms' of 1965, which returned control to central sectoral ministries. By 1980, 87 per cent of Estonia industrial output was being produced by enterprises either fully or mostly controlled by Moscow.

In 1988, fifty-nine of the around 300 state industrial firms were all-union enterprises controlled by about twenty Moscow-based ministries or departments, mostly in the fields of energy and fuel, chemicals, petrochemicals, machine building and metallurgy. A second group of 169 firms was under the mixed subordination of all-union and Estonian authorities. This included the important sectors of light industry, food processing, and forestry and wood products. Finally, the remaining sixty-three enterprises, which together employed around 63,000 workers and accounted for less than 10 per cent of industrial output, fell under Estonian control. These were in sectors such as peat, construction materials and some light industry. During the last years, the mixed subordination enterprises have been eliminated in Estonia and are now formally under full republican control. However, as all-union ministries continued to be the key input suppliers and output purchasers, the *de facto* independence from Moscow increased to a much lesser degree.

E. Major sectoral developments

a. Agriculture

Before independence, most agricultural land was owned by the descendants of Baltic–German feudal lords. One of the first acts of the new Estonian government was a land reform in 1919, whereby property was redistributed from large estates to tenant farmers. By 1939, there were almost 140,000 farms, as compared to around 52,000 in 1919. A thriving agricultural sector became the mainstay of the economy, with total output doubling and milk production trebling during the independence period.

Immediately after World War II, agricultural production fell to about one-half of the pre-war level and suffered another disastrous blow in 1949 with the start of forced collectivisation and the subsequent enlargement of farms. The number of collective farms fell from 2,989 in 1950 to 150 in 1985. Resistance was strong and about 12 per cent of the rural population was deported.

In spite of the excessive size of farming units, a certain recovery in agricultural production began in the early 1950s and accelerated in the 1960s. Today, production is highly concentrated in about 325 collective and state farms, employing an average of 300 persons each. This structure has only begun to change during the last two years, when measures were undertaken to restore private farming. By early 1991, 4,000 private farms had been established.

Agricultural productivity is low by Western standards, but high relative to other Soviet republics. Better performance in part reflects the shorter period of collectivisation and the memory of pre-war conditions. It may also reflect higher investments and the importance of agricultural experimentation in Estonia as compared to elsewhere in the Soviet Union.

Finally, as might normally be expected at that stage of development, the agricultural population declined, falling to one-half of the pre-war level. Today, agriculture employs around 12 per cent of the labour force and generates about 25 per cent of total net material production.

Under Soviet rule, products of animal husbandry, that is meat and dairy products, continued to be the major products. Present agricultural production is described in Chapter 12.

Food products currently constitute about 25 per cent of total Estonian exports with about one-third of the milk and meat production being sold to other union republics. Heavy mechanisation and dependence on imported inputs (fertiliser, fodder, machinery and fuel) makes agriculture highly vulnerable in case of disruptions in the availability of all-union resources. Therefore, the key strategic objective in agriculture is the reduction of dependence on the Soviet Union for deliveries of feed grain. However, the fixed state procurement prices have not provided adequate incentives for local farms to deliver grain. In 1991 it is expected that grain production will total 900,000 tons. This should be supplemented by 760,000 tons of imports of which 626,000 will be feed grain.

As in the Soviet Union in general, the output from private plots became over time a significant percentage of total agricultural output from the 1960s onwards. However, this was relatively less important in Estonia than in the Soviet Union as a whole.

b. Industry

During the period of independence, Estonian industry was concentrated in textiles, oil-shale mining and shale products. While textiles had already been well established, the largely state-sponsored shale-related activities became significant only after World War I. Other important sectors were phosphorite mining, forestry and wood processing. Changes in industrial structure, particularly the decline of some traditional industries, resulted from the 1924 Soviet embargo.

During the war, much industrial capacity was either plundered or destroyed. What remained was rapidly nationalised in 1945 and then concentrated into fewer and larger firms.

Traditional activities were complemented by new growth sectors, particularly electricity generation, machine tools and metallurgy, and chemicals. Existing concentrations of industry were supplemented by totally new industrial centres, especially in the oil-shale region, with expansions almost entirely based on immigrant labour. Light industry and food industry remained particularly important. Table 4.4 gives a broad overview of the sectoral composition and structure of industry.

Estonian light industry has long focused on textiles and particularly on cotton fabrics. Textile production has been concentrated in or near the northeastern city of Narva. In 1941 the Red Army destroyed many mills, causing immediate post-war output to fall far below pre-war levels. Textile output eventually recovered and was complemented by greater production in garments and footwear.

In 1989, textiles accounted for around 12 per cent of total industrial employment. However, as this sector is very labour intensive, and based on raw materials imported from distant parts of the Soviet Union, there is a question as to whether or not it reflects Estonia's longer-term comparative advantage.

Development of the energy sector, initially based on peat, began in the nineteenth century. Oil-shale was first mined in the 1870s, but did not become an industrial input until 1916. Its development during independence, mostly for the production of oil and gasoline, even allowed Estonia to become an oil exporter.

After the war, a further expansion of this sector followed Estonia's full integration into the Soviet northwest energy system. Electricity generation was developed through the construction of two new shale-fired power plants near the Russian border. The feedstock for these plants comes from seven nearby mines and four open-cast pits. The annual output of shale electricity is about 16 Twh (terawatt-hours). While oil-shale is a relatively costly form of energy, and thus possibly uneconomic at world prices for inputs and outputs, it represents one of few indigenous energy sources in the Baltic area.

Machine-building and metalworking grew in relative importance over the post-war period, although its share of Estonian industry stayed below the

Table 4.4 Estonia: industrial structure, 1989

	share of industrial production	no. of enterprises	employees (thousands)	average employment/ enterprise
Electrical energy	6.0	10	7.2	720
Fuel industry	2.6	14	11.3	807
Chemicals	9.2	17	16.2	953
Machinery/metalwork	14.4	46	58.2	1,265
Timber, pulp, paper	9.1	48	28.0	583
Building materials	3.6	21	14.3	681
Light industry	26.4	45	43.3	962
Food industry	23.9	51	28.2	553
Others	4.8	28	14.6	521
All enterprises	100	284	221.3	779

Source: Estonian Statistical Yearbook, 1990.

Soviet average. During independence, a key sector had been production of railroad equipment. Over time, this general sector has become more diversified, with important products including electric and electronic products (especially motors) and oil industry equipment, mostly produced in Tallinn. Today, over one-fourth of industrial workers are employed in this sector.

The food products industry, already important during independence, continues to be central. It employs about 14 per cent of the industrial labour force and produces around one-fourth of the measured value of industrial output.

Relative to the pre-war period, forestry has declined in importance. The wood-products industries, with a focus on woodworking (furniture and ski production), are based increasingly on imported inputs. Other important products are plywood, fibre board and particle board. Timber, wood products, and pulp and paper sectors together employ about 13 per cent of the industrial labour force.

Chemicals are largely derived from indigenous oil-shale and phosphorite fertiliser resources. Main products are fuel oils with other outputs including solvents, asphalt binder and oil coke. The chemical industry employs about 7 per cent of the industrial labour force.

Finally, in construction materials, the Soviet period saw the expansion of the large cement plant at Kunda which has now become a major source of environmental pollution.

The immediate future of Estonia's industry is uncertain, depending on how political relations between Estonia and Moscow develop. The most important problem in the short term is the uncertainty about material supplies. As Moscow no longer guarantees supplies even to all-union enterprises, and has sharply curtailed deliveries of imported inputs, most factories are forced to by-pass the centre and develop 'horizontal links' with other enterprises.

Soviet wholesale prices were deregulated as of 1 January 1991. As a result, the cost of inputs has risen sharply for many enterprises, often by as much as 50–200 per cent. Still others have failed to secure required inputs at all. Therefore, it is likely that industrial production will fall in the short term. In its prognosis for economic development during 1991, the Estonian goverment warns that industrial production may fall by as much as 12–15 per cent.

c. Foreign trade

During the inter-war period, Estonia primarily exported meat and dairy products (in some years, butter alone comprised over one-third of total export value), textiles, garments and forestry products. Among its major imports were cotton, textiles, iron and steel, and chemicals. Germany and Great Britain were major trading partners.

The effect of fifty years of Soviet rule and control over the Estonian economy, and of its complete integration into the Soviet economic structure, is best shown by the fact that Estonia's direction of trade turned 180 degrees from West to East. Although few reliable statistics are available, about 90–95 per cent of exported goods are currently sold to other Soviet republics, about one-half going to Russia. Of the remaining part, 1989 statistics show 50 per cent sold to socialist countries, 36 per cent to the West, and 12 per cent to developing countries. In relation to the Soviet Union, Estonia is a very open economy. In 1966, both imports as a share of consumption and exports as a share of production were around 30 per cent.

Currently, the main export items are electrical power, meat and dairy products. Other important sectors include light manufacturing, food processing, machine-building and metallurgy, wood products, pulp and paper, building materials and chemicals.

In services trade, tourism has performed well and has potential for further growth. However, the hard currency from much of this trade has been absorbed by the central agencies and ministries in Moscow.

According to the Estonian Institute of Economics, merchandise imports totalled around 3.5 billion roubles in 1989, with over 90 per cent coming from other Soviet republics. Chapter 7 provides a detailed discussion of the Estonian balance of payments and the statistical weaknesses which colour the interpretation of reported figures.

In recent years, foreign-trade organisation has undergone some changes. Until 1987, all foreign trade in the Soviet Union was centralised in all-union foreign-trade organisations. In that year, direct trade with Estonia was made possible with the establishment of Estimpex, the first enterprise of its kind in the USSR. In 1989, all republics and enterprises in the Soviet Union were allowed to enter into direct foreign-trade agreements. By 1991, 3,200 enterprises, organisations and cooperatives had direct foreign-trading rights.

F. Recent economic policy and institutional reform

a. Estonia as an economic laboratory

In the 1970s and early 1980s, Estonia spearheaded a number of economic experiments which inspired many of the changes that were later implemented throughout the Soviet Union. The first of these took place in agriculture as early as the mid-1970s. Around 1985, further experiments followed in the service sector, light industry and individual enterprises. Finally, a wage reform was implemented in 1987.

The 1975 agricultural reforms were at first only organisational. Estonia became the first republic to establish regional agro-industrial associations to coordinate the whole chain of agricultural production and distribution within each region. In 1982, three ministries and 'state committees' were amalgamated into one Ministry of Agriculture. Estonia also pioneered self-financing in agriculture which made profit the most important of a reduced number of plan indicators and gave farms the right to sell above plan production at a 50 per cent premium above state procurement prices. In 1987, there was a further initiative towards vertical integration in 'agrofirms' and 'agroindustrial associations'.

The service-sector reforms of 1985 attempted to substitute contracts for vertical plans and directives. The different service establishments under the Ministry of Services were united in associations, one for each type of service (for example dry cleaners, barbershops etc.). These associations were to conclude collective agreements with each establishment under its direction. The establishment, in its turn, would conclude individual agreements with employees, leasing out facilities, arranging social insurance payments and so on. On the whole, the service experiment had positive results. In the first year, services supplied to the general public increased and the number of complaints decreased dramatically. The experiment also involved contradictions that could only be solved by further liberalisation. Still, the experiment was judged successful enough for the Soviet government to introduce the same system in all republics in 1986. Although the service experiment largely became irrelevant in 1987, when Soviet laws on individual work and cooperatives were introduced, it had prepared Estonians for the greater freedom that these laws offered. For this reason among others, new enterprise forms developed particularly fast in Estonia.

Parallel with the service experiment, the Estonian authorities cautiously encouraged individual entrepreneurs in handicrafts production. By March 1985, 757 such entrepreneurs were registered. Since it proved difficult to control the revenues of these entrepreneurs, it was suggested that the municipal authorities take an active role in overseeing private enterprise. This proposal was introduced in the Union laws on individual enterprise (1987) and cooperatives (1988) which were largely based on Estonian experiences.

Estonia also pioneered the reform of the hierarchical branch-orientated production structure by a reorganisation of its light industry starting in early 1985. At that time, this was the only significant industrial sector which the republics controlled. This experiment was inspired by the East German

'Kombinate'. It reduced the number of plan targets from over twenty to just three — profits, gross production and an investment limit and gave enterprises and the ministry itself much more freedom and flexibility. The experiment also contained contradictory elements. On one hand, individual enterprises were allowed to retail their own products, bypassing the traditional trade organisations. At the same time, the Ministry of Light Industry in many respects strengthened its position as a monopolist. On the whole, supply was too limited to create active competition among the enterprises. Partly to address the problem of competition, the Estonian government in 1987 started to pursue a policy of encouraging small-scale state enterprises with production aimed at local markets. The light industry experiment was later extended to other branches of industry. Thus, industrial associations were formed out of enterprises in the food industry, local industry and the woodworking industry.

Beginning in 1987, Estonia was also the testing ground for a wage reform, designed to decentralise decisions on wage-setting and to tie wage developments closer to changes in productivity. Although the economic results of the experiments may have been limited, they were instrumental in obtaining a special status for the enterprises and organisations involved, thus freeing them from much of Moscow's influence. In this respect, the experiments can be seen as a direct forerunner to the discussions of regional economic self-accounting and, later, economic independence.

b. From experiments to independence: the recent evolution of Estonian economic policy

Many of the Estonian experiments were made official Soviet policy at the plenum of the Central Committee of the CPSU in June 1987. It soon turned out, however, that the centre was prepared to yield very little real influence to the republics.

A July 1987 decree of the Central Committee of the CPSU and the Council of Ministers foresaw the transfer of industries producing consumer goods to the republics but also strengthened the control of Moscow over key sectors of the economy like energy production and petrochemicals.

Disappointment over the failure of the June plenum seriously to address the issue of relations between the centre and the republics prompted a number of leading Estonian economists and public figures to initiate work on an Estonian reform programme with the object of transferring as much economic authority as possible to the republic. The effort was spearheaded by the publication in September 1987 of an ambitious reform proposal formulated by a group of economists (Edgar Savisaar, Miik Titma, Siim Kallas and Tiit Maade). Savisaar, now Prime Minister, was then an official of the State Planning Commission but was dismissed as a result of his initiative. Siim Kallas was later appointed Governor of the Central Bank.

Called IME (the Estonian acronym for 'Self-Managed Estonia' which also translates to 'miracle'), the proposals contained the key assumption that decentralisation of economic management would enable Estonia to use its resources and productive capacity more efficiently. The authors mentioned two principal sources of inspiration: on territorial management, Khrushchev's sovnarkhoz reform between 1957 and 1965, and on foreign economic participation, the special economic zones in China. The proposal suggested that:

— the economy should be managed primarily by financial and monetary instruments, with prices reflecting true costs;
— all public property within the boundaries of Estonia should be controlled by Estonian authorities, allowing adjustment of production to local interest and local resources;
— economic exchange with other republics and foreign countries should be based on market principles and mediated through a convertible Estonian currency;
— Estonia should manage its own tax and budget system, making only a lump-sum contribution to the central budget for services rendered by the union;
— all organisations, enterprises and local government organs should be accountable for their own finances;
— different forms of property and enterprise schemes should be developed, including the participation of foreign capital;
— the influx of labour from other parts of the Soviet Union should be limited; and
— economic management by the government should be limited to strategic considerations.

The proposal initiated a fervent debate both within Estonia and between Estonia and Moscow. As public support mounted for the IME concept, the government and the Estonian Communist Party (ECP) were forced to accept most of the ideas. Two competing commissions — one led by the Director of the Institute of Economics of the Estonian Academy of Sciences, Rein Otsason, and the other by Savisaar — presented more detailed proposals which were amalgamated into a Concept on Self-Accounting (*khozraschet*) for the Estonian SSR. In May 1989, a law on Self-Accounting for the Estonian SSR was adopted, marking the real starting point for Estonia's economic reforms.

In taking this step, Estonia had assumed the lead among the Baltic republics in pushing for economic reform and autonomy. In fact, the leading role played by proposals for economic reform has been one characteristic of the Estonian political process. In the period preceding outright calls for political independence, economists and those with experience in managing the old economic system thus had a leading role.

For a while Moscow seemed to favour another, less radical proposal on regional self-management that would primarily have been limited to re-arrangements of the budget system. However, the Estonian model — later supported by Latvia and Lithuania — prevailed. The Baltic republics successfully worked in the all-union Supreme Soviet for the adoption of a decree on the transfer of Lithuania, Latvia and Estonia to 'self-accounting'. This decree, adopted in July 1989, was only a preliminary step towards the

Law on Economic Independence, which was finally passed in November 1989. This law went a long way in responding to Baltic demands, while in practice most issues still remained unsettled.

First, the law stipulated that the economic independence should be implemented within the framework of all-union legislation. The threat posed by this paragraph was, however, diminished by the inclusion of a rider that all-union legislation on economic questions would only extend to the Baltic republics to the extent that their move towards economic independence was not counteracted.

Second, the right to use land and natural resources remained ambiguous in the law. The republics were given the right to own and use the land and natural resources on their territories but only under the condition that the use would be in the interest of the Union as well as the republic.

Third, in the monetary and financial sphere, the republics were only given the right to 'administer' the financial system but not to take over the assets of the branches of Soviet banks on their territories. The branches of the Soviet Gosbank were specifically excluded from control by the republics, and the controversial issue of separate currencies was not addressed. The question of financial management has created some of the most bitter conflicts between Estonia and Moscow, partly because of the ambiguous wording of the law.

Fourth, the question of taxation authority was not regulated in detail. However, Moscow has not, as many Estonians feared, insisted on the right given by law to tax subjects in the Baltic republics directly on the basis of all-union legislation.

Fifth, the law foresaw a transfer of all-union property to the republics on the basis of mutual agreements. Military installations, important oil and gas pipelines, and 'other subjects of all-union significance' were to remain with the Union. Subsequent negotiations failed to define which enterprises should be considered to be of all-union significance. An agreement between Moscow and the three republics on the transfer of some enterprises was signed in February 1990, but its implementation was unilaterally stopped by Moscow after the Supreme Councils of the three republics adopted independence declarations. Of twenty-one enterprises that were to be immediately transferred to Estonia, only one seems to have changed hands. Similarly, Moscow's concession to transfer two banks to local control stalled. Gradually, however, the failure of Moscow to guarantee supplies to the all-union enterprises has made the enterprises themselves less hostile to losing their all-union affiliation.

Finally, on prices and wages the law gave little room for action by the republics. They could only establish 'differentiated conditions' within the framework of a unified Soviet price and wage system. Moscow tried to enforce its authority in this field by objecting to Estonia's first unilateral price increases on alcoholic beverages, fruits and vegetables in January 1990 but soon dropped its objections. Over time, as the need for radical price reform grew dramatically, Moscow has moved towards a position where it lets the repubics implement necessary price increases, making them — rather than Moscow — subject to any popular dissatisfaction.

Within Estonia the progression of economic reform since the adoption of the IME programme in May 1989 has been thorny and full of conflict and can roughly be subdivided into four different periods:

The first period was dominated by legislation on the reform. The IME programme had been launched in 1988 under the old undemocratically elected Supreme Soviet. However, at that time the government of Bruno Saul, which had discredited itself by open hostility to regional self-accounting, was forced to resign under public pressure. Saul was replaced by the ECP Ideology Secretary, Indrek Toome, who quickly embraced economic autonomy. The new government formed twenty-two working groups, dominated by state officials and charged with the drafting of legislation for regional self-accounting in preparation for its introduction on 1 January 1990. At the same time, Rein Otsason, the leader of one of the two groups that prepared a draft of the self-accounting bill, was appointed chairman of the Estonian Planning Committee (Gosplan). The objectives of the work in this period were limited: it was still believed that economic independence could be attained within the framework of the Soviet Union.

The second period was one of reconsideration and further preparation. It began with the appointment of Savisaar as chairman of the Planning Committee in the autumn of 1989. As the performance of the working groups had been disappointing, they were dismissed, and the preparation of the reform was moved to the Planning Committee.

It soon became obvious that a comprehensive package of legislation would not be ready by the beginning of 1990. At the same time, conflicts began to develop between the government and the Planning Committee with the latter forcing the pace of reform. Another source of disagreement resulted from the Soviet Law on Economic Independence for the Baltic Republics. Whereas the Government believed the law would create the conditions for Estonia to pursue its independent reform, Planning Committee specialists pointed out the inconsistencies.

In the third period, the reform movement stagnated. For many reasons, including the disappointment that real economic autonomy would not be achieved on 1 January 1990, economic issues were pushed into the background. Some conflicts also developed between the Supreme Council and the Planning Committee. The Supreme Council first delayed the implementation of a number of tax laws that had been proposed by the committee and later changed the date of introduction of the reform to 1 July 1990, when it was believed that a new budget and taxation system would be ready. Finally, the campaign for the Estonian Supreme Council elections in March 1990 moved attention away from economic issues.

In February 1990 the Soviet and Baltic governments agreed to give republics greater control over foreign trade operations, acquisition of foreign credits and creation of their own currency reserves. But here too, Moscow failed to yield control of any part of the relevant infrastructure. The customs and banking system remained under its control, and only very recently did Moscow actually permit some local banks to conduct international banking operations.

However, following the adoption of declarations of independence, or of a transition period to restore independence, by all three Baltic republics (in Estonia on 30 March 1990) Moscow halted implementation of the Law on Economic Independence, ceasing active attempts to achieve economic sovereignty within the Soviet system. Sanctions were imposed on all three republics. The first action taken against Estonia was in the sphere of banking, where the so-called 'war of banking' developed (see Chapter 6 for further discussion). There was also a blockade on the delivery of certain key commodities such as feed grain.

The result of developments during this period was a political and economic radicalisation. Following the elections in March, Savisaar was elected Prime Minister to replace Toome.

The fourth reform period, roughly from the summer of 1990, could be characterised as one of crisis. The sanctions from Moscow, of which the blockade against Lithuania was only the worst example, led the Baltic leaders to conclude that economic autonomy would be impossible to attain without political independence. Very few important steps towards reforming the economy were actually taken. Prices remained regulated. Little progress was made in gaining control of the financial and monetary system. Privatisation was a long way from being launched.

On the contrary, in order to counteract the total collapse of the economy, there were moves towards a strengthening of the administrative regulations of the economy such as rationing and a decree that forced state enterprises to sell 80 per cent of their output to the state. The Ministry of Material Resources continued to allocate inputs to Estonian enterprises. Most importantly, the insecurity and the inability of Estonia to gain control of key sectors of the economy, such as the banking sector, made it virtually impossible for Estonia to restructure and develop stable trading relations with the West.

c. Present Estonian reform plans

In 1991, the Estonian government plans to give priority to changing the price, wage and tax system, parallel with measures to disengage the Estonian economy from that of the Soviet Union by the introduction of customs barriers, immigration quotas etc. Although privatisation is one of the first priorities, the fact that Estonia has remained part of the Soviet monetary system casts serious doubts on the prospects for implementing a large scale privatisation in the near term (see Chapter 8). The government's agenda on economic reform consists of the following main elements:

— the creation of an independent banking system to make it possible to pursue an independent financial policy;
— the creation of mechanisms to regulate and balance the labour and consumer goods markets;
— the reinstatement of property rights of the Estonian government to those objects that will not be privatised (mainly infrastructure and heavy industry);
-— the launching of a land reform;

— the balancing of foreign trade in hard currency;
— support for the 'crisis sector' (that is key industries);
— improvement in accounting, both at enterprises and for national accounts.

The evolution of the Estonian independence process was more clearly related to the development of proposals for economic autonomy than in the other two Baltic countries. As a result, there was a more focused development of a detailed economic reform programme.

As many of the Estonian reforms are furthest along, they are used as case studies in other parts of the current volume. The reader will find a discussion of Estonian monetary and banking reform in Box 6.1 and of fiscal system reforms in Box 6.3.

One especially difficult aspect of the overall reform process has been price reform and the compensation for price increases. While some legislation on prices has been adopted, it does not amount to a fundamental dismantling of the system of centralised price formation.

A Law on Prices was adopted in December 1989 and was later followed by a decree spelling out some further details. The law preserves for the government the determination of prices for a wide range of goods: those that are covered by state orders or state purchases, those that are sold or purchased according to intergovernmental agreements and those deemed to be of state or social importance. Other prices have to be approved by the government, although the intitiative to change them may come from the enterprises themselves; this includes prices of necessities (as defined by the government) and goods or services provided by monopolists. The latter are defined as any company with a market share of more than 20 per cent for any one product. Not surprisingly in an economy as small as Estonia's, and with an investment pattern that has favoured large-scale production units, most producers were deemed monopolists. As a result, the limit was subsequently raised to 50 per cent.

Since the Law on Prices, Estonia gradually moved towards the most liberal price system in the Soviet Union, but the process was not smooth. The Soviet government initially seemed eager to defend the prerogatives of the centre with respect to price formation and price regulations, but it gradually yielded as it became obvious how politically dangerous the question of price increases is. Local authorities in neighbouring regions of Russia, most importantly Leningrad, also objected to the first price increases, since they would encourage Estonians to go to those areas to buy cheaper consumer goods. That oppositon also abated after the local authorities — like Estonia more than a year before — introduced a residency requirement for the purchase of most consumer goods.

Estonian trade unions also opposed some of the early price increases and succeeded in thwarting them for some time. Gradually, however, they have accepted the necessity of price increases. The problem seems to have been defused by the signing of a general agreement between the government and the trade unions in February 1991.

The most serious challenge, however, has come from the Russian-speaking minority, primarily in Tallinn and the northeast. The issue of price increases has been a rallying point for interests that oppose the Estonian government, and in many of the strikes and other manifestations that have taken place since early 1990, the issue of price increases has played an important part.

For this and other reasons price reform has not advanced as far as was expected from the outset. In absence of a concerted move to liberalise prices completely, most price changes that have taken place have been administrative price rises. Further legislation on the price system was shelved in August 1990 because it was concluded that a comprehensive price liberalisation could be disastrous without first establishing a customs service and a new tax system, privatising public property, reforming wages and introducing a compensation scheme. However, prices of fruit and vegetables were decontrolled in January 1990, and prices for fish and many services went up somewhat later. (The price rise for fish was not planned by the Estonian government but came in response to a unilateral attempt by Moscow, as a part of the dispute on the budget, to shift the burden of subsidising fish from the centre to Estonia.) Most prices were sharply raised as a result. For example, potatoes went up from 10 kopeks to 1 rouble per kilo and herring from 70 kopeks to 5 roubles per kilo.

On 15 October 1990, subsidies on meat and milk products were abolished. In a further move, prices of energy, transport, telecommunications services and most agricultural products were raised on 1 January 1991. Although these moves were accompanied by a compensation scheme described below, they were successfully used against the government during the Baltic crisis of January 1991 and forced the Estonian government to declare a general price freeze at that time. The next step would have been to raise rents on 1 July.

No decisions have been taken on wholesale prices, but even in the absence of any formal liberalisation, they have increased sharply. Price limits are based on profitability levels of the enterprises which are easy to manipulate. Furthermore, an increasing proportion of wholesale trade is being conducted through direct contacts between enterprises rather than through the traditional material supplies system. Even the government in Moscow recently allowed contracts at free prices above state orders. This caused a sharp increase in input prices which put retailers, who are still bound by fixed retail prices, in a difficult position together with those enterprises that produce finished products. Much production is being stockpiled which has caused a further deterioration of supplies in the retail sector. Only the large all-union enterprises have been largely unaffected since they mostly produce intermediate goods that are delivered to the Soviet market.

Thus, the issue of price reform was in mid-1991 at a stalemate. The government discussed alternative proposals for price reform, but a comprehensive liberalisation will probably have to wait until other important parts of the economic reform have been introduced. This would include a flexible anti-monopoly law more appropriate to a small economy than the clumsy 20 or 50 per cent rules applied so far.

In the long run, it would be wise for the government to distance itself from decisions on pricing. Instead of price reponsibility being transferred to enterprises, local councils have been given some authority to establish price limits, and it seems likely that they will take over many of the regulatory functions when most prices have been decontrolled. Meanwhile, inflationary pressure is building up. It is widely expected that retail prices will increase by 2.5 to 3 when they are deregulated in Estonia.

One precondition for price reform that has been put into effect, however, is a compensation scheme. In doing this, the government has implicitly declared the purpose of a retail price reform to be changing of relative prices and increased flexibility rather than achieving balance between the aggregate availability of goods and incomes. The compensation scheme adopted in the autumn of 1990 is expected to cover 85 per cent of the additional costs incurred by the public owing to higher prices. It consists of six parts:

(i)   direct compensation to 'risk groups', that is pensioners, single mothers, etc.; 750,000 people will receive forty roubles per month on average for a total of 315 million roubles;

(ii) local municipalities will receive thirty-six million roubles to distribute to approximately 85,000 people from the poorest families;

(iii) salaries of approximately 200,000 workers in the public sector will be increased for a total of sixty million roubles for the first half of 1991;

(iv) the minimum wage has been increased from 100 to 135 roubles per month;

(v)   the minimum pension has been increased from eighty to 100 roubles per month; and

(vi) enterprises have been permitted to raise wages and to compensate themselves through further increases of the prices of their products (in the future, however, there will be restrictions on wage increases).

Box 4.1   Estonian price indices

In the Soviet context, Estonia is very advanced in the construction of price indices. Beginning in the fourth quarter of 1989, a cost of living index has been constructed. However, in contrast to the international practice in which the index reflects the cost of living of a typical household, the Estonian index is based on the consumption basket of a citizen near the poverty line. While including over 100 different types of goods and services, it takes no account of luxury goods prices.

While relatively sophisticated, the index has two weaknesses which should colour its interpretation: first, as with all price indices, quality changes and unclear product definition make it impossible to ensure full comparability of goods over time. The most disaggregated data show implausible price falls for several types of goods. However, as this factor could just as well lead to overreporting in other cases, it should not systematically bias the overall index.

Second, as with all Soviet measures, the index is based on prices in state stores and does not capture the grey and black markets which have been playing a greater role in the economy. While state stores sell some goods at free prices, most free price sales take place elsewhere. In recent years, in which unofficial markets have experienced both growing volumes and premiums (ratios of prevailing prices to official prices), the official index understates the actual rate of inflation.

The index shows that relative to the fourth quarter of 1989, the Estonian cost of living in the last quarter of 1990 had risen 60.2 per cent. This can be subdivided into a 100 per cent rise in food product prices, a 22.3 per cent rise in industrial goods prices, and 19.5 per cent rise in the cost of services. In greater detail, the biggest price rises occured in potatoes and vegetables, which partly reflect price liberalisation in state stores, to a level close to those in the private markets. At the other end, prices of communications and fabrics remained unchanged.

The index also shows that inflation has accelerated. From the third to the fourth quarter of 1990, prices rose by 21.4 per cent or at a compound annual rate of 117 per cent.

To compare this performance to earlier periods, one must rely on general Soviet price indices. As price developments used to be fairly uniform across the Soviet Union, this will not be far off the mark. However, as inflation was underreported even in earlier years, official data will give only rough estimates. The annual rate of Soviet retail price inflation during 1986–90 was well within single digits.

In controlled economies there is an important distinction between actual inflation and inflationary pressure. The former would be captured by a well-designed price index. The latter also includes repressed inflation, or the price rises which would occur were all prices freely set but which is prevented by price controls.

In the Soviet Union, repressed inflation and the general goods shortages it brings have arguably been even more important for consumers' welfare than open inflation. This is by nature difficult to measure, but one indicator often used is the relative growth rate of personal income and retail sales. If the former rises faster than the latter, this can be seen as evidence of 'forced savings' owing to the unavailability of desired goods. Estonian estimates for 1990 show incomes rising by 35 per cent, while nominal retail sales increased only 25 per cent.

The qualitative picture, as described by the Eesti Konjunkutuuri-instituut (Estonian Market Institute), gives further evidence of growing repressed inflation. In 1988, currency reform rumours and other factors led to the hoarding of certain goods such as sugar. By 1989, shortages, black markets and 'speculation' (resale of goods purchased at a low controlled prices in the free market) became more prevalent. The government responded by erecting some barriers to purchases by non-Estonian residents. By 1990, hoarding of goods, either as a store of value or to acquire goods which could later be exchanged for other items, became indiscriminate. By the end of 1990, the consumer goods market was almost empty.

G. The social situation

a. Health

Life expectancy in Estonia has remained more or less at a constant level since the 1960s which may be taken as an indication that the health situation has not significantly improved. Whereas life expectancy was higher than in Finland during the interwar years, Estonia now lags far behind. In 1988, life expectancy at birth was 67 years for men and 75 years for women (71 years for the entire population). The corresponding figures for Finland were 71, 79 and 75 years.

In 1989, there were 48 physicians and 122 hospital beds per 10,000 inhabitants, and 26,000 abortions were recorded, that is 67 per 1,000 women between the ages of 15 and 49. The latter figure is down from an average of about 95 in the early 1980s.

Although infant mortality is only half the average for the Soviet Union (12.4 per 1,000 compared to 24.7 in 1988), this figure remains about twice as high as for the Scandinavian countries. Moreover, preliminary statistics for 1989 and 1990 indicate an increase. The measures for this are unclear, but one hypothesis is that the effects of the anti-alcohol campaign, which initially led to a sharp drop in infant mortality, have begun to wear off.

The most striking feature of statistics on causes of death is the exceptionally high proportion of deaths by accident and unnatural causes; in 1989 such causes represented 31 per cent of deaths among the working-age population which is almost double the level in Sweden. Part of this may be explained by misreporting, but it may also be an indication of for example, alcohol abuse. The number of accidental deaths did go down sharply after the anti-alcohol campaign.

b. Education

Of 1,000 inhabitants fifteen years or older, 117 had completed higher education, 474 had completed general secondary education, and 210 had completed less than a secondary education. In 1989–90, there were 634 general-education high schools with 227,500 students. There are six higher-education institutions with 26,300 students. In 1989, 13,800 students studied in vocational schools.

c. Housing

More than one-third of the housing stock was lost during the war. During the subsequent decades, the combination of slow construction and a high rate of immigration led to a decline in per capita living space and to serious housing shortages. As rural populations have not generally increased, shortages have been most acute in urban areas, especially in the new shale-mining cities. Also, the more ready allocation of housing to immigrants than to local residents on waiting lists became a source of ethnic tensions.

Subsequently the volume of housing has increased. In 1988, the average living space per person was 18.8 square metres in urban areas and 27.5

square metres in the countryside. Urban housing in 1989 consisted of 22.2 million square metres, of which 18.3 was in the state and social sector. Living space in the countryside is almost equally divided between the state and private sectors.

Housing quality is still poor by Western European standards. In the cities and towns, 96 per cent of units have running water, 68 per cent have hot water and 82 per cent have central heating. The subjective indicators are certainly worse, with units suffering from poor construction, lack of maintenance and dearth of materials. While much of the old city of Tallinn was renovated for the 1980 Olympic Games, few people live there and few other residental areas have seen such renovation and repair.

III The reform process

5 The inherited system and the reform agenda

A. Background

In describing the economic situation of Estonia, Latvia and Lithuania in Chapters 2, 3 and 4, the reforms that have already been launched were summarised. In this and the following chapters some of the main issues which will confront all three republics in implementing existing and developing further economic reform will be explored in greater depth.

Examination of the reform process must begin with an assessment of the legacy inherited from the Soviet planning system. Moreover, the trajectory of the reform process within the Soviet Union itself will condition the options open to the Baltic republics in the future. This is the case even though political independence now has opened a wider range of opportunities for economic policy making in the Baltic states.

After their incorporation into the Soviet Union, the three republics were forced to adopt the Soviet economic system of planning and management. Neither a smooth nor a speedy process, it was begun in 1940, interrupted by the war and restarted once the Germans were driven out and resistance (especially in Lithuania) eliminated. As in other countries of East-Central Europe, at first the communists promised to respect small-scale property but then eliminated the 'petty bourgeoisie' and collectivised agriculture.

By 1950 the three republics were barely distinguishable in their economic organisation, and in their political system, from the other Soviet republics. Whatever the formal powers granted the 'sovereign' republics under the constitution, known then as the 'Stalin constitution', the Soviet Union was in fact governed as a unitary state, controlled by and through the unitary party. Even formally, under the party's rules, the republican party organisation (for example the Latvian party committee) had no more rights *vis-à-vis* the Central Committee than had any provincial party organisation. The so-called democratic centralism was a sham, all party 'elections' were a mere pretence; the party leadership nominated the supposedly elected party secretaries (of Latvia, of Georgia, of Leningrad, etc.) and could and did dismiss them. There were 'Supreme' Soviets at the centre and in the republics, but the 'elections' were for the only candidate, nominated in practice by the Communist Party apparatus, and any and every resolution was voted for unanimously. The government, like any other social–political organisation, was dominated by the party, and this was indeed inscribed in the constitution of the USSR itself (until January 1990). All officials, deputies, ministers, editors, senior managers were on the party's nomenklatura, that is their appointment was either made or had to be approved by the appropriate party committee (for all important posts it was the Central Committee).

The economic administration was divided between the party apparatus (for example the Central Committee contained divisions corresponding to the principal branches of the economy) and the economic ministries which were responsible for various industries and for construction, agriculture, trade, finance and so on, with Gosplan as the chief coordinator of the plan. Republics too had their Gosplans. Ministries were of three kinds: union, union–republican and republican. The first of these exerted direct control over enterprises from Moscow within the borders of any and all republics. The second involved so-called 'dual subordination': a large group of enterprises were under both the Council of Ministers of the given republic and the union–republican ministry in Moscow. Finally, republican ministries (for example of local industry) had no direct superior in Moscow.

Most of the ministries were responsible for a wide range of activities. Thus for example, the Ministry of Coal Industry made mining machinery, and its construction department might build, say, a hospital or a dwelling-house. Some items — for instance material-handling equipment or refrigerators — were produced in enterprises under literally dozens of different ministries, including ministries specialising in military hardware. Many ministries and enterprises made their own components to lessen dependence on (often unreliable) 'outside' suppliers.

In 1957, Khrushchev sought to destroy the 'ministerial' centralised system and established so-called sovnarkhozy (regional economic councils), which were supposedly in direct control of enterprises in their localities. At first there were 103 sovnarkhozy, and the smaller republics, including Latvia, Lithuania and Estonia, were each a sovnarkhoz. So, on paper, they acquired much more direct control over economic life. But in reality the centralising logic of the system reasserted itself. Left to themselves, each republic or region inevitably tended (in the absence of any market mechanism) to give priority to its own needs at the expense of other regions. To counteract this, the all-union Gosplan and Gossnab (the State Committee of Material–Technical Supply) acquired power over resource allocation, and the Baltic sovnarkhozy were soon complaining that their powers over resources were extremely limited. After some re-centralisation, the sovnarkhozy were abolished after Khrushchev's fall, and the economic ministries were recreated in 1965.

Their recreation was part of the so-called 'Kosygin reform', which was supposed to achieve some degree of decentralisation of power to management, giving greater stress to profits and to contracts with customers. However, this failed to alter the centralising basis of the system, since prices continued to bear no relation to scarcity or use-value, and so the profitability criterion could not function. The dominant criterion remained the fulfilment of plans, which were compulsory and included plans for output, deliveries to specified customers, supplies of inputs from specified suppliers all at fixed prices.

The logic of centralised planning can be best seen in wartime. In Great Britain too, say in 1943, there was material allocation, fixed prices, severe limitations on the market so as to concentrate resources for the priority purpose of waging war. It was the Polish Marxist economist Oscar Lange who defined the Soviet planning system as 'a war economy *sui generis*'. It was best suited to impose the priorities of the political leadership. However, already under Khrushchev, and under Brezhnev, those priorities became diluted: not just heavy industry and arms but also housing, agriculture, consumer goods and services. The economy grew more complex. The number of decisions to be taken vastly exceeded the capacity of the planning system. It has been quipped that to prepare a plan for next year which was fully balanced and disaggregated with the help of computers might take 30,000 years. So plans were not balanced or disaggregated, had to be repeatedly altered and became internally inconsistent. The production plan, the supply plan and the financial plan were issued from different offices and could contradict each other. There were endless problems of inter-sectoral coordination. Thus, for example, a large increase in output of mineral fertiliser was not accompanied by the needed increase in storage space, means of transport and machines to spread the fertiliser.

A massive critical literature pointed to various forms of waste. Thus plans expressed in tons penalised economy of metal, and plans in roubles encouraged higher cost and prices. Economic ministries became autonomous interest groups, and investment resources were allocated not where they were most needed but in response to the influence of the minister or local party secretary. Vast resources were frozen in uncompleted investment projects, uncompleted because more were started than there were resources available (labour, materials) to finish them. The system supposedly was based on the notion that the compulsory plans incorporated the needs of society, of industry, of agriculture and of the consumer. In practice, the sheer size of the task of planning rendered impossible the task of incorporating detailed needs in the plans. There was no direct feedback from the user to the producer despite much discussion about the desirability of direct horizontal links. Technical progress suffered because, on the one hand, risk was not rewarded (and novelty necessarily involves some risk of failure), and on the other it proved very difficult to incorporate innovation, and also quality, in quantitative plans. Planning authorities and the party leadership at all levels demanded that enterprises exceed earlier production levels. Innovation often involves temporary interruption of production and was therefore discouraged by pressures coming from the command structure. Agriculture too suffered from the attempt to impose plans on state and collective farms, plans which frequently failed to take into account the specific circumstances of the locality.

By the early 1980s the system entered a period of stagnation, partly concealed by statistical exaggeration. An important contributory factor was the burden of the arms race which diverted into this unproductive sector a disproportionate share of the best technology and the most talented technologists.

So Gorbachev inherited a system which was malfunctioning and in a real sense had lost confidence in itself. The following long extract from an article by Nikolai Shmelev (*Novyi mir*, no. 6, 1987) expressed in particularly vigorous terms the situation as the reformers saw it, and Gorbachev expressly stated that he agreed with its analysis (though not with all its practical recommendations).

We are still dominated by the conception that the existing system of economic and property relations is the embodiment of Marxism–Leninism in practice, fully consonant with the nature of socialism as a social formation.

Marx and Engels elaborated the theoretical bases of revolution, showed its objective inevitability, but as for what shape the economy would take after victory, on this they only had guesses (*dogadki*) . . . They left us virtually nothing which could be considered as practical advice about the methods of reaching the aims [of socialism]. The prerevolutionary works of Lenin were also in the main devoted purely to politics . . . and not to what will have to be done to organise a full-blooded economic life after the revolution. Thus the revolution caught us without a thought-out or complete economic theory of socialism. . . . It is essential to realise that the cause of our difficulties is not only or not solely due to the heavy burden of military expenditures and the very expensive global responsibilities of our country. If we expended them correctly, even the remaining resources would be sufficient for maintaining a balanced and technically progressive economy and for satisfying the traditionally modest needs of our population. However, prolonged attempts to break up the objective laws of economic life, to suppress the age-long natural stimuli for human labour, brought about results quite different from what was intended. Today we have an economy characterised by shortage, imbalances, in many respects unmanageable, and, if we were to be honest, an economy almost unplannable. . . . We have one of the lowest levels of labour productivity of any industrial nation, especially in agriculture and in construction, since through the years of stagnation the working masses have reached a state of almost total disinterestedness in freely-committed and honest labour . . .

Apathy, indifference, thieving . . . have become mass phenomena, with at the same time aggressive envy toward high earners. There have appeared signs of a sort of physical degradation of a sizeable part of our population, through drunkenness and idleness. Finally, there is a lack of belief in the officially announced objectives and purposes, in the very possibility of a more rational economic and social organisation of life. Clearly all this cannot be swiftly overcome — years, maybe generations, will be needed.

B. The reform process in the Soviet Union

The failure of the 'Kosygin' reform, and of a number of other attempts to 'further perfect' the centralised planning system, led an increasing number of economists to insist on a radical reform of the market type since the only alternative to the planning of output and allocation from above was to allow enterprise managers to determine their own output and inputs by negotiation with customers and suppliers. However, in 1985 a five-year plan was drafted and in 1986 a more ambitious version was adopted, envisaging accelerated growth. The plan incorporated unrealistic targets, including a large-scale investment programme to reconstruct obsolete industrial capacity, the attempt to implement which contributed to the subsequent inflation. It is now recognised that this attempt to plan along traditional centralised lines conflicted with the objective of marketisation. The very existence of such a plan was used as a means of slowing down the reform process. Where to draw the boundary between plan and market was unclear. Initially, market socialism became the goal. Private enterprises could not be allowed to employ anyone (to avoid 'exploitation') and the existence of some cooperatives was not to challenge the dominance of state property. Gradually more radical voices were heard, both in the Baltic republics and in Russia itself, arguing that markets and competition were inherently inconsistent with state ownership, that there should be a capital market, a labour market, and (by 1989) that extensive 'privatisation' was necessary. However, there was (and still is) opposition to such ideas, not only among 'bureaucrats' but also among ordinary citizens brought up to regard the market and private trade as forms of 'speculation'. The net effect of the attempts to change the system was a deteriorating economy, shortages, fears of chaos and disruption. S. Shatalin, L. Abalkin and many other leading economists spoke of a looming catastrophe; to cite Shatalin (*Pravda*, 23 February 1990): 'It is not a question of saving socialism, communism or any other -ism, it is now a matter of saving our country, our people.' Why did this situation arise?

First, it must be recognised that the task of 'marketisation' was highly complex. Even if everyone agreed on the reform model, even if there were no opposition, the difficulties would be very serious: lack of training and experience; lack of market infrastructure; and lack of the needed information flows. But there was not and is not agreement about a viable reform model; there was and is opposition to the necessary measures. This opposition comes from several sources: ideologists (markets and socialism were seen by Marxists as inherently incompatible); some party and state officials in the nomenklatura who feared for their status and privileges; and also those ordinary citizens who have absorbed the principles of egalitarianism and resent the enrichment of others. This 'anti-mercantile' spirit has non-Bolshevik roots, one finds it in Dostoevsky and also in the ideas of Solzhenitsyn. In these respects the Baltic republics have somewhat different traditions which may explain why they have moved ahead faster on the road to the market.

Second, the steps taken were half-hearted, inconsistent and contradictory. To give some examples, in 1987 a 'law on state enterprises' in the Soviet Union was adopted which supposedly greatly increased managerial autonomy. However, no attempt was made to make radical changes in the price system, and so profitability could not act as a rational guide to action. Instead, it was decided to replace the compulsory plans by so-called 'state orders' (*goszakazy*), with enterprises free to dispose of any output in excess of these priority state orders. In practice these orders incorporated the bulk of productive capacity, and, because supply of scarce materials was linked with these orders, management sought *goszakazy* rather than a risky independence. This meant that the centralised production and supply planning system remained with just a change in terminology. However, the loosening of controls over enterprise finances, unaccompanied by a hardening of the budget constraint, and with interest rates on credits at absurdly low levels, led to two undesirable consequences: a substantial increase in money wages and also the starting of too many enterprise-financed investment projects. These contributed to a growing shortage both of producers' goods and of consumers' goods.

Another example of weakness in the reform strategy was the (correct) decision to allow cooperative enterprise; the law on cooperatives adopted in 1988 was not at fault. But operating under conditions when most materials were still subject to administered allocation, and with growing imbalances in the consumer market, the cooperatives were often unable to obtain inputs through legitimate channels and were able (or were forced) to charge very high prices which led to their unpopularity and to pressures to limit and heavily tax their activities.

Also in 1988, measures were introduced to create so-called 'republican *khozraschyot*', that is to make closer links between the plans and finances of the various republics and the functioning of enterprises located on their territory. From the standpoint of the functioning of the Soviet economy as a whole, this was unwise in the sense that 'marketisation' logically called for managerial decision-making within an all-union market rather than a transfer of authority from bureaucrats in Moscow to bureaucrats in republican capitals. However, action at the republic level was necessary because of the failure to act at the union level. These measures coincided with the growth of nationalist separatism and gradually, especially in 1990, this had the effect of weakening the *goszakaz* system. All-union economic powers diminished, the republics began to control the movement and sale of goods but without any real move towards a market. This in turn led to the disintegration of the material supply system.

Finally and decisively, the failure to deal with prices was accompanied by a fatal loosening of financial policies. The budget deficit grew, from a modest level of about fifteen or so billion roubles in the early eighties to as much as 100 billion in 1989. The causes were many: the fall in the oil price in 1985–9 sharply reduced revenues from foreign trade; the campaign against alcoholism reduced revenues while pressure to spend more on health, housing and pensions plus the cost of the Chernobyl disaster and of the Armenian earthquake increased expenditures. Efforts to cut back investment and military spending had only modest results. Failure to tackle the highly subsidised retail prices of food, while prices paid to the producers were raised, led to ever higher subsidies, still further unbalancing the budget. The deficit was covered by various forms of money creation. With purchasing power rising much faster than the supply of goods and services at the state-fixed prices both management and labour reacted by hoarding, which further emptied shops and storehouses. The rouble lost effective purchasing power. Various forms of barter developed, as did corruption and an economic mafia. Yet a move towards a market economy requires money in which buyers and sellers have some confidence.

In relation to stabilisation policies, political changes ('democratisation') did not help matters. On the contrary, fear of popular protest led to the postponement of necessary increases in prices, and popular pressure for more spending proved irresistible. The politics of balancing the budget and increasing taxes pose difficulties in many democracies, not least in the United States. An acute observer, Igor Klyamkin, put the Soviet dilemma well. Writing in *Komsomolskaya Pravda* (23 January 1991), he noted that in the absence of private property in the means of production, the citizens see

themselves primarily as consumers and have long learned to expect the
authorities to be providers.

> So if in such a society one introduces representative democracy, the elected
> parliaments cannot avoid becoming societies of angry consumers, which demand
> redistribution of revenues at the expense of other groups . . . But since the bosses
> must take away in order to give, and there is no one they can take from, they have
> only one solution: to print more new money and to divide it among all claimants.

This is what Albert Hirschman has called 'conflict inflation'.

An effective, comprehensive programme to move towards a market
economy ideally should contain a whole number of interrelated measures:
stabilised money; radical price reform (including a very sharp rise in prices
of highly subsidised 'necessities'); a big reduction in the budget deficit; a
totally different banking system with positive real rates of interest; the
legalisation of at least small-scale private enterprise; some move towards
currency convertibility with free exchange rates, more joint ventures; real
capital and commodities markets; strict financial discipline; and, also
measures to provide protection for those who will inevitably suffer from
these measures: the unemployed, pensioners, children in poor families etc.
There must also be some clarity as to the objective to be reached: a 'socialist'
market with a large state-owned sector or the speediest restoration of
capitalism, albeit 'with a human face'. Most of the above measures were
proposed in the '500-day' reform programme put forward in 1990 by
Shatalin and Yavlinsky, modified by Aganbegyan, and by the proposals of
Ryzhkov and Abalkin, but there was disagreement about timing and
sequence and also on the relative role of the union and the republics, with
Yeltsin seeking an independent and radical role for the Russian republic. No
effective action was taken.

However, by 1990 there arose another obstacle. To take all these
measures requires political power — authority to impose them — and the
power mechanism no longer functioned. Poland's 'shock therapy' could be
accepted by the people because it was imposed by a government of national
trust. The Soviet Union was still ruled by Communists. Though the party's
position had been gravely weakened, no other coherent group had emerged
at the centre as a serious alternative. Nationalist separatism was strong, and
not only in the Baltic republics. The legitimacy of the regime had been
undermined: loud voices were being raised in Russia to the effect that the
October revolution of 1917 was a tragic disaster. The collapse of the
economy was blamed on the ruling party, and on Gorbachev personally. The
system clearly was a failure. How, then, could the Soviet government
mobilise the people to carry out a revolutionary change in the way the
economy and society works?

With the Soviet government losing legitimacy and with no clear reform
programme set in place, the economy continued to deteriorate. Output
plummeted. Oil production, the key Soviet foreign exchange earner,
continued to fall. The foreign trade deficit and the level of indebtedness
continued to rise. The republics, in trying to protect themselves from the
consequences of the disruption of links, inevitably further disrupted these

links. By summer, preliminary indications furthermore pointed to a poor harvest, holding out grim prospects for the winter.

Clearly it was an untenable situation. Though Gorbachev in early 1991 still seemed to rely on support from the conservative forces, the army and the KGB, in July he attended the G7 summit in London holding out new assurances of radical reform hoping for international assistance. The two fundamental issues remained unresolved, however: political democratisation and the fate of the union.

Was there to be a union at all, other than as a loose federation of genuinely sovereign states, which delegate upwards only those powers and resources which then choose to provide? Such a model was implied by the '500-day' Shatalin-Yavlinksy plan and was denied by the Ryzhkov-Abalkin reform version.

Some republics clearly rejected even the loosest confederation, but after long negotiations eight republics were ready to sign a union treaty. It implied the disintegration of the Soviet Union and was thus unacceptable to the conservative Soviet forces. On the eve of its signing, 17 August, eight conservative leaders attempted a coup, while President Gorbachev was vacationing on the Crimea.

The decisive resistance led by Russian President Boris Yeltsin caused the ill-prepared coup to fail. This watershed in Russian history and in the history of the peoples living under the Soviet Union will not be analysed here. Suffice it to say that the Soviet Union, as we have known it, is now gone. The question is still open as to what the political future holds and what economic and other agreements some of the constituent republics will want to make.

For the Baltic states, of course, the August event radically changed the possible scenarios.

C. Possible scenarios

At the time of writing this study, we could hardly dare hope for such a rapid recognition of the independence of Estonia, Latvia and Lithuania. Independence has now widened the options available to the Baltic states of implementing radical economic reform and establishing economic sovereignty.

Membership in the international financial institutions — the International Monetary Fund, the World Bank and the European Bank for Reconstruction and Development, in particular — is now imminent. Multilaterally coordinated support, both technical assistance and financial assistance, will now be forthcoming. Bilateral cooperation, like that already initiated with for example Sweden and Denmark, can now be developed with more countries.

Many difficult policy choices still remain, of course, for the Baltic governments but they can count on developing and making use of all economic policy instruments available to sovereign nations. Choosing the optimal course of reform will, however, still depend to a large degree on developments in the Soviet Union, its republics and whatever new organisation they might agree upon.

Basically, two scenarios present themselves — one involving comprehensive reform and eventual recovery in Russia and elsewhere, and one involving weak political leadership, disorganised reform and continued economic decline. The second scenario, not at all an unrealistic one, would severely complicate Baltic economic transformation. The likelihood of the first scenario will depend on a decisive outcome of the political power struggle in favour of the reformers and the agreement between Russia and other republics on some basic economic cooperation. The Baltic states have declared that they would not be party to such an agreement on a par with other republics. However, it is clear that the Baltic states would benefit from open trading relations with other former Soviet republics. That is also the stated policy objective of the Baltic governments.

With independence, the Baltic states will be able to benefit from cooperation with Western governments. Estonia, Latvia and Lithuania will become members of the international financial institutions, in particular the International Monetary Fund, the World Bank and the newly created European Bank for Reconstruction and Development. As economic reform gathers momentum also financial assistance will be possible, including balance-of-payments support and more specific support for trade and investment. However, significant Western trade and investment support will crucially depend on the implementation of comprehensive economic programmes. Already many ideas are put forward, like that by the Nordic Investment Bank of a Baltic Investment Bank, to increase the flow of risk capital. Prospects for industrial development will to a large extent hinge on the possibility of this facilitating access to Western capital, technology and entrepreneurial skill.

As Estonia, Latvia and Lithuania now embark on developing their domestic economic reform programmes, the prospects for transformation will to a large extent depend on what external economic relations can be developed. These issues are further explored in the next three chapters. They were written with Baltic independence in mind. That perspective has now taken on new realism. However, the transition problems remain and need to be analysed.

Before going on to the following chapters, there follows below an account of the scenarios as we perceived them during the first half of 1991. It is retained because it throws light on the predicament of the Baltic states, what has determined their policy choices so far and the considerations they might be giving the transitional issues as they build their sovereignty.

The most considerable uncertainties conditioning any discussion of the Baltic reform process, writing in the early months of 1991, relate to the situation in the Soviet Union.

During the coming period, the Baltic governments will need, along with the process of extending their political sovereignty, to take steps to clarify their position *vis-à-vis* the Soviet Union with respect to a number of questions, including fiscal arrangements, the allocation of external assets and liabilities, ownership of union enterprises in the republics, the terms of future trading relationships etc. The instruments of national economic policy-making will need to be created and policies designed and implemented in a number of key policy areas.

The political and economic aims of the three Baltic governments are clear: to achieve both *de jure* and *de facto* political independence and to transform their economic systems into mixed economies of a Western type, integrated into the world economy.

As elsewhere in East–Central Europe, the problem is not the destination but the route to it. For the Baltic republics, the difficulty of getting to the economic destination is even greater than it is for countries like Hungary and Poland. The problem of transformation and sequencing is broadly similar to that facing Hungary, Poland and Czechoslovakia, but the Baltic republics have the additional problem of an uncompleted struggle to escape from Moscow's administrative and financial control.

At present, the Moscow connection presents four main dangers:

1. the possible use of force to re-impose Soviet power;
2. the possible use by Moscow of an economic blockade;
3. the side-effects of a collapse in the level of Soviet economy; and
4. the dangers attendant on incorporation in the present Soviet monetary system, with the supply of roubles out of control.

The rest of this chapter explores the options facing the Baltic governments by breaking down the question 'What is to be done?' into several slightly less daunting questions. This is done by considering the implications of likely scenarios of developments over the near future.

The Baltic economies are experiencing a modest fall in output and quite substantial open inflation, roughly in line with the Soviet Union. The present tight link with the fortunes of the Soviet Union is unbreakable in the short run, given the significant share of output deliveries to the Soviet Union, the tiny share of output delivered elsewhere (including to one another), the heavy usage of production inputs imported from the Soviet Union and the Baltic republics' incorporation in the rouble currency area.

Even in the recent past, however, there has been some increase in economic independence. The gains have been greatest in Estonia, where the government has had some success with both financial autonomy at home and careful negotiation with Moscow. Estonian budget revenues covered expenditures in 1990 and are planned to do so again in 1991. Some Estonian and Latvian banks have been able to establish correspondent accounts abroad, with Soviet Gosbank/Vneshekonombank agreement. In addition, the internal use of the Finnish mark, the Swedish krona and other foreign currencies has become quite widespread in Estonia and elsewhere. Enterprises in the Baltic republics, like enterprises in Russia and other republics, also have bank accounts abroad — illegally, so far as Soviet Gosbank is concerned.

None the less, financial autonomy is limited. It is the opinion of some Baltic policy-makers that Baltic currencies could only be introduced with Moscow's agreement. One reason is simply that consignments of the new money, printed abroad, could be confiscated by the Soviet-controlled customs on their way into the country. More generally there is a lack of gold, hard currency and goods inventories and crucially of confidence in the future to support new Baltic currencies, even if they were well-managed. Meanwhile, Moscow retains control over the supply of roubles to the republics.

Moreover, the Union authorities have suspended negotiations over future ownership of all-union enterprises. Negotiations with Moscow at the technical level have been constructive, but when proposals go to the top leadership, nothing is decided.

To enforce its rules, Moscow maintains the following instruments for controlling Baltic behaviour: the Army; the KGB (including border guards); the customs service on the Baltic coast; direct administration of at least some all-union industry, especially that part of it that comes under the Military–Industrial Commission (an estimated 5–15 per cent of industrial employment in the Baltic republics) and the monetary system.

The Union's control of ports and transit traffic is of great importance, not only for Moscow's ability to operate a blockade, but also for the ability to withhold potential hard-currency earnings that Baltic republics could derive from port and other transit services related to Soviet-bound imports and Soviet-origin exports and to Scandinavian–Central Europe freight flows. The Latvian Department of Foreign Economic Relations estimates, for example, that conventional charges on export cargoes through its ports would yield $1.2 billion a year.

A point to be stressed, so far as Moscow–Baltic economic relations are concerned, is the fluidity of the whole situation surrounding re-negotiation of a new Union Treaty. Here the Baltic republics may be able to exploit inter-republic coalitions. The Union authorities have organised economic negotiations with the Baltic republics into three separate commissions (by republic). The Baltic republics try to maintain a unified negotiating stance through meetings of the Baltic Council and other frequent contacts. They also are committed, in principle, to creating a common market and to close coordination over prices and 'rules of the game' generally but in practice have often failed to keep in step (for example over retail price increases or the assumption of part of Soviet foreign debt-service).

The Baltic republics have also developed several networks of bilateral and multilateral arrangements with other republics. So far the latter are largely of a declaratory, morale-boosting character and do not constitute serious alternatives to dealing with the centre or strong coalitions for conducting that bargaining. They might, however, develop into more effective coalitions.

Over the next couple of years, four main scenarios are conceivable, so far as the Moscow connection is concerned.

(i) *Backlash*: a military crackdown and/or economic blockade to crush independence movements, combined with a clear tendency to maintain and strengthen centralised administration of the Soviet economy.

(ii) *Authoritarian reform*: a crackdown and/or blockade, closely followed by the adoption of strong marketisation and privatisation policies under an authoritarian regime.

(iii) *Drift*: a continuation of the present muddle; neither crackdown or liberalisation, and no resolution of the negotiations for independence either.

(iv) *An independence deal*: the Baltic republics find themselves negotiating, or on the way to negotiating, a deal with Moscow under which the Soviet Army, the KGB and the Soviet Customs withdraw; budget and monetary independence is agreed, along with independent central banks; and deals are struck over the ownership and control of all-union enterprises. This scenario does not necessarily entail all these things happening within a couple of years; a clear move and agreement in principle about goals would suffice.

Backlash. There is not much to be said about this scenario. If it happens, neither Western nor Baltic governments can do much about it. It cannot be ruled out, but the events of January 1991 suggest that at least two considerations make it unlikely: the Baltic population's readiness to resist, even suicidally; and Western governments' readiness to signal disapproval and apply sanctions — withholding aid, withholding or wihdrawing most-favoured-nation tariff treatment of Soviet exports and offical credit support for Western capital-goods exports etc. These sanctions probably have only marginal effects on the Soviet economy. Some present Soviet policy-makers such as Prime Minister Valentin Pavlov may have written off Western economic cooperation in advance as expendable. None the less, the Soviet leadership as a whole still seems to exhibit a nervous sensitivity to such signalling.

Authoritarian reform does not seem a serious possibility. It is true that there has been some discussion in Moscow of economic modernisation under authoritarian political rules as an option. South Korea, Singapore and even Pinochet's Chile have been quoted as models. What makes this scenario implausible for the near future is that the people who would try to make it work would be those like Gorbachev, Pavlov and the whole of the early-1991 top leadership whose power base is the party–state apparatus. That apparatus would be dispossessed by systematic de-nationalisation. Its members' collective distaste for radical reform is already apparent.

It is true that there may be a substantial number of nomenklatura members who, as individuals, are attracted by the prospects of so-called 'nomenklatura privatisation'. But the top leadership (primarily Politburo and Cabinet) draws its authority from the institutional structure of regional party committees, the Army, KGB and the military–industrial sector. The leaders will, therefore, be concerned about the survival of those institutions, with something like their present powers, although not necessarily about the survival in post of all the individuals who currently staff them.

Drift. It is usually easier to imagine the present state of affairs continuing — in any country — than to imagine it changing drastically. Perhaps that makes the prolongation of the present mess seem more likely than it really is, particularly as failure to adopt effective policies is leading to increasing economic decline — the system is not so much drifting as sinking. Still, there does seem to be a strong political logic to this scenario. The Union authorities hold most of the levers of power; their institutional interests bias them against either real economic transformation or a break-up of the empire; and they see Baltic secession as the first of the dominoes. In those circumstances, the Baltic republics cannot by their own efforts acquire substantial economic independence. The question is, rather, what can they do to protect their modest living standards, maintain some movement towards economic liberalisation and prepare the ground for a better deal later on, and what the implications for Western business and governments might be.

Whether an *independence deal* is likely in the near term will only become evident by mid-1991. Meanwhile, it is worth considering what might, over the next two years, create a movement towards it.

The most realistic assumptions seem to be: that the Baltic republics' economic reform prospects while they are *de facto* part of the Soviet Union depend on Moscow; that the present Soviet leadership is unlikely to preside over a marketisation of the Soviet economy; and that *de facto* Baltic economic independence depends on a constructive deal being reached with Moscow. The question is, what are the factors that could facilitate a movement towards a deal, as against either a crackdown or a continuation of the present muddle?

Two factors suggest themselves:

(1) the outcome of the Gorbachev–Yeltsin power struggle;
(2) the possibility of a sharp fall in Soviet output and of accelerating inflation.

In the Gorbachev–Yeltsin contest, each of the contestants has come to stand for interests and causes with which they were not so clearly associated two to three years ago.

In early 1991 Gorbachev seemed to have become the champion of the party–state apparatus. It seemed more evident than it was before that he is on the central control side of the market/plan divide. And it is clear that he will fight for a strong Union.

Yeltsin has emerged, for the time being, as the only leading politican who both has a base of popular support and espouses liberal causes. The latter include the idea of a loose confederation of successor-states to the present Soviet Union.

The Shatalin '500-day' programme, with which Yeltsin aligned himself in 1990, had a section on an Economic Union of Sovereign Republics. It envisages a relatively weak centre, or rather a centre whose powers and funding are delegated to it by agreement among the republics. Republics that would not accept the framework of the new confederation could opt out and seek associate status if they wished. The policy positions Yeltsin has adopted recently have been consistent with this. In general, the democratic opposition in Russia accepts the Baltic republics' right to secede and is sympathetic to the mainstream elements in the Baltic popular fronts.

There seems, however, to be no immediate prospects for a resolution to the power struggle in Moscow. Furthermore, even if the democratic opposition were to gain influence the policy outcome would still be unclear. At the moment the opposition is greatly lacking in political cohesion. And there is no guarantee at all that, in office, the democrats would be effective economic policy-makers. Their appeal comes partly from their being against the old authorities; the behaviour so far of the democrat-dominated city councils of Leningrad and Moscow, and of the Russian republic parliament, suggests that they are unwilling to lose popularity by pursuing tough economic policies.

What is most important for the Baltic republics in the near term is the way that coalitions of republics may influence their bargaining position with Moscow. Yeltsin aimed originally at outflanking Gorbachev on economic policy and on the terms of a Union Treaty by getting the '500-day' programme adopted by all republics' parliaments. This did not happen, and even the Russian parliament — which did adopt it, albeit as a programme for the Soviet Union — did not then act consistently with it.

Meanwhile Yeltsin has been trying to construct an alliance of four big republics: Russia, Kazakhstan, Belorussia and the Ukraine. The Baltic republics have an interest in the success of such a large-republic coalition as long as it aims to turn the present Soviet Union into something like the Shatalin programme's Economic Union. If, however, Yeltsin and his allies settle for some kind of power-sharing deal with Gorbachev, within roughly the present federal structure, the Baltic could lose out. The embryonic coalition between them, Georgia, Moldavia, Armenia and (overlapping with the Yeltsin coalition) the Ukraine might provide some assistance to Baltic interests in the event of a Gorbachev–Yeltsin deal. But the main hope, from a Baltic point of view, must be that Yeltsin continues to do what Gorbachev accuses him of doing — trying to break up the Soviet Union. But even if he keeps at it, it will not be an easy task.

The second obvious influence on events is the level of economic activity in the Soviet Union. If during 1991 the fall in output accelerates, the conservative policies now being pursued by the Gorbachev–Pavlov leadership will be further discredited. At the same time, policy-makers in the Baltic republics are bound to have mixed feelings about a sharp fall in Soviet production levels. Some fall in output between 1990 and 1991 is unavoidable. For example, it is clear that a fall in Soviet grain deliveries to Estonia will reduce Estonian meat and dairy produce output, just as a fall in oil deliveries will affect electricity generation. If such reductions are the result of a general decline in the Soviet economy, and not just of supply cuts concentrated on the Baltic republics, they will be part of a sequence of events that will weaken the Union government.

Similar considerations apply to inflation. On the one hand, the Baltic republics can do little to insulate themselves from a further loss of faith in the rouble, but on the other hand, it will do the Union authorities no good and strengthen the case for separate Baltic currencies.

How likely these developments are is another matter. A conservatively inclined Union leadership cannot be expected to push through a real transformation of the economic system, but it might have some success in macroeconomic stabilisation. One precedent for this is the Jaruzelski regime in Poland after the imposition of martial law which restored production levels after the drastic fall in economic activity during the first Solidarity period of 1980–1.

On the other hand, the stabilisation measures so far attempted by the new Pavlov government, such as the withdrawal of 50 and 100 rouble notes, have been disastrous.

There is one other possibility that is relevant to both declines in output and spiralling inflation. Economic deterioration precipitates a hard-right coup in which the centrist Gorbachev is ousted and the new leadership is ready to disregard outside opinion altogether and use force. This cannot be ruled out. On the other hand, it rather looks as though the hard right, like the democratic opposition, lacks the confidence and coherence to take over and impose its own policies.

Thus the options available to the Baltic republics in negotiating a deal with Moscow are narrow.

The more consolidated the position that can be presented to Moscow, the better. There is extensive consultation already between the three Baltic republics, but neither their internal economic policies nor their bargaining stances in Moscow have been tightly harmonised. Administered increases in state retail prices have been neither simultaneous nor identical despite the calls for a Baltic common market. There is a growing use of residents-only rationing and of customs controls at intra-Baltic borders. Budget, foreign-currency and other deals have been negotiated or at least proposed to Moscow independently. There is an urgent need for more work on coordination, perhaps by means of a joint standing commission, attached to the Baltic Council, of officials involved in these negotiations.

The option of broader coalitions has been mentioned earlier. The Tallinn Assembly of Heads and Representatives of Governments, and the various bilateral and multilateral economic cooperation agreements between Baltic and Soviet republics, are intended as open-ended arrangements for building up a network of alliances and economic links that bypass the Union authorities. Practical benefit has yet to come from these arrangements, but it would be natural to develop them further. In particular, it would be possible to develop within these arrangements various joint negotiating positions *vis-à-vis* the centre and not just to concentrate on by-passing Moscow.

The near-term priorities in the Baltic economic negotiations with the Soviet Union seem to be generally agreed upon but not the ways of achieving them. To secure *de facto* economic independence, or at least to move towards it, the Baltic republics are seeking deals with the union on:

1. The budget: a transition to a single, pre-determined payment to Moscow is sought, allowing local control of revenues and expenditures; Estonia and Latvia have gone a long way towards this, but the coordination of Baltic approaches seems less than it should be.
2. Foreign-currency debts and reserves: the Shatalin programme adopted the principle that there should be an agreed share-out of existing Soviet Union debt and reserves among republics, after which new foreign credits should be raised (a) jointly among 'interested parties' only or (b) by individual republics on their own account, but not by the Economic

Union of Sovereign Republics on its own account. The fact that Latvia is negotiating over a deal of this sort while Estonia and Lithuania refuse to do so (and are only observers on the new Union–Republic Foreign Currency Committee) is another example of the lack of joint negotiating positions.

3. All-union enterprises: the draft Estonian–Union deal in which these enterprises become Estonian state enterprises committed to future deliveries to Moscow presents (in its basic principle) a formula worth continued, joint Baltic negotiation. However, it is worth pointing out that many of the 'imports' of the Baltic republics seem to be for the enclave of all-union enterprises. Given that many of these enterprises are in heavy-industry branches whose share in Soviet Union output has recently declined, and will decline further if real structural adjustment gets under way, it would be unwise to accept delivery commitments at or close to recent-past levels.

4. Port services and transit traffic: here there could be strong, joint Baltic bargaining, using agreed formulae based on standard international shipping and port services' charges, to get hard-currency revenue from Moscow. This issue has the attraction of being one that should in principle be an acceptable negotiating matter for Moscow.

5. Soviet troops: some budget flows from Moscow towards the support costs of 'closed institutions' in the Baltic republics are already part of the system; this provides a slender foundation for negotiating towards a 'foreign-base' type of deal, in which troop ceilings and agreements on their use might later be included and financial remuneration in the form of leases be obtained.

The forces at work on the policy environment in the coming period can be summarised in a simple diagram:

	POLITICAL DEPENDENCE	POLITICAL INDEPENDENCE
COMMAND ECONOMY	1	2
MARKET ECONOMY	3	4

The goal of the Baltic republics has been to move from quadrant 1 to quadrant 4: from command economies within the Soviet Union to independent market economies. Even while the Baltic republics are part of the Soviet system, movement from command to market relationship (from 1 to 3) is feasible, depending on the evolution of Soviet policy. In the transition, pushing the economy as far as possible in the market direction, within the limits imposed by the functioning of the Soviet system, will be a useful step towards the eventual goals. However, there are also situations in which the republic governments find it necessary to use some of their increasing authority to defend Baltic interest by direct command-type interventions (e.g. rationing and other controls over purchases), that is there may be cross currents pushing toward quadrant 2.

The difficulty in describing and analysing policy options in the coming period is that in relation to both political and economic axes conditions are likely to be transitional — the movement away from the command economy will be less than complete, including ineffective market arrangements (for example barter) and the instruments of national economic policy are only partially under the control of Baltic governments.

Much of the discussion therefore has to address policy-making under transitional conditions which are uncertain before the achievement of full independence. This is the case, for example, in Chapter 6 in which fiscal and monetary policy issues look very different if the Baltic republics are still subject to partial Soviet Union control than if they have achieved independence, with the freedom to create the normal instruments of national macroeconomic policy.

For the time being, Baltic policy-makers are forced to accept the limitations of the rouble environment. It has been argued that there is little they can do in the fundamental business of transforming their economies. If they decontrol prices, it has been suggested, other republics or the Union will place administrative controls on the flow of goods into their territory, and their own population will react adversely to higher prices without significantly increased supplies.

Similarly, it has been argued that attempts at local macroeconomic stabilisation are futile when there is no local control over the money supply. Balancing the republic budget, minimising the compensation of households for price increases and generally taking a tough line over subsidies and social spending will cause local pain without local gain.

Privatisation, too, is seen as vulnerable to purchasing by non-Baltic individuals and enterprises awash with roubles. Moreover, the present situation of extreme uncertainty is an impediment to the development of a new business sector, apart from small-scale wheeling and dealing in a shortage environment and a probably small total of special cases where long-term business developments are possible even now.

It is true that having separate currencies and therefore adjustable exchange rates against the rouble would alleviate these problems — as long as the new currencies were sound. But this would require both a far-reaching deal with Moscow and the conditions necessary to develop sound currencies.

On the other hand, several transformation measures look feasible even now.

The first is the development of the legislative framework of a mixed economy. Here especially, the case for close coordination is obvious because it is important to produce an identical — or at least highly mutually compatible — environment of commercial law in the three republics. This is an area where technical assistance from the West could play a large part.

Also, it should not be assumed that incompatibility with Union and Russian Federation legislation is in itself a merit. In fact, much of the new Soviet Union legislation, even though it has defects and in many cases has so far only a paper existence, is more liberal than is generally supposed. Some of it is in place before equivalent Baltic legislation; it should not be ignored or contradicted for the sake of contradiction.

In the area of denationalisation of state property, much has been debated, legislation has been enacted but so far little has been implemented. The reasons for this and further policy options are considered in Chapter 8.

There may be more scope for action to de-control prices than is sometimes suggested. Already, in the case of retail food prices, state and market prices are less far apart than they are in Moscow and Leningrad. What will happen in cross-border arbitrage depends strongly on the peasant-market and black-market levels elsewhere.

Rationing and border controls can of course help to insulate Baltic prices and incomes from the Union environment, but these are not the kinds of devices that recommend themselves to market reformers.

More generally, policies which accelerate the growth of a new enterprise sector capable at trading, providing services and manufacturing outside the old centralised system are likely to create a real institutional basis for greater real economic autonomy. For that reason there is a real Baltic interest in developing the parallel economy which breaks many of the rules which still operate in defence of the old system.

6 The macroeconomic reform process

A. Introduction

In the transition from a planned to a market economy, a difficult but crucial policy requirement is the matching of the enterprise and sector-level reforms with successful macroeconomic stabilisation. Stabilisation measures are necessary to avoid explosive inflationary pressures as planning controls are released and to create the conditions necessary for an orderly liberalisation of external trading relationships.

The difficult challenge arises from the need to implement firm macro-economic policy measures at the same time as the required macroeconomic policy instruments are being created. The case of the Baltic republics is further complicated by the fact that their process of reform starts with the crucial macroeconomic policy instruments under the control of the Soviet authorities, and in turn the Soviet authorities have badly mismanaged them.

In this chapter, three key aspects of the Baltic macroeconomic reform process are examined. First, the existing institutional setting and macroeconomic policy environment are described. Second, the long-run institutional reforms required in a move to a market economy are explored. Finally, aspects of the medium-term, transitional macroeconomic policy agenda are discussed.

B. Fiscal and monetary questions under central planning

On the surface, the Baltic economies appear to possess many of the institutions required to operate a market economy: banks, tax policies, government budgets, wage policies etc. However, the nature of centrally planned economies (CPEs) makes them work very differently from their market economy equivalents so that substantial institutional reforms are now required.

To better understand the needed changes, it is useful to explore the role and form of 'macroeconomic policy' in a 'pure' CPE which can be analysed in relation to the impact on three broad sectors: domestic enterprises, foreign trade and domestic households.

In such an economy, the overriding mechanism for determining the levels of production of or input deliveries to *domestic enterprises* is the central plan. This can be the five-year version describing broad trends or the detailed annual version giving enterprise-level instructions. In spite of numerous attempts to give profitability an increased role as a plan target, the *de facto* key planning targets and commands have remained the physical quantities of inputs and outputs.

As the plan is the primal determinant of enterprise behaviour, money held by enterprises cannot be permitted an active role in acquiring goods. Money not backed by a previous plan allocation gives no claim to resources, while the existence of a given activity in the plan means that banks must finance it. For enterprises, money represents neither a means of exchange nor a store of value, serving merely as a passive unit of account through which plan fulfilment can be checked. The banking system, therefore, acts as an administrative arm of the planning organs rather than as an active allocator of credit.

Plan fulfilment is monitored by providing the enterprise with sufficient funds to meet specific plan targets and ensuring that the funds are used fully and in the specified ways. For example, funds allocated to pay wages should not be used for investment purposes.

In a 'pure' CPE, a tax system would not be strictly necessary. As the owner of all means of production, the state naturally receives all enterprise revenues, eliminating the need to raise funds in other ways. Likewise, with full administrative control over domestic prices and wages, the state can tax or subsidise by directly changing any single wage or price. Finally, as enterprises respond to quantitative plans more than price signals, tax changes would in any case not affect their behaviour. When tax systems have been used in such economies (for example modest payroll taxation), this has been motivated either by the administrative efficiency of an overt tax system or by deviations in actual economies from the 'pure' CPE model.

In a CPE, *foreign trade* is an integral part of the process of input procurement and output sale and must be arranged along lines consistent with the management of the domestic economy. It would be inconceivable for foreigners to be free to convert money into goods (leading to exports) or goods into money when domestic firms are precluded from doing this. There are two main reasons for this.

First, in a consistent plan, the output of a given sector will be fully allocated as an input to another sector for domestic final use in consumption or investment or for export. If foreigners were free to purchase or sell in the domestic market, and behaved differently than planned, at least one of the domestic plan allocations would not be met. This could in turn lead to the spread of surpluses or shortages through other sectors of the economy.

Second, a hallmark of Soviet-type planning is a conscious effort to isolate the domestic economy from the 'world' relative price structure. As domestic prices, chosen to achieve a domestic goal, will not always reflect the scarcity values of goods, unrestricted foreign purchases or sales can be harmful to the domestic economy. These transactions are precluded, and the differences between domestic and world prices sustained, by granting the monopoly on foreign trade to a state agency. This office trades abroad at world prices and in the home market at different domestic prices, acting like a vacuum lock between the two markets. Imports sold for a higher domestic price or exports purchased at a lower domestic price than the rouble equivalent of the world price at the prevailing exchange rate will generate profits for the state monopoly. Similarly, lower domestic import prices or higher domestic export prices generate a loss. Any net profits or losses accrue to the government budget.

The foreign trade office is required to fulfil an import and export plan and to maintain the differentiated domestic price structure at any cost, that is it cannot act as a profit maximiser. As the exchange rate will have little effect on the behaviour of anyone except tourists and diplomats, it has nearly no impact on economic decisions. The sole exception could be in determining the countries from which planned imports are purchased and to which exports are sold.

Finally, the *household sector* is the only one which is not subject to detailed planning. Except when goods are rationed or, as in recent years, simply unavailable, households are free to spend their incomes in any legal way. Macroeconomic policy in the household sphere is thus concerned with ensuring that total after-tax household income (mainly wage payments) leads to a level of aggregate demand which allows the planned supply of consumption goods to be purchased at official prices.

To achieve this, the monetary circulation of households is separated from that of enterprises with the sole link being through wage payments. Administrative control on wage payments is thus a prime mechanism for ensuring aggregate balance in the household sector and the economy as a whole.

Of course, the Soviet system has always deviated from the ideal model. The central plan never achieved the desired level of consistency, the plan targets emerged only after a lengthy bargaining process between various levels and many of the actors in the economy were less disciplined than the model implied. During the period of *perestroika*, the deviations from the archetypical CPE have further increased because the planning mechanism has been dismantled or has gradually broken down, either owing to a legally sanctioned devolution of powers to enterprise managers or simply from a growing proclivity to ignore directives from higher authorities.

One form this has taken is the formation, by state enterprises, of parallel 'cooperative' firms which operate under more flexible rules. By subcontracting to these cooperatives, which can pay much higher salaries, and which can be paid from several different enterprise funds, monies which were earlier frozen within the enterprise are pried loose and enter the household circulation sphere. Yet, as real production has recently either stagnated or declined, the greater stock of money chasing a smaller stock of goods has increased inflationary pressures.

As this process unfolds, the collapse of planning accelerates. When shortages grow, central authorities lose their best lever for ensuring plan fulfilment — the ability to deliver required production inputs.

Another symptom of this breakdown is the explosion of inter-enterprise credit. As described above, an important control lever of the planning committee is the direct allocation of investment funds. Once enterprises begin financing each other, usually via the establishment of a 'commercial bank' of which they are a partial 'owner', the centre loses another important lever of control.

It is this macroeconomic environment that the Baltic republics share with the Soviet Union and which provides the difficult context in which macroeconomic reform has to be implemented.

C. Long-term goals of macroeconomic reform

The long-term goal of macroeconomic reform is to create the appropriate instruments for the implementation of macroeconomic policy in a market economy. While there are differences among economists about how macroeconomic policy instruments should be used (for example regarding the relative weight to be given to fiscal and monetary tools and alternative views about balancing the budget and public sector borrowing), there is much wider agreement about the required institutional framework.

In the *monetary sphere* the first requirement is the development of a two-tier banking system, with a clear distinction between the central bank and commercial banks. The central bank would be responsible for managing the instruments of monetary policy, through interventions to affect the liquidity of the commercial banking system and through direct or indirect influence on interest rates. It should also be responsible for supervision of commercial banks and have sufficient powers and staff to carry out that task. Bank supervision primarily involves steps to monitor the solvency of commercial banks and, where necessary, to intervene to check practices which would lead to insolvency. This is likely to require guidelines and instructions about the balance of portfolios as between different classes of business to ensure bank liquidity and diversify risk but should not involve the assertion of a view about any particular client or transaction. As a matter of prudence, of course, no commercial bank should handle its portfolio so as to make its own solvency dependent on its business with a few clients.

Supervision will be particularly important in the transitional period, when there will be many new banks, and even established bankers will be learning a new business. The vulnerability of financial institutions has been a weak point in most market economies at some stage of their history. Experience in the United States in the 1930s and in recent years demonstrates the potential for banking failure to generate problems for the economy at large.

The primary goal of monetary policy is to sustain high levels of real economic activity under conditions of reasonable price stability. Economists may debate about what this implies for short-term management of the money supply and in particular what growth in the money supply is consistent with the primary policy goals. However, for small open economies such as the Baltic republics, whose currencies are unlikely to be held as an asset by foreigners, it can be concluded that money-supply growth should remain close to the potential real rate of growth.

Whether such a target can be easily achieved will depend on the *fiscal stance* of the government. If public-sector borrowing goes beyond the level which can be accommodated by the financial system within target money supply growth rates, pressure will be put on the central bank to increase the growth in the money supply to undesirable levels. The consequences of funding large public sector deficits by printing money are by now writ large in the Baltic consciousness as the negative impact of Soviet over-expansion of the rouble has been directly experienced.

The government's fiscal stance will depend, on the spending side, on the degree to which public spending can be constrained by trimming public-sector employment and reducing subsidies. On the revenue side, the critical factor is the degree to which a flexible tax system can be created — in particular one which is reasonably income elastic so that the government's revenues expand automatically with growth in the economy. At the same time, the incidence of the tax system should not be such as to discourage effort and innovation or required structural change. The main difficulty will be to create a new tax base and capture a reasonable tax take from the developing private sector without imposing tax levels or administrative controls which choke its growth.

In relation to the *exchange rate* policy over the long term, two fundamental points to be noted are that:

(a) the external value of the currency will be linked to the achievement of stability in the domestic economy;
(b) the most effective single policy tool to shift the Baltic economies from an excessive degree of integration in the Soviet system to greater involvement in the international economy is likely to be a realistic exchange rate, which reflects the scarcity of foreign exchange.

There is less urgency at this stage of discussing the specific details of longer-term policy options, such as alternative exchange regimes (for example fixed versus floating rates), as much of the discussion will remain hypothetical until the basic questions of relationships with the Soviet Union are resolved. However, some of the longer-term possibilities can be illustrated by placing the current situation in its historical context; for this purpose, a short case study of the monetary history of modern Estonia is presented at the end of this chapter (Box 6.1).

D. Medium-term transitional macroeconomic issues and options

After the 'pure' CPE described above is partially reformed and decentralised, as is increasingly the case in the Baltic republics, the role and ideal form of macroeconomic control begins to resemble more closely that in market economies. If the main features of a sensible long-term macroeconomic policy are relatively clear, defining the agenda during the transition itself is more complex. Therefore, the most pressing issues to be tackled by the Baltic republics relate to monetary, fiscal and foreign-exchange arrangements in the medium-term transitional period. This section explores these issues.

Regardless of the prevailing forms of ownership, the growing decentralisation of a previous CPE reduces the government's ability directly to control enterprises. This means that general direction of the economy must be increasingly achieved through indirect macroeconomic policies.

The need for a new system of taxation and active monetary policy becomes even more urgent as reform allots a growing role to the private sector, for at least four reasons:

1. Without a tax system, relative growth of the private sector will erode the real resources at the disposal of the government. The maintenance of a reasonable level of government expenditure, financed by non-inflationary means, requires that taxes be collected from the new private activities.
2. Fiscal policy becomes a major potential tool for stabilising the private economy, and a flexible tax system would make this more effective.
3. As private enterprise generates a widening range of income and wealth levels, the tax system may be used to maintain a desired level of equity and provide the government with the means of providing a social safety net for groups severely affected by structural change.
4. As economic decision-making is decentralised to private economic actors, money takes on its functions as a medium of exchange and store of value. This requires management through an active monetary policy.

Furthermore, as enterprises in this setting will be largely motivated by considerations of profit, and will have wide choices of activities and markets for input purchases and output sales, the *exchange rate* will begin to have a real impact on decisions. Appropriate exchange-rate policy thus becomes important as a way of ensuring that decentralised enterprise decisions take account of the value of foreign exchange to the economy as a whole.

However, the ability to use macroeconomic policy in a partially reformed Baltic economy is curtailed by several factors. First, given the continued important role of the state sector, and the relatively 'soft' budget constraints it faces, indirect policies such as dearer credit or higher taxes may not induce as lively a response as in economies with more private ownership. It may thus be necessary to maintain some direct quantitative controls.

Similarly, with a state-owned commercial-banking sector also facing a soft budget constraint, the ability of central banks to influence the supply of credit, via control of interest rates and/or monetary aggregates, may also be limited so that quantitative limits on commercial bank's credit allocation may be justified.

a. Fiscal policy issues

i. CHOOSING THE FISCAL STANCE IN A FEDERAL SETTING

For independent states restricted to self-financing within a well-functioning international loan market, the need for *fiscal responsibility* is well understood and easily argued. While they are in a different situation, the same approach is also suggested for the Baltic republics by the fact that, even before full economic sovereignty, the foundations for effective national economic policy regimes are already being laid. Developing a reputation for fiscal prudence and for allocating government resources through tight budgeting will facilitate policy-making after independence. In this spirit, the Baltic governments have made moves to construct national budgets on a sound financial basis. (As this is a new exercise, and as the consequences of recent and future price reforms are difficult to predict, it is not possible to predict outcomes in the immediate future.)

On the other hand, in the disorganised federal setting in which the Baltic republics have been operating, it may appear more rational in the short term for the Baltic governments to adopt a less responsible stance. The dissipation of all costs and benefits throughout the Union, without a compensating well-functioning federal structure, provides little incentive for republican governments to make efforts to improve macroeconomic performance, even if their growing powers allow this. The republican governments have not yet had to bear the full consequences of their macroeconomic policies. (Similarly there is no link between the amount of foreign exchange at the disposal of any republic and the foreign-exchange earnings of that republic.)

Politically, there is also little point in republican governments taking unpopular decisions (for example cutting subsidies or raising taxes) if the benefits are dissipated throughout the union, especially when these republics do not see their long-run future in the Soviet Union.

Economically, as credit is now provided at a very negative real interest rate, rational behaviour would argue for taking as many loans as possible and leaving the real costs to creditors in other union republics. At the moment, if any of the republics succeeds in financing a fiscal deficit, leading to an increased supply of roubles, only a small share of the negative effects is felt within that republic itself (except as regards Russia). The weakness of the mechanisms subjecting republic-level behaviour to Union macroeconomic goals is one underlying cause of the heightening chaos in the Soviet economy.

Faced with this situation, Union authorities have attempted to tighten credit availability to republican governments and to enterprises. For example, interest payments were introduced for funds made available to republic-level banking institutions by Union banks. However, in the early months of 1991 there was no indication that the flow of credit was being cut off and that republics were being forced to adopt tighter financial policies.

ii. ISSUES IN TAX POLICY

Regardless of the fiscal stance adopted, the Baltic governments will have to make several choices about the form and organisation of the taxation regime. In doing so, several principles should be adhered to.

First, there will be a great virtue in keeping the tax rules as simple as possible. This simplifies the development, interpretation and implementation of the tax changes and the administration and enforcement of tax laws. It also signals that the government intends to focus on broad guidance of the economy rather than on its detailed planning. The latter will also add credibility to any claims by these governments that they have adopted a radically different *modus operandi* from their predecessors.

The virtues of simplicity should be remembered when studying the tax systems of other countries as possible models. These have emerged over decades of minor amendations and extensions and should not be used as models for a new tax system. In particular, in a period in which both the institutions of government and the enterprise system are changing so fast, the primary criterion in designing new taxes is the administrative feasibility of the proposed system.

The second criterion is that taxes should be created which can generate revenues from the growing private incomes without excessive policing.

Without a capacity to tax the fast expanding private circuit of incomes, stabilisation will not be possible. However, taxes based on elaborate policing or a high degree of voluntary compliance are not likely to work very well in the transitional context, in which private businesses should be encouraged to operate freely.

This suggests that fine tuning of the tax system to take account of equity or distributional goals will hardly be possible during the transition period. For example, a greater emphasis on excise taxes on popular items in inelastic demand (for example tobacco, alcohol, sugar) and of simple, non-progressive personal taxes is likely to be more appropriate than schemes that would be ideal on distributional grounds.

Sales taxes can also be used to soak up some of the potential 'rents' in the system where there is, for example, a large gap between the official and market prices for items and where 'freeing' of the price will not in itself rapidly increase supply.

One area in which liberalisation is likely to have a dramatic effect on personal wealth and income is the privatisation of real estate and land and the commercialisation of rents. A sophisticated property-tax system requires an expensive and time-consuming property valuation. However, that should not preclude the introduction of property taxes based on simple principles (for example square metres of land, or space depending on use and location, broadly defined).

iii. CONTROLLING EXPENDITURES

In relation to public expenditures, the Baltic governments will face two conflicting sets of pressures. On the one hand, the achievement of macroeconomic stability, the difficulties of introducing a new currency and successful establishment of new banking and foreign-trade regimes will require fiscal and monetary conservatism.

On the other hand, during the inevitable dislocations of the transition period, when democratic forces are gradually emerging, and with the constraints on government not yet fully appreciated by political activists, there will be strong popular pressure for programmes requiring increased government direct expenditures and subsidies. If unrestrained, this would lead either to crippling tax hikes or to inflationary financing of the deficits, either of which could quickly threaten the reform process itself.

To resist such pressures and maintain a coherent fiscal regime, it will be crucial for each Baltic government to define an overall vision, or set of consistent and well-understood basic principles, to guide fiscal policy choices. Most important, governments will have to establish the credibility of this overall scheme by overtly rejecting claims for assistance which fall outside the agreed programme. To achieve this, the government budget and allocations within agreed budgetary ceilings must become a more important part of the political process than has been the case in the past. This will enhance the importance of the finance ministries, the power of which should be increased along with their new strategic role.

Another way to enhance this credibility would be to define legal restrictions on the government's ability to spend and/or to use debt financing, for example through a quantitative limit on the central-bank financing of public-sector deficits.

An important step in fiscal, monetary and enterprise reform is separation of the finances of state enterprises from the state budget, or a 'hardening' of the budget constraint. Formally, the first step in this process is now completed with the recent elimination of most subventions to state enterprises from republican budgets.

The practical importance of this step has, however, been reduced by two factors. First, if enterprises have free access to bank credits to meet their cash requirements, the end of budgetary support will mean little. Under a 'hard-budget constraint', access to credit should only be given to firms with a proven ability to repay the principal costs and interest set at or close to positive real interest rates. If, in practice, firms can borrow whatever they require, they are relieved from making business decisions taking the product and input market conditions into account.

Second, all-union enterprises currently continue to receive finance from union-level finance institutions so that introduction of the hard budget constraint will depend on a change in Union financial practices. For the governments of the Baltic republics, caution in hardening budget constraints is likely to arise from the immediate real cost of enterprises cutting down their operations and/or workforces and, in the extreme, facing bankruptcy because of the budget crunch. In the immediate future, facing enterprises with strict financial constraints is likely to produce sharp increases in unemployment. As disorder in the Soviet economy grows, input shortages will increasingly constrain supply, reducing cash flows. If credits are not readily available, enterprises will have to reduce cash outflows, most notably the wage bill, in line with the reduction in cash inflows.

The social tensions that may arise from bankruptcies and rising unemployment will cause great concern, particularly in the complex political situation the Baltic governments are facing. However, successful structural change will only be achieved by shifting a substantial part of the workforce and capital stock to new tasks. The objective should be to ease the process of adjustment by opening up new opportunities as fast as possible rather than subsidising or protecting jobs which have no future.

At the end of this chapter there are two case studies on budgetary development in Lithuania and Estonia to illustrate issues currently being confronted (Box 6.3 and 6.4).

b. Money and banking issues

As the republics, in those areas in which they currently exercise control, work to develop a sound basis for future national economic policy-making, they will also need, in the transitional period, to seek means to protect themselves from the effects of policy failures in the Soviet Union.

In particular, there is a need to insulate these economies from the growing repressed ('monetary overhang') and open inflationary pressures emanating from the Soviet Union which have their source in the policies of both the Union and other republican governments, to which the Baltic states remain largely subject.

This insulation has so far been attempted by physical controls on the transfer of commodities out of the republics, either by establishing inter-republican border controls or through attempts to limit sales to non-residents through the use of ration cards.

The main problem with these strategies, in addition to the real practical problems of implementation, is that they are quite contrary to the spirit of developing markets. From this perspective, a more effective approach would be for the republics to establish market clearing prices, while defending the welfare of residents through salary adjustments and, in the case of the non-employed, direct payments. In turn, the difficulty with that strategy is that market clearing prices would reflect the full impact of inflationary pressures emanating from the Soviet Union.

An alternative strategy is to counter these pressures through new monetary instruments. As Estonia has in many ways pioneered the monetary reforms in the Baltic republics, most issues of implementing such reforms will be discussed in the case study of Estonian money and banking at the end of this chapter (Box 6.1). In another account (Box 6.2) the Latvian experience from the introduction of the lat in the 1920s as related by the famous economist of Estonian origin, Ragnar Nurkse, is given as a background. In addition, a few more remarks should be made.

The focus of the monetary debate has been the introduction of real or surrogate national currencies. From an economic perspective, this is motivated by the pursuit of macroeconomic stabilisation goals described above. The motivations have also had a political dimension, with the introduction of a currency viewed as an important symbolic statement of national sovereignty.

The most clear-cut means of achieving some insulation, is through overt establishment of national currencies. These have been widely discussed since the Estonian IME proposal of September 1987. As independent countries all three states are set on introducing own currencies as soon as possible.

Many factors complicated the introduction of such currencies before independence. Not only were there physical limitations to their introduction (border controls etc.) but the remaining opportunities for Soviet authorities to interfere with foreign transactions was likely to impair convertibility of the currency. It is difficult to establish confidence in the currency under such uncertain political and economic conditions. For example, if the size of the transfer to the all-union budget is uncertain, so will be the size of the public-sector borrowing requirement, the rate of money growth and the rate of inflation.

A real national currency could be introduced in several ways. It seems likely that a simple one-for-one conversion would face the republics with their own monetary overhang. To deal with this problem, the new currency could be introduced through a monetary reform, which could confiscate and/or temporarily freeze a part of monetary savings. This would ideally be closer in form to the comprehensive East German reform of 1990, than the bungled Soviet scheme of January 1991, which was limited to retiring fifty and one-hundred rouble notes. It would, for example, be possible to issue the new currency for roubles to residents up to a certain specific amount and at a somewhat unattractive rate.

What to do with the roubles acquired by the monetary authorities would depend upon negotiations with the Soviet Union, which would also have to address the issue of the future exchange rate with the rouble, payments arrangement etc.

Less than full-blown currencies are not as desirable economically but possibly easier to implement politically. One such half-way house to a true currency, which has been discussed in the Baltic republics and already implemented in the Ukraine, would be a generalised rationing system. This would involve issuing 'coupons' along with salary payments, in such a way that the coupons cover only part of the roubles. It would then be stipulated that, within the republic, roubles would have to be matched by coupons to complete a purchase. It is also conceivable to issue coupons to cover a fraction of accumulated financial savings. If such coupons were transferable between holders, they would work as a quasi-money alongside the rouble, and indeed an exchange rate in terms of roubles could be expected to develop.

Such a scheme amounts to a *de facto* wage cut when applied to flows, or a monetary reform when applied to savings, but with one important twist. Namely, the 'uncovered' roubles are not confiscated and can be used by the residents outside the republic.

Of course, if the exercise is carried to the point of issuing coupons to be in permanent circulation as part of the resident's asset holdings, the effect is so close to the creation of an actual currency it could be argued that it would be less confusing to go the final step and issue a currency as such.

An alternative strategy would be for the republics to legalise or even promote foreign currency use alongside the rouble. This has already happened spontaneously, especially in Estonia. This would be similar in effect to issuing a new national currency against 100 per cent backing in foreign exchange (with the important difference that with 100 per cent foreign exchange-backed currency, the issuing agency or currency board enjoys the interest to be earned from the foreign-exchange holdings).

The advantage of such a policy, if combined with a *de facto* freeing of foreign trade, is that it would provide a considerable boost to foreign exports and, therefore, a shift away from dependence on the Soviet economy. However, as it involves infringement of Union laws, it could only be pursued if those laws were to be modified, or the Union authorities were willing not to apply them (as, to a large degree, is currently the case).

In the transitional period, encouraging an uncontrolled foreign-exchange/foreign-trade market alongside official transactions would provide a powerful force for structural change. It would be advantageous to the republics that foreign exchange stay under control of republic residents rather than being surrendered to Union authorities. And as it would be a parallel market, it would not require any official intervention to set or defend an official exchange rate.

A move to such a regime was signalled in Estonia in March 1991, when the Bank of Estonia announced the establishment of a legal market for the household sector to buy and sell foreign exchange. Sales by households of hard currency would be simple and unlimited, whereas the quantity of hard currency which could be attained would be restricted in value and limited to those possessing valid foreign-travel documents. The initial plan is to establish a spread of 7 per cent between buying and selling rates.

From an economic perspective, the ideal choice of which transitional currency regime to adopt will depend critically on the evolution of macroeconomic developments in the Soviet Union. If the Soviet economy were to be successfully stabilised, the rouble overhang removed or frozen and the growth in money supply held in check, the economic need for separate currencies would diminish. Transactions with the Soviet Union could be made and cleared in roubles, and the problem for the Baltic republics would be how to earn roubles to purchase required goods or how to settle any balance (if in convertible currencies, for example, at what exchange rate?).

If, as now seems more likely, the Soviet Union enters a period of high and escalating inflation, the arguments for a separate currency as a possible way of isolating the republics' economies from these tendencies becomes even more acute.

Any system of coupons, quasi-money or parallel markets in foreign exchange would not, however, resolve the question of how transactions with the Soviet Union, particularly for the supply of raw materials and intermediate goods, are to be conducted. This can only be resolved by developments in the Soviet system as a whole, negotiations with Soviet Union and republic governments and inter-enterprise negotiation. Even though independence now means that there are no reasons for any half-way measures and that the governments can concentrate on how to introduce full-fledged convertible currencies, this will not diminish the need for economic negotiations with the Soviet Union on how transactions should take place during a transitional period. What can be hoped for is, of course, that reform in the Soviet Union itself will proceed quickly so that normal international payments relations can prevail.

c. Central-banking reform

All three Baltic republics have recently established their own central banks. As these are still in an embryonic phase, decisions still have to be made about their organisation, and particularly, about their relationsip with the government.

As noted above, one clear principle is that the roles of the central and commercial banks must be clearly separated, as it is not appropriate for a central bank charged with supervising the commercial banks to be at the same time competing for business with them.

One sphere where this separation is of necessity blurred is in financing the government. Central banks often act as the government's banker. In an economy with a large public-enterprise sector, with finances not clearly separated from the state budget, the central bank can in this role only too easily find itself taking on business which should more properly be the concern of the commercial banks. A conscious policy is required to hive off commercial-banking functions from the central bank.

Another institutional issue which should be tackled early in the transition process is defining the status of the central bank *vis-à-vis* the government. Here, the range of international practice, both in terms of legal status and *de facto* operations, is wide. In many countries the central bank is seen largely as an instrument of the finance ministry, possibly with the right to give independent advice and even publicly to express a view but ultimately subject to the government's instruction. This is basically the situation in Britain. In other cases central banks have great autonomy in managing monetary policy, notably in the United States, Germany and Switzerland.

Given the many uncertainties in the Baltic economies, it would be advisable for the Baltic republics to create strong central banks with a good deal of real autonomy in managing monetary policy. This would build confidence in the currencies and act as a check on the governments in their fiscal behaviour in the transitional period, in which it may be only too easy to release short-term financial constraints by resorting to the printing press.

E. Exchange-rate issues

Looking to the future, when the three republics have introduced national currencies, the governments will have an important policy tool at their disposal through the possibility of adjusting the exchange rate. While it would be premature to discuss the details of alternative exchange-rate policies, it may be of interest to examine the basics of the potential role of exchange-rate policy, as this illustrates certain of the underlying issues relating to the Baltic external economic relations discussed later in Chapter 7.

Once a separate currency is established, the exchange rate takes on great importance as a way of promoting exports and economising on the use of foreign exchange for inputs. The exchange rate translates the foreign exchange earned from exports and the foreign currency used for imports into domestic prices. An exchange rate which places a high value on foreign exchange in terms of domestic currency stimulates exports because it makes exporting profitable to domestic producers. Also, by lowering Baltic wages in terms of hard currencies, it can boost competitiveness. An exchange rate which realistically reflects the scarcity of exchange encourages structural adjustment through expansion of exports. At the same time, devaluation protects the domestic market from foreign competition.

Exchange-rate policy offers a potential way to reduce the overall dislocation from structural change. A sufficient devaluation relative to hard currencies, by lowering Baltic wages when expressed in foreign currencies, can preserve competitiveness and allow enterprises additional time to restructure.

The beneficial effects of an active exchange-rate policy are shown by comparing the recent experiences of the former German Democratic Republic and of Poland. In East Germany, the exchange rate at which wage levels were translated into West German marks kept wages high relative to the productivity of East German workers. East German products could not find a Western market with the result being a sudden collapse in real levels of output and exports and very rapidly growing unemployment.

In Poland, on the other hand, the zloty was initially strongly devalued, enhancing the external competitiveness of Polish products. While a more rational price structure rapidly developed, Polish firms were also given some breathing space to begin the necessary adjustments. The result has been an initial strong growth in real Polish exports to hard-currency markets, a smaller drop in output levels and more modest rates of industrial unemployment than in the East German case.

Furthermore, exchange-rate adjustment which could potentially reverse the initially incorrect choice of parity, a not unsurprising outcome given the great uncertainty surrounding the true competitiveness of these economies during the transition, is ruled out in the East German case. This loss of the exchange-rate instrument has faced the eastern part of Germany with an unpleasant choice between protracted unemployment and emigration unless a massive inflow of capital can increase productivity and sustain the balance of payments. However, capital flows may be limited given the high real wage level.

The exchange rate can be used most straightforwardly to influence trade with market economies. However, at the moment, Baltic trade is predominantly with the Soviet Union. Under existing conditions, an exchange rate between Baltic currencies and the rouble would influence transactions by tourists and petty trading but would have little effect on the much more important transactions between enterprises. However, as the Soviet economy reforms, the exchange rate will become important for an increasing proportion of transactions.

In the current situation of monetary disequilibrium, rouble oversupply and lack of convertibility even within the Soviet Union, acquired roubles cannot easily be used to purchase goods at market prices. Most transactions still take place at administered prices or under barter arrangements, under supply-constrained conditions of scarcity. The availability of goods at official prices is not guaranteed.

Under these conditions, the 'exchange rate' between new Baltic currencies and the rouble does not in itself have much meaning unless it is also established what the roubles can be used to purchase.

At some point, a crucial choice will have to be made whether exchange rates will be fixed or flexible and which currencies if any to peg to. As the underlying complex issues are well analysed in the economic literature, they are not examined here in any detail. However, a few basic points deserve to be made. Namely, while general floating is possible, as is fixing to a single currency or basket while floating against *all* others, pegging against both the rouble and a hard currency is impossible, especially if Soviet inflation accelerates. By promising to convert roubles into Baltic currency and then into dollars, the Baltic central banks would effectively undertake to guarantee the convertibility of the rouble. Even if these banks had massive reserves, and they do not, this would be unsustainable whenever the free-market rouble–dollar rate fluctuates. If the implicit rouble–dollar rate fixed by a Baltic central bank differed from the market rate, massive arbitrage transactions would take place at the expense of these banks.

This variant is implicitly the source of frequently held Baltic fears that 'we cannot have our own currency, for non-residents will purchase all of our currency and one day flood our market with them'. As this dual peg, reminiscent of failed nineteenth-century bimetallic standards is an unrealistic option, the resulting fears are also ungrounded.

A fixed exchange rate can act as a nominal anchor for an economy when other macroeconomic policies are targetted to maintaining the rate. Its main potential problem could be the present dearth of hard-currency reserves at the Baltic central banks. If attempts are made to set the exchange rate for the Baltic currencies too high, the lack of reserves will have serious consequences. The adoption of new currencies will be quickly followed by a balance-of-payments crisis. However, if the Baltic currencies are initially undervalued relative to hard currencies, and if macroeconomic policy is credibly tight, the lack of reserves could be less of a problem. With no fear of immediate devaluation and with positive real interest rates from tight monetary policy, hard currency now held as cash outside the banking system could be converted into Baltic currency denominated deposits.

The attraction of flexible exchange rates is that no reserves are required at all. However, any economy requires a nominal anchor of some sort. Under flexible exchange rates, this could be a pre-specified rate of domestic money growth. In the initial Baltic situation, this may be particularly difficult to achieve as control of base money will be imprecise, the link of base money to broader monetary aggregates will be uncertain and the level and changes in money demand will be poorly understood and predicted.

One of the variants described above can be attained immediately or through a more gradual approach. To some degree, the latter is already taking place with the growing relative role of currency auctions such as have been conducted by the Bank of Estonia on a monthly basis since mid-1990. These work in conjunction with the surrender requirements more fully described in the next chapter. Exporters must convert a given percentage of receipts at the low official exchange rate and can either use the remainder or sell this in the auction. On the import side, some firms have access to rationed inexpensive foreign exchange with any remaining requirements supplied by the auction market. Similar results could be achieved by allowing a free market in foreign exchange to coexist with the official system.

A transitory two-tier regime has some drawbacks in that it continues the administrative allocation of some foreign exchange, possibly through uneconomic criteria.

F. Wage policy

In a private-ownership economy, the interests of the enterprise owners facing hard-budget constraints provide an effective counterweight to wage demands. When overall demand policies are suitably restrictive, macroeconomic balance can usually be achieved through these policies alone.

In predominantly state-owned economies, especially where excess demand under controlled prices combines with labour shortage, this natural brake on wage growth is absent. In an attempt either to hire additional workers or to deflect possible labour unrest, an enterprise facing a plan target, but with little danger of bankruptcy (that is one facing a soft-budget constraint) will be ready to grant large wage increases. If these cannot be passed on as higher prices, the resulting losses will most likely be covered by higher subsidies. In such a setting, traditional stabilisation measures may not have the desired effect.

The development of extensive private ownership to introduce an effective counterweight will take time. As stabilisation cannot wait that long, it may be necessary to maintain some form of wage growth restrictions in the coming years. This could take the form of either quantitative wage norms or an excess wage tax on increases above a given norm. An argument against such a policy would be that it hinders relative wage adjustment at a time when this is required by structural changes. However, the reform process itself may founder if inflation is not brought under control.

Box 6.1   Money and banking in Estonia

a. The historical background

When Estonia became independent in February 1918, the country inherited a part of the old tsarist-Russian banking system, which in no way was adapted to the needs of Estonia as an independent country. Besides this, the ten commercial and ninety-one cooperative banks which then existed in Estonia had lost most of their assets as their holdings in Russian currency and securities had been wiped out.

The monetary situation of the country was chaotic. Several currencies were in circulation simultaneously. The temporary German occupation in 1918 left both reichsmarks and ostmarks behind, and roubles of different kinds were still in circulation: tsarist roubles, ostroubles, duma-roubles and Kerensky-roubles. Besides this, several municipalities and big companies had issued their own money.

On 9 December 1918, an Estonian currency was introduced and made the only legal tender. As in Finland, it was called the mark and it was kept on parity with the Finnish mark. On two occasions, this made it possible to borrow mark notes from Finland temporarily as the capacity to print Estonian notes was insufficient.

Gradually the note-printing capacity improved and was heavily utilised, among other things for financing the rapidly growing budget deficit. In 1918–20 Estonia was involved in a war against the Bolsheviks and against mercenary troops hired by the Baltic–German nobility (the *Landeswehr*).

Although the war was won by the Estonians in 1920, inflation continued. The exchange rate of the Estonian mark against the United States' dollar rose from ten marks at the start in 1918 to 375 marks four years later. This remained the stable rate for the rest of the independence period.

In 1927 a monetary reform was implemented. A new currency unit, the kroon, equal to 100 old marks, was introduced. The kroon was divided into 100 cents. In connection with the monetary reform Estonia was granted a 7 per cent stabilisation loan of £1.36 million by the League of Nations.

The main part of this loan was invested in gold which was deposited in London. On this basis the kroon was made convertible to gold at a rate of 1 kroon = 100/248 gram of fine gold which was equal to the gold content of the Swedish krona.

In 1927 Estonia also received a loan of 7 million Swedish crowns from the Swedish Match Company. In return the company was given a monopoly of the Estonian market. The loan was used mainly for the construction of two new railway lines.

The loans from the League of Nations and from the Swedish Match Company, along with a minor Swedish government loan for purchase of agricultural equipment in the 1920s, were the only international credits received by the Estonian government for commercial purposes. Besides this, during the war years 1918–20, loans had been granted by the United States, England and France for the purchase of war equipment and food for Estonian military forces.

In 1939 the total unpaid foreign debt of Estonia amounted to about $30 million, roughly equal to Estonia's commodity exports in 1939.

The gold standard introduced in Estonia from the beginning of 1928 worked in a satisfactory way until September 1931, when both England and Sweden devalued and abandoned the gold standard. Estonia cancelled convertibility in gold but tried to avoid devaluation with the help of exchange restrictions and import controls. This policy turned out to be a mistake, and in June 1933 the kroon was devalued by 35 per cent to the same external value as the Swedish crown. On that level the exchange rate of the kroon was maintained until the end of Estonian independence in 1940.

As the exchange-rate level established in 1933 implied a considerable undervaluation of the kroon, it had a favourable effect on the trade and tourist balances of Estonia. During the latter part of the 1930s Estonia's gold and foreign exchange reserves increased gradually.

The development of an Estonian banking system was started with the establishment of a central bank, Eesti Pank, in February 1919. During the first year of its existence, Eesti Pank acted as a universal banking institution dealing not only with the typical central bank functions but also receiving deposits from the population, granting all kinds of credits and undertaking foreign-exchange operations. In 1927 the total amount of credits granted by Eesti Pank was twice as high as the credits of all commercial banks together. On the deposits' side Eesti Pank was three times as big as all the commercial banks together.

In connection with the currency reform of 1927 Eesti Pank was reorganised. Its functions were confined to those of a traditional bank of issue. Its loan portfolio was transferred to a newly established government-owned mortage bank. Eesti Pank also ceased to pay interest on deposit accounts. Private savings accumulated in Eesti Pank were transferred to a newly established State Savings Bank, which competed for private savings with the private commercial and cooperative banks. Eesti Pank was organised as a joint-stock company. Two-thirds of its shares were held by the Estonian Government, and the rest were in private hands.

During the first years of independence, a large number of new private commercial banks were established. An optimistic assessment of the country's economic future combined with unsatisfactory public control of the banking business led to big credit losses for many of these new banks. Within a few years most of the newly established banks, as well as some of the older ones, had to close down. Also during the Great Depression in the 1930s some banks were in difficulties and needed government support to survive. There were no foreign banks in Estonia, but one commercial bank had close ties to a big German bank. During the latter part of the 1930s banking conditions gradually improved. The deposits of both the commercial and the cooperative banks almost doubled between 1933 and 1939.

A typical feature of the banking system in Estonia was the existence of a large and growing number of cooperative banks. Whereas the number of commercial banks declined from fifty-five in 1925 to twenty-four in 1939, the number of cooperative banks grew at the same time from 143 to 219. The cooperative banks were small local institutions dealing with all kinds of domestic banking business. They were served by a central organisation in Tallinn. Their total deposits in 1939 roughly equalled those of the commercial banks.

b. The banking system under Soviet rule

Before the changes of the past two years, banking activities in Estonia were totally in the hands of the local offices of the six big Moscow banks, including the central bank of the Soviet Union, the Gosbank. These local offices operated with monopolistic rights in their special sectors of the economy and were firmly controlled by their head offices in Moscow. Most of the funds flowing to them were put at Moscow's disposal, and it was decided from Moscow to what extent these funds were redistributed to Estonia.

The intermediary in this transfer of funds to and from Moscow was the Estonian office of the Gosbank. It also provided a clearing service for payments between banks in Estonia and those in other parts of the Soviet Union. All short-term credits to Estonian enterprises (except agriculture) were channelled through the Gosbank office. In this way the office provided the Estonian economy with the necessary supply of money. But the Gosbank's office took no active part in monetary policy in the traditional sense of the term. All decisions regarding the supply of money and the level of interest rates etc. were made in Moscow. In the field of foreign exchange and international operations, all practical functions have been taken care of by a special bank — the Vneshekonombank in Moscow.

The local banks' offices in Estonia — the so-called special republican banks — are the following:

(1) Bank of Industry and Construction
(2) Agricultural bank
(3) Housing and Social Bank
(4) Savings Bank.

A fifth local bank office, for foreign trade, Vneshekonombank, liquidated towards the end of 1990 after the centralisation of all its functions in Moscow earlier the same year.

The first three special banks offered different sectors a banking service of various kinds. They took care of the liquid funds of their customers — enterprises, authorities and institutions — without paying any interest. A certain proportion of these funds were paid to the Gosbank, the rest was lent directly to the customers after the approval, in each individual case, of the head office in Moscow. As a rule, these special banks granted only long-term loans of more than one year. The interest paid by the customers was very low. Until recently, it was only ½ per cent per year. Now the rate has been raised to 6–9 per cent and a further increase is generally expected.

The Agricultural Bank granted both short-term and long-term credits to the agricultural sector. It operated the second largest network of offices after the Savings Bank. This was the reason why the Agricultural Bank was used for payments of the main part (about 80 per cent) of all government budgetary allocations.

As indicated by its name, the Housing and Social Bank was serving the housing and social infrastructure sectors. It took care of these sectors' liquid funds and served them with credits. About 20 per cent of all payments according to the allocations through the government budget were executed by the bank. Credits to private households were granted on a very limited scale and only for housing purposes.

The Savings Bank operates a large number of small local branch offices (about 300). It has no lending activity in Estonia. The accumulated funds are handed over to Gosbank's office and from there lent to the Soviet Government in Moscow. The Savings bank paid interest on its customers' holdings, 2 per cent for sight deposits and 3 per cent for time deposits. In the past year interest rates have risen sharply.

The only alternative way for private households to earn interest was through purchase of government bonds. These did not give any fixed interest, but an amount corresponding to 3 per cent of the bonds outstanding was distributed by lot among the savers.

c. Recent changes and the present situation

The first important change in the banking system as described above was the establishment of the first independent commercial bank in Tartu in December 1988, the Tartu Kommertspank. A group of representatives of different government-owned and cooperative enterprises and of other institutions had tired of the slow and bureaucratic procedures in the existing banking system. They succeeded in obtaining the necessary licence from Moscow and started operations as the first 'private' bank in the whole of the Soviet Union. In the beginning the bank was organised as a cooperative enterprise, but later it was changed to a joint-stock company.

The example of Tartu Kommertspank was followed elsewhere, and today there are 12 commercial banks operating in Estonia. Their accumulated volume of credits amounts to approximately 500 million roubles or about 25 per cent of the outstanding credits of all banks in Estonia.

The commercial banks pay interest on the deposits of their customers, at present from 6 per cent and upwards. Paying interest has made it possible for them to attract a rapidly growing volume of deposits which has led to a corresponding growth of their credit business.

The two biggest commercial banks have received a special licence from Moscow to transact foreign business. They have opened accounts with banks abroad, initially in Sweden and Finland. The scope of their foreign operations, however, is still quite small because most of Estonia's earnings of foreign exchange are handled by the Vneshekonombank in Moscow. The Estonian banks have to follow the rules issued by Moscow because otherwise they risk losing their licences and being excluded from banking transactions with other Soviet banks.

While the government-owned special banks worked without any equity capital, the commercial banks have to fulfil certain minimum equity requirements.

One important consequence of the establishment and growth of commercial banks was that competition was introduced on the otherwise monopolistic credit market in Estonia. For the first time, both depositors and borrowers were given the opportunity to choose among alternatives.

So far, the commercial banks have not been subject to any regular public control. It is true that they have to apply for establishment licences from both the Gosbank in Moscow and from the Eesti Pank in Tallinn, but in their current operations they are practically free from official supervision, although it is prescribed in the banking legislation. Combined with the fact that to a large extent they have had to rely on inexperienced staff, the result has been that in many cases the quality of their loan portfolios has become less satisfactory. According to the Estonian office of the Gosbank, in some banks the share of loans which have not been properly served by the commercial bank's borrowers is alarmingly high (up to 50 per cent of the total loan stock).

The next step in the development of Estonian banking came when an Estonian central bank — called Eesti Pank — was established as of 1 January 1990. Since then Estonia has had two central banks.

The establishment of the Eesti Pank is to be seen against the background of the Soviet law of 27 November 1989 which granted the Baltic countries a certain degree of economic autonomy. Among other things the law says that the Baltic republics have the right to organise their own banking systems. An exception is made for central banking, which would still be administered from Moscow. Estonians found it difficult to understand how an independent banking system could be established without a central bank.

So far the central bank functions of the Eesti Pank have been very limited. It controls the establishment of new banks through a system of licences and buys and sells foreign exchange at free-market rates. In November 1990 the Eesti Pank started borrowing money against certificates with a five-year maturity and 6½ per cent of interest. So far about forty-five million roubles have been borrowed out of the planned total of sixty million. The funds have been used for granting credits to Estonian and foreign banks and to Estonian enterprises.

d. 'The banking war'

The growing political tension between the Baltic republics and Moscow probably contributed to a number of measures being taken by banks in Moscow which in Estonia has become known as 'the banking war'. Instead of allowing Estonia to take care of the special banks as foreseen in the law of 27 November 1989, the banks in Moscow tightened their grip on Estonian banking.

One of the measures taken by Moscow was the issuing of a law in the beginning of 1990 which submitted the Savings Banks to the control of the Gosbank in Moscow. Through this move the only institution which administered the savings of the Estonian public was excluded from that sector of banking which, according to the November 27 law, should have come under Estonian control.

Another measure was a change in the system of payment transfers between banks in Estonia and those in other Soviet republics. In March 1990, direct transfers between these banks were stopped, and all transactions were ordered to go via Moscow. This centralisation led to enormous delays in payments. Documents were piled up in Moscow, and Estonian enterprises lost a lot of business. Three months later the rule was somewhat mitigated. Instead of having to go via Moscow, transactions with other Soviet republics are now made through Gosbank's office in Tallinn.

The third measure taken by Moscow was to concentrate all foreign payments from the Tallinn office of the Vneshekonombank in Moscow. The result was similar to that of the centralisation of domestic payments. Transactions were severely delayed. Additionally, the allocations of foreign exchange were reduced.

According to the existing rules, a large part of the export earnings of Estonian enterprises should be delivered to Vneshekonombank in Moscow at the official rate of exchange. From the foreign-exchange holdings thus accumulated in Moscow, allocations are made for approved imports and other purposes. A very limited amount of foreign exchange is put at the Estonian government's disposal. As a rule, foreign exchange is not made available for Estonians who travel abroad for other than official purposes.

The most important source of foreign exchange in Estonia, the passanger traffic between Tallinn and Helsinki and the hotel business in Tallinn, is largely in the hands of the Moscow-owned Intourist, whose foreign-exchange income goes to Moscow exclusively.

While 'the banking war' was still going on in mid-1991, certain changes were taking place which tended to loosen the ties between Estonian banking and Moscow. In the first place, the three special banks in Tallinn — the Bank for Industry and Construction, the Agricultural Bank and the Housing and Social Bank were undergoing gradual change. They have all — with Moscow's consent — been converted to joint-stock companies. In the case of the Housing and Social Bank a majority of shares are owned by the Estonian government, whereas the other two banks are owned by a number of their largest customers. In the case of the Bank for Industy and Construction a special solution has been found. The Moscow-owned office still formally exists but the actual business has been mostly transferred to a commercial bank established within the framework of the bank, using the same localities and the same staff. The idea is by retaining its old branch office to keep open some favourable credit channels from the old parent bank in Moscow.

The two other special banks have been changed to commmercial banks according to the Estonian law. Like other commercial banks they have to deposit a certain proportion of their disposable funds at the Gosbank's local office. If needed they can strengthen their lending capacity by borrowing from the Gosbank's office up to certain limits.

e. The Estonian 'kroon'

One question which the Eesti Pank has been dealing with is the introduction of an Estonian currency. In November 1989, the Estonian government decided that a currency — called the 'kroon' divided into 100 cents, as in independent Estonia — should be established. The Governor of the Eesti Pank held out the prospect of the kroon being introduced before the end of 1989. After a design competition among Estonian artists, an order was placed with a printing office abroad. At present the production of bank-notes is reportedly going on.

The Estonian government decided to establish an Estonian currency for several reasons. One reason was the growing weakness of the rouble. As a result of the increasing budget deficit of the Soviet Union, the country was increasingly flooded with money, making a balanced economic development impossible.

If Estonia is to introduce a functioning market economy, the existing price and wage controls should be abolished. This is impossible without a barrier to separate the Estonian economy from the rouble-flooded Soviet economy. A separate currency could establish such a barrier, making the rouble a foreign currency.

Another reason for an Estonian currency is the irrational exchange-rate policy of the Soviet Union. The official exchange rates applied by the Vneshekonombank in Moscow imply a more or less strong over-valuation of the rouble. Through this policy exports are discouraged and imports made more profitable. If separated from the rouble area, Estonia would have the opportunity to introduce a more realistic exchange-rate policy, better adapted to the country's need of balanced foreign trade.

Further, there was a strongly felt need to stop the growing drain of consumer goods in short supply from Estonia to other parts of the Soviet Union. The supply of consumer goods had always been better in Estonia than in most other Soviet republics. With the growing surplus of purchasing power this difference was increasingly levelled out. If the rouble were to become a foreign currency, it could no longer be used for purchases in Estonian shops.

The Estonian government is now set on introducing the kroon during 1992. The proposal from mid-1991 does not recommend any fixed date but proposes a solution as soon as possible, and recommends a conversion rate of 1:1. It presumes two essential conditions for the implementation of the currency reform: the achievement of stable trade relations with the other Soviet republics and satisfactory guarantees against excessive inflation. It suggests the appointment of a high-level commission consisting of three to four people including the prime minister and the president of the Eesti Pank for the implementation of the project.

Box 6.2 Latvia: successful economic stabilisation in the 1920s

Among the most urgent tasks of all Baltic governments now is to stabilise their economies. This includes the reduction and control of inflation, the attainment of balance of payments equilibrium, and separation from the financial chaos of the rouble zone.

Prognoses concerning these steps are often pessimistic, with a lack of experience with the market economy, absence of required institu-tions, and lack of foreign reserves cited among possible reasons for failure. To counterbalance such concerns, it is useful to remember that several countries have emerged from even deeper economic and financial chaos to achieve stability and rapid economic growth. While the post-World War II West German monetary reform and the resulting *Wirtschaftswunder* constitute the most legendary case, another success story is found much closer to home.

In 1946, the League of Nations commissioned Professor Ragnar Nurkse of Columbia University in New York, to prepare a study on 'The Course and Control of Inflation'. Based on the post-World War I experience of Europe, this influential book aimed to draw the lessons from that period for the countries again emerging from war. Nurkse, the greatest Estonian economist ever, singles out the Latvian stabilisation as a 'complete success'. Describing the European experience in general, he writes:

> There is no close correlation at all between the extent of reconstruction needs and the degree of inflation in the different countries. If such a correlation had existed, Latvia, for example, would perhaps have the worst inflation record, having had much of her equipment removed, her factories blown up and her farms destroyed not only in the fighting between Imperial Germany and Czarist Russia but also in the subsequent civil war within her borders and in her war of liberation against both Soviet Russia and irregular German troops. Yet Latvia, without foreign aid, put a definite stop to inflation in the early summer of 1921 (less than a year after making peace with Russia) and was one of the very first countries to stabilize her currency.

He further notes that Latvia was burdened by an accumulation of foreign debt, and also by the need to restructure its provincial economy to one befitting an independent state.

Nurkse attributes much of this success to the existence of an effective tax system. In circumstances much like those of the present, where the Latvian government hardly can print money and has little access to loans, tax revenues were the only way to finance government expenditures. The government of the new republic quickly established a war profits tax, various indirect duties, a progressive income tax, and other measures to ensure adequate revenues.

In spite of this effective tax system, the 1920 introduction of the Latvian rouble (not unexpectedly) tempted the government to use the apparently 'less painful' method of financing some expenditures through monetary emission rather than taxation. The result was a home-grown inflation which reached extreme levels in early 1921.

When the government finally responded with a serious attempt to stabilise the economy, the existing tax system proved to be a great asset. In fact, it had meanwhile been strengthened further by a step which Nurkse describes as a 'first' in Europe. In May 1921, Latvia established the 'accounting lat' as the unit for assessing all taxes. As this unit was tied to currencies fixed in terms of gold, all tax rates were in effect given in terms of hard currency. As revenues in roubles would now grow automatically with depreciation and inflation, budget balance became easier to maintain. This lessened the need for new monetary emission which was at the root of the inflation problem.

By using this tax system to cover expenditures, Latvia was in mid-1921 able to restore budgetary balance, dampen inflation and stabilise the exchange rate, all without foreign assistance. With the abolition of exchange controls and the introduction of a lat currency tied to gold, convertibility was achieved by early autumn 1922.

Thereafter, Latvia experienced no great difficulty in maintaining the peg to gold, in spite of minor fluctuations in the balance of payments. In fact, the Latvian government was able to run budget surpluses for six years after stabilisation. As the government became a net supplier rather than demander of credit, these surpluses enhanced the access of private traders, farmers and industrialists to investment funds. Omitting the gold received as reparations from Soviet Russia, Latvia would only receive its first foreign loan in 1928.

Lest the story look too simple, Nurkse traces the Latvian success not only to tough policy decisions and a solid tax base, but also to an important bit of good luck. Namely, while the prices of most Latvian raw materials imports were then falling, the price of flax, a key export item, held up well (exports from Russia, a major competitor, had virtually ceased). This helped support the balance of payments in the same way as would a foreign loan.

This experience has three main lessons for current economic policy in Latvia and the other Baltic states. First, while success is not certain, there is also no prior reason why a determined government could not restore the economy to stability and financial health over a relatively short time period. As in 1919, Latvia once again has an independent tax system which, while probably far from perfect, has proved successful in generating revenues. Even without strong export prices like those of the 1920s (and these should not be expected), Latvia will now have greater access to foreign financing and technical assistance. Also, the knowledge of past success should boost the confidence of the Latvian officials and public in the ability to succeed.

Second, the 1920–1 experience with home-grown inflation shows that an independent currency is by itself neither good nor bad. Even with a strong tax system, the Latvian government began to print money rapidly once this option became available. During the upcoming difficult period of restructuring, the government will again face pressures to spend more than it can collect in tax revenues. If the lat is not to lose its value as fast as is the rouble, the government's ability to finance expenditures via monetary emission must be curtailed. This is best done through a central bank which is strong and independent.

Finally, while the experience from the 1920s stresses the need for avoiding government budget deficits, it says little about the ideal level of spending and of taxes. This will be decided on the basis of other factors, including the need to finance a social safety net and the need to maintain incentives for economic growth.

Box 6.3 Budgetary changes in Lithuania

Until 1990, the Lithuanian state budget was fully integrated with those of the other republics as well as the all-union budget of the Soviet Union. In 1991, the budget became completely separate, while 1990 was a year of transition. Local finance ministry officials report that they formerly did little more than process data from Moscow, whereas now they have to calculate everything within Lithuania. Box table 6.3.1 presents a summary of the state budget for the 1980s.

Box Table 6.3.1 The Lithuanian budget, 1980–9 (million roubles)

	1980	1985	1986	1987	1988	1989
Revenue	2,633.9	3,850.1	4,244.5	4,081.8	4,533.9	4,835.1
turnover tax	1,487.5	1,647.9	1,714.1	1,696.7	1,904.6	2,073.3
as %	56	43	40	42	42	43
profits of state enterprises	489.1	718.5	781.7	770.0	739.9	741.8
as %	19	19	18	19	16	15
Expenditure	2,557.5	3,802.5	4,171.0	3,967.6	4,398.2	4,725.9
subsidies	1,550.8	2,505.8	2,669.7	2,503.8	2,737.9	2,929.3
as %	61	66	64	63	62	62
social security & education	902.6	1,170.8	1,234.3	1,341.6	1,441.9	1,606.0
as %	35	31	30	34	33	34
memo items:						
surplus	76.4	47.6	73.5	114.2	135.7	109.2
net transfer to all-union budget	− 81.7	− 49.3	− 117.9	− 284.6	− 56.4	10.0
as % of NMP:						
revenue	45	51	54	49	51	53
expenditure	44	51	53	48	49	52
surplus	1	1	1	1	2	1

Source: Lithuanian Statistical Yearbook, 1989.

The major revenue sources for the state budget have been the turnover tax and profit deductions from state enterprises, although the relative importance of the turnover tax diminished during the decade owing to the increasing tendency for prices of retail goods to increase more slowly than production costs. Revenue was obtained increasingly from other taxes, mainly on incomes, and from social security payments.

The main item of expenditure was accounted for by subsidy payments to agriculture to compensate for retail prices below production costs. The divergence of centrally determined prices from those

Box table 6.3.2 Revenue generated in Lithuania, 1990 (million roubles)

	Total revenue	From USSR budget	From Lithanuian budget Total	of which: State	Local
Turnover tax	2,074.9	457.0	1,618.0	1,453.6	164.4
Transfers from:					
All-union enterprises	508.5	113.4	395.0	335.4	59.6
Republic enterprises	731.3	—	731.3	585.7	145.6
Local enterprises	93.3	—	93.3	—	93.3
Income tax from firms and institutions	157.7		157.7	9.5	148.2
Income tax from wages	579.1	127.8	451.4	212.6	238.8
Tax on priv. producers	70.6	—	70.6	—	70.6
Tax on single persons	26.0	—	26.0	—	26.0
Agriculture tax	3.1	—	3.1	—	3.1
Income from forestry	4.8	—	4.8	—	4.8
Lottery income	7.1	1.2	5.9	4.3	1.6
Other taxes	55.3	—	55.3	34.6	20.7
Other revenue	156.1	—	156.1	100.3	55.8
State tax	41.8	—	41.8	—	41.8
Total	4,509.6	699.4	3,810.2	2,735.9	1,074.3
%	100.0	15.5	84.5	60.7	23.8

Source: Lithuanian Ministry of Finance.

which would apply in a market environment and from costs of production has meant that a large proportion of budget expenditure and revenues consists of payments to producers to compensate for the excess of production costs over retail prices and taxes to extract much of the excess of retail prices over production costs. Expenditure on health and education comprised most of the remainder of budgetary expenditure.

The Lithuanian budget for the period prior to 1990 incorporated both the state budget as well as the local administration budget. The budget was usually broadly in balance. A number of transfers took place between the republic and the all-union budget, not all of which were detailed in the old budget format. The transfers shown in Box table 6.3.1 were largely the result of transfers of enterprises between all-union and republic ministries or other special one-off payments. The payment of a percentage (22 per cent) of certain taxes and profits from all-union enterprises directly to the all-union budget was not recorded in the old budget presentation. In 1990, which was something of a transitional year, these payments comprised over 15 per cent of all revenue originating within Lithuania. Box table 6.3.2 shows the revenue side of the 1990 Budget in detail, along with the allocation of revenue among the all-union, republican and local authority budgets.

Box table 6.3.3 Draft Lithuanian budget, 1991 (million roubles)

(a) Revenue	Total	%	State	Local admin.
Profits tax	745.46	14.33	542.50	202.96
Excise tax	3,234.35	62.17	3,234.35	—
Personal income tax	680.00	13.07	272.00	408.00
Land tax	393.90	7.57	34.90	359.00
Other revenue	148.65	2.86	31.20	117.45
Total	5,202.36		4,114.95	1,087.14
%	100.00	100.00	79.10	20.90

(b) Expenditure Item		%
Education	340.4	8.3
Culture	84.3	2.0
Health	173.9	4.2
Sport	4.5	0.1
Social security	63.0	1.5
Science & technology	52.7	1.3
Road maintenance	76.0	1.8
Productive investment	278.0	6.8
Defence	86.9	2.1
Administration	59.2	1.4
Legal system	14.9	0.4
Police	157.4	3.8
Executive government	93.3	2.3
Special programmes	2.4	0.1
Capital investment	317.2	7.7
New projects	2.1	0.1
Others	74.0	1.8
Price compensation	2,067.9	50.3
Transfer to local budgets	166.8	4.1
Total	4,114.9	100.0

Source: Lithuanian Ministry of Finance.

The 1989, 1990 and 1991 budget presentations are not strictly comparable as the systems, methodology, legislation and revenue measures have been changing significantly over the past two years. The apparent reduction in the overall size of the budget, from 4.8 billion roubles in 1989 to 3.8 billion roubles in 1990, does not take account of some payments, noticeably pensions, which were paid directly from the all-union budget in 1990. The 1990 breakdown details the allocation of resources among the republic, local administration and the Soviet Union.

Box table 6.3.3 presents the initial draft of the projected 1991 Budget, which is the first to be prepared completely independent of the overall all-union budget on the premise that Lithuania is once again an independent state and that no transfers will be made to the Soviet Union. This position is being maintained by the Lithuanian authorities, although it is likely to be a topic for discussion if negotiations on Lithuanian independence break the political impasse and proceed to economic matters. The Soviet Union has recently implemented large tariff increases on a number of import and export commodities, and this revenue accrues to the authorities in Moscow. These new tariffs, effective on 10 January include: coffee 600 per cent, tea 500 per cent, US cigarettes 1,000 per cent and clothing 210 per cent. Moscow's control over this customs revenue is one reason for Lithuania's view that it should not make any payment to the all-union budget in 1991.

The draft 1991 budget has already (March 1991) been through a number of revisions as a result of policy changes and the delay in the implementation of certain reform measures. The decision to abort the price adjustments put forward by the Government of Prime Minister Prunskiene in January 1991 had immediate consequences for the budget. The Government had intended to make no subsidy payments to producers in 1991 by allowing retail prices to increase sufficiently to cover production costs and profit and sales margins. A number of prices were to be allowed to be fully market determined. As compensation for the impact of the price increases on consumer expenditure, payments were to be made directly to wage and salary recipients as well as those receiving direct state payments (pensions, scholarships etc.).

The decision to reverse the January 1991 increases made it necessary to continue to pay large subsidies to producers and as a result the budget was running a deficit in the first two months of 1991, as against the original projection of balance both over the year as a whole and during the year. This deficit has been funded by borrowing from the banking system. Republican debt to the Agro-Industrial Bank of the Soviet Union, which had reached 150 million roubles at the end of 1990 largely as a result of a deficit in that year, has reportedly risen to over 800 million roubles, although some of this amount is currently in dispute. The reported increase in the debt would indicate a very sizeable deficit during the first two months of 1991 as a result of the failure to proceed with the price reform, delays in the finalisation of some revenue measures and delays in payments.

A revised budget projection is currently in preparation based on the currently approved price reform and compensation package. However, further adjustments are likely both as a result of the Soviet price reform package and as a result of developments during the year. The currently approved Lithuanian price reform and compensation package, detailed below, involves higher compensation payments than those envisaged when the original draft budget was prepared, and to maintain a balanced budget for the year, tax revenue will have to be increased and/or some expenditures reduced.

The Lithuanian branch of the Agro-Industrial bank is in the process of being separated from Moscow to be constituted as an independent commercial bank. In this new guise it is exercising its independence and prudence by attempting to limit borrowing by the Lithuanian government. The authorities believe that there are currently no other options for deficit funding, although the development of government debt instruments is under active consideration for the future. The government's intention is to use some of the proceeds from the proposed privatisation of state assets to repay the outstanding debt to the banking system. Maintaining a conservative fiscal stance and not having recourse to the banking system will be necessary if Lithuania succeeds in introducing its own currency and establishing an independent monetary and exchange-rate policy. Unfortunately, there still appears to be some confusion over the desirability of government borrowing for budgetary purposes, with the view being expressed that a large portion of the funds in the banks were from Lithuanian individuals and enterprises and can, therefore, be used by the government.

Despite the inevitable changes to the budget numbers, the broad structure can be expected to remain largely unchanged. The main source of revenue is the excise tax levied on: petroleum products, expected to raise around 1 billion roubles; alcohol and tobacco, also expected to raise around 1 billion roubles; and the products of light industry. The revised budget projections are expected to increase the target excise tax yield to 3.4 billion roubles. The other major sources of revenue are from the new Lithuanian taxes on profits (taxes on legal persons), incomes (taxes on physical persons) and land. These are all new taxes, recently promulgated by the Lithuanian government and it is too early to assess their impact. They are all modelled on existing taxation legislation in OECD countries. Some of the revenue measures appear to have been hastily prepared and require amendment, others are still being finalised, and the net result is of an inadequately integrated package of legislation dealing with companies, investment and taxation. Some deficiencies are recognised by the authorities, with particular problems being faced with the profit tax.

A law on taxation of profits was approved by the Supreme Council in July 1990 and a tax rate of 35 per cent was set in October. Provisional income tax and land tax laws were also approved in October 1990. These are to be the major sources of taxation revenue, along with the turnover tax, which is being transformed into an excise tax as a possible first step towards a value-added tax. A taxation inspectorate was established in June 1990 to ensure the effective functioning of the new taxation system. The profits tax rate at 35 per cent is lower than the ruling Soviet rate of 45 per cent, of which 22 per cent should go to the Soviet Union and 23 per cent to the Republic. The Lithuanian law allows for 20 per cent of the profits tax yield to go to local administration and 80 per cent to the state budget. The provisional income tax law is intended to be in effect for 1991 and 1992; incomes up to 100 roubles are exempt from taxation, while above that level the system is progressive. It is modelled on that of Sweden, but the rates are lower!

On the expenditure side of the draft 1991 budget the major item is the transfer payments to compensate for the impact of price increases on consumers, accounting for 50 per cent of projected expenditure. The currently approved higher levels of compensation payments will increase both the total level of compensation payments and its proportion of total expenditure. The projected framework of price increases will also require some continuation of subsidy payments to producers in some areas. These are likely to amount to around 700 million roubles or one-third of the total of compensation and subsidy payments. The budget only shows the costs of compensation payments made to direct government employees and those receiving other forms of support from the state (pensioners, students etc.). Employees will receive their compensation payments directly from the enterprise as part of an increased salary payment. Payments to children will be made from the social insurance budget, which is detailed separately by the authorities. The income of the social insurance fund derives from a payment of 30 per cent of wages and salaries payments and an additional 1 per cent from employees.

Capital expenditure is separately identified in the 1991 budget at under 8 per cent of total expenditure. This level allows for no new capital projects and is purely a continuation of ongoing construction projects. Casual observation suggests that much construction activity is at a standstill.

Lithuanian law obligates all enterprises in Lithuania to pay taxes to the Lithuanian budget, regardless of subordination. All enterprises are currently reported to be adhering to the Lithuanian law which may not be surprising as the Lithuanian tax rate is less than the Soviet Union rate! In the case of enterprises belonging to the military–industrial complex, the Lithuanian authorities have no means of checking whether the correct level of payments is being made. In addition, some activities which the Lithuanian authorities would like to fund from the republican budget are continuing to insist upon funding from the all-union budget: for example, the hospital at Ignalina.

Box 6.4 Fiscal and budgetary issues in Estonia

The Estonian system of taxation has undergone thorough changes since the end of 1989, and most of the new taxation system took effect on 1 January 1991.

Estonia was the first Soviet republic to introduce, in 1990, a 'one-channel' budget system; whereby all taxes on Estonian territory are to be collected by Estonian authorities and payment for any services rendered by the Union transferred directly from the Estonian budget in the form of a lump-sum payment each year. The new system, largely modelled on the Federal Republic of Germany, was spelled out in the Law on Taxation, which was adopted in December 1989.

Until 1990, the Estonian budget was entirely formed on the principles of the central Soviet budget. The most significant recent development had been the growing importance of the turnover tax at the expense of the corporate tax. This was owing to the recentralisation of the Soviet economy from the early 1970s, after the demise of the 1965 reforms. These reforms had given increased autonomy to the enterprises, in part via a corporate income tax which allowed the retention of some revenue. The turnover tax, however, is an arbitrary tax (the difference between wholesale and retail prices) that is used to transfer the enterprises' profit, in part or in full, to the state budget. Its scope was increased to curtail the independence of the enterprises, leaving a diminishing share of 'free' profits to tax by corporate income tax or to use at the enterprises' own will.

In 1990, in spite of the switch to a one-channel tax system which required all enterprises to pay taxes to Estonia alone, the taxes imposed remained largely the same as in the all-union tax system. This was one of the first real steps towards economic independence for Estonia.

The only new tax introduced in that year was an excise tax on alcoholic beverages (at a 20 per cent *ad valorem* rate), beer (50 per cent), and tobacco (100 per cent). The resulting additional revenues of 188.2 million roubles were used to increase salaries of those working in health care, education, sports etc. by an average of fifty roubles per month. These sectors had had extremely low salaries throughout the Soviet Union. In 1989, average wages in Estonia were 270 roubles per month, but only 179 roubles in health care and 193 roubles in education and cultural professions. By comparison, average wages were 293 roubles in industry, 299 roubles in agriculture and 357 roubles in construction.

Only in January 1991 did Estonia introduce its own tax system that notably differed from that of the Soviet Union.

This involved introduction of the following taxes:

(i)   indirect taxes, including an excise tax on luxury goods and a turnover tax. This consists of two parts; the more important value-added tax of 7 per cent of the price of the sale and a simple sales tax of 3 per cent that may be imposed by municipal authorities;

(ii) direct taxes, including a corporate tax, an income tax for individuals and a special tax for taxable subjects who do not declare their income;

(iii) land and natural resource taxes;

(iv) a social tax in the form of a payroll tax;

(v)   an environmental fee, imposed on environmentally damaging activities; and

(vi) government fees.

Other envisaged forms of taxation yet to be introduced are:

(i)   customs duties (taxes on foreign trade have hitherto been transferred directly to the union budget); and
(ii) a capital tax (not yet introduced because there are not yet any taxable capital accumulations).

The marginal rate for the personal income tax is 16 per cent for incomes up to 4,800 roubles per year, that is for most tax-payers. For incomes between 4,801 and 12,000 roubles it is 24 per cent and above that 33 per cent. Incomes up to 1,200 roubles per year are not taxed.

The corporate tax rate is also progressive and depends on net profit. The marginal rate is 15 per cent for net profits up to 500,000 roubles per year, 23 per cent for net profits between 500,000 and 1,000,000 roubles and 30 per cent above that. Such a system will theoretically favour small enterprises, but many observers warn that rules on depreciation etc. are not sophisticated enough to prevent large enterprises from hiding profits. For this reason, they may turn out to pay less than smaller and more vulnerable enterprises. The social tax is 20 per cent of the total payroll.

The bulk of revenue from indirect taxation goes to the state budget; local councils can only impose a 3 per cent sales tax. Of the corporate tax, 65 per cent goes to the state budget and 35 per cent to local budgets. The individual income tax goes entirely to the local budgets; thus, there is no state income tax. The municipalities also receive revenue from the land tax, whereas the tax on natural resources is channelled to the state budget, with only a minor share going to the municipalities. Revenues from the social tax (payroll tax) and the fee for environmental pollution are not included in the budgets but are accumulated in separate extrabudgetary funds. The system is obviously designed to strengthen local councils. The cities in the northeast complain, however, that the new system will put them at a disadvantage because they have an even larger share of Estonia's industrial production than would be their share of local tax revenue largely based on personal incomes.

Apart from the new taxes, the most important change was the significant strengthening of local municipality budgets. Whereas they previously received almost all funds through transfers from the republican government (a minor share came from taxing local industries), they have now been given an independent tax base.

Thus, the municipal budgets receive all revenues from personal income taxes (around 363 million roubles) and 35 per cent of corporate income tax revenues (about 105 million roubles). They may also themselves impose a 3 per cent sales tax above the mandated value-added tax. The latter will be used to cover an expected financing gap of approximately 85 million roubles.

Tax revenues will account for about 70 per cent of the total local revenue with the rest still transferred from the government in Tallinn (about 226 million roubles). It needs to be emphasised that the municipalities are still relatively weak in relation to the centre; of the total tax revenues in the republic, only about 27 per cent is collected by the municipalities directly, and another 11 per cent is channelled to them through transfers.

The municipalities will also receive fees and land-lease revenue estimated to total twenty-one million roubles. Total municipal expenditures are estimated at 800 million.

Another important novelty is the creation of an extrabudgetary social fund from which social insurance and welfare expenditures, including pensions and compensation for price rises, are to be paid. The main source of revenue for the social fund is the social tax (20 per cent of the payroll of all enterprises), which is expected to raise 680 million roubles. In addition to this, there will be a transfer from the state budget of 315 million roubles.

The following important tendencies can be noted on the expenditure side of the budget:

(1) The share of the budget used for subsidising enterprises has decreased dramatically from 62.6 per cent of the budget in 1985 to 24.3 per cent in 1991.
(2) Instead, expenditures for social purposes have increased from 34.6 per cent in 1985 to 67.5 per cent in 1991.
(3) The expenditures for administration have also increased, in particular in 1991. The main reason for this is the need for additional financing of the Supreme Council. From 1990, all ministries are also financed through the state budget. They were previously financed by enterprises subordinated to them.
(4) Still, Estonia was to pay a contribution to the centre, but this amount had not been determined when the Estonian Supreme Soviet approved the budget. For 1991, Moscow has demanded the sum of 1,438 million roubles; of this, 863 million was said to refer to 'union taxes' (corporate tax, turnover and excise tax and the newly imposed sales tax), and 575 million are supposed to be paid to an all-union economic stabilisation fund (288 million of the latter item is said to cover interest payments on the internal debt of the Soviet Union). In 1990 Moscow insisted on a transfer that was roughly twice the amount that Estonia was estimated to have contributed previously. This resulted in Moscow imposing sanctions on Estonia: centralised subsidies on fish products, grain, and feed grain were suspended. (This move may have speeded up Estonia's decision to carry out a price reform on 15 October.) An agreement was finally reached in October that Estonia would pay 240 million roubles as its contribution to the central budget.

Moscow has not tried to interfere with the implementation of the new Estonian legislation on taxation despite its disregard of Moscow's interests. The Estonian tax department stopped reporting to union authorities. The remaining conflict was over the size of Estonia's centralised contribution to the union budget. Most enterprises accepted to pay tax according to Estonian laws, with the possible exception of 4–5 secret military enterprises, the books of which are not accessible to Estonian authorities. The main reason for the compliance of many enterprises seems to have been that they would pay less according to Estonian law.

It is difficult to conclude how the new system will change the incidence of taxation, since a proper corporate tax system did not exist at all previously. The stated goal is a total tax burden of approximately 30 per cent of national income. On the whole, individuals will pay more under the new system (both direct and indirect taxation have increased), whereas enterprises will gain. Still, many enterprises previously had very low tax rates set more or less individually, and they may therefore suffer. For this reason, the Ministry of Finance has created a special commission for tax benefits which reviews applications from individual enterprises. Special consideration will be given to enterprises with large contracted investments.

Enforcement of the new tax system may be a problem and will require the creation of a large tax inspectorate. Private individuals will file their first income tax returns in 1992. Enforcement of the personal income tax is not seen as a major problem; of the 360 million roubles collected last year, all but ten to fifteen million was retained by employers. Increasing reliance on second sources of income may, however, create a serious problem in the future. The enterprises will file quarterly returns, except for the VAT, which is calculated on a monthly basis. This may become a serious bottleneck.

Any foreign-owned or partly foreign-owned firms registered before 1 December 1990 will retain the benefits they had when founded to maintain the conditions that prevailed when the investment was made. Enterprises with foreign participation registered after this date will be treated on a case-by-case basis. All taxes are payable in roubles with equivalent amounts of foreign currency recalculated according to 'commercial' exchange rate for enterprises and the 'tourist' exchange rate for individuals. The tourist rate is also used for calculating the social tax.

7 External economic relations

A. Introduction

Some of the most difficult problems regarding the economic prospects for independent Baltic states concerns their external economic relations.

Currently Estonia, Latvia and Lithuania are tightly integrated into the economy of the Soviet Union. The rest of the Soviet Union supplies a very high proportion of inputs and finished goods used in the Baltic states, which in turn supply a high proportion of their output to other Soviet republics. There is a similarly dense set of interconnections in their service sectors.

The first problem is to sort out the existing pattern of transactions between the Baltic states, the rest of the Soviet Union and the rest of the world. Estimation of existing external economic flows is difficult because of a number of problems of coverage and interpretation.

Regarding commodity trade, the most difficult problem relates to the prices at which the trade is valued. The picture varies, for example, according to whether existing rouble prices are used, or valuation is based on some approximation to world prices. Also, some commodity transactions are incompletely covered (for example, military production).

Available data suggests that the existing commodity trade balance with the Soviet Union is negative and becomes more so if adjusted to world prices.

The Baltic states perform important transport service functions in relation to the Soviet economy. Some rough estimates are possible regarding the magnitude of these flows, the effect of which is to make the current account of the Baltic balance of payments more favourable.

The Baltic states have also made fiscal transfers to the Soviet Union. There are issuses of principle about how such transactions should be handled in the balance of payments. At one extreme, they might be seen as a net unrequited transfer to the Soviet Union and, as such, resources spent outside the Baltic republics and potentially transferable to other uses. Alternatively, the transfers might be interpreted as payments for services provided to the republics which would have to be provided one way or the other whatever future political arrangements prevail.

In this chapter these problems have been resolved as far as reasonably possible to provide a plausible picture of the existing situation. To use such estimates as a guide to prospects for the future involves heroic assumptions.

The first such relates to the likely trajectory of Soviet trade. The Soviet economy is now in crisis, and Soviet policies are in a state of flux. Dramatic changes in the external trade regime have already been implemented, in particular dismantling the CMEA and shifting trade with ex-CMEA partners to a world price basis. Massive financial assistance is being sought from the West, and there has been a degree of opening to private foreign investment.

Moreover, crisis and reform in the Soviet economy is dramatically changing the availability and demand for goods.

Irrespective of any action by the Baltic states, the trading relationship with the Soviet Union may be subject to great changes, which, in turn, will change the potential costs the Baltics would incur consequent to their own actions. Also, the rest of the world is itself subject to change — shifts in the world petroleum price, for example, change any benefits from access to Soviet fuel at fixed prices.

There are also the uncertainties relating to the nature of future relations agreed between the Baltic states and the Soviet Union. These could range from a continuation of trading and service links on terms not varying greatly from the existing system to a messy divorce leading to an abrupt break in trading links. If economic good sense prevails, worst-case scenario should not be the outcome. More cooperative options would be to the benefit of both the Soviet Union and the Baltic states. However, a political break with the Soviet Union must be assumed to have some short-term costs in terms of loss of markets and access to some important inputs (most notably petroleum) at favourable prices.

Also, bargaining has already taken place regarding the distribution of the external debt among the republics in the event of independence. Other capital adjustments debated include payment of reparations to the republics for past burdens and claims on the Soviet gold reserves as against payments to the Soviet Union for capital assets transferred to the republics. Such matters will essentially be resolved in a bargaining process in which objective valuation will be but a marginal input.

There is also the question of the Baltic gold, the gold reserves of the independent Baltic states that shortly before the Soviet occupation were transferred to the West. Though not insignificant, the eventual access of the gold will not change future scenarios to a very great extent.

The most difficult problem, however, in composing scenarios for the Baltic external payments' accounts relates to longer-term dynamic effects. There will be short-term costs, of which estimates of orders of magnitude can be made from available data. Deterioration in the external payments' situation is likely to be severe, and external support during transition will be an important need. However, while the potential costs can be estimated, it is impossible to make any sensible estimate of the likely positive response to new market opportunities as the Baltic economies are opened up to world markets. There is a danger that projection has an inbuilt pessimistic bias in that while potential costs are readily identifiable, market-orientated adjustments are inherently unpredictable.

Any conclusions about the future are therefore necessarily problematic. A very difficult external balance position can be expected in the short term both because of deterioration in the Soviet economy and as a consequence of independence. It is likely that the Soviet Union will seek to strike some hard bargains.

In the medium term, the small absolute size of the Baltic republics will be to their advantage in seeking external assistance. Their problems, even if severe in per capita terms, may still appear manageable to outside partners.

Over the longer term, more important than any attempt at dubious statistical crystal-ball gazing is recognition that the profile of the future balance of payments will respond to the policies adopted. Attention should concentrate on policies which encourage a swift adjustment of the economy to the needs and opportunities of the new economic situation rather than on exercises in pseudo-planning, which claim to project what is inherently unpredictable.

B. Quantitative measures of external relations

a. The level and composition of trade

The dominant features of Baltic trade are a high, often inefficient, interdependence with the Soviet Union, and very limited trade with the rest of the world (much of which is conducted through state foreign-trade organisation intermediaries). The commodity composition of trade reflects an excessive degree of industrialisation and the limited development of services. Difficulties to be overcome in future trade relations arise from the great dependence on energy and metal imports from the Soviet Union and the sizeable (yet variable) differential between Baltic and world-market product quality.

Like many of the economies of Eastern and Central Europe, the Baltic economies have high overall levels of trade, even when one accounts for their small size. This is a natural result of the centralised planning process which led to extreme specialisation. As one plant very often serves the needs of the whole Soviet market, trade flows are naturally significant. In other words, 'openness' reflects not the response of trade to market opportunities, but rather to Soviet planning decisions. Moreover, given the highly monopolistic structure of production, the Baltic republics and the Soviet Union are mutually dependent in ways not captured by trade shares.

Like the rest of the Soviet Union, the Baltics are relatively isolated from world trade; 85–95 per cent of Baltic trade occurs with other Soviet republics.

Roughly 50 per cent of Baltic exports outside the Soviet Union were to CMEA members, roughly a third to Western countries and the remainder to developing countries. Trade with CMEA members was conducted largely through state foreign-trade organisations which negotiate large, rather complex deals. Although direct trade ties (that is trade which does not require intermediation through state foreign-trade organisations) have expanded, the Soviet Union state foreign-trade monopoly still retains control over the bulk of trade flows.

In terms of the commodity composition of trade, there are similarities among the three Baltic republics (see Tables 7.1–7.4). Given this broadly similar structure of the three Baltic economies, their trade relations can be examined as a single unit. Tables 7.5–7.8 provide a value and percentage breakdown by branch and trading partner for Baltic imports and exports in 1987. About 82 per cent of imports and 91 per cent of exports are inter-republic flows with the rest accounted for by imports and exports outside the

Table 7.1 Domestic exports of commodities by republic, 1988 (percentage shares of total exports)

	Estonia	Latvia	Lithuania	Russia	Ukraine	Belorussia
Total (million roubles)	2,715.10	4,515.20	5,430.70	69,224.20	40,055.20	18,221.70
Industry	98.59	93.76	97.91	98.95	94.69	97.66
Electric power	4.78	1.66	3.02	0.71	0.40	0.14
Oil and gas	0.23	0.14	5.65	10.80	0.86	6.35
Coal	0.00	0.00	0.00	0.67	0.64	0.00
Other fuels	0.54	0.01	0.01	0.00	0.00	0.00
Ferrous metals	0.22	2.30	0.56	7.76	15.39	1.08
Nonferrous metals	0.30	0.30	0.15	4.40	2.28	0.38
Chemicals and petrochemicals	11.65	13.98	6.61	11.92	8.23	12.34
Machinery	19.70	28.05	32.49	39.17	39.19	42.18
Wood, paper and pulp	4.71	2.96	4.49	6.03	1.03	2.49
Construction materials	1.08	1.33	1.32	1.66	1.82	1.27
Light industry	29.40	17.69	25.75	9.23	6.51	20.41
Food industry	23.93	21.98	16.96	3.75	16.33	9.29
Other industry	2.04	3.35	0.89	2.84	2.02	1.72
Agriculture	1.09	2.27	2.02	0.48	4.19	2.14
Other sectors	0.32	3.97	0.07	0.57	1.12	0.20
	100	100	100	100	100	100

Source: Vestnik statistiki, no. 3, 1990; estimates by Stuart Brown.

Table 7.2 Foreign exports of commodities by republic, 1988 (percentage shares of total exports)

	Estonia	Latvia	Lithuania	Russia	Ukraine	Belorussia
Total (million roubles)	245.90	330.90	527.10	33,313.50	6,880.10	1,695.50
Industry	99.72	91.31	99.87	96.28	96.05	99.48
Electric power	0.00	0.00	0.00	0.30	7.63	1.24
Oil and gas	0.77	0.00	33.90	28.38	6.06	20.09
Coal	0.00	0.00	0.00	2.11	10.06	0.00
Other fuels	0.24	0.21	0.19	0.00	0.00	0.04
Ferrous metals	0.28	3.20	0.49	4.50	27.78	0.86
Nonferrous metals	0.00	0.11	0.02	4.78	0.66	0.07
Chemicals and petrochemicals	4.23	9.64	2.09	8.51	9.15	18.37
Machinery	13.46	35.81	26.86	23.81	22.14	46.40
Wood, paper and pulp	10.37	9.06	4.38	9.18	0.59	1.89
Construction materials	0.94	1.21	1.37	0.50	0.44	0.60
Light industry	22.00	3.33	3.43	4.38	3.46	4.05
Food industry	46.12	27.93	26.85	3.44	6.81	1.17
Other industry	1.30	0.32	0.28	1.39	1.28	4.71
Agriculture	0.16	2.76	0.13	0.91	0.57	0.09
Other sectors	0.12	5.93	0.00	2.80	3.38	0.44
	100	100	100	100	100	100

Source: Vestnik statistiki, no. 3, 1990; estimates by Stuart Brown.

Table 7.3 Domestic imports of commodities by republic, 1988 (percentage shares of total exports)

	Estonia	Latvia	Lithuania	Russia	Ukraine	Belorussia
Total (million roubles)	3,047.2	4,632.8	6,238.5	68,963.9	36,431.6	14,171.4
Industry	97.65	97.29	98.65	93.77	98.72	96.79
Electric power	0.95	2.88	1.46	0.76	0.43	0.96
Oil and gas	8.61	10.57	16.79	2.33	10.76	12.71
Coal	0.11	0.06	0.31	0.27	0.81	0.42
Other fuels	0.01	0.00	0.07	0.04	0.01	0.01
Ferrous metals	4.57	8.66	5.93	9.23	6.61	9.38
Nonferrous metals	2.88	2.94	2.89	2.30	5.21	2.86
Chemicals and petrochemicals	14.94	13.55	12.30	8.97	11.50	13.93
Machinery	32.71	33.80	34.75	30.23	35.86	33.37
Wood, paper and pulp	2.65	3.01	3.50	1.15	4.34	2.70
Construction materials	1.28	1.61	1.43	1.09	0.94	1.69
Light industry	16.60	10.85	12.55	16.76	13.47	9.65
Food industry	10.07	6.81	4.83	19.05	6.10	7.30
Other industry	2.23	2.54	1.84	1.58	2.69	1.82
Agriculture	1.88	2.52	1.29	5.73	0.67	2.38
Other sectors	0.47	0.19	0.06	0.50	0.61	0.83
	100	100	100	100	100	100

Source: Vestnik statistiki, no. 3, 1990; estimates by Stuart Brown.

Table 7.4 Foreign imports of commodities by republic, 1988 (percentage shares of total exports)

	Estonia	Latvia	Lithuania	Russia	Ukraine	Belorussia
Total (million roubles)	661.40	958.40	1,249.10	66,901.20	13,430.70	3,672.40
Industry	79.48	84.63	83.80	89.88	90.52	83.56
Electric power	1.57	0.00	0.00	0.00	0.00	0.00
Oil and gas	0.00	0.00	0.06	1.18	0.45	0.06
Coal	1.09	2.54	2.87	0.42	0.89	0.35
Other fuels	0.00	0.00	0.00	0.00	0.00	0.00
Ferrous metals	2.10	1.04	1.93	3.75	3.76	1.73
Nonferrous metals	0.05	0.00	0.42	1.87	1.23	1.40
Chemicals and petrochemicals	10.86	9.38	5.56	8.20	8.70	10.62
Machinery	22.27	11.63	28.95	36.74	26.20	31.63
Wood, paper and pulp	1.39	2.18	1.49	2.01	3.25	2.36
Construction materials	1.30	0.40	0.77	0.86	0.69	0.80
Light industry	24.75	27.12	21.26	20.75	27.21	22.55
Food industry	13.50	29.32	19.99	12.80	16.65	11.48
Other industry	0.60	1.02	0.52	1.31	1.50	0.57
Agriculture	18.85	15.23	16.20	8.36	7.91	14.92
Other sectors	1.66	0.14	0.00	1.76	1.57	1.52
	100	100	100	100	100	100

Source: Vestnik statistiki, no. 3, 1990; estimates by Stuart Brown.

Table 7.5 Imports of goods to the Baltic republics in 1987 (million roubles)

	Import total	Import from the USSR	From Russia	1	2	3	4	5	6	7	8	9	10	11	Total imports from outside USSR
Electricity prod.	84.2	94.2	80.8		3.3		17.0	8.0	3.2	19.6	0.7	1.9	5.7		
Metallurgical ind.	1,284.6	1,221.3	942.6	204.5	16.5	2.1			0.3						62.7
Fuel industry	1,642.5	1,591.6	1,294.3	44.6	251.1	0.7									56.9
Chemical and petrochemical ind.	1,786.2	1,526.6	1,061.3	187.8	194.0	16.8	17.8	5.8	12.2	13.2	0.3	4.3	11.7	0.6	259.6
Machine-building and metal-processing	4,818.2	4,324.7	3,028.5	758.4	316.1	17.6	15.4	12.7	14.4	42.7	16.3	3.7	37.3	1.8	493.4
Forest, wood-processing, paper and pulp	436.0	389.9	336.7	21.3	25.7	0.1	0.4	0.4	0.4	4.1	0.1		0.5		46.1
Building material industry	182.8	164.0	98.2	27.8	32.1		1.4		0.3	3.2	0.7		0.3		18.8
Light industry	2,273.1	1,504.6	547.5	160.7	235.9	63.1	127.3	119.4	22.3	38.0	78.1	44.8	16.9	49.9	768.6
Food processing industry	1,276.6	701.6	148.6	118.7	83.7	24.3		63.8	37.9	185.6	9.0	4.4	24.4	1.4	574.3
Meat and dairy products	24.0	21.0	3.5	11.4	4.9		0.3			0.9					2.9
Fish industry	24.2	23.7	23.5	0.1		0.4								0.1	0.5
Milling industry	110.8	103.4	91.2	10.4	3.3	0.6	2.2	2.5		1.9					1.4
Other branches	258.9	238.2	159.9	37.5	26.3	5.4	1.3	3.2	1.9	4.6	0.6		3.1		20.8
Agriculture	663.4	235.1	111.0	57.7	6.0	0.1	22.3		4.4	15.6	7.3	0.6		1.5	428.3
Other sectors of material prod.	31.5	30.3	25.9	2.1	1.7		0.2			0.2					1.2
Total	14,902.8	12,166.6	8,014.7	1,643.2	1,200.8	131.3	206.0	215.9	97.3	329.7	113.0	59.7	99.9	55.3	2,736.2

Key: 1. Ukraine; 2. Belorussia; 3. Uzbekistan; 4. Kazakhstan; 5. Georgia; 6. Azerbaijan; 7. Moldavia; 8. Kirghizia; 9. Tadjikistan; 10. Armenia; 11. Turkmenia.

Source: Official statistics, estimates by Stuart Brown.

Table 7.6 Imports of goods to the Baltic republics in 1987 (in % according to deliveries)

	Import total	Imports from the USSR	From Russia	1	2	3	4	5	6	7	8	9	10	11	Total imports from outside USSR	% of total imports from USSR	% of total imports from outside USSR
Electricity prod.	100.0	100.0	96.1		3.9											0.6	
Metallurgical ind.	100.0	95.1	73.4	15.9	1.3	0.2	1.3	0.6	0.3	1.5	0.1	0.1	0.4		4.9	8.6	2.3
Fuel industry	100.0	96.5	78.5	2.7	15.2	0.9	1.0	0.3	0.7	0.7		0.2	0.7		3.5	11.1	2.1
Chemical and petrochemical ind.	100.0	85.5	53.4	10.5	10.9	0.4	0.3	0.3	0.3	0.9	0.3	0.1	0.8		14.5	12.0	9.5
Machine-building and metal-processing	100.0	89.8	64.1	15.7	6.6		0.3	0.3	0.3	1.0			0.1		10.2	32.3	18.0
Forest, wood-processing, paper and pulp	100.0	89.4	77.2	4.8	5.9		0.1	0.1	0.1	1.0			0.1		10.6	2.9	1.7
Building material industry	100.0	89.7	53.7	15.2	17.6		0.7		0.2	1.7	0.4		0.2		10.3	1.2	0.7
Light industry	100.0	66.2	24.1	7.1	10.4	2.8	5.6	5.3	1.0	1.7	3.4	2.0	0.7	2.2	33.8	15.3	28.1
Food processing industry	100.0	55.0	11.6	9.3	6.6	1.9	5.0	5.0	3.0	14.5	0.7	0.3	1.9	0.1	45.0	8.6	21.0
Meat and dairy products	100.0	87.9	14.5	47.6	20.6		1.3			3.9					12.2	0.2	0.1
Fish industry	100.0	97.9	97.2	0.3										0.4	2.1	0.2	
Milling industry	100.0	96.7	82.3	9.4	3.0	0.3	2.0	1.0		1.7	0.2		1.2		1.3	0.7	0.1
Other branches	100.0	92.0	61.8	14.5	10.1	0.2	0.5	0.5	0.7	1.8	1.1	0.1			8.0	1.7	0.8
Agriculture	100.0	35.4	15.7	8.7	0.9	0.8	3.4		0.7	2.3	0.1				64.6	4.5	15.7
Other sectors of material prod.	100.0	96.2	22.2	6.8	5.5	0.4	0.5			0.6				0.2	3.8	0.2	
Total	100.0	81.6	53.0	11.0	8.1	0.9	1.4	1.4	0.7	2.2	0.8	0.4	0.7	0.4	18.4	100.0	100.0

Key: 1. Ukraine; 2. Belorussia; 3. Uzbekistan; 4. Kazakhstan; 5. Georgia; 6. Azerbaijan; 7. Moldavia; 8. Kirghizia; 9. Tadjikistan; 10. Armenia; 11. Turkmenia.

Source: Official statistics, estimates by Stuart Brown.

Table 7.7 Exports of goods from the Baltic republics in 1987 (million roubles)

	Total exports	Exports to the USSR	From Russia	1	2	3	4	5	6	7	8	9	10	11	Total exports to outside USSR
Electricity prod.	190.9	190.0	109.1	0.1	81.7					4.2	0.5		0.5		
Metallurgical ind.	159.0	141.3	100.7	17.1	14.3	0.8	1.4	1.0	0.7	0.1		0.1	0.1		17.8
Fuel industry	314.1	91.6	72.3	3.7	14.3	0.5	0.7								222.5
Chemical and petrochemical ind.	1,132.4	1,074.1	557.6	183.5	127.9	23.5	66.4	23.1	21.0	28.1	11.5	9.6	9.6	12.4	59.4
Machine-building and metal-processing	3,577.6	3,289.5	1,806.4	758.2	320.0	60.8	124.7	38.7	34.9	52.1	21.9	17.3	32.4	21.1	288.1
Forest, wood-processing, paper and pulp	536.9	451.4	261.0	81.5	26.4	9.3	20.6	13.9	11.9	7.6	3.7	8.4	3.1	3.9	85.4
Building material industry	135.6	124.3	80.1	6.4	20.5	5.0	4.5	0.9	2.3	1.5	0.1	0.1	2.9		11.3
Light industry	2,933.7	2,979.8	1,550.6	522.6	169.2	140.9	150.4	60.3	35.8	85.2	34.6	31.7	77.6	20.9	53.9
Food processing industry	930.0	811.6	599.8	85.3	42.6	17.9	28.3	6.2	7.1	5.0	8.2	6.2	3.7	1.5	18.4
Meat and dairy products	1,112.7	1,056.3	973.6	3.8	2.8	4.2	3.1	24.9	17.5	4.9	0.2	0.2	9.7	5.3	56.3
Fish industry	830.3	635.5	365.5	103.0	72.8	14.8	27.3	19.9	6.9	9.2	3.5	4.6	4.6	3.3	194.9
Milling industry	46.6	46.6	38.5	2.5	0.8	3.5				1.3					
Other branches	221.8	214.5	117.4	35.4	22.4	6.9	8.9	3.4	3.3	3.4	2.5	2.5	3.7	4.6	7.3
Agriculture	239.0	196.2	69.1	10.6	36.3	23.4	34.1	7.2	4.9	1.4	0.4	0.4	1.0	7.4	42.8
Other sectors of material prod.	34.5	13.6	6.7	2.3	3.0	0.4	0.2			0.1	0.9				20.9
Total	12,295.0	11,217.0	6,714.4	1,816.2	955.1	311.9	470.6	200.5	146.3	203.9	87.7	81.1	148.9	80.5	1,079.0

Key: 1. Ukraine; 2. Belorussia; 3. Uzbekistan; 4. Kazakhstan; 5. Georgia; 6. Azerbaijan; 7. Moldavia; 8. Kirghizia; 9. Tadjikistan; 10. Armenia; 11. Turkmenia.

Source: Official statistics, estimates by Stuart Brown.

Table 7.8 Exports of goods from the Baltic republics in 1987 (in % according to receivers)

	Total exports	Exports to the USSR	From Russia	1	2	3	4	5	6	7	8	9	10	11	Total exports to outside USSR	% of total exports to USSR	% of total exports outside USSR
Electricity prod.	100.0	100.0	57.2	0.1	42.8											1.6	
Metallurgical ind.	100.0	99.8	63.3	10.8	9.0	0.5	0.9	0.6	0.4	2.6	0.3	0.1	0.3		11.2	1.3	1.6
Fuel industry	100.0	29.2	23.0	1.2	4.6	0.2	0.2	2.0	1.9	2.5	1.0	0.8	0.9		70.8	2.6	20.6
Chemical and petrochemical ind.	100.0	94.8	49.2	16.2	11.3	2.1	5.9							1.1	5.2	9.2	5.4
Machine-building and metal-processing	100.0	91.9	50.5	21.2	8.9	1.7	3.5	1.1	1.0	1.5	0.6	0.5	0.9	0.6	8.1	29.1	26.7
Forest, wood-processing, paper and pulp	100.0	84.1	49.6	15.2	4.9	1.7	3.8	2.6	2.2	1.4	0.7	1.6	0.6	0.7	15.9	4.4	7.9
Building material industry	100.0	91.7	59.1	4.7	15.1	3.7	3.3	0.7	1.7	1.1		0.1	2.2		8.3	1.1	1.0
Light industry	100.0	98.2	52.9	17.8	5.8	4.8	5.1	2.1	1.2	2.9	1.2	1.1	2.6	0.7	1.8	23.9	5.0
Food processing industry	100.0	97.8	72.3	10.3	5.1	2.1	3.4	0.8	0.9	0.6	1.0	0.8	0.4	0.2	2.2	6.8	1.7
Meat and dairy products	100.0	94.9	88.0	0.3	0.3	0.4	0.3	2.2	1.6	0.4			0.9	0.5	5.1	9.0	5.2
Fish industry	100.0	76.5	44.0	12.4	8.8	1.9	3.3	2.4	0.8	1.1	0.4	0.6	0.6	0.4	23.5	6.8	18.1
Milling industry	100.0	100.0	82.6	5.4	1.7	7.5				2.8						0.4	
Other branches	100.0	96.7	52.9	16.0	10.1	3.1	4.0	1.5	2.1	1.5	1.1	1.1	1.7	2.1	3.3	1.8	0.7
Agriculture	100.0	82.1	28.9	4.4	15.2	9.8	14.3	3.0	2.1	0.6	0.1	0.2	0.4	3.1	17.9	1.9	4.0
Other sectors of material prod.	100.0	39.5	19.4	6.6	8.7	1.2	0.7			0.2	2.6				60.5	0.3	1.9
Total	100.0	91.2	54.6	14.8	7.8	2.5	3.8	1.6	1.2	1.7	0.7	0.7	1.2	0.7	8.8	100.0	100.0

Key: 1. Ukraine; 2. Belorussia; 3. Uzbekistan; 4. Kazakhstan; 5. Georgia; 6. Azerbaijan; 7. Moldavia; 8. Kirghizia; 9. Tadjikistan; 10. Armenia; 11. Turkmenia.

Source: Official statistics, estimates by Stuart Brown.

Soviet Union. On the import side, the overwhelming fact is the high degree of dependence on the Russian Federation, accounting for almost 54 per cent of total trade and 66 per cent of intra-Soviet trade. For those branches in which imports are significant shares of Baltic consumption, Russia's share is particularly pronounced in ferrous and nonferrous metallurgy (73 per cent), fuel (78 per cent), chemical–petrochemicals (53 per cent), machine-building and metal-working (64 per cent), forestry, pulp and paper products (77 per cent) and construction materials (54 per cent).

The Ukraine and Belorussia represent the next two largest sources of Baltic imports with an 11 per cent and 8 per cent share, respectively. Both are significant suppliers of milk, meat and other food products, construction materials, chemical–petrochemical products, and in Belorussia's case, petroleum products.

The overall branch structure of total imports and foreign imports is given in columns 18 and 19, respectively (Table 7.6). Inter-republican trade with the Baltic region involves an emphasis on machinery while the structure of foreign imports is tilted toward light industry and food products. The most important single import at a three-digit classification is refined petroleum products.

On the export side, less than one-tenth of the total value of Baltic exports went outside the Soviet Union in 1987. Russia is the dominant importer of Baltic products, followed by the Ukraine and Belorussia. Important branches for Baltic exports are machinery (29 per cent) and light industry (24 per cent). Although processed food and fish products are significant (roughly 22 per cent), unprocessed agricultural crops account for a very minor share of interrepublican and foreign Baltic exports. In terms of more disaggregated product classifications, leading Baltic exports include radio–electronic products (985 million roubles), fish and fish products (830 million), knitted wear (680 million), meat and meat products (669 million) and wool manufactures (627 million).

b. The balance of goods and services

In principle, the balance of payments' accounts for each Baltic republic should record the principal trade balances on goods and services as well as the capital flows between each republic and the rest of the world. As constituent parts of the Soviet Union, individual Soviet republics until recently have not attempted to estimate systematically their own balances of payments. Presently, Estonia appears to be furthest along in developing a notion of a payments balance and making estimates for the principal sub-balances.

Such efforts began with the publication in 1990 by the Soviet statistical agency, Goskomstat, of comprehensive data on merchandise trade balances by republic, both for interrepublic and foreign transactions. To estimate a current account of the balance of payments, republican authorities must also estimate the balance-of-services' trade.

To explore Baltic trade and services balances Goskomstat data on merchandise trade and financial flows can be used, supplemented by the

Table 7.9 Estonian balance of payments (million roubles)

	1988 Income (1)	Expenses (2)	Balance (3)	1989 Income (4)	Expenses (5)	Balance (6)
Merchandise trade	2,961.0	3,708.6	−747.6	2,832.5	3,487.7	−655.2
Interrepublican	2,715.1	3,047.2	−332.1	2,641.8	2,835.8	−194.0
Foreign	245.9	661.4	−415.5	190.7	651.9	−461.2
Services	304.9	117.8	187.1	248.9	23.4	225.5
Cash flows	303.7	116.7	187.0	247.7	22.0	225.7
Retail trade	277.0	92.3	184.7	207.6	0.0	207.6
Foreign tourism	5.2	7.9	−2.7	3.9	5.8	−1.9
Post office	2.1	1.4	0.7	2.0	1.9	0.1
Recreation	17.9	13.7	4.2	17.4	14.3	3.1
Other	0.3	0.3	0.0	16.8	0.0	16.8
Recreation						
(non cash)	1.2	1.1	0.1	1.2	1.4	−0.2
Financial-credit transactions	1,541.6	833.3	708.3	1,624.6	931.5	693.1
Interbudgetary transfers						
Turnover taxes to all-union budget	0.0	45.0	−45.0	0.0	208.7	−208.7
Turnover taxes with merchandise	181.8	35.3	146.5	47.0	−0.0	47.0
Transfer payments	82.8	41.7	41.1	54.3	65.6	−11.3
Profits to all-union budget	0.0	271.9	−271.9	0.0	203.0	−203.0
Population income tax	0.0	0.0	0.0	0.0	0.0	0.0
Central government borrowings	0.0	2.3	−2.3	0.0	3.2	−3.2
Subsidies for food	111.8	5.7	106.1	166.8	0.0	166.8
Contributions for science	29.1	0.0	29.1	108.1	0.0	108.1
SS payments for pensions	241.4	0.0	241.4	313.5	0.0	313.5
Contributions for capital investment	39.9	0.0	39.9	24.8	0.0	24.8
Other contributions	0.0	0.0	0.0	57.4	49.9	7.5
Payments to all-union ministries						
Out of profits	53.1	50.3	2.8	69.2	69.4	−0.2
Depreciation	12.7	67.7	−55.0	6.9	73.7	−66.8
Payments to social security budget	292.8	9.0	283.8	272.7	6.5	266.2
Payments for exported goods	417.5	0.0	417.5	463.0	0.0	463.0
Settlements for credit	77.6	0.0	77.6	28.3	0.0	28.3
Other	1.1	304.4	303.3	12.6	251.5	−238.7
Total	4,806.3	4,658.6	147.7	4,706.0	4,442.6	263.4

Source: Estonian Institute of Economics.

more detailed Estonian estimates. The latter are shown in Tables 7.9 and 7.10, which describe the overall balance of payments and the current account balance, respectively.

With respect to merchandise trade, the data suggest that the Baltic republics run deficits on both interrepublican and foreign trade and hence

Table 7.10 An estimated Estonian current account (million roubles)

	1988 Balance	1989 Balance
Merchandise trade	−423.8	−335.9
Interrepublican	−179.9	−147.0
Foreign	−243.9	−188.9
Services	187.0	225.5
Cash flows	186.9	225.7
Retail trade	184.7	207.6
Foreign tourism	−2.7	−1.9
Post office	0.7	0.1
Recreation	4.2	3.1
Other	0.0	16.8
Recreation (non-cash)	0.1	−0.2
Unilateral transfers	−223.6	−112.4
Interbudgetary transfers	−187.5	−122.2
Turnover taxes to all-union budget	−45.0	−208.7
Transfer payments	−43.4	−14.5
Profits to all-union budget	−271.9	−203.0
Subsidies for food	106.1	166.8
Contributions for science and capital investment	69.0	140.4
Payments to all-union ministries	−52.2	−67.0
Social security settlements	−42.4	47.3
Payments to social security budget	−283.8	−266.2
Social security payments for pensions	241.4	313.5
Other	56.2	26.3
Current account	−404.2	−196.5
Adjusted current account*	−13.2	2.0

* merchandise plus services plus *negative* of unilateral transfers.

Source: Table 7.1.

overall trade deficits. This is true whether the balances are expressed in established domestic prices, prices incorporating revisions proposed for the thirteenth Five-Year Plan, prices which incorporate wholesale price increases beginning on 1 January 1991 or so-called 'world market prices' from Soviet statistics. Judgements on the usefulness of these data for assessing the future economic potential of Baltic states (and their future balances of payments) are impossible without some mention of the principal biases in these various measures.

The overall (interrepublic plus foreign) merchandise trade balances in

Table 7.11 Inter-republican and foreign trade balances by republic, 1988 (million roubles)

Republic	Imports	Total Exports	Balance	Imports	Domestic Exports	Balance	Imports	Foreign Exports	Balance
Estonia	3,708.6	2,961.0	−747.6	3,047.2	2,715.1	−332.1	661.4	245.9	−415.5
Latvia	5,591.2	4,896.1	−695.1	4,632.8	4,515.2	−117.6	958.4	380.9	−577.5
Lithuania	7,487.6	5,957.8	−1,529.8	6,238.5	5,430.7	−807.3	1,249.1	527.1	−722.0
Russia	135,865.1	102,537.7	−33,327.4	68,963.9	69,224.2	260.3	66,901.2	33,313.5	−33,587.7
Ukraine	49,862.3	46,935.3	−2,927.0	36,431.6	40,055.2	3,623.6	13,430.7	6,880.1	−6,550.6
Belorussia	17,843.8	19,917.2	2,073.4	14,171.4	18,221.7	4,050.3	3,672.4	1,695.5	−1,976.9
Uzbekistan	12,327.1	10,486.9	−1,840.2	10,623.7	8,957.2	−1,666.5	1,703.4	1,529.7	−173.7
Kazakhstan	16,420.1	9,164.8	−7,255.3	13,686.4	8,337.1	−5,349.3	2,733.7	827.7	−1,906.0
Georgia	6,492.9	5,900.8	−592.1	5,218.4	5,508.1	289.7	1,274.5	392.7	−881.8
Azerbaidjan	5,672.2	6,782.0	1,109.8	4,258.2	6,357.5	2,099.3	1,414.0	424.5	−989.5
Moldavia	6,080.4	5,057.5	−1,022.9	4,986.5	4,800.3	−186.2	1,093.9	257.2	−836.7
Kirghizia	3,744.8	2,595.4	−1,149.4	2,971.8	2,536.8	−435.0	773.0	58.6	−714.4
Tadjikistan	3,492.4	2,358.7	−1,133.7	3,022.6	2,025.2	−997.4	469.8	333.5	−136.3
Armenia	4,876.4	3,767.0	−1,109.4	4,017.6	3,683.1	−334.5	858.8	83.9	−774.9
Turkmenistan	2,918.2	2,634.2	−284.0	2,486.0	2,389.2	−96.8	432.2	245.0	−187.2
Total	282,383.1	231,952.4	−50,430.7	184,756.6	184,756.6	0.0	97,626.5	47,195.8	−50,430.7

Source: Vestnik statistiki, no. 3, 1990.

established domestic prices for the Baltic republics in 1988 are given in Table 7.11. In 1988 Estonia, Latvia, and Lithuania ran overall deficits of 747 million, 695 million and 1.53 billion roubles, respectively. To put these balances in perspective, it should be noted that only five of the Soviet republics ran positive trade balances in domestic (interrepublican) trade and only Belorussia and Azerbaijan succeeded in achieving positive overall balances in 1988. This relates to the contribution of foreign trade to the overall balances. Despite a modest surplus in foreign-currency prices, the overall Soviet foreign-trade deficit in 1988 in domestic prices was over 50 billion roubles with not a single Soviet republic in surplus. The difference largely reflects very low domestic prices for the Soviet Union's predominant foreign-exchange earner, energy, and very high prices applied to most consumer imports. In per capita terms, among the thirteen republics running negative overall balances, Estonia, Latvia and Lithuania occupy second, sixth and third place, respectively, in terms of the size of these balances.

However, these trade balances do not capture real interregional (and foreign) commodity flows, owing to distortions underlying Soviet domestic prices. Soviet domestic prices are administratively set, highly differentiated according to non-economic criteria and extremely rigid. Prices may under- or overestimate the real opportunity cost of interrepublic (and foreign) commodity and service flows.

Such distortions vary in size and pattern by republic, reflecting disparate industrial structures. Owing to the vagaries of Soviet pricing principles, the major part of net output produced in sectors of heavy industry and agriculture is realised in the prices of products of other sectors, primarily in the textile and food industries. Because turnover tax is highest for final consumer manufactures, it disproportionately augments exports in republics specialising in such manufacture. Thus, for example, large alcoholic beverage exporters (importers) bias trade balances upward (downward) owing to the roughly 90 per cent of value added attributable to turnover tax on alcohol.

By contrast, owing to the Soviet practice of levying subsidies at the location of production rather than consumption, the presence of subsidies reduces the value of exportables. Thus, export volume for large net agricultural exporters is downwardly biased thanks to the high percentage of subsidies contained in the retail price. For example, as a major agricultural producer and exporter, Lithuania in 1989 paid out subsidies of 2.1 billion roubles or 44 per cent of its entire budget for the production of milk and meat. These subsidies represent approximately 30–40 per cent of the product's value. Of this sum 600 million (28 per cent) was paid to producers for goods which were exported.

Furthermore, for certain republics the domestic prices used in the official valuations of commodity exports and imports differ from those at which such goods are transacted. For example, Estonian economists argue that Estonia's merchandise trade balance is downwardly biased for this reason. Others maintain that the prices assigned to specific goods in interrepublican trade frequently are either less than their costs of production or less than the prices at which they are sold within the producing republic.

Table 7.12 Republic trade balance adjustments, 1988 (billion roubles)

Republic	Turnover taxes	Subsidies	Purchases by migrants	Total adjustments
Estonia	– 0.1	0.2	0.3	0.1
Latvia	– 0.2	0.4	0.5	0.2
Lithuania	– 0.4	0.8	0.5	– 0.1
Russia	– 3.4	– 5.1	0.1	8.2
Ukraine	– 1.2	1.6	– 0.4	– 1.9
Belorussia	– 1.1	1.7	0.6	– 0.9
Uzbekistan	1.5	0.0	– 0.4	0.5
Kazakhstan	0.2	1.0	– 0.5	0.5
Georgia	0.6	– 0.3	– 0.7	– 0.8
Azerbaijan	1.8	– 0.4	– 0.4	1.0
Moldavia	0.9	0.3	0.6	1.2
Kirghizia	0.3	0.1	0.0	0.1
Tadjikistan	0.4	– 0.1	0.2	0.3
Armenia	0.2	– 0.3	– 0.2	– 0.5
Turkmenistan	0.5	0.1	– 0.2	0.9
Total	0.0	0.0	0.0	8.8

Source: Vestnik statistiki, no. 3, 1990.

In addition, some aspects of commodity trade are apparently not covered in Moscow's data. For example, at least three big enterprises directly subordinated to the all-union ministries provide no statistical data to Estonian authorities. Moscow supplements these data with statistics on such all-union enterprises.

An additional bias in the trade balances involves purchases by travellers moving between republics whose purchases of local goods are not captured as exports in official statistics. Finally, the peculiar treatment of foreign trade in official statistics can distort republican trade balances.

In response to criticisms that recorded trade-flow prices are biased measures of interrepublican resource transfers and foreign-trade flows, Soviet authorities have provided several alternative valuations of republican trade balances. For example, Table 7.12 provides Goskomstat re-estimates of republican merchandise trade balances for 1988, with turnover taxes and subsidies redistributed based on value added and purchases by travellers netted out. The last column shows that such adjustments worsen Russia's balances by 8.4 billion roubles annually. In contrast, the balances of Estonia, Latvia and Lithuania improve by 400, 700 and 900 million roubles, respectively.

Goskomstat has also estimated republican trade balances in 'world market prices' for 1988 (Table 7.13), showing Russia as the only Soviet republic with a positive overall trade balance. In comparison to valuations in (pre-1991) domestic prices, trade deficits in Lithuania, Latvia and Estonia worsen by 2.17 billion, 600 million, and 600 million, respectively. In per capita terms in 1988, Lithuania exhibits by far the largest negative balance of all

Table 7.13 Foreign and inter-republican trade, 1988 (in domestic and world market prices) (million roubles)

Republic	Domestic prices			World prices			WP/DP	
	Imports	Exports	Diff	Imports	Exports	Diff	Imports	Exports
Estonia	3,700	3,000	−700	3,200	1,900	−1,300	0.865	0.633
Latvia	5,600	4,900	−700	5,000	3,700	−1,300	0.893	0.755
Lithuania	7,490	5,960	−1,530	7,800	4,100	−3,700	1.041	0.688
Russia	135,860	102,540	−33,320	101,900	132,700	30,800	0.750	1.294
Ukraine	49,860	46,940	−2,920	47,400	44,500	−2,900	0.951	0.948
Belorussia	17,840	19,920	2,080	18,500	16,400	−2,100	1.037	0.823
Uzbekistan	12,320	10,490	−1,830	10,500	8,000	−2,500	0.852	0.763
Kazakhstan	16,400	9,100	−7,300	15,600	9,000	−6,600	0.951	0.989
Georgia	6,490	5,900	−590	5,300	3,400	−1,900	0.817	0.576
Azerbaijan	5,700	6,800	1,100	5,100	4,600	−500	0.895	0.676
Moldavia	6,100	5,060	−1,040	5,100	2,500	−2,600	0.836	0.494
Kirghizia	3,770	2,560	−1,210	3,200	2,100	−1,100	0.849	0.820
Tadjikistan	3,490	2,330	−1,160	2,800	1,700	−1,100	0.802	0.730
Armenia	4,880	3,760	−1,120	3,600	2,200	−1,400	0.738	0.585
Turkmenistan	2,900	2,600	−300	2,400	2,400	0	0.828	0.923
Total	282,400	231,860	−50,540	237,400	239,200	1,800	0.841	1.032

Source: *Vestnik statistiki*, no. 4, 1990; and authors' estimates.

Table 7.14 Effect on terms of trade and GNP of a shift to world market prices

	(1) world/ domestic price ratio (from Table 7.13)	(2) terms of trade effect (calculated from (1))	(3) exports to Soviet Union as share of GNP 1989	(4) effect on GNP (calculated from (2) and (3))
Estonia	exports 0.633 imports 0.865	– 26.8	0.501	– 13.4
Latvia	exports 0.755 imports 0.893	– 15.4	0.469	– 7.2
Lithuania	exports 0.688 imports 1.041	– 33.8	0.473	– 16.0

Source: Vestnik statistiki, no. 4, 1990; and for column (3) Commission of the European Community: *European Economy*, no. 45, 1990.

Soviet republics (– 1,000). Estonia exhibits the next largest negative per capita balance (– 813) with Latvia in fourth place (– 480).

However, the prices used are not world market prices but rather Soviet foreign-currency prices averaged over trade with the West, developing countries and members of the CMEA. Nevertheless, since these prices are closer to actual world market prices, they are probably more realistic indicators of future external resource constraints than trade balances valued in Soviet domestic prices. According to these figures then, a shift to foreign-currency trade balances could result in terms of trade deteriorations of 27 per cent in Estonia, 15 per cent in Latvia, and 34 per cent in Lithuania (see Table 7.14). The terms of trade could be even less favourable if Russia ultimately charges the Baltics actual world market prices for fuels, and adjustments for quality deficiencies in manufactures are made. It will also make a significant difference to the Baltic economies if the Soviet Union insists on settlement in hard currency rather than in heretofore inconvertible roubles.

Straight calculations based on estimates of Soviet trade with the Baltic republics as a share of Baltic GNP suggest an effect on national income on the order of half the terms of trade effect, that is about 10 to 15 per cent. On the basis of alternative assumptions, a 'guesstimate' of the immediate impact of an abrupt shift to world market prices suggests a 20 per cent reduction in total Baltic domestic expenditure. Again, let it be pointed out that these figures are nothing but illustrative calculations based on the only available statistics.

c. Factors countervailing the negative external position

There are a number of factors that countervail the picture of a very weak external position given in the previous section. One set of factors is the potential of earnings from services. Another set pertains to the dynamics of

Table 7.15 Estimates of turnover from transit traffic via the Baltic republics
(1989/90 traffic level, world market prices in millions of US $)

Shipping	420
Ports	230
Road traffic	70
Railway traffic	460
Total	1,280

Source: Estimates by Peter Broch.

changing prices, composition and volume of cross-border trade, a process
that has already begun.

The most significant item missing from the current account as discussed
in the previous section is trade in services. This is a significant source of hard
currency earnings so far hardly tapped at all by the Baltic states. Three
different sources are likely to be of specific importance: transit traffic,
tourism and people working abroad.

Given the importance of Baltic ports in maintaining supply lines to Russia
and other republics, negotiation over tolls and port charges could yield the
Baltic states substantial revenue. Some indications of magnitude of transit
traffic are given in Chapter 13. Using the traffic volumes set out in that
chapter and using long-term marginal cost estimates as a proxy for realistic
pricing, estimates of turnover (Table 7.15) from transit traffic via the Baltic
states can be derived.

Significantly higher estimates have been made, even two to three times the
US$1,280 million suggested in the table. However, even the table's estimate
does not provide a very solid basis for estimating future revenue prospects,
given uncertainties about developments in the Soviet economy, the ability of
Soviet republics to pay and the possibility of diverting trade to other routes.

Estimates of possible returns from the tourist trade and from workers'
remittances are impossible at this stage. The potential of these sources
depends, of course, on the unknown dynamics of future development.
Already today, however, a significant growth is noticeable. Tourism income
was previously monopolised by the Moscow-based tourist agency. This has
already changed with hard-currency earnings staying in the Baltic states. The
tourist sector has obvious potential, both for culturally interested visitors
and seaside resort vacationers, but income will depend on new investments
and radically improved services.

An unknown number of Baltic nationals work outside the Baltic states.
They may have found short or seasonal jobs, with or without work permits,
in Finland and Scandinavia, and also in Poland and Germany, for example.
As borders become more easily penetrable this source will gain in importance. It is likely to become an important issue between the neighbouring
countries. Though migrant labour may cause some strain, studies from other
parts of the world suggest that it is beneficial to the region as a whole. In
this context it should be noted, also, that an increasing number of Baltic

nationals earn foreign exchange from services provided within the Baltic states, for example business consultancies.

Income from tourism and labour abroad mostly becomes part of the increasing volume of foreign exchange already circulating within the Baltic states and the Soviet Union. A significant part, however, is saved in bank accounts abroad. Again, no estimates are as yet possible.

The second major set of facts that countervail the negative external position concerns the dynamics of a changing trade pattern. Though future external economic relations are further discussed in the final part of this chapter, the effects of changes already under way on the picture of the current account that has been given in the previous section needs to be brought out.

First of all, the prices at which goods actually are traded has already started to change, both the officially set prices and the prices set on the free or 'black' market or negotiated in various kinds of deals. Between firms within the Baltic states and with Russia and the other republics barter or hard-currency settlement may in fact already predominate. To the extent that this is taking place, some movement is already being made towards world market prices. A corresponding adjustment in the terms of trade will then also have taken place.

Changes in the volume and composition of current account transactions, as distinct from their prices, are also likely to be substantial. Indeed large changes in cross-border flows among Soviet republics are already under-way, but they are not yet well-documented. Some general tendencies can however be identified.

First, in the former Soviet Union as a whole, within a shrinking total output, there has been a shift in the structure of production in 1990–91 towards consumer goods at the expense of investment goods and material inputs to investment goods. This is connected in part with priority changes originating at the centre (e.g., large cuts in investment funded from the union budget) and partly with a shift in behaviour at the enterprise level as central control has weakened, leaving enterprises increasingly concerned to fend for themselves, 'themselves' in this context usually meaning the working collective.

Second, all-union enterprises, including some in the officially-designated military sector (originally under the Soviet government's Military-Industrial Commission or VPK), have been taken over by the republics or turned into purportedly non-state corporations, often in a form of *nomenklatura* privatisation. In the case of the Baltic states, where these enterprises were often mainly staffed by ethnic Russians and located in ethnic-Russian enclaves, some running-down of these production units is especially likely.

If the detailed cross-border commodity flows for Estonia (Tables 7.16–18) provide some guidance with respect to all three Baltic states, both these changes would tend to improve the constant price trade balance with the Soviet Union.

As discussed in Chapter 11, the Baltic states' industrial structure is more concentrated than the Soviet average on the food, clothing and textile industries (though not otherwise as closely similar to one another as is often

Table 7.16 Net flows of goods across Estonian borders, through state channels, in physical terms, 1989–90 ('000 tons unless otherwise specified)

product	1989 actual	1990 expected
meat	59.0	39.5
dairy produce	442.3	400
eggs (mn. units)	61.2	55
potatoes	21.7	33.8
vegetables	– 3.5	– 0.9
electricity ('000 kWh)	7,467	7,210
peat (in briquettes)	4.5	2.0
residual fuel oil	– 1,523.2	– 1,584
kerosene	– 121.6	– 120
hard coal[a]	– 371.1	– 369.9
diesel fuel	– 583.2	– 595.2
benzine	– 506.8	– 531.1
bricks (mn)[b]	14.7	32.7

Notes: [a] most if not all from Poland; [b] 'wall-building materials in brick-equivalents'.

Source: Estonian Republic Ministry of Economics, *Ekonomika Estonii v 1991 godu*, Tallinn, November 1990.

Table 7.17 All-Union industry consumption of selected net-import items, in Estonia, 1990 (%)

residual fuel oil	46.5
kerosene	3.1
hard coal	7.6
diesel fuel	41.2
benzine	9.9

Source: ibid.

suggested). The importance of military industry was substantially less in these republics than in the rest of the Union — a circumstance that may be helpful to the Baltics if military production assets are likely either to be the subject of ownership claims from Moscow or to be run down.

The effects of probable Soviet troop withdrawals on the Baltic states' current-account balances with the Union are unclear. Reports have referred to estimates of 400,000 Soviet military personnel in the region, equivalent to 5 per cent of the population. The return of those troops (very few of whom are Baltic conscripts) to Russia and other republics would reduce Baltic import requirements (e.g., of fuel) and probably boost potential food exports. On the other hand, the past intra-budget financial flows that relate to Baltic troop support costs are not clearly documented, and the continued

Table 7.18 Production and cross-border flows of consumer goods, Estonia, 1990 (1990 retail prices, million roubles)

	production	imports	exports	balance
non-food	1,817	748	1,024	276
food	1,742	259	536	277

Source: ibid.

maintenance of Soviet bases in three states might have been the subject of negotiations yielding substantial revenues for the Baltic states.

Discussions of inter-republic goods flows have stressed the disruptive effect of the new trade barriers between republics. The fact that proportional reductions in officially recorded economic activity in the Baltic states in the first half of 1991 seemed to be of the same order of magnitude as those in the Soviet Union as a whole suggests that in early 1991, at least, there was no *prima facie* evidence that the Baltic states were suffering especially badly in this way.

Inter-republic trade barriers apart, the existing branch and regional patterns of supply would change dramatically if the shift to a market economy gathered pace. This is partly because the structure of final output would continue to change rapidly, partly because material input usage per unit of a given line of final output is likely to fall, and partly because the geographical pattern of deliveries, even with the existing patterns of final output and input usage, would be subject to stronger economic pressures to make it cost-effective.

In this context it may also be noted that suggestions have been made that imports to the military-industrial sector are recorded in the republican trade statistics, while their consumption by structures alien to the Baltic economies and the export of goods, for which they were inputs, are not. If this is so, it might possibly significantly change the conventional picture of Baltic trade.

There may therefore be more scope for shifting to alternative (local, or otherwise accessible) sources of supply, even in the short run, than is usually thought. One reason for supposing this is that Soviet studies of industrial concentration, showing extremely high measures, exaggerate the scale of the monopoly problem. They are based on official supply data on commodity flows, which cover only shipments between enterprises. But there is plentiful evidence of an unusually high degree of vertical integration within Soviet industrial enterprises, as each has sought to safeguard itself against the unreliable supply system by producing its own components and specialised equipment, if possible, in circumstances in which under market conditions these would be brought in from specialist suppliers. The concentration of production, though probably still high, is therefore less high than the concentration shown by inter-enterprise deliveries. The internal 'self supply' production units within large Soviet enterprises will often be inefficiently small, but at least in the short run there should be more potential sources of supply of most production inputs than the official supply data indicate. In general, given their relatively consumer-orientated production structures, the sum of Baltic enterprises may be somewhat better able to adjust to supply disruptions within a generally fragmenting economic space than the average of Soviet producers.

To sum up this sub-section: it appears that in the short run the Baltic economies' transactions with the rest of the former Soviet Union would probably result in a current account balance that was less unfavourable for them than that which developed under the old order.

d. Transfers, the capital account, debts and assets

To complete the overall picture of the balance of payments, estimates of goods and services flows must be supplemented by data on transfers and capital flows. The interpretation of these figures, and the ways in which they interrelate are conditioned by some specific aspects of the Soviet situation.

It has been in the nature of the Soviet centrally planned economy that money and credit are passive means of accounting and have not represented claims on resources without an accompanying order in the central plan. Given that financial transfers have not served the same function in determining claims on real resources as in a market system, such data as exists on purely financial flows between republics of the Soviet Union are not very revealing. There may have been significant real resource transfers, through government resource allocations or enterprise resource allocations, but this will not be accurately measured by any available financial data.

In considering the capital account, the question of the relationship of Estonia, Latvia and Lithuania to the international assets and liabilities of the Soviet Union are crucial.

There is at present confusion in the Soviet Union as to who is to resume responsibility of the Soviet debt. Though the West is likely to exert considerable pressure on the republics and whatever economic community that may emerge not to default, the Baltic states clearly have refused to take any responsibility for the debt or to participate in the servicing of the debt.

Before independence, at least Latvia did at some point negotiate taking upon itself a share of Soviet debt, corresponding to its share in population or national income. This was part of a strategy to gain control over foreign currency transactions, demonstrate credit-worthiness and obtain new credits. Now Latvia has dropped out of these negotiations, reflecting perhaps a judgement that there would be no net benefit obtainable from negotiating on the matter.

Presumably, any acceptance of a share of the Soviet debt would entail a claim on a share of the Soviet international assets. Would there be any advantage for the Baltic states in negotiating with the Soviet Union or a successor-organisation on this matter? Unfortunately the data on gold reserves and on indebtedness to the Soviet Union are subject to very wide margins of error, so that definitive judgement at present is impossible.

Possibly these figures will be available in the near future, possibly negotiations would be feasible. However, the strategy adopted by Estonia, Latvia and Lithuania is more likely to be determined by the denial of the legality of the incorporation of the Baltic states into the Soviet Union and the political circumstances in the Soviet Union than net calculations of costs and benefits.

A net asset is, certainly, the gold that the Baltic states can claim from the West. Shortly before the Soviet occupation of the independent Baltic states, most of their gold reserves were transferred from their central banks to Western central banks for safe-keeping. Gold was received by at least Great Britain, France, Sweden and the Basle-based Bank for International Settlement (of which the central banks of the occupied Baltic states remained *de jure* members). Some of the gold still remains in the West. Sweden turned the gold it had received from Estonia (3 tonnes) and Lithuania (1 tonne), over the the Soviet Union in 1940. Great Britain sold 14 tonnes of Estonian gold in 1968 as part of a settlement with the Soviet Union. A clear picture of the total amount is not yet at hand. According to some accounts, that include the gold that was turned over or sold, the Baltic states may lay claims on 28 tonnes. At $350 an ounce the market value would be some $315 million. The Baltic states have, however, not brought up this issue in public yet.

As this chapter so far has shown, Estonia, Latvia and Lithuania are still a long way from having even a rough picture of their balance of payments. Though new research will provide a better picture, many issues will not be sorted out until a clearer economic separation follows the political independence from the Soviet Union. It will be without a good knowledge of the external economic relations that the Baltic governments will have to choose new policy directions.

C. Changing external economic relations

Independence has opened new policy options for changing the external economic relations of Estonia, Latvia and Lithuania. Sovereign trade policies can be put in place, opening the countries to new markets in the Nordic region, in the rest of Europe and in the world as a whole. While opportunities are offered, risks and difficulties will be substantial.

Opening any economy that has been cut off from the world market presents a demanding adjustment phase that must be overcome. The Baltic transformation is, however, made the more difficult because of the dependence on the Soviet economy where the reform process itself is quite unclear.

Given the state of flux in the reform process of the Soviet Union, Russia and the other republics and in determining what successor-organisation, if any, they may choose to create, this final part of the chapter can only try to give some perspective to the future reform process.

a. Cooperation with the former Soviet republics

In the Soviet Union, while the centre still retained effective control over most critical economic instruments, control over several aspects of economic policy, including prices, budgets, banking and foreign exchange, was vigorously disputed between the union and republican governments. Of direct relevance to Baltic external economic relations has been the burgeoning movement of direct cooperation among the republics. From a low level, formal ties among the republics appear to be growing steadily, reflecting both economic and political considerations. These interrepublic links have been formalised during the past year in agreements signed by the Baltic republics with a majority of the remaining, now former, Soviet republics.

These agreements have the declared aim of 'deepening the mutually advantageous economic ties (among two republics) on the basis of equal rights'. In large part they represent an immediate response to the crisis of supply deliveries, containing provisions guaranteeing interrepublic deliveries not lower than the level of 1990. The intention is to conclude treaties, agreements or protocols in the following areas: general economic problems and financial-credit policy, the social sphere and national culture, the production of consumer markets, scientific–technical progress and fundamental research, ecology, material–technical supply, agriculture, industrial structuring, migration and so on. (See, for example, 'Agreement on Economic and Cultural Cooperation between the Estonian and Georgian Republics'.)

There are two potential problems with these agreements. First, their implementation may run counter to the apparent desire to protect republican markets through border controls and export licenses. Also, republican governments will have to assign state orders to enterprises to fulfil intergovernmental barter-type trade agreements. All of these policies, while understandable as attempts to stabilise the domestic market using the limited instruments available to the Baltic governments, if abused could retard the development of an autonomous enterprise sector and horizontal interenterprise links.

Agreements between the republics reflected a perceived need to forge closer economic ties so as to cope with the declining ability to maintain centralised supplies to enterprises and households. In addition, from the perspective of certain republics, increased interrepublican ties strengthened their political bargaining power with the centre. Thus, the simultaneous trends of weakening central control over both economic and political developments in the country, on the one hand, and intensified cooperation among republics and sub-republican entities, on the other, had important implications for the Baltics' success in weathering potential embargoes or other hostile actions.

Nevertheless, the extent of interrepublic cooperation should not be exaggerated. Obstacles to expanded interrepublic links reflect at once dissimilarities and similarities among the 15 union republics. Given widely disparate resource endowments (including that of human capital), unequal labour productivities and living standards and significant variations in political and economic cultures among the republics and regions of the Soviet Union, one sub-group of republics favours some form of revamped union, another dissociation from the union altogether and a middle-group of republics and regions is capable of moving in either direction depending on political circumstances. Russia will clearly dominate any conceivable economic agreement, but it may yet convince some of the new sovereign republics to join it in some new ex-Soviet economy community. The national aspirations must, however, not be underestimated.

b. Cooperation between the Baltic republics

Despite sharing political aspirations, the three Baltic republics had up until independence achieved a disappointingly low level of economic cooperation. Given the challenging economic road ahead, there should be scope for cooperating among them to smooth the adjustment process. Upon independence one of the first joint declarations by the three governments was not to erect trade barriers between the countries. This was an important statement which will need to be followed by close cooperation in practically all fields.

A Baltic Council has been formed which earlier oversaw twenty-one working groups on different aspects of potential cooperation among the Baltic republics (Baltic Council on Cooperating Committee, 1990). According to their own assessments, practical progress has been slow in the majority of working groups and virtually nonexistent in some. In particular, the working group on foreign economic ties noted that failure to conclude agreements has slowed progress in other areas such as developing a common trade nomenclature system and better information coordination.

More generally, there appears to have been little progress in laying the infrastructure for progress in the direction of a free trade area or customs union facilitating free goods' and services' trade and movement of labour and capital. In addition, despite the solid economic arguments in favour of a coordinated monetary and credit policy or even a common currency, such coordination has not existed.

Despite the formal commitments to expanded cooperation, the limited progress in this direction can be explained by several factors. First, as argued in Chapter 1, despite their common historical experience *vis-à-vis* the Soviet Union, the Baltic states differ in important ways.

Second, given their broadly similar industrial structure, producers in these states are natural competitors. However, this should not be taken as an argument for anything less than open trade between the Baltic states; in the post-war world economy there has developed a marked trend toward greater intra-industry trade. This is characterised by increased specialisation within broadly similar commodity groups, despite the existence of comparable factor endowments. However, such trade tends to flourish in societies which have reached a stage of development in which product variety becomes increasingly demand-led.

c. Future external economic relations

Top priority in the Baltic reform process will be to liberalise foreign trade. Control over economic borders and over foreign exchange is essential. A sovereign trade regime must be established enabling direct trade ties with foreign concerns and taxation and tariff policies attractive to foreign investors and conclusive to domestic industrial adjustment and expansion.

Exposure to foreign business standards in advertising, marketing, and quality control through foreign travel and interaction with foreign businessmen will be critical. In addition, the Baltic republics should be emphasising development of an accurate system of statistics and accounting.

In many ways, the Baltic challenge is similar to that facing developing countries with a history of excessive import substitution. A closer alignment of relative domestic prices with those of world prices for tradeables and the choice of an appropriate active exchange-rate regime are crucial for providing the informational environment in which firms can assess opportunity costs. The history of small socialist countries which have implemented foreign-trade reforms strongly suggests that guaranteeing the proper incentives for export stimulation, including direct trading rights and foreign-exchange retention are necessary but not sufficient conditions for expanded integration in the global economy and greater national competitiveness.

Equally crucial is allowance for a steady increase in import competition. This can reduce monopolisation, forcing producers to better monitor costs and quality, break bottlenecks and lower the input costs for export production and help transform the domestic price structure in a more efficient direction. In the longer term, freeing up the economy contributes to gains related to the transfer of marketing know-how and innovation.

In opening up the economy, the implicit commodity-specific quota arrangements that underlie all trading systems in Soviet-type economies should be eliminated and converted into a more transparent and uniform tariff system.

Although it is unrealistic to expect enterprises, which have functioned in totally sheltered markets, suddenly to face world market competition without protection, firms will never become competitive if high tariff barriers are maintained indefinitely.

Thus, a principal policy goal should be an orderly, staged reduction in the degree of protection. Furthermore, bold moves toward internal currency convertibility and nondiscriminatory access to foreign exchange (at a fixed or variable rate), and ultimately complete convertibility on current account, will help capture the gains from freer trade.

In principle, one would like to project what the structure of Baltic external relations will look like after independence. However, a concrete picture would require quite heroic assumptions concerning the degree to which the Baltic republics will remain dependent on Soviet trade, the extent to which they are able to raise product quality and locate niches in the world market and the likelihood of net capital inflows from abroad (including the Soviet Union) in the form of official and bank credits and direct investment. All of these factors have important time dimensions involving the speed of structural and systemic change which are difficult to anticipate.

Additional uncertainties include the shares of Soviet external debt and the share of Soviet gold and other assets which the Baltic states might choose to negotiate. Finally, the distribution of competing property claims among the

198   *The reform process*

Baltic states and the other republics will have to be negotiated and resolved. Given the uncertainties attending all of these elements, the best one can do is to identify certain realistic trends that can potentially alter the major sub-balances of the balance of payments.

The current tight links with the Soviet Union suggest both the danger of profound disruptions from sudden disengagement and the longer-term costs of maintaining the lop-sided industrial structure inherited from the Baltic republics' need to serve the Soviet market. The optimal degree and pace at which the Baltic states reduce their economic ties with the Soviet Union will depend largely on reform in the Soviet Union itself. Meaningful change in the Soviet Union will render many of the existing arrangements between the Baltic and Soviet economies redundant while opening up new trading possibilities.

The adoption of market-type reforms will necessitate greater alignment of relative domestic prices with world market prices. Moreover, once greater enterprise autonomy is achieved, including the imposition of harder-budget constraints, a different pattern of domestic investment and resulting evolution in industrial structure can be expected. Such an effort to realise gains from proper specialisation based on comparative advantage will significantly alter the quantities exported and imported both in Baltic–Soviet trade as well as Baltic–world trade.

A factor of overriding importance is the dependence of all three states on oil and natural gas imports from the Soviet Union. Whether or not such energy resources are imported from the Soviet Union in the future or instead from another source, the average prices for such imports will rise dramatically. This will place enormous pressure on the Baltic states to economise on energy use.

Once savings from reducing imports are exploited, the Baltic states will have to expand manufacturing exports significantly. This raises an additional salient feature of current Baltic trade — the low average quality of Baltic exportables in relation to contemporary world market standards. Since this problem reflects systemic factors which are difficult to change quickly, the Baltic states will be forced to consider sizeable reductions in average export prices to remain competitive. However, since much of world trade today is dependent on marketing, packaging and other aspects of quality even more than price, the Baltic states may initially find it difficult to market their manufactures. For example, Lithuania could significantly expand food exports were its packaging and advertising raised to world standards.

Alternatively, they may be forced to lower their prices to the point that anti-dumping petitions are filed. Such petitions lodged against socialist countries (even those in the midst of market-type reforms) are notoriously difficult to anticipate, arbitrary in the criteria used to calculate 'fair value' and thus represent a serious source of uncertainty and export impediment.

An onerous trade barrier facing the Baltic economies is the European Community's Common Agricultural Policy. Moreover, Baltic agriculture is highly dependent on imported inputs (fertilisers, fodder, machinery and fuel) which makes it vulnerable in case of disruption in the availability of resources or increased input prices.

Given such factors, the Baltic states may find it most expedient initially to specialise in groups of consumer and producer durables in which they have some production experience, targeting less competitive markets in Eastern Europe and the developing world.

However, owing to existing quality differentials between Baltic consumer and producer durables and world-class products, as well as transport cost and market familiarity factors, the natural market initially will remain the present Soviet Union. Some Baltic manufactured consumer goods, especially light industrial products, are outmoded in the world market but still have an edge in the Soviet market. At present, the Soviets remain, to some extent at least, dependent on Baltic manufacturing sectors, particularly in high technology. Soviet authorities have traditionally allocated a sizeable share of imported capital equipment to Baltic production lines owing to their generally more effective use there. Therefore, they are likely to view the Baltic republics as important sites for assembling complex manufactures for exports. They will also continue to require access to Baltic port facilities.

However, given the scarcity of hard currency in the Soviet Union, if settlement of trade balances is transferred from a rouble to a dollar world-market price basis, the Soviets will be less inclined to accept lower-quality Baltic products over competing Western varieties unless Baltic prices are adjusted for quality. Therefore, with the prospect of significant competition for the Baltic states in the Soviet as well as East European markets, the distinction between 'hard' Western and 'soft' Eastern markets in certain respects is likely to become progressively obsolete.

The Baltic region has a potential to generate a modest income from tourism and as an intermediary facilitating Soviet–Western economic cooperation. For example every year 120–140,000 tourists visit Estonia (80 per cent from the West) with — until now — most of the income and hard currency going to Moscow. In addition, the export of Baltic labour to Scandinavia and mainland Europe may generate some foreign exchange in the form of remittances. However, these revenue sources are unlikely to cover Baltic import needs, as there is no way around a broader expansion of Baltic manufactures, agricultural and service exports.

The likely deficit in the current account will require a net capital inflow. The Baltic region offers specific advantages to foreign investors including favourable geography, a relatively skilled (and cheap) labour force and the rudiments of a market culture. With independence at hand, the inflow of private capital should increase. An influx of greatly needed Western managerial, marketing and technical expertise would be greatly facilitated by membership of the main international economic organisations. As economic reform gathers momentum and develops into full-fledged reform programmes, official financial support in the form of balance of payment and trade is also likely to be forthcoming.

8 Enterprise reform and the institutional framework

A. Reforming the system

In a textbook model of a market economy, numerous actors facing a resource constraint, and taking the prices of inputs and outputs as given, make independent decisions in pursuit of their economic self-interest. It is the totality of these decisions which in turn determines the composition of aggregate economic activity.

When the actors are individuals, households or small firms, this model is not far from reality. Even in a highly sophisticated economy, individual or household producers play an important role, especially in agriculture and the services sector. In the Baltic economies, such activity could be found even at the height of the centrally planned system, but only in a 'grey zone' between the officially approved state-owned sector and the illegal black market. To move towards an enterprise sector appropriate for a full market economy, the Baltic republics confront the challenge of developing a policy framework to encourage the growth of small-scale business.

Many other economic activities, however, require the mobilisation and management of numerous workers and large amounts of capital. In Western market economies, this is primarily done by large, professionally managed, privately owned joint-stock companies.

In the Soviet system, such activites, at least outside the agricultural sphere, have been conducted by state enterprises. Often much larger than their Western counterparts, they were in turn grouped into huge so-called associations. These were responsible to a parent ministry, which would appoint the top management and issue instructions about general business decisions. Such structures of state ownership, and the monopolised environment of central planning in which firms operated, and which determined much of their behaviour, are described in Chapter 5.

As in Western corporations, the locus of day-to-day business decisions in state enterprises is hard to determine from the legally defined relationships alone. Especially in recent years, many managers have achieved considerable autonomy in controlling their companies. The top executives of large concerns have become an important political force, exerting pressure on the very authorities which should exercise 'ownership' rights over the firms.

The movement of the Baltic republics from this environment to one resembling Western market economies, involves three dimensions of enterprise reform:

(i)   changing the structure of ownership and control;
(ii) changing the external environment to which the enterprise responds; and

(iii) changing the internal operation of the enterprise.

Enterprise reform should involve a coordinated exercise, with mutually reinforcing changes made simultaneously in all three areas. This is best shown by the failure of earlier partial reform efforts, not only in the Soviet Union but throughout Central and Eastern Europe. Until 1988, the Soviet reform debate was focused on an abortive attempt to change enterprise behaviour through altering either the external environment or the incentive structures within enterprises, while keeping intact the system of state-owned property. For Estonia, the most 'experimental' of the Baltic republics, the results of such attempts are described in Chapter 4.

This search for a 'third way' might be seen as a revival of the vision of 'market socialism' first expounded some fifty years ago by Oskar Lange and Abba Lerner. However, while Lange–Lerner 'market socialism' exists as a theoretical model, there are no examples yet of its successful implementation in 'reforming' planned economies.

A limited willingness to alter property relations was first shown in 1988, when so called 'cooperative' (private) activity was liberalised. However, the environment in which the new firms operated was largely unreformed, supply of inputs remained dependent on access to state-controlled sources and managerial and worker attitudes changed slowly. Not unexpectedly, these firms soon faced many difficulties and had little immediate impact on the aggregate economy.

The political developments since that time have widened ideologically the choice of the feasible goals of reforms and the paths to their achievement. Nevertheless, the actual reform path will still be constrained by political realities, including the balance of interests within the republics and the continuing limits on manoeuvre resulting from Soviet policies. As a result, implementation in practice is unlikely to follow a theoretically appropriate ideal sequence.

In addition, not only the path but also the long-run targets of the economic transformation may differ from the textbook model of a market economy. The choice of reform programme is often discussed in terms of identifying an existing 'model' to emulate. Scandinavian social democracy, with its limited state ownership but extensive redistribution via the tax system, is often presented as a desirable goal. Others see the small Baltic economies playing a regional role akin to that of Hong Kong or Taiwan in Asia and advocate taking a private and very liberal direction. Still others set their sights on a corporatist economy, with a continued role for state ownership and public interventions, of which France or Italy still have strong legacies. One may also recall that, for example, the capitalist British economy operated for many decades with an extensive public sector (now partly dismantled). Market economies have operated with varying balances between private and public ownership, and the actual balance struck has been a legacy of political decisions based on both ideological choices and pragmatic responses to *ad hoc* problems.

However, while useful in some respects, the search for a 'model' can be counterproductive for two reasons. First, the actual balance between public and private ownership, or between *dirigisme* and *laisser-faire*, is the outcome of a long and specific historical process in which much more than conscious ideological choices were involved. Attempts to follow closely these 'models' in other times and places are likely to fail.

Furthermore, the differences between Western industrial economies are much smaller than the gulf between the Baltic economies and any one of these 'models'. The former are all reasonably well-functioning market economies with developed institutions and a long history of private owner-ship. Until the Baltic republics have made clear and decisive steps in the direction of a market economy, the differences between, say, the Swedish and French models are miniscule compared to the leap which the Baltic republics must make to reach any one of them.

Only a bold prophet would predict where the balance between public and private ownership will be in ten years' time in the Baltic republics or in the other Eastern European economies. However, experience of reform so far in the Communist economies suggests that a substantial shift in ownership is the necessary condition for the creation of an effective market. Whatever the theoretical possibilities of 'market socialism', a decisive change in ownership is needed really to transform the practices and culture of a planned economy and spur entrepreneurship and structural change. How much private owner-ship might be sufficient to leven the stodgy dough of the inherited system would depend on how far the state-owned enterprise system can itself be made to respond to the stimuli of the market.

B. Privatisation issues

All three Baltic republics aim at extensive privatisation. In none of them has the process yet gone far, except on paper. Necessary laws have either been adopted or are under active discussion. However, formidable problems must be overcome in implementation.

As the magnitude of the transformation is enormous, as there are few historical precedents, and as the processes are as much political as economic, it is not surprising that opinions on all aspects of privatisation vary among politicians and within the population. Not unexpectedly, this diversity of views has led to major delays in passing laws on property and ownership and in the implementation of privatisation.

At the heart of the problem is the legitimacy of the property rights which might be created. The most fundamental source of legitimacy of private ownership is that it works. Mature market economies typically combine dispersed ownership of part of the stock of large corporations, with a suffi-cient concentration of shares, and thus of wealth, in the hands of a few individuals or institutions to exercise effective control. In these economies, some of the largest shareholders are financial institutions (e.g. insurance companies, pension funds), which act on behalf of their many clients.

However, to create a property-owning system at a stroke is another matter. A strong private sector may emerge from a combination of privatisa-tion, liquidation of existing firms and new business development. In the

Baltic republics, as throughout Central and Eastern Europe, these processes have gone further on paper than in practice. The general difficulties of this transformation are further complicated by the particular political and economic linkages of the Baltic republics still tied to a Soviet Union in deep crisis.

a. Key choices in privatisation

The development of a privatisation programme requires difficult choices in several areas. First, which individuals or groups will have the right to acquire privatised assets? Should the initial participation be primarily restricted to the citizens or residents of each republic, as is common in many countries, or should Soviet or non-Soviet foreigners also be allowed to participate? In the latter case, there is the hope of substantial financial inflows, but a fear that foreigners or existing non-Baltic managers may acquire the lion's share of assets.

The attitude towards Western investment in the Baltic republics is ambivalent. In general, it is favoured in principle. The expectations about its positive impact on living standards are often far greater than is warranted, at least in the short term. The modest volumes of actual foreign investment, a feature of most Eastern and Central European economies, are often lamented. At the same time, there is unease about the acquisition of existing assets by foreigners. These attitudes have led to a notably more liberal stance towards new foreign investment than to foreign participation in the privatisation of existing assets.

Second, all three Baltic republics have passed laws providing for a mixed economy in which a number of different forms of property coexist. Thus, decisions must be made about which state enterprises will remain under public ownership and which will be divested. The Baltic governments must also develop methods for managing or holding the assets remaining in the state sector.

Third, will the privatisation process aim to create widespread share ownership of medium- and large-scale firms, or the concentration of shares in a few hands to improve the control of managers by owners? Or will the focus be on the growth of institutional investors, such as insurance companies, mutual funds and pension funds, which are at the same time large owners of other firms, while themselves being widely held? As the one does not preclude the other, the choice is one of emphasis.

Fourth, should the process of privatisation be decentralised or strictly controlled by the government authorities? Centralisation may seem illiberal and, when taken to an extreme, slow down the process. On the other hand, a more decentralised, spontaneous process is hard to control and open to manipulation by enterprise managers, to whom it gives a great deal of power.

Fifth, what role should enterprise managers and workers play? Should they receive shares at a discount or be treated as any other citizens?

Finally, there are many choices to be made on the sequencing of privatisation with other reform steps. For instance, should privatisation precede or follow price liberalisation and actions to enhance competition? On the one hand, it is nearly impossible to determine the 'true' value of enterprises in a distorted price environment very different from that which will prevail in the long term. Purchasers of firms which run into difficulty after price decontrol or enhanced competition will be resentful and could lobby against these moves. However, delay until after the development of a more comprehensive market environment could be self-defeating, as private ownership in itself is a means of promoting competitive market conditions.

There are also questions about the link between privatisation and stabilisation. Some argue that given the severe repressed inflation in the Soviet Union, and the dubious way in which many roubles were acquired, extensive privatisation through sale of assets must be avoided or at least delayed until establishment of stable local currencies. There is a fear that sale of assets will attract a flood of currency from the Soviet Union, leading to loss of control over real assets in exchange for a piece of paper of uncertain value. More generally, the success of privatisation would be facilitated by a functioning, stable fiscal and monetary system and financial markets.

Others, including the Bank of Estonia, have made proposals that privatisation be used as the prime means of monetary stabilisation. In one way or another, the Baltic governments would exchange real assets for monetary liabilities, reducing the monetary overhang without the need for currency reform. This raises questions about the precise link between the two steps, as stabilisation is best done rapidly, while privatisation will be a more lengthy process.

A related question concerns any funds generated by sale of public assets and the control of their use. Should these monies be withdrawn from circulation, placed in special funds controlled by legislatures or used to balance the state budget under weak fiscal structures?

b. Methods of privatisation

Among the most crucial choices to be made is how assets will be transferred. While each country will use several methods simultaneously, they will differ in the degrees of emphasis on sale versus free distribution. The former includes methods such as initial public offerings, case-by-case private placement with domestic or foreign individuals or groups, controlled auctions (with bids among selected investors) and various forms of open auctions.

Advocates of sale methods claim that these will put shares in the hands of active investors who will take a strong interest in the workings of the firm. They see extensive free distribution in small chunks as delaying, or even preventing, the concentration of shares into hands of effective owners.

Other benefits include the raising of government revenues at a time when fiscal systems are weak and avoiding the high administrative costs of dispersing ownership in very small units. For firms for which auction methods are feasible, and where valuation is only required to set a reserve price, privatisation programmes can be quickly prepared and implemented.

Free distribution encompasses three broad methods:

1. the 'sale' of shares for vouchers allocated at no cost or for a nominal fee;
2. the 'bundling' of relatively small fractions of shares from many companies into privately managed mutual funds, the shares of which are disbursed to the public; or
3. the agglomeration of controlling sums of shares into holding companies, the shares of which are similarly distributed to the public.

Free distribution to the public can be combined with allocation to financial intermediaries. Some equities could be given to banks as part of a recapitalisation process and others given to pension funds which are themselves privatised. Still others could be distributed to mutual funds which could be used to compensate previous owners.

Supporters of free distribution often argue that the main beneficiaries of sale arrangements will be black marketeers and the nomenklatura, with the latter combining their existing wealth and banking connections to buy up a large holding. Whether free allocation will prevent or simply delay this result is less clear. While a concern throughout Eastern Europe, this has an added Baltic dimension, with concern that sales might hand over important segments of industry to speculators from other parts of the Soviet Union just at the moment when greater national independence is being sought.

Proponents of free distribution also argue that even with dispersed ownership, the threat of takeover attack if assets are not employed very effectively will induce managers to act efficiently. Advocates of the mutual fund/holding company strategies further stress that, by avoiding the need for difficult and politically contentious asset valuation, the speed of privatisation can be accelerated. The opaque valuation procedures required for most cash or voucher sales of large firms can result in accusations that the national wealth has been sold at bargain prices. Sales would be very risky for purchasers, as true enterprise value is very uncertain in a rapidly changing environment.

Mutual funds and holding companies differ in that the former, being portfolio investors, will be few but hold shares in many companies. Holding companies would be several, each having controlling interest in a smaller subset of firms. The mutual fund approach is more likely to avoid the risk of heavy-handed intervention and reduced competition which can occur with holding companies.

Any free distribution scheme must specify the rule for allocating vouchers or shares. This can either take the form of uniform disbursements to all adult citizens or residents or some rule linked to years of employment and even sectors of employment as has been discussed in Estonia.

In the intermediate term, before new institutions have had time to evolve, the effectiveness of all privatisation schemes will be constrained by the inadequacy of capital markets, both the absence of established and well-understood equity markets (that is stock exchanges) or a developed structure of financial intermediaries.

c. Possible delays to privatisation

The process of privatisation will be impeded by various factors. Many are common to all countries undergoing this process, but others are more specific to the Baltic situation.

Among the former is the weak, undeveloped state of the financial markets which must play a central role in any implementation of privatisation. This will have effects on the speed, efficiency and equity of the procedure.

Another factor common to all reforming economies is a dearth of private capital relative to the book value of enterprises as discussed for Lithuania below. This holds even after subtracting any estimate of the 'monetary overhang' of excess roubles which has received much attention. The great imbalance in domestic versus foreign purchasing power is one reason for aversion to foreign participation in privatisation. Methods designed in response to this problem include leveraged buyouts and all free distribution methods.

Finally, the process can be slowed down on both equity and efficiency grounds. The former include the requirement of detailed valuation to avoid sale at excessively low prices. The latter include the attempt to raise revenues via sale rather than free distribution.

A difficult problem of great political importance is the right of former owners to reclaim or otherwise be compensated for their nationalised property. While less of an issue in Russia, where the confiscations occurred sixty or seventy years ago, it has been important throughout Central and Eastern Europe. It may well be even more acute in the Baltic republics, where nationalisations were overtly imposed by a foreign occupying power and where older citizens and their children well recall what they once owned. The process of restoring former owners can thus be seen as the economic counterpart of restoring political independence.

While the nationalisations have been declared illegal in all three countries, the extent and form of actual denationalisation and restitution is very much unresolved. This process is likely to be time consuming and the scope for conflicts is wide. Interim improvements or degradation to property will influence valuation. Persons who have lived in houses or apartments for years or decades may make counterclaims. If physical restitution is made impossible because of the fear of new injustices (for example when land has subsequently been built on or is being used productively), the amount of financial compensation must be decided. The privatisation commissions charged with deciding these issues will be faced with difficult choices.

The Baltic governments have developed some practical solutions to minimise the delays which can arise from denationalisation. These include a broad acceptance of the principle of financial compensation in difficult cases. Estonia has adopted a two-track approach, in which those firms or properties with no evident pre-1940 precursors can be identified and begin to be privatised while other claims await resolution. Businesses with potential claims by previous owners can also be leased out, pending the resolution of these claims.

Other stumbling blocks have been more specific to the Soviet sphere and often beyond the control of Baltic governments. Unlike in Yugoslavia and Czechoslovakia, where the right of constituent republics to undertake privatisation has been unambiguously declared, the Soviet government continued to demand control over privatisation of many assets located in the Baltic republics. With an unclear inter-governmental division of jurisdiction over the process, both levels claimed the right to transfer or sell the same industrial enterprises. This 'war of the laws' has pervaded all aspects of Baltic economic reform, showing how the lack of definition of political sovereignty can slow down the process of real change.

This has created problems particularly in privatising the so-called all-union enterprises, which are large and together make up an important segment of Baltic employment, capital and output. Even if the legal uncertainties concerning these firms were resolved, their extreme integration into the Soviet economy would remain as a problem. The possibility of restructuring will depend crucially on the nature of commercial relations with the Soviet economy, and proper asset valuation is impossible without some idea of the terms and conditions under which future trade with Soviet enterprises will take place.

As noted above, the combination of yet undefined citizenship laws for each republic, the absence of exchange controls on capital accounts with the Soviet Union and the other Baltic republics and the financial chaos of the rouble zone are further impediments not faced by the sovereign countries of Central and Eastern Europe.

C. Privatisation: implementation in practice

Each republic has gone through considerable policy debate and substantial legislation, in sequences which are rather similar, but have so far achieved only modest success in implementing privatisation. Much is still unresolved and remains to be done, both conceptually and practically. There are differences in the goals and methods of privatisation, with free distribution of shares receiving more support from the Lithuanian government than those of Estonia and Latvia.

a. Privatisation in Estonia

Enterprise reform in Estonia was formalised by adoption of the Enterprise Law in November 1989. This important step, one of the first results of the IME ('Self-Managed Estonia') programme, allowed a pluralism of ownership forms, including private property without limitations. The law contained some idiosyncrasies in response to the political environment of the time. Adopting a careful attitude towards Moscow, it trod the fine line of recognising 'property of the Soviet Union' without calling it 'all-union'.

It also envisioned a new form of firm termed 'popular enterprise'. This was seen as an intermediary step between all-union and republican subordination and was designed to make their desired transfer of control less threatening to Moscow and the current directors. It sought to end the virtual extra-territorial status of such enterprises by bringing them under Estonian control but without requiring Estonian management. A further, unstated motivation for this form was that, at least initially, most Russian work collectives were believed to be against privatisation. The law did not force the issue but did leave the door open for future transformation into joint-stock companies.

The ground for privatisation was further prepared by the adoption of a Law on Property in June 1990 which began the definition of property rights. A Law on Leasing was adopted in October 1990. A very important step was adoption by the Supreme Council, in December 1990, of a decree declaring illegal the major acts of nationalisation and collectivisation of the 1940s. While this in principle restored the property rights of former owners and their heirs, the actual return of property will not be automatic but will involve formal application and proceed according to special laws. This is expected to play an important role in housing privatisation, but it is estimated that only 10 per cent of fixed-capital productives will be subject to claims by former owners.

The government's philosophy of privatisation was spelt out in a Concept for the General Principles of Privatisation, presented to the Supreme Council in October 1990. This states the main goals of privatisation as increased freedom and entrepreneurship and the emergence of a middle class. It does not envisage major concessions for firm employees and sees the sale of shares as the main vehicle of transfer. Rules for privatisation will differ among industry, agriculture, transportation, housing and social services.

The government envisages free distribution as playing a secondary role, using vouchers in privatising a limited fraction of state property. This could take a form where vouchers are issued in rough proportion to active working years, possibly with some adjustment across professions. The government expects the process to take five to six years to implement, after which 65–70 per cent of all current state property will be in private hands. Given the emphasis on sale of assets, and the valuation which is required, this may be somewhat optimistic. Various other parties have presented alternative concepts, and the final structure of the privatisation programme is still in flux.

The government concept has identified and proposed solutions for several problems in the process. First, it views return of farmland to previous owners who do not plan to cultivate it as a problem and wishes to use only financial compensation in those cases. The amount of compensation which can be paid is uncertain with some politicians favouring a forwarding of these claims to the Soviet government, which bears the real responsibility for the nationalisations.

Similarly, the government may seek to require the new owner of any privatised property to continue using it in its present way. For example, barber shops could be instructed to continue in this activity for up to five years. While it is true that pre-liberalisation price signals may induce a very distorted economic structure, such restrictions go strongly against the aim of restructuring and perpetuate the government's role in the micro-decisions of enterprises. It might be better to accelerate price reform and the development of a free market for real estate which would give incentives for inefficient users of property to sell to those capable of putting it to better use.

The Estonian attitude towards rouble purchases is also ambivalent. The government wishes to reduce these, and as a result has put off large-scale privatisation. Conversely, the monetary-reform concept of the Bank of Estonia sees privatisation as a vehicle for establishing Estonia's own currency. Still others fear an inordinate delay in privatisation if establishment of a new, stable money is a pre-requisite.

The government envisages three stages of privatisation. The first includes divestiture of enterprises in trade, services and catering (under a December 1990 law on small privatisation), widespread privatisation of housing and farms and the experimental privatisation of a few large enterprises. This stage has commenced, including a limited privatisation of housing. It should be possible to replicate the Tallinn initiative to sell off apartments. If tenants of publicly owned flats are faced, as in Hungary, with the alternatives of low-priced purchase or to become sitting tenants with a rent increase to realistic levels, the privatisation of housing could be speeded up. In its initial conception, the government intends to sell flats only to people born in Estonia or to those having resided there for more than twenty-five years.

The second stage will include privatisation of most remaining small and medium-sized enterprises, following a previous settlement of most questions concerning return of and/or compensation for nationalised property, citizenship laws and residency requirements. The final stage will be the comprehensive privatisation of large enterprises.

The privatisation process will be managed by the State Property Department, which has the valuation of enterprises as its most controversial task. Valuation will be necessary for public offerings and for setting reserve prices for auctions. It is envisaged that a mixture of sale techniques will be used. There is also some potential role for management-designed schemes. These appear to have been introduced to appease Moscow and the directors of all-union enterprises, reducing their fear that privatisation would bring their loss of control.

b. Privatisation in Latvia

The Latvian government's ownership reform programme has the main stated goals of enhancing economic efficiency, achieving a wide distribution of shares and ensuring the bulk of control by permanent residents of Latvia. It is pragmatic and comprises several measures, but the focus is on identifying potential active owners who could effectively manage the property. The acquisition of assets by certain groups, for example an enterprise's employees, at well below fair valuation, is to be avoided.

A number of mechanisms are envisaged, including cash sales (either lump-sum or by instalment), sales leveraged through bank credit and the creation of a special 'state redemption fund' to provide financial support for the purchase of state property.

In response to concerns about disposal of funds, it is proposed to create a special fund for the receipts generated from privatisation under direct parliamentary control. Accumulation of such funds could be associated in some way with the future issue of a new Latvian currency. There have also been suggestions to use some part of the funds for small business development.

While free distribution is downplayed in the government scheme, the Latvian Popular Front (LPF) has alternatively proposed a voucher auction system. All citizens over 18 years of age would, for a nominal fee, receive voucher 'points' which would be registered in their documents and be non-transferable. These could be used to bid for shares in state-supervised auctions, with groups of citizens being allowed to amalgamate their points to buy blocks of shares. The approximate price of shares would be indicated by the total number of points being bid for them. Some important details of the system remain to be worked out, including the time at which acquired shares would become tradeable.

The government's pre-independence programme had three broad steps. The first is dividing ownership between Soviet, Latvian and municipal governments. The Soviet government would, for the moment, control sectors such as telecommunications, transportation, defence contracting and certain 'strategic' resources. The Latvian government will own most enterprises in light manufacturing, consumer services and tourism, as well as most of the agricultural facilities. Municipalities will formally own local minor public services. This stage has already commenced.

The second step would be quick privatisation of some properties and small enterprises (for example restaurants, shops and retail outlets). Enterprises which were expropriated without compensation after 1940 will be returned to their original owners, while other small businesses will be auctioned to Latvian citizens and foreigners.

The final stage would involve the start of large-scale privatisation. 'Ownership' and supervision of the enterprises will be taken from sectoral ministries. Once they have overseen the 'denationalisation' of each enterprise (in consultation with a new inter-ministerial commission), including the selection and installation of new management, many ministries will be abolished. From this point on, enterprise finances will formally be separated from the state budget.

While the intent of these reforms appears sensible, a number of important questions remain unanswered. Does separation from the state budget mean the conversion of all debt to equity, or that all subsidies will end? How will the inter-ministerial commissions be chosen and what power will they have? While the handling of each transaction by these commissions might have political merit because of its apparent fairness, it does not itself solve the valuation problem.

c. Privatisation in Lithuania

The Lithuanian Supreme Council passed an act in December 1990, describing forms of property and placing private property on an equal footing with other forms. A law on privatisation was passed in March 1991 and envisages a number of elements. Property confiscated in the 1940s will be restored to original owners or their heirs with the precise rules governing this process to be described in a separate law. The eventual goal is the privatisation of 60–70 per cent of state property. Other goals include widespread share ownership, initially maintaining most shares in the hands of Lithuanian citizens and residents and minimising the share going to former Communist Party officials and black marketeers.

While a range of methods is under consideration, the actual mixture has yet to be decided. Options being considered include sale by auction, private negotiated agreements, sale at a discount to employees and flotation of issues on the stock exchange or through financial institutions. The government also plans the transfer of about 20 per cent of state property to the public free of charge, making this method more important than in the present plans of the Estonian and Latvian governments.

The government estimates that only 5 per cent of depositors control one-half of all savings-bank deposits, and that total savings accounts of around seven billion roubles amount to only 15 per cent of the book value of enterprises to be privatised. A free allocation is seen as necessary for making the process both rapid and equitable.

It is envisaged that all Lithuanian citizens will receive vouchers depending upon their age. Those above thirty-five should receive 5,000 roubles' worth, while those under eighteen should get 1,000 roubles' worth. The total face value of about eight billion roubles amounts to one-fifth of the book value of the Lithuanian assets to be sold. Vouchers will be non-transferable and valid for a limited period of time. These can be used to buy shares in all assets and real estate, except farmland. Vouchers can also be supplemented with cash but only in quantities less than or equal to the face value of vouchers.

In the transitional period, it is also proposed to lease out some medium- and large-scale enterprises, with a view to subsequent sale, and to incorporate some enterprises into foreign joint ventures.

The government programme is seen as having two stages. In the first, privatisation will cover small enterprises in trade, services and catering, some housing and farms, some middle-sized enterprises and a few large firms on an experimental basis. Sale will be made for roubles, hard currency and vouchers under special rules. This will be completed with the creation of an independent Lithuanian financial system and currency (litas).

The second stage will see privatisation of remaining medium- and large-scale enterprises with any sales against litas or hard currency.

The process will be managed by specially created Privatisation Commissions, which operate both nationally and at the town and district levels. Privatisation in certain socially important sectors (medicine, education, housing and agriculture) will be covered by special rules.

D. New business development

The restructuring of the Baltic economies will come as much from the establishment of entirely new businesses and lines of activity as from the privatisation and restructuring of existing firms. Present enterprises often have outdated technologies and capital equipment and would be better liquidated. New firms could build on the released capital, labour and land, supplemented by foreign resources and technologies used in new and innovative ways. This would bring needed structural transformation to the Baltic economies as well as providing a flexible base for achieving greater economic autonomy. It will be important for the Baltic governments to create an environment in which new small- and medium-scale enterprises can flourish and grow.

Some formal steps have already been taken. While initially, only the transitional form of 'cooperatives' was allowed, subsequent legislation has permitted joint-stock companies, partnerships and individual proprietorship on a more straightforward basis. Many former cooperatives have responded by changing into such businesses.

Formal encouragement of the enterprise sector at the early stage will also require the elimination of unnecessary government-induced sources of uncertainty. Rules, regulations and licences should be scrapped, except where they can be justified as fulfilling a specific need or function in the market economy. Arbitrary powers of search and surveillance, such as those given to the KGB by the Union government, should be abolished. Business is hardly encouraged by an atmosphere in which it is virtually assumed to be misbehaving unless it can prove otherwise.

A difficult but needed step is changing the attitudes to profit and entrepreneurship which have been ingrained during fifty years of Communist rule. In a chaotic environment in which bureaucratic delays and input shortages hamper new business development, some new firms will reap very high profits. This will occur as much from high prices under general excess demand, and the exploitation of quirks in the irrational price structure, as from real entrepreneurial ability.

In this environment, private businesses are easily labelled as 'profiteers' or 'speculators' and could be blamed by populist politicians for shortages and other economic ills . This would be a great mistake, as development of new businesses could be the fastest route to building the flexibility required to increase economic autonomy. Also, many of these same people will form the very crucial commercial class once comprehensive stabilisation and liberalisation have made its normal development possible.

In principle, a distinction might be made between 'genuine' private business and those activities which are essentially parasitic on the state sector. The seemingly high profits of the former would be no more than the return which astute businessmen would earn operating in any economy experiencing great disequilibrium and have the function of moving the economy towards a better balance. By contrast, profits derived from diverting resources from their intended official use, or getting privileged access to scarce goods at official prices to resell them at higher market prices, are rents from the failures and irrationalities of the official system.

However, in practice it is hardly possible to separate the business sheep from the goats. Campaigns against so called 'speculators' are as likely to net the productive businessman as the black marketeer. The best way to curb black markets is to reduce the systemic malfunctions which create the potential rents for those with privileged access. This includes greater price flexibility and the encouragement of more entrants to provide added competition rather than imposing further restraints on the private sector. New firms pursuing new business opportunities can begin to alleviate the scarcities underlying these high profits.

In the transition period, establishment of markets is more likely to succeed if market activities are fully accepted, 'warts and all'. While some regulations may be introduced as the system subsequently takes root, an initial overly fastidious approach to private business will stifle the animal spirits of capitalism before they have played the required role in creating structural change. With stifling regulations businessmen are also likely to find it necessary to break the rules in order to pursue legitimate business objectives, further eroding an already low respect for the law.

Another crucial development will be the greater liberalisation of foreign trade. Foreign competition can raise the dynamism of the enterprise sector, accelerate restructuring and import a more rational price structure than the one currently prevailing. Most important, for small economies like those of the Baltic states, import competition is probably the only effective method of reining in monopoly power. The alternative to extensively breaking Baltic industrial firms into enough units to generate domestic competition will almost surely leave undersized and inefficient firms.

While foreign investment will have a useful role in the transformation process, especially in bringing new technology, the performance of the Baltic economies is likely to depend particularly on the emergence of a national enterprise sector. Foreign investment should not be overemphasised. With competition from many other countries, attracting large amounts of foreign investment through subsidies and tax breaks can be expensive and would not at the moment counterbalance the inherent riskiness of investing in the present Soviet environment. More important, foreign investors are likely to be attracted by, and be more effective in, a setting in which a national enterprise sector is thriving and actively supported.

E. Selecting and managing state-sector enterprises

The extensive privatisation of the large-scale sector will take some time, even after the fundamental political relations between the Baltic republics and the Soviet Union are clarified. Therefore, an important part of the medium-term policy agenda concerns the management of those large-scale state firms which await privatisation or those which will remain in the state sector. With the public focus on independence and privatisation, this issue has received less attention than it deserves.

At a general level, it is recognised that many public enterprises should be 'commercialised', or turned into state-owned joint-stock companies, with managers supervised by an independent board of directors. This can be seen as an attempt to induce state enterprises to operate somewhat more like commercial firms, responding to market constraints and opportunities and bearing greater responsibility for their profitability.

The success of commercialisation is also linked to price liberalisation. In a distorted price structure, a 'hardening' of firm-budget constraints by ending cheap credits or subsidies could lead potentially profitable firms to be closed down. At the same time, actually wasteful enterprises could make large profits. A corollary to placing commercial demands on management is freeing those which are not 'natural monopolies' from price controls and other political interference on non-commercial grounds.

An important benefit of commercialisation is that it clarifies the ownership of the firm. This is currently ambiguous and has led to managers acting like owners and making major decisions on the disposition of state assets. Answerability of managers to a board of directors, however imperfect, may at least prevent some gross abuses. These could include excessive salary payments, poor leasing agreements for state property and the signing of joint-venture agreements which enrich the present management and employees at the expense of the firm's long-term interests.

However, while successful instances of commercialisation can be drawn from Western experience, state enterprise reform by itself is unlikely to produce the required efficiency gains in the Baltic economies. The successful operation of state-owned firms in a predominantly private economy arises from a very different environment and incentive structure than that facing a public firm in a largely state-owned economy. This is well demonstrated by the drawn out, unsuccessful attempts at enterprise reform in Eastern Europe and many developing countries. Even when governments have promised to impose a 'hard-budget constraint', they have only too often retracted and provided subsidies or cheap credit instead of closing down firms when they make losses.

While a good deal of autonomy can be fostered in day-to-day state enterprise management, this is less possible in decisions over the size and use of capital-investment funds. The 'investment hunger', large numbers of unfinished capital projects and poor ex-post returns from investments have been persistent characteristics of state-owned firms. This in turn has spillover effects in the macroeconomy with high credit demand fuelling inflation. As a result of planning failure, general scarcity is combined with excess capacity.

Thus, the Baltic governments face a short-term dilemma. It is surely not desirable to resurrect the rigid system of investment planning and physical targets which prevailed under central planning. At the same time, when state-sector firms are still monopolistic and strict market discipline does not operate, excessive autonomy can also lead to poor performance and the stripping of state assets. In the transitional period, state-owned firms will have to be faced with a balance of autonomy (for example in pricing and production decisions) countered by some restrictions (for example on the wage bill and credit and foreign exchange allocations).

It should also be understood that even if privatisation is greatly extended, the governments will still need to play a key role in the provision of reliable infrastructure and public utilities. For the success of the business sector, the most important direct interventions by the public sector relate to the provision of power, transport infrastructure, water, and telecommunication and postal services.

F. The institutional and policy environment

As the economies move on to a market basis and their centres of gravity shift towards the private sector, it will become increasingly important to create an institutional environment and policy regime which enable the enterprise sector to play a creative role in the economy and to use resources efficiently.

The first requirement for a thriving enterprise sector is a reasonable degree of certainty that present and future governments will be supportive of the sector. This is not primarily a matter of legal guarantees, which can always be withdrawn, as the development of a solid public understanding and support for the role of business. This will become more possible as the new enterprise sector is seen to play a productive role. But it may also require an exercise in education, particularly within the bureaucracy, about the role of the enterprise sector in a market economy.

The need for bureaucratic understanding is important, as a requirement for reform is a conscious and systematic change in the bureaucracy's own activities, rescinding unnecessary restrictions and regulations.

The government and legislatures must also take positive steps to develop a formal set of 'rules of the game' to provide an appropriate context for commercial activity. Thus, an important part of the institutional environment is a modern system of commercial law. In all three countries, a sustained effort is under way to develop company, property and other laws. Attention is also being focused on incentives to encourage foreign investment, including legal definition of the rights of investors in joint ventures and wholly owned projects. The creation of the minimum legal structure is an important and necessary first step.

In the transitional period, particularly before the achievement of economic sovereignty allows the implementation of comprehensive reform, the Baltic governments may encourage partial reforms which lie within their power. In particular, the encouragement of free and parallel markets in foreign exchange, commodities and property may provide flexibility in the economy and begin to provoke structural change, even before the implementation of full liberalisation.

For many of the crucial institutional requirements, the government itself may need to do little in the way of positive intervention. Credit and equity transactions can take place between actors in the enterprise sector, for example, without the need for any government intervention. The government should, however, give clear signals that such developments are acceptable. The introduction of positive real interest rates by the monetary authorities will also contribute to the development of capital markets.

Important financial institutions are likely to remain in the public sector. They should be commercialised and private business should enjoy access to their facilities, along with public enterprises, on a non-discriminatory basis. However, there may be a case for public support of credit facilities for some classes of borrowers (for example small businesses, farmers) and for some purposes (for example export credits).

The development of capital markets is important for the longer-term development of the enterprise sector — including access to credit and the development of a market in equities to increase the liquidity of asset holdings.

Perhaps the most crucial factor for any given enterprise is that the process of liberalisation is proceeding at a fast pace across the board. For example, a firm will be more able to expand if there is an active property market through which office and factory space can be acquired, and there is a lively collection of other firms offering needed services. The development of a dense, mutually supportive pattern of business activity will be especially important for the success of small and medium-scale firms.

A crucial aspect of the environment affecting enterprise performance is macroeconomic policy. The development of a set of stable macroeconomic policies, as set out in Chapter 6, would provide important support to the enterprise sector. This would ideally be combined with development of orderly, competitive markets so that inputs can be acquired and outputs sold through open markets rather than through inefficient and uncertain barter transactions. This implies decontrolling prices and moving state-owned enterprises on to a market footing so that access to their outputs and facilities and the possibility of selling to them can be freely available to all enterprises.

The decontrol of prices and full ability of firms to choose products, customers and input sources will level the playing field for the growth of all enterprises and eliminate the privileges and loopholes whose exploitation gives 'business' a bad name.

For the Baltic republics, the ability to undertake real enterprise reform is crucially tied to developments in the Soviet economy. The extreme integration of these economies with the Soviet Union was described in Chapter 7. Any efforts at enterprise reform will come to nought if firms must continue to operate in the deepening crises and economic irrationality currently characteristic of the Soviet system. It is increasingly difficult for firms to operate in the hiatus created by the breakdown of the command system and the failure to replace it with a real market.

Privatisation, commercialisation or small-business development will not occur or have their intended effect with exploding money supply, heightened supply constraints and a movement from central planning — not to a market economy — but to barter trade. Despite the anachronistic attempts of Soviet authorities to reverse private-sector developments and restore the role of the state, the disintegration will continue as output declines reverberate throughout the system. Therefore, as much as is possible, the Baltic republics should support the Soviet reform process, while at the same time taking steps to achieve real economic independence.

Another important area of activity is the improvement of skills and changing the business culture of industrial managers. Having operated in an environment of chronic shortages in which it was easy to sell products but difficult to acquire inputs, the current breed of managers is experienced in troubleshooting, bookkeeping and production management but has little knowledge of product pricing, marketing and finance.

Improvements can come through training, encouragement of professional activities (such as associations of managers) and staff development systems which emphasize commercial performance rather than political affiliation in hiring and promotion decisions. The accelerated development of domestic management consultancy would also aid this process.

However, the greatest strides in managerial practice would result from two less direct and glamorous steps. Successful stabilisation of the Baltic economies would remove the excess demand which has resulted in the atrophy of commercial skills, restoring a need for marketing and design while ending the pressure to scavenge for inputs. Once this is achieved, the best way for learning is through actual experience in producing under market conditions. After some initial experience in this new business world, more formal courses and training would benefit those that wish and are able to continue to learn.

IV Sectoral issues

9 The labour market

A. The labour-market situation

a. The Soviet labour market

This chapter describes the Baltic labour markets and discusses some aspects of possible developments and policies in this area during the initial transition period of the Baltic economies.

Until the present, participation in the labour market has been more or less compulsory for the working-age population. The Soviet constitution provided that every able-bodied Soviet citizen had a right and obligation to work. The absence of other major sources of income, especially from property, has also resulted in high participation rates. Nevertheless, there has been considerable freedom of choice on the supply side. Individuals have been able to choose their profession and place of work and change jobs on their own initiative. Though many factors particular to the Soviet society have limited real choice, incentives such as wages, other benefits and working conditions have played an important role. The geographical movement of the labour force has also been influenced by relative living standards (in particular the availability of housing, consumer goods and services) among regions and the administrative regulation of residence permits (*propiska*).

The level and composition of labour demand have been centrally regulated. The right to employ people has been restricted to state enterprises and organisations and to collective farms (*kolkhozy*). Employers have not been subject to strict financial discipline in their labour requirements. The crucial determinants of the employment level have been certain imperative physical plan targets (in particular production targets) and various restrictions (particularly since the 1965 Kosygin reform on wage budgets which have been very loosely linked to enterprises' overall results). The Soviet command model, with its emphasis on extensive growth of certain priority sectors of the economy (heavy industry, the defence industry), combined with inefficient resource usage at the micro-level, has guaranteed increasing employment. Since the mid-1960s the number of jobs has exceeded available labour resources. 'Shortage' of manpower has been particularly pronounced in the Baltic republics, European Russia, Siberia and the Far East.

Wages have been set and closely monitored by the centre. At the micro-level, however, there has been a certain discretion in modifying relative wages through the use of premiums and setting of piece-rate norms. It must be remembered that in the Soviet economy money and access to goods have not been directly related. Workers' remuneration has partly been in the form of differentiated 'access to goods and services' offered by the employer. For instance, big enterprises have had their own social services, recreation facilities and special shops.

a. Ethnic composition of the labour forces in the Baltic republics

A special characteristic of the Estonian and Latvian labour forces is that a large part consists of non-Balts, whereas the Lithuanian population is ethnically quite homogeneous. In the past Lithuania had a much higher natural population growth than Estonia and Latvia (on average 1 per cent per year in Lithuania compared to about 0.2 per cent per year in the other Baltic republics between 1959–89), but in recent years the Lithuanian pattern has moved closer to that of the others. In addition, immigration has been much lower in relation to the existing population.

The decline of the share of ethnic Estonians and Latvians is due to deportation, emigration, low reproduction in the population and immigration, mostly of labour, from the rest of the Soviet Union. In the beginning of the 1970s, net immigration to Estonia was about 8–9,000 per year. In the latter part of the 1970s and the early 1980s, the numbers declined to about 5–6,000 per year. Immigration to Latvia from other Soviet republics was particularly high during the 1960s and 1970s. In the 1980s, net immigration was about 9,300 per year.

The attitude towards immigration among Estonians and Latvians is negative. Of course, a drop in the share of the native nationality from over 90 (in Estonia) and 75 (in Latvia) to 60 or close to 50 per cent in fifty years is dramatic. The allegation that immigrants have received preferential treatment in the distribution of housing is often mentioned in discussions. While native Estonians and Latvians may wait for over twenty years to get a separate flat, immigrants have been granted flats within three to five years after their arrival. The reason for this is that native inhabitants have somewhere to live (with parents, in communal flats) and usually their living space is above the minimum living space per person which means they are not considered preferential cases. Immigrants commonly live in enterprise dormitories during their first years. Also, enterprises build their own housing and contribute to municipal housing construction, giving them the right to a certain percentage of flats. A particular problem mentioned by several officials in Latvia is that many persons choose to settle there after reaching retirement age.

In 1988–9 measures against the import of labour were taken in both Estonia and Latvia, and immigration declined sharply. In 1988 and 1989 net immigration to Estonia fell to 1,800 and 1,200, respectively. In 1990, a law on immigration in Estonia and a decree in Latvia led to emigration exceeding immigration in that year, in Estonia by 3,200.

Ethnic Estonians still prevail in rural areas. According to the population census in 1989, they constituted 87 per cent of the rural population. The share of ethnic Latvians in the Latvian countryside is 72 per cent. In many urban centres, however, Estonians are in a minority. In Riga, the capital of Latvia, the share of Latvians dropped to 36.5 per cent in 1989. During the Soviet period, the eastern part of Latvia was increasingly populated by Russians. The cities Rezekne and Daugavpils have only 35 and 13 per cent Latvians, respectively.

In Estonia and Latvia, the 'Russian-speaking' population (as the non-ethnic Balts are usually called) dominate the industrial labour force. Statistical data from 1987 give their share in the industrial work force in Estonia as 57 per cent and in Latvia as high as 62 per cent. These high percentages are largely owing to the all-union enterprises, where the Russian-speaking share of the labour force is often around 80 per cent.

Also Russian-speaking labour predominates in such key sectors as transportation. In 1987, its share in Estonia was 70 per cent in railway transportation and 85 per cent in sea transportation, while the share of Latvians in transportation is 20–25 per cent. In Riga, only 14 per cent of the police are Latvians.

Thus, there is a particular type of segmentation in the Estonian and Latvian labour markets. A large share of the Russian-speaking population works predominantly in blue-collar jobs in industry and controls certain vital sectors of the economy. Estonians and Latvians predominate in agriculture, services and small-scale industry. The striving towards economic independence and a market economy affect these segments differently. In particular, it appears that there are mainly Estonians and Latvians in activities with good prospects in a transformed economy, while the Russian-speaking population is largely occupied in production which the Balts would like to reduce or reshape radically. The future of the Russian-speaking management and workers in all-union enterprises will also depend on their own response to the changing economic environment. Some managers of all-union enterprises show interest in developing their firms as more autonomous units in a liberalised economy. Also there are instances of Russian-speaking workers taking the initiative to form industrial cooperatives with the intention of becoming private businesses. In both Estonia and Latvia there is a risk of increased social and national tensions if unemployment rises unevenly in different segments of the labour market.

Even in Lithuania, there are areas where non-Lithuanians dominate. Between the wars, southeast Lithuania was under Polish rule and in the Vilnius region 40 per cent of the population is still Polish. Vilnius itself has a Lithuanian majority of 51 per cent, but 20 per cent of the capital's population is Russian and 19 per cent Polish. In the early 1980s, net immigration to Lithuania rose sharply from about 6–7,000 a year to 12–13,000 a year. This reflects large investment projects launched by Moscow in the republic. The building of the nuclear power station at Ignalina is one example. The population in the nearby town Snieckus grew from 9,800 in 1981 to 22,000 in 1985, only 9 per cent of whom are Lithuanian. The port town of Klaipeda has a large Russian minority; according to the latest census 28 per cent of the population is Russian and 63 per cent Lithuanian. However, the dominance of the titular nationality in the population means that the ethnic segmentation in the labour force is not as pronounced as in Estonia and Latvia. In 1987, the share of Lithuanians in the industrial work force was 71 per cent. As elsewhere, all-union enterprises have a relatively large share of Russian-speaking labour.

In Vilnius, several officials mentioned the large number of commuters entering the city each day (about 36,000, which corresponds to about 30 per cent of the city's labour force), of which the greater part come

Table 9.1 Labour force participation, 1989 (per cent)

TP = Total population
M = Men
W = Women

Age group	Estonia			Latvia			Lithuania		
	TP	M	W	TP	M	W	TP	M	W
16–19	36	39	32	37	39	35	29	33	25
20–4	79	80	77	81	82	81	76	79	73
25–9	93	96	90	94	97	91	92	97	88
30–49	96	97	95	96	97	94	95	97	93
50–54	90	92	88	90	93	88	88	92	84
55–9	67	83	54	66	86	51	62	86	43
60–4	43	52	38	41	52	34	33	44	25
65–9	29	36	25	26	35	22	19	27	14
70+	9	13	8	8	13	6	5	11	4
16–54/59[1]	86	87	85	87	88	85	84	86	81
16–64	80	85	77	83	85	77	78	83	72

Notes: [1] Working-age age groups according to Soviet standards; normal pension age is 60 for men and 55 for women.

Source: Calculated from population census, 1989.

from outside Vilnius but also from Belorussia. Since working in a city for five years gives the right to a flat, the local government has recently tried to restrict enterprises' ability to invite labour. The quotas have been limited to about 1,000 in total per year. Moreover, enterprises have had to pay 21,000 roubles to invite a person permanently.

b. Labour force participation

In 1989, 850,000 persons were employed in the Estonian economy. The corresponding figures for Latvia and Lithuania were 1,459,000 and 1,901,000. The working-age groups according to Soviet standards are 16–54 years for women and 16–59 years for men. In addition, in all three countries many old-age pensioners continue to work after reaching retirement age.

Labour force participation is high (see Table 9.1). According to the 1989 population census, 80 per cent of the Estonian population aged 16–64 years is employed. In Latvia the figure is 83 per cent and in Lithuania 78 per cent. The employment figures for the working-age age groups was 86 per cent in Estonia, 87 per cent in Latvia and 84 per cent in Lithuania. The working-age groups account for 89 per cent of the total labour force in Estonia, 87 per cent in Latvia and 92 per cent in Lithuania, the remaining 11, 13 and 8 per cent being persons beyond retirement age.

The low labour force participation among the youngest age groups, 16–19 years-of-age, reflects the fact that most young persons continue their education after the ninth year of general school. They can choose between continuing into the 10th and 11th year of general school to get full secondary education, vocational training in a vocational training establishment or beginning a specialised secondary education.

Among those aged 20–24 years, there are also many still in education. In this age group, 79 per cent participate in the labour force in Estonia, 81 per cent in Latvia and 76 per cent in Lithuania. Persons entering higher education and higher specialised education do not enter the labour market until they are 23–24.

In the age groups 25-54 labour force participation is over 90 per cent. At the age of 55, many women leave the labour market and retire on pension which results in the drop in labour force participation to 67 per cent in the 55–59 age group in Estonia, to 66 per cent in Latvia and 62 in Lithuania. At 60 years of age men have the right to retire, and labour force participation declines further. In the 65-69 age group, 29, 26 and 19 per cent participate, while the numbers for 70 and over are 9, 8 and 5 per cent, respectively.

Women in the working ages participate in the labour market almost to the same extent as men. The labour force participation of working-age women in Estonia is 85 per cent, while that of working-age men is 87 per cent. In Latvia and Lithuania these figures are 85 and 81 for women, respectively, and 88 and 86 for men. Labour force participation is slightly lower in Lithuania than in the other two Baltic republics.

For the age group 55–59, the female participation rate drops from almost 90 to 54 per cent in Estonia and to 51 per cent in Latvia because of the lower female pension age. Lithuanian women work to a lesser extent after retirement than Estonian and Latvian women. The labour force participation for those aged 50–54 drops to 43 per cent. Among those aged 55–60 only one-fourth stay in the labour market. The lower participation rate among women aged 20–29 is largely an effect of these being the prime child-bearing ages.

The major reason that old-age pensioners continue to work after reaching the retirement age is that pensions are very low. In Estonia the average monthly state old-age pension was 105.2 roubles in 1989 which corresponds to 38.9 per cent of the average monthly wage (270 roubles) in the state sector the same year. For former collective farmers the average monthly old-age pension was 90.8 roubles a month in 1989. About half of the state old-age pensioners and three-fourths of the collective farm pensioners had pensions under 100 roubles a month in 1987.

In Latvia, the average monthly state pension was 94 roubles in 1990 which corresponds to 35 per cent of the average monthly wage in the state sector (268 roubles, first six months 1990). For collective farm pensioners the average pension was 80 roubles in 1990. About 60 per cent of state pensioners and 90 per cent of the collective farm pensioners had pensions under 100 roubles a month in 1987.

In Lithuania, the average monthly state pension was 95.6 roubles in 1989 which corresponds to 39 per cent of the average monthly wage (244.1 roubles) in the state sector the same year. For former collective farmers the average monthly old-age pension was 78.6 roubles a month in 1989, 31 per cent of the average monthly pay in collective farms (257 roubles).

c. Hours worked

There are no regular statistics on hours worked. However, it is known that part-time work is rare in the Soviet Union, with only about 1 per cent of the labour force reported as working part time in 1987. The major reason is that jobs are almost exclusively offered on a full-time basis. However, given the poor consumer goods' distribution system, in practice much time has to be spent shopping, which means that in many cases fewer than the official 41 hours a week are worked.

Assuming this to be the case in the Baltic republics as well, the majority of those participating in the labour market work full time. This makes the participation rates of women very high in comparison to other developed countries. For instance, in Sweden where female labour force participation is around 80 per cent, almost 50 per cent of the employed women work part time (fewer than 35 hours per week).

On the other hand, many people hold several jobs. In 1988, 43,000 persons or 6 per cent of the state labour force held several jobs in Estonia, 4.7 per cent in Latvia and 4.2 per cent in Lithuania. These figures have increased since work in the private sector has been permitted.

B. Structure of employment

In the Baltic republics, as elsewhere in the Soviet Union, until 1986 only employment in the state sector and collective-farm sector was considered productive employment. In 1986, a law on 'individual work' permitted individuals to be self-employed. Cooperatives were allowed on an experimental basis in Estonia the same year. In 1988, an all-union law on cooperatives was adopted which allowed a group of people to form cooperatives and to employ people. The liberalisation of foreign trade beginning with the reform in January 1987 has resulted in new forms of joint ventures with the West.

The major share of employment is still in the state sector. According to the official data from the population census in 1989 (see Table 9.2), in all three republics the state sector employed close to 90 per cent, with the kolkhoz sector employing about 10 per cent (12 per cent in Lithuania), and the 'private sector' only about one per cent.

These figures significantly underestimate the number of people employed outside the state and kolkhoz economy. They do not reflect the rapid development of cooperatives and new firms, discussed below.

Neither do the figures include persons primarily employed in private subsidiary agriculture which number officially about 5,000 in Estonia, 12,000 in Latvia and 24,000 in Lithuania. However, many more people are in fact engaged in private subsidiary agriculture. Of persons revealing two major sources of income, 41,000 in Estonia, 11,000 in Latvia and 202,000

Table 9.2 Employment structure according to census data, 1989 (number of persons; per cent of total in brackets)

	Total	State	Kolkhoz	Cooperative	Self-employed	Private employment
Estonia	850,471	756,929	84,657	7,099	1,569	217
	(100)	(89.0	(10.0	(0.8)	(0.2)	—
Latvia	1,458,554	1,293,580	149,968	11,244	3,409	353
	(100)	(88.7)	(10.3)	(0.8)	(0.2)	—
Lithuania	1,901,232	1,647,598	229,023	15,046	8,474	1,091
	(100)	(86.7)	(12.0)	(0.8)	(0.4)	(0.1)

Source: Population census, 1989.

in Lithuania cite private subsidiary agriculture as their second source of income. In Estonia, of people with two sources of income, 28,000 say private subsidiary agriculture is their major source of income. The same claim is made by 75,000 in Latvia and 167,000 in Lithuania. In the first group the majority is working in the state or kolkhoz sector. The majority of the second group, however, is composed of people who have pensions and benefits as a second source of income. The fact that they regard the private plots as their major source of income indicates the insufficient level of pensions and benefits.

Table 9.3 provides more information on total employment in the state sector. More detailed information on sectoral employment is provided elsewhere, particularly in Chapter 11 on industry and Chapter 12 on agriculture.

During 1988 and 1989, state-sector employment declined by about 3 per cent in Estonia. In Latvia, the decline was 2 per cent in 1988, 3.5 per cent in 1989 and in 1990 it is assumed to be 6.4 per cent. In Lithuania, state employment decreased by 3 per cent in 1989.

There are several reasons for this decline. In 1988, a new all-union enterprise law gave enterprises some incentives to economise on labour. Another reason may be that it is increasingly difficult to import labour from outside the republics.

The major reason, however, is the rapid growth of the number of people engaged in the non-state economy. Since 1988, when activity outside of the state and kolkhoz economy could start to expand, the number of people employed in cooperatives, joint-stock companies and other forms of independent firms has risen rapidly.

Official statistics on employment in cooperatives suggest that by mid-1990, 47,000 people worked in Estonian cooperatives, 159,000 in Latvian and 78,000 in Lithuanian cooperatives. This would suggest that in Latvia, where the development apparently has been the most rapid, about 10 per cent of the labour force has been employed in the cooperative sector.

The cooperatives are further discussed in Chapter 11 (Table 11.4 gives a statistical overview). It should be noted in this context, however, that many

Table 9.3 Employment in the state sector, 1985–90

	1985	1986	1987	1988	1989	1990
Estonia						
Total employed (thousands)	718	725	716	695	675	626
Annual change (per cent)		1.0	− 1.2	− 2.9	− 2.9	− 7.3
Latvia						
Total employed (thousands)	1,231	1,237	1,239	1,213	1,171	1,096
Annual change (per cent)		0.5	0.2	− 2.1	− 3.5	− 6.4
Lithuania						
Total employed (thousands)	1,563	1,580	1,600	1,591	1,545	na
Annual change (per cent)		1.1	1.2	− 0.6	− 2.9	

Sources: Statistical yearbooks and officially provided data.

cooperatives have been formed in direct connection to state enterprises, and workers might now be counted in the cooperative sector although their tasks remain essentially the same. It should also be noted that in Lithuania the cooperative as a special form of enterprise has ceased to exist.

Apart from being employed in cooperatives, people can be self-employed. In Estonia, these were 11,200 in 1988, primarily engaged in handicrafts. In Latvia the numbers in self-employment were 700 in 1985 and 3,900 in 1989, while 11,300 individuals were self-employed in Lithuania in 1989.

In the beginning of April 1990 there were 1,400 private farms in Estonia and 5,400 in Latvia. The number of private farms in Lithuania is about 4,000 and another 18,000 persons have applied to get land.

C. Wages and non-wage benefits

a. Wages

The average monthly wage in the state sector in 1990 was around 300 roubles in Estonia, 268 roubles in Latvia and 271 roubles in Lithuania. Wages have risen significantly since then. Expecting price rises in January 1991, many Lithuanian enterprises increased wages by 50–100 per cent. After years of stable money wages, significant increases have occurred since 1988 (Table 9.4). This pattern can be observed for the Soviet Union as well and is linked to the transition process started in 1987. It might be noted that all figures relate to nominal wages before taxes. Previously, Soviet wage-earners paid a flat income tax of about 13 per cent. In the Baltic republics, progressive income taxes have been introduced, and in addition inflation has diminished the real value of a given nominal wage.

Wage differentials among sectors are in fact significant. As in the Soviet Union, average earnings are highest in construction, transport and industry, and lowest in education, health and most services. In the latter women-dominated sectors, average pay has until the recent past often been well

Table 9.4 Average monthly wage in the state sector, 1985–90 (roubles)

	1985	1986	1987	1988	1989	1990
Estonia	215.1	221.1	229.0	249.2	270.2	340.7
annual change (per cent)		2.8	3.7	8.8	8.4	26.1
Latvia	195.9	201.4	208.9	227.0	249.9	268.0[1]
annual change (per cent)		2.8	3.7	8.7	10.1	na
Lithuania	190.0	194.7	204.1	222.6	244.1	271.3[2]
annual change (per cent)		2.5	4.8	9.1	9.7	na

Notes: [1] First six months. [2] First nine months.

Sources: Statistical yearbooks and officially provided data.

below 200 roubles a month. Though the Soviet system has paid scientists relatively well, wages have been low in service and communication sectors important for economic modernisation. Also within industries, there has been little economic incentive to do creative work, with heavy blue-collar work often being paid more than engineering and other professional skills.

This general picture is likely to change with the emergence of a functioning labour market. Changing government priorities, increasing enterprise autonomy and the emerging private sector are contributing factors. Already now, earnings are considerably higher in the private sector. A visit to a joint venture in Riga revealed that the lowest salary was about 350 roubles per month and the highest 1,500 roubles per month. A particular problem for governments is to retain competent staff, who often could earn far more in the private sector.

The Estonian government seems to have refrained from regulating wages for employees outside budget-financed organisations. The government only sets the minimum wage, which is 135 roubles a month since 1 January 1991. This wage is based on calculations of a social minimum, 125 roubles, and 'physical' minimum of 100 roubles, based on calculations of a minimum consumption basket.

The Lithuanian government is preparing a reform of basic salaries in budget-financed institutions. Wages are to be raised by 50–100 per cent. The cost of this rise will be 600 million roubles of which 413 should be paid by the state budget and the rest by the employers. The new wage scales were to be introduced by 1 March 1991. A visit to a dairy near Klaipeda revealed they would double their wage fund as soon as their prices were raised.

b. Non-wage benefits

Monetary incomes are not a clear indicator of people's real incomes. In addition to wages, employees have access to an important range of non-wage benefits. Depending on where they work, they may have differentiated access to otherwise difficult-to-get goods, services and housing. This is not the nomenklatura system of preferential benefits for the old party and power structure but a regular feature of the Soviet economic system.

Enterprises, particularly large ones, may have their own distribution systems for food stuffs and consumer durables, their own child-care facilities, recreation facilities, vacation homes and even hospitals. Often still more important is the fact that many enterprises provide their employees with apartments. In the Baltic republics, this has often particularly been the case with the immigrant labour force.

The importance of non-wage benefits is naturally very difficult to measure. One estimate indicates that they may correspond to about 30 per cent of incomes. Their importance also means that they constitute a significant constraint on labour mobility and consequently on the emergence of a functioning labour market.

A particular problem, therefore, in the transition process is that enterprise restructuring, which necessarily entails labour displacement and unemployment, will be hampered by the lack of functioning markets for the non-wage benefits, particularly the lack of a housing market. Further, the fear of unemployment will be exacerbated by the risk of losing access to such benefits. Neither will it be possible to compensate for those benefits.

D. The labour market in transition

a. Unemployment risks

In the short term the major threat to employment does not come from economic reforms (as privatisation or fundamental restructuring of the economy) but from the breakdown in the material supply system. State enterprises with state orders have some guaranteed supplies, but the shortage of inputs has always been a problem for the new private sector. Shortage of agricultural machinery also hampers private farming.

A second threat comes from the regulation of prices. Prices for raw materials have risen much more than prices for final products. For example, after the all-union rise of wholesale prices from 1 January 1991, the Estonian government temporarily froze the prices on goods and services supplied on the Estonian market, threatening enterprises with bankruptcy.

So many factors in the transformation being uncertain, any unemployment projections will be not much more than guesswork. Nevertheless, the Baltic governments have made some estimates of possible developments.

In the Estonian goverment's outlook on the labour market for 1991 there are two scenarios. The first alternative assumes that no radical change for the worse concerning production conditions takes place. In this case, it is assumed that unemployment will occur mainly because of job-changing and frictions. According to this alternative, about 30,000 persons (3.5 per cent of the labour force) would be in need of help to find jobs. About half of these, 16–17,000, would be helped by active labour-market measures to get jobs, and 13–14,000 (1.6 per cent of the labour force) would be in need of unemployment benefits.

In the alternative scenario, which involves a sharp disruption of production activities, 130,000 persons (15 per cent of the labour force) are assumed to lose their jobs and be in need of help. It is presumed that some of these would be helped by their employer, but 10,000 persons are supposed to find jobs outside the republic and 30–40,000 working pensioners would have to retire. Restricting the possibility of holding several jobs and assuming that 13–20,000 will find new jobs or become self-employed, this alternative foresees that 20–30,000 persons would be in need of unemployment benefits. These two scenarios represent extreme alternatives.

In Latvia, projections of unemployment if privatisation goes quickly range from 23–48,000 (1.6–3.3 per cent) of the labour force after the start of privatisation to 60–70,000 (4–5 per cent of the labour force) after 3–4 years. Other 'guesstimates' of coming unemployment are in the range of 5–10 per cent of the labour force. During the past four years the number of vacancies reported to the Employment Services has declined, from about 31,000 in 1987 to 18,000 in 1991 (about 70 per cent of all vacancies are said to be reported). There are particular worries about displaced white-collar workers and new school-leavers.

According to one Lithuanian projection, 105–140,000 persons in the labour market 1991 will be in need of assistance. It is supposed that of these 19,000 could be offered retraining and 10–17,000 public relief works. This would mean that 80–111,000 would become unemployed (4.2–5.8 per cent of the labour force in 1989) and would be in need of unemployment benefits. The basic reasons for the projected unemployment are material supply problems as well as the start of privatisation and its assumed effects. So far, displacements are said to have particularly hit women with higher education for whom the Employment Service has had difficulty in finding new jobs. The old practice of administrative placement of graduates from higher education has been abandoned and finding jobs for these was mentioned as a special problem.

In a longer-term perspective, the development of employment depends on how successful the republics will be in restructuring their economy and particularly to what extent old work-places will be replaced with new ones.

b. Labour market policies in Estonia

In Estonia, labour-market questions used to be dealt with by the Republican State Committee on Labour and Social Questions. This Committee was subordinated to the All-Union State Committee on Labour and Social Questions in Moscow. The Estonian government has replaced this committee with a Ministry of Social Affairs. Within the ministry there is a small Labour-Market Department consisting of a general director and a staff of five persons.

The department is working out a draft law on employment. An all-union law on employment was adopted January 1991. This law regulates the status of unemployment, gives directions for minimum benefits as well as recommendations regarding active labour-market policies. It defines as unemployed a person who is searching for a job but cannot find one for reasons beyond his or her control. Registration of unemployment was started in May 1991. According to a Government Decree of 4 January 1991 unemployment benefits will be 80 per cent of the minimum wage and will be paid, after the person has been registered for seven days at the Employment Service, for a maximum of 180 days. The decree provides for subsidies to those who employ various categories of weak job seekers and funds for redundant workers to start their own business. Benefits and other outlays on labour-market measures are to be financed from the Social Fund, which is financed by a social tax on employers.

Local authorities are responsible for providing employment service in a district. Employment Services are on a self-financed basis: enterprises and organisations pay for their use. Fees are related to the size of the enterprise's work force and are usually paid on a yearly basis. The local government pays for services for job seekers who have been laid off for reasons beyond their control, and the Employment Service can also provide special services for which the job seeker pays himself like searching for and getting a job in another district within the republic or in another republic. The Tallinn Labour Exchange also provides assistance to those interested in jobs in the West.

As the Employment Services are self-financed and do not receive money from the republican budget, almost no information is available on job seekers and vacancies at the republican level. Data at the Labour-Market Department of the Ministry of Social Affairs and at the Department of Labour and Wage Statistics of the State Statistical Committee are therefore far from complete.

Data from the Tallinn Labour Exchange for 1989 and 1990 suggest that the number of job seekers turning to the Employment Service has diminished. In 1989, 11,000 persons applied to the Employment Service, in 1990 8,600. Most of the vacancies are for blue-collar jobs, while most of the job seekers are white-collar workers. A particular problem was women with higher education who had been laid off from administrative positions. Another category with particular difficulties in finding jobs is persons approaching retirement age.

b. Labour-market policies in Latvia

Labour-market policies in Latvia are under the auspices of the Republican Centre of Employment Service under the Department of Welfare (formerly the Republican State Committee for Labour and Social Questions). As in Estonia, the Services are still financed by fees from employers.

The Republican Centre has worked out a draft law on employment for the Latvian republic. This law proposes that benefits and active labour-policy measures should be paid from the Employment Fund, which should be financed by the social security budget and from the state budget. The social security budget is to be used for unemployment benefits and social benefits to members of the families of the unemployed and to cover retraining costs, including stipends, to those taking part in these programmes. For 1991 110 million roubles (1.5 per cent of the social security budget) have been set aside for labour policies. The social security budget is financed by a social tax on employers which is 37 per cent of the wage fund.

Support from the state budget would provide funds for subsidies to employers for creating new work places, for creating special work opportunities for women with small children, invalids, elderly people, for rehabilitation centers of invalids, for rehabilitation centres for people who have been imprisoned and who have lost working discipline, for public relief work and to cover the expenses of the employment services.

Under the draft law a person is considered unemployed if he cannot earn his living from work for reasons beyond his control and is registered with the local employment service. In addition, the person must fulfil at least one of the following criteria: (1) to have worked for at least twelve weeks during the year before becoming unemployed; (2) to be re-entering the labour market after maternity leave or after a period devoted to taking care of sick members of the family, invalids or the elderly; (3) to be a first-time job seeker. The state guarantees free services of the employment service, free retraining in case of unemployment, opportunity to take part in public relief work and unemployment benefits.

There is a proposal to introduce quotas to promote employment of invalids. There is also a provision for tax reductions if the employer hires a person under 29 years of age without professional training, a person who has been unemployed for more than six months or a former convict. Employers must notify the Employment Service every month of their vacancies.

Unemployment benefits are paid from the fourteenth day of registration at the Employment Service for a maximum of 26 weeks (6 months) during a 12-month period, on the condition that the unemployed visits the Employment Service at least twice a month. Benefits are not paid to displaced workers who get severance payment from their employer. Benefits are disbursed by the local social security authorities.

Persons are not eligible for unemployment benefits if they have quit their jobs of their own volition. If the unemployed does not accept a suitable job offered by the Employment Service he loses the benefit for one month. After a second rejection of a job offer, the unemployed loses the right to benefit. The unemployment benefit is 90 per cent of the Latvian minimum wage.

c. Labour-market policies in Lithuania

In Lithuania, the Ministry of Social Security is responsible for labour-market questions. Employment services operate throughout the republic. A basic idea of Lithuanian labour policy is to give a great deal of authority to the Employment Service. The Employment Service should assist people in finding jobs, register the unemployed, handle the payments of benefits and organise retraining and public relief works.

The Employment Service is to receive its resources from the Employment Fund which is basically financed from the social security budget. Thus, the old system of services depending on employers' fees will be abandoned. Three per cent of the social security budget will be transferred to the Employment Fund which is under the Employment Service's jurisdiction. The social security budget is financed by a social tax of 30 per cent on the wage funds and 1 per cent of employees' wages. In addition, it is hoped that the fund will get money through voluntary contributions from employers, subsidies from the republican state budget and fines from employers who do not fulfil certain obligations. The Employment Fund should cover all costs related to employment service and unemployment: unemployment benefits, public relief works, the running of the services, credits to unemployed wishing to start their own business, courses of retraining and stipends to those participating.

A Lithuanian Law on Employment was adopted on 13 December 1990 according to which a person is unemployed if he cannot earn his living from work for reasons beyond his control, is registered with the local Employment Service and is ready to take a job in accordance with his professional training or is willing to undergo retraining and requalification. The state guarantees free services of the Employment Service, free retraining in case of unemployment, the opportunity to take part in public relief work and unemployment benefits.

There are special guarantees for socially exposed groups — persons under 18 years of age, women with children below 14 years of age (and men bringing up children of the same age on their own), persons who have less than 5 years left to retirement age, persons who return from imprisonment and invalids. Employers are to be given work position quotas (up to 5 per cent of their jobs) for these categories. If they cannot provide jobs for these kinds of job seekers when asked by the Employment Service they must pay fines to the Employment Fund corresponding to 12-months' average wage at the enterprise.

If more than 10 workers are to be laid off within a 30-day period, the Employment Service should be notified 3 months in advance. The Employment Service has the right to postpone lay-offs for 6 weeks. Employers may be compensated from the Employment Fund. Employers must report their vacancies to the Employment Service every month.

Unemployment benefits are paid from the 8th day of registration at the Employment Service and are paid for a maximum of 6 months during a 12-month period. Persons who have been employed for at least 24 months during the past 3 years are eligible for benefits. The unemployed gets 70 per cent of his average monthly wage during the first 2 months, 60 per cent during the next two months and 50 per cent during the last two months. Persons who have 5 years or less left to retirement can get benefits for another two months.

Persons ineligible for unemployment benefits have a right to social benefits according to the Law on Guaranteed Incomes.

Persons are not eligible for unemployment benefits if they have quit their jobs on their own initiative, if they do not accept a suitable job or if they do not visit the Employment Service regularly to get job offers.

E. Social policies

The economic transformation involves risks not only of large unemployment but also of declining purchasing power when prices rise following market

Table 9.5 Pensioners and pensions, 1985–9, Estonia

	1985	1986	1987	1988	1989
Number of pensioners: (thousands)	352	358	363	367	378
of which:					
Old-age pensioners	265	272	278	282	287
of which:					
State-pensioners	231	239	245	250	na
Collective farmer pensioners	34	33	33	32	32
Average size of old-age pension (roubles per month):					
State-pension	93.9	na	na	100.2	105.2
Pension of collective farmer	64.3	na	na	74.1	90.8

Sources: Statistical yearbooks and officially provided data.

reform. Consequently, social policies — compensation schemes, pensions, social security systems — have become increasingly important.

In Estonia, the October 1990 price rise was accompanied by compensation schemes. People with fixed incomes got about 35–40 roubles a month in compensation. In connection with the price rises on bread, meat and milk products in January 1991, the Latvian government also introduced compensation. Enterprises had to pay wage compensation to their employees using their own means. Compensation to persons employed in budget-financed organisations, students and mothers on maternity leave were paid from budgetary means. Compensation to working people was 66 roubles a month, 46 roubles to non-working pensioners and to students, 45 roubles a month. The compensation is based on the idea that subsidies previously paid to producers should now be paid to the consumers.

Work has been undertaken to calculate changes in the population's living standard. In Latvia it was estimated that the subsistence minimum rose from 101.4 to 158.5 roubles a month after the increases in bread, meat and milk prices. If all prices are increased, the estimated future subsistence minimum is 209 roubles.

The pension and social security system in the Baltic republics has been determined by all-union laws and regulations. The pension system was based on the pension law of 1956 for state pensioners and that of 1964 for collective farm workers. This system was very outdated and a new pension law was adopted on the all-union level in 1990. In the old system only people who had participated in the labour market were eligible for an old-age pension. Civilian state employees were eligible for an old-age pension upon reaching age 60 (men) and 55 (women), provided that they had spent at least 25 years (men) or 20 years (women) in state-sector employment. Pension depended on earnings in the last 12 months before retirement. Minimum and maximum pensions were stated in absolute terms.

According to a draft law, the Estonian minimum old-age pension will be increased from 100 to 115 roubles. The maximum pension will be 60 per

Table 9.6 Pensioners and pensions, 1985–90, Latvia

	1985	1986	1987	1988	1989	1990
Number of pensioners: (thousands) of which:	586	592	603	614	616	625
Old-age pensioners of which:	440	449	459	469	na	na
State-pensioners	356	368	380	391	na	na
Collective farmer pensioners	84	81	79	78	na	na
Average size of pension (roubles per month)						
State pension	77.1	82.2	84.5	87.1	89.4	94.1
Pension of collective farmer	45.4	53.2	54.7	60.8	62.3	79.7

Sources: Statistical yearbooks and officially provided data.

Table 9.6 Pensioners and pensions, 1985–9, Lithuania

	1985	1986	1987	1988	1989
Number of pensioners: (thousands) of which:	761	776	790	807	841
Old-age pensioners of which:	548	563	577	594	626
State pensioners	353	371	387	407	440
Collective farmer pensioners	195	192	190	187	186
Average size of old-age pension (roubles per month):					
State pension	82.8	na	na	90.4	95.6
Pension of collective farmer	49.7	na	na	58.7	78.6

Source: Officially provided data.

cent of the wage earned before retirement or a maximum of 6 times the minimum pension.

The Latvian government adopted a new pension law in November 1990. Latvian citizens will have a right to a pension if they have permanent residence status in Latvia. Foreign citizens and residents without citizenship who come to Latvia after 1 January 1991 will receive a pension provided they will have worked for enough time.

Maternity-leave regulations have been changed. Mothers continue to get 112 days paid by the employer, 100 roubles per month until the child is eighteen months old and a benefit of 40 roubles per month until the child is 8 years old. If childcare facilities are not used, the mother is paid 70 roubles a month for staying home until the child is 3 years old. If the child does not use a childcare facility between 3 and 7 years of age, an extra child allowance of 50 roubles per month is paid. Child allowance is 50 roubles per month for children.

In order to finance the new pensions and other social reforms, the social tax has been increased from the earlier average level of 4–15 per cent to 37 per cent of the wage fund.

Pensions in Lithuania are still regulated by the all-union pension law. In contrast to the other two republics, the work on a new pension law does not seem to have come very far.

F. Assessment

Short-term effects on employment appear primarily to be owing to distortions in the material supply system and other problems linked to the rather chaotic situation in all of the Soviet Union. Estimates for unemployment rates in the three republics are around 5 per cent for 1991. So far it is primarily white-collar workers, women and persons near retirement who have been displaced and have had difficulties in finding new jobs.

Long-term effects are difficult to foresee since much depends on the political development in the Soviet Union. Structural changes entailing displacement of workers and need for retraining and re-education can be expected. The speed with which such changes take place is crucial in determining how many people will lose their jobs and the ability of the governments to cope with unemployment. The same applies to privatisation and its potential effects.

All three states have ambitions to modify the negative effects of unemployment. Employment policies have been worked out for how the unemployed are to be assisted in finding new jobs. There is, however, no capacity to cope with the occurrence of mass unemployment. Therefore, it is of great importance that the institutions for implementing labour-market policies are developed as fast as possible. First, this involves increasing the number of Employment Services and their staff, providing training for the staff and procuring equipment which allows the Services to provide information on job seekers and vacancies efficiently. Second, systems for retraining have to be worked out to facilitate active labour market policies as much as possible. The governments wish to offer retraining to displaced workers, but there is at present no regular system to achieve this. A particular problem is that persons with quite good white-collar positions will be made redundant because they have an education not relevant to a transformed economy. These persons need re-education.

There is also a desire to modify the effects of the transition through social and compensatory policies. However, monetary compensation will often not be sufficient to mitigate the effect of price increases and rising unemployment. Many goods and services have been provided only through the enterprise and the extra benefits employment has entailed. The loss of a job means the loss of more than monetary income. Since the reform process has only begun and the transitional difficulties regarding employment and welfare are yet to come on a significant scale, one can only speculate on the scale of popular resentment and possible labour market unrest that could follow.

10 The environment

A. Introduction

Concern about the environment was expressed in public debate in the Baltic states even before the independence movement started and has been a pivotal force behind the political events of the last two to three years. One of the objectives in the Baltic states' struggle for independence has been to seek republican control over natural resources. For many of the Estonians, Latvians and Lithuanians, large industrial complexes and power plants have become negative symbols of Soviet domination in their republics. Most Baltic people regard the centrally designed Soviet industrial policy as arbitrary exploitation of their domestic resources. In the elections to the Baltic Parliaments in the winter and spring 1990, the environment was one of the most debated issues. As a result, green movements are now represented in the Parliaments of all three republics.

Most ecological problems in Estonia, Latvia and Lithuania are similar to those of other industrialised economies. However, some features typical for centrally planned economies make the situation of the Baltic republics different from countries in Western Europe and North America. Land, water, raw materials and energy are free or underpriced. Consequently, industrial production in the three republics has a high intensity of raw material and energy use which makes it exceedingly polluting. Treatment of waste water and air pollution is either insufficient in capacity or based on rudimentary technology. Despite a fairly well-developed system of environmental inspection, little has so far been done to reduce emissions from industry and other polluters. Since enterprises are subordinated to central ministries, it is often difficult to determine who should be held responsible for violation of environmental laws and regulations. Local as well as republican authorities have until now had very limited influence on economic activity on their territory.

The state of the environment in the Baltic states (with regard to pollution of water and air, land degradation, waste management etc.) is comparable to that of the countries in Eastern Europe, although an overall assessment probably concludes that the situation is less acute in the Baltic countries. With the exception of northeastern Estonia, the region does not have the type of complex and serious environmental problems which now are recognised in Saxony, northern Bohemia or Upper Silesia in East-Central Europe. There is no doubt, however, that there are several environmental problems in the Baltic states which call for immediate action.

The figures presented in the following are from official statistical sources in Estonia, Latvia and Lithuania. In most cases, they are estimates based on collected data from individual enterprises. Consequently, the given figures must be regarded as preliminary and indicative only.

B. Pollution of water, air and land

a. Water

With the exception of northern Estonia, the Baltic countries have abundant resources of surface water and groundwater. For example, Lithuania has an average annual river flow of 25.9 billion cubic metres (m³), or 7,000 m³ water per person a year available which is well above the European average (1,710 m³), and over ten times more than in Czechoslovakia or Poland.

Despite these favourable geographical conditions, water pollution in rivers, lakes and the Baltic Sea is the most acute environmental problem in the Baltic states. There are three major sources of polluted water: insufficiently treated sewage from towns and municipalities, industrial sewage and agriculture.

Of the three republics, Estonia and Lithuania are the largest water users. In 1989, their total water consumption was 3,014 and 4,355 million m³ respectively. Most of this, about 80 per cent, was used as cooling water for thermal power plants. The rest of the consumption was divided more or less evenly among industry, households and service, and fish breeding. A small share was used for agricultural purposes. The same year, Latvia's water consumption was 650 million m³. Of this, 36 per cent was used by industry, 30 per cent by households and 26 per cent for agriculture and fish breeding (see Table 10.1.)

Per capita use of water varies considerably between the three states. The figures for Estonia (1,916 m³) and Lithuania (1,139 m³) are several times higher than those for Latvia (241 m³). Per capita consumption in the countries of East Central Europe is in the range of 350–550 m³.

According to official statistics for the year 1989, Estonia discharged 517 million m³ of used water in need of treatment. Latvia discharged 367 million m³ and Lithuania 450 million m³. In Estonia, about half of the water in need of treatment was 'standardly' treated (that is discharged after treatment to a concentration of pollutants lower than permittable levels according to Soviet criteria). In Latvia this share was only 30 per cent in the same year, and in Lithuania it was even smaller — 25 per cent. The remaining part of the waste water in the three republics was insufficiently treated or discharged without any treatment.

Existing sewage treatment capacity is far from sufficient. Several Baltic towns have no sewage treatment facilities at all. Moreover, most of the available sewage treatment plants are equipped only with mechanical and biological treatment. Biological–chemical treatment is only available in very few cases which means that nutrients can not be handled. Some industries, like food processing or metallurgy, have their own treatment plants where waste water requires special treatment. However, most enterprises channel their sewage directly to the municipal treatment plants, despite the fact that these plants lack appropriate equipment to treat industrial sewage.

Construction of new treatment plants is slow. Equipment has to be imported. During the recent years it has become more difficult to purchase equipment from the Soviet Union, since production of sewage treatment facilities is much smaller than demand. More sophisticated technology, for

Table 10.1 Water consumption and sewage discharge, 1989 (million cubic metres)

	Estonia	Latvia	Lithuania
Total extracted water	3,328	733	4,355
from underground sources	456	320	506
Utilised total	3,014	650	4,327
Per capita	1,916	241	1,139
Total discharge of waste water	3,248	579	4,075
Not needing treatment:	2,726	212	3,625
Sewage in need of treatment	517 (100%)	367 (100%)	450 (100%)
(a) standardly treated	271 (52%)	110 (30%)	114 (25%)
(b) insufficiently treated	192 (37%)	257 (70%)*	124 (28%)
(c) untreated	54 (10%)		211 (47%)

* Untreated or insufficiently treated.
Sources: Environment '89, Estonian Nature Management Scientific Information
Centre, Tallinn, 1990; *Latvian Environmental Statistics*, Riga, 1990 (in Latvian);
Lithuanian Environmental Statistics, Vilnius, 1990 (in Lithuanian).

instance for chemical treatment, is only available for convertible currencies.
Funds for hard-currency imports are still controlled by Moscow. Not
surprisingly, after the Baltic republics' independence declarations such funds
have not been readily available.

Another problem is the maintenance of existing treatment plants. Lack of
money and interest means that equipment is not maintained as it should be.
Spare parts are difficult to get. Inadequate training of the staff also causes
low efficiency of operation.

Agricultural production generates specific problems of water pollution.
Pigs and chickens are bred at large farms, usually with between 10,000 and
50,000 animals. These farms produce huge amounts of manure, which is
stored before it is spread out on the fields, often without control of the
actual load on the soils. Leakage from stored manure, as well as from the
fields, contaminates the ground water near the farms. Drinking water from
dug wells in such areas contains high concentrations of nitrates.

In *Estonia*, the rivers belonging to the catchment area of the Gulf of Finland
in the northern part of the country are the worst affected by water pollution.
Groundwater quality is unstable in several settlements. Measured concentrations of nitrates have been up to 30 mg per litre, or even 100 mg per litre
in extreme cases. In the northeast the level of groundwater has sunk as a
result of the oil-shale mining. About 350 million m³ of water are pumped
out of the mines each year. Another serious problem in this area is highly
alkaline water leaking from stored ash at the thermal power plants in Narva.
As a result of polluted seawater and unfavourable changes in the natural algae
communities, the spawning and living conditions for many fish species have
worsened along the Estonian part of the Baltic coast. The situation is worst
in the Gulf of Riga and in the eastern part of the Gulf of Finland.

Some of the largest towns and settlements in Estonia do not have sewage
treatment plants, among them Tartu, Rakvere, Kuressaare and Tapa. In

Table 10.2 Discharge of sewage from major Baltic towns, 1989 (million m³)

	Total discharge of sewage	Routinely treated	Untreated or insufficiently treated	as % of all in republic
Estonia	527	271	246	100
Tallinn	117	3	114	46.3
Kohtla-Järve*	295	237	58	23.6
Harju*	19	7	12	4.9
Rakvere*	11	5	6	2.4
Narva	28	25	3	1.2
Latvia	367	110	257	100
Riga	171	14	157	61.1
Liepaja	22	0	22	8.6
Daugavpils	21	3	18	7.0
Jurmala	22	7	15	5.8
Jelgava	10	7	3	1.1
Lithuania	450	114	336	100
Kaunas	89	0	89	26.5
Vilnius	88	0	88	26.2
Klaipeda	46	—	46	13.7
Šiauliai*	21	11	10	3.0
Panevešys*	22	13	9	2.7

* Districts.
Sources: Same as Table 10.1.

Tallinn and several other towns existing treatment facilities are working inefficiently. Kohtla-Järve (including the district of Kohtla-Järve) and Tallinn together produce 80 per cent of all Estonian waste water in need of treatment. The major industrial polluters are the Oil-shale Chemical Production Association in Kohtla-Järve (which among other pollutants discharges about 500 tons of phenols each year), the pulp and paper plants in Tallinn and Kehra, the Phosphorite Production Assocation in Maardu, the cement plant in Kunda and several plants processing agricultural products (see Table 10.2).

In *Latvia*, the Lielupe River basin is considered to be the most polluted area. The main pollution load comes from the towns of Olaine and Jelgava where about one-third of the waste water is disharged into the river without treatment. Another source is the Sloka pulp and paper plant near Jurmala. The Lielupe River flows into the Gulf of Riga which in turn is one of the most polluted parts of the Baltic Sea. The major reason for the bad state of the Gulf of Riga is sewage from Riga. In 1989, the town of Riga dumped almost 160 million m³ untreated waste water into the Gulf. That was 61 per cent of the total amount of untreated sewage in Latvia that year.

Municipal sewage is the most significant source of pollution in inland and coastal waters in Latvia. Hardly any Latvian town has sufficient capacity to handle its waste water. Besides Riga, the ports of Liepaja and Ventspils are

Table 10.3 Discharge of nutrients, oil and phenol to the Baltic Sea, 1989[1] (tons)

	Nitrates	Phosphorous	Oil products	Phenol
Estonia	10,350	588	240	523
Latvia	7,155	944	640	2[2]
Lithuania	7,770	881	540	—[2]
Total	25,275	2,413	1,420	525

[1] Discharged directly to the sea or transported by rivers.
[2] The figure for Latvia is probably underestimated; from Lithuania there is no
information available.

Source: Same as Table 10.1; additional information from the Estonian Ministry of
Environment.

the major towns polluting the Baltic Sea. Liepaja only treats a small part of
its sewage biologically: the rest is handled mechanically. In 1989, swimming
was prohibited along the seashore of Liepaja (the same happened to several
beaches along the Gulf of Riga). In Ventspils new treatment capacity was
installed in 1988. However, parts of the town's sewage is still discharged
untreated.

Groundwater pollution is mainly caused by agricultural production
complexes of the same type as in Estonia. A major source of groundwater
contamination is the chemical and biochemical industry in Olaine. Concentrations of toxic pollutants in the groundwater at several hundred times
permissible levels have been recorded.

Lithuania has the worst standard of sewage treatment of the Baltic
republics. In 1989, the two largest towns, Kaunas and Vilnius, accounted
for 177 million m³ or about 40 per cent of the total amount of waste water
in need of treatment in the country. Kaunas does not have any treatment
facilities at all, and in Vilnius the sewage is only mechanically treated.
Despite the bad state of sewage treatment, most inland waters are still free
from severe pollution. However, contamination of wells around large
agricultural production complexes has become a growing problem in the last
ten years.

On the Baltic Sea coast, the sewage from the town of Klaipeda which is
discharged into the Curonian Lagoon is inadequately purified. This includes
waste water from the Klaipeda sulphate pulp mill. Another source of pollution is leaking oil from the harbour, which is used for oil export. At the
south of the Curonian Lagoon, a total amount of about 80 million m³ of
polluted water flows from the towns Sovetsk and Neman in the Kaliningrad
administrative area through the mouth of the Neman River each year.
Further north, at the seaside resort of Palanga, waste water from the refinery
in Mazeikiai, 90 kilometres inland, is piped into the Baltic Sea. This water
is cleaned in Mazeikiai, reportedly to acceptable standards. Unfortunately,
interference from untreated water coming from Palanga causes the Mazeikiai
water to be dumped too close to the shore which spoils the beach.

The total annual discharge of nitrogen and phosphorus to the Baltic Sea from the three republics is estimated at about 25,000 tons and 2,400 tons, respectively (see Table 10.3).

According to an agreement within the so-called Helsinki Convention from 1988, the countries around the Baltic Sea have committed themselves to reduce their total discharge of pollutants into the sea by 50 per cent by 1995. Although this agreement was signed by the Soviet Union and not by the individual Baltic republics, they have declared their intention to meet the requirements set in 1988. However, the Baltic governments have at the same time made clear that they will not be able to do this without foreign assistance to purchase new sewage treatment equipment. At a meeting in Ronneby in Sweden in September 1990, the signing parties of the Helsinki Convention decided to prepare a joint action plan by the beginning of 1992 with the aim of improving the ecological situation of the Baltic Sea. This plan will suggest priority areas for investment in environmental protection.

a. Air

Estonia is the largest emitter of air pollution among the Baltic republics. In 1989, it produced a total of 1,050,000 tons of solid particles and gaseous pollutants; 210,000 tons of this was sulphur dioxide (SO_2) which corresponded to a per capita emission of 131 kg SO_2. This was one of the highest levels in Europe; higher than in Poland and more than five times the Swedish level the same year. More than half of the Estonian emissions come from stationary sources. Apart from sulphur dioxide, different kinds of solid particles are the worst pollutants. These emissions, in turn, are concentrated in the area between Talinn and Narva in the northern part of the country where most of the industry is located. More than 80 per cent of the air pollution in Estonia originates from this region (see Tables 10.4 and 10.5).

In Narva the two thermal power plants fuelled with oil-shale together account for almost a third of the total emissions in Estonia. Both of the plants have equipment for dust filtration but lack technology for desulphurisation and gas cleaning. Thanks to a high content of calcium oxide in the shale which reacts with sulphur during the combustion process, up to 80 per cent of the sulphure content in the oil-shale is fixed. This reduces the emissions to the air significantly but produces large amounts of ash.

Latvia has no air polluters comparable with those in Estonia. About 40 per cent of all emissions from stationary sources (159 thousand tons) are generated in the four towns Riga, Liepaja, Ventspils and Daugavpils. In recent years, pollution from stationary sources has decreased. Between 1986 and 1989 it dropped by 25 per cent, mainly as a result of the use of natural gas instead of oil in thermal power plants. Traffic is the major source of air pollution in Latvia, accounting in 1989 for roughly 70 per cent of total emissions.

In *Lithuania*, total emissions into the air were estimated to about one million tons in 1989, 431,000 tons being emitted from stationary sources. As in Latvia, the major source of air pollution is traffic. The main stationary polluters are the oil refinery in Mazeikiai, the cement factory Akmencementas

Table 10.4 Air pollution, 1989 (thousand tons)

	Estonia	Latvia	Lithuania
Total emitted	1,050	585	approx. 1,000
From traffic	474	426	approx. 570
From stationary sources:	576	159	431
(a) solid particles:	261	38	44
(b) sulphur dioxide (SO_2)	210	59	188
(c) nitric oxides (NO_x)	23	12	44
Total per capita (kg)	668	217	270
SO_2 per capita (kg)	134	22	51
SO_2 per km^2 (kg)	4,656	926	2,883

The figures given for traffic emissions should be regarded as rough estimates.
Source: Same as in Table 10.1.

in Akmene, the fertiliser plant Azotas in Jonava, and the thermal power plant in Elektrenai. Together with the district of Trakai, to which Elektrenai belongs, the districts of Akmene and Mazeikiai account for over half of all emissions from stationary sources in Lithuania.

All three republics have declared that they intend to follow the international convention signed by the Soviet Union on reduction of sulphur dioxide by 30 per cent from the level of 1980 by 1993. There is also an agreement between the Soviet Union and Finland that the Soviet side shall decrease air pollution by 50 per cent in the regions close to Finland, including Estonia, by 1995 at the latest. However, Estonia will not be able to fulfil these agreements without foreign assistance, unless it reduces its production of electricity from oil-shale by almost half. Latvia and Lithuania, which are only affected by the first convention, may be able to achieve sufficient reduction if their electricity and heat production plants are converted completely to natural gas.

c. Other problems

There are virtually no processing plants for residuals and solid waste from industrial production in the Baltic republics. Only a minor share of the industrial waste is recycled and returned into production, most being dumped together with household waste at unchecked storage sites. Hazardous waste, like toxic chemicals or radioactive substances, are with few exceptions stored at places inadequately protected from leakage.

For example, in Estonia, oil-shale processing for chemical products produces more than 1.6 million tons of slags and sludge annually. The power stations in Narva generate more than 8 million tons of ash. There are about 400 dumping sites in Estonia covering a total area of 550 hectares where 2.5 million tons of household waste and more than 10 million tons of industrial waste are disposed each year. The dumping site at the chemical–metallurgical plant in the town of Sillamäe, located directly on the Gulf of Finland, is considered one of the largest environmental threats in Estonia. In

Table 10.5 Air pollution from the most polluting towns, 1989 (stationary sources, thousand tons)

	Total emitted	of which:		% of total emissions in republic
		solids	SO$_2$	
Estonia	576	262	210	100
Narva	312	162	125	54.2
Kunda	64	56	6	11.1
Kohtla-Järve District	50	12	21	8.7
Tallinn	39	6	21	6.8
Latvia	159	38	59	100
Riga	30	—	—	18.9
Liepaja	15	—	—	9.4
Daugavpils	9	—	—	5.7
Ventspils	9	—	—	5.7
Lithuania	424	41	188	100
Trakai District	83	—	—	19.6
Akmene District	76	—	—	17.9
Mazeikiai District	67	—	—	15.8
Vilnius	32	—	—	7.5
Kaunas	26	—	—	6.1

Sources: Same as for Table 10.1.

1989, 45,000 tons of slags, parts of it highly toxic, were produced at this enterprise.

All three republics are planning to build combustion plants for hazardous and toxic waste. Preliminary contacts have been made with foreign specialists in this field, but finance of such projects has yet to be identified.

Mining of phosphorite and processing into phosphate fertilisers at the enterprise Estonian Phosphorite in Maardu near Tallinn was long considered one of the most urgent environmental problems in Estonia. After strong public protest the Estonian government decided to stop mining by 1991 and reprofile the enterprise for production of superphosphate and some other products based on imported raw materials. As a result air pollution and generation of solid waste have already been subtantially reduced.

Monitoring of forest damage has only recently started in the Baltic republics. Preliminary estimates suggest that about 60 per cent of the pine forest in Estonia and Lithuania, and about 50 per cent in Latvia are damaged to some extent. Serious damage with dying trees has only been recorded in a few places. In Estonia the worst damaged areas are in the heavy industrialised northern region, especially near the towns Tallinn, Kiviöli and Maardu. Lithuania gets a large share of its air pollution deposits from Eastern Europe.

Not much is known about the impact on the environment from military activities in the Baltic region. In December 1989, more than 100 tons of air-plane fuel leaked out from a Soviet army airport in western Estonia, 32 tons of which contaminated the river Pärnu. Similar but smaller accidents have also been reported from military airports in other parts of the Baltic region.

C. Environmental management

In the 1980s, the development of environmental policy in the Baltic republics more or less moved along the same lines as in the Soviet Union. In 1988, a Soviet state committee for environmental protection, Goskompriroda, was founded. It was given the major responsibility for nature protection and environmental policy and has basically the same powers as a ministry. Simul-taneously, corresponding committees in the different republics were created. One year later, after the elections to the Soviet Parliament, a special ecological commission was established at the Supreme Council (the perma-nent body of the Parliament). The commission is formally independent of the government and is an important authority for the evaluation of new regula-tions and laws on environmental protection before they are approved in the Supreme Council.

In 1989 and 1990, Goskompriroda supervised the preparation of an environmental protection programme for the Soviet Union. The ambitious programme was expected to be discussed in the Supreme Council sometime at the beginning of 1991. Because of the confused political situation in the Soviet Union, however, discussion of the programme has been delayed. In March 1991 it was still not clear if it would be approved.

A combined system of taxes, limits and charges is envisaged. A limit would be imposed on each enterprise for the use of natural resources accord-ing to its specific needs. A certain tax would be levied for the use of resources up to this limit, for instance ten roubles for each ton of gravel within a limit of a thousand tons. If consumption were to exceed the limit, a higher tax would have to be paid for each unit above the limit, for instance thirty roubles a ton. A similar system would be introduced for the discharge of waste water, air pollution and solid wastes.

The money collected from the charges would be divided among local, republican and all-union funds earmarked for investments in environmental protection. Furthermore, environmental administration and control of enter-prises and other economic organisations would be decentralised to the local and regional level. The role of the all-union Goskompriroda is to be limited to general policy-making, preparation of laws and regulations and inter-national contacts.

At first sight, the Soviet environmental programme and the economic measures connected with it seem to be over-ambitious. It presupposes a complicated network of administrative and fiscal control on local and regional level. However, the local and regional administration lack the required experience and organisation to handle these tasks. The likely response of enterprises to financial penalties is also uncertain as long as enterprises are subordinated to ministries.

⌐Since the spring 1990 declarations of independence, the Baltic republics have gone further to reform their systems of environmental protection and are now trying to pursue their own policy independent of the Soviet Union.⌐ However, in many aspects, the Baltic republics are now implementing ideas of environmental control similar to those being discussed at the central level in the Soviet Union. ⌐Taxes on the use of natural resources and new charges for pollution (according to the system described earlier) were introduced in Estonia and Latvia on 1 January 1991. In Lithuania they are expected to be introduced later the same year.⌐

The organisation of nature protection and environmental control has been significantly changed in all three republics. The environmental committees created in 1988 in the Baltic republics only existed for a short period. They were reorganised at different stages in 1989 and 1990. The result of these changes was the creation of a Ministry of Environment in Estonia and an Environmental Protection Committee in Latvia and Lithuania. Besides these administrative bodies, there are environmental commissions working in the Parliaments in each republic.⌐

⌐*Estonia* has chosen an administrative model comparable with that of many European countries. The guidelines for environmental protection and use of natural resources are given in two laws: On the Order of the Use of Natural Environment and Resources from 16 December 1989, and On the Protection of Nature in Estonia from 23 February 1990. Presently, specific laws on fishing and hunting, forest, water and waste management are being prepared.⌐

⌐The Ministry of Environment, which started its work in the spring of 1990, is responsible for the overall organisation of environmental protection and use of natural resources. It prepares economic regulations and laws. The ministry also conducts environmental inspection. The information collected through this inspection system and the 19 local Environment Protection Offices will be elaborated and presented in regular reports by an information department at the ministry. Local authorities are responsible for environmental protection and utilisation of natural resources in their territory. They issue limits to enterprises and organisations for the use of water and other resources. Further, they carry out the environmental control on the spot.

At the beginning of 1991, it was not yet clear how the taxes and charges collected were to be distributed among local and republican authorities. Another question to be solved is how the environmental control at the local level should be organised in relation to the inspection service at the republican level. ⌐

In *Latvia*, the approach to environmental management is somewhat different from that in Estonia (and that in most European countries). The main body for environmental protection is the Environmental Protection Committee. It was founded in July 1990 and has the same responsibilities as its Estonian counterpart. The organisation of nature protection and environmental control also follows the Estonian pattern, with basically the same division of responsibilities among local, regional and republican levels. However, the Latvian committee is subordinated directly to the Parliament, is independent of the government and consequently has greater formal authority than a ministry. It is intended that this system will give environmental protection preference over other questions. The Latvian government is thereby forced to consider the environmental impact of all proposals it submits to the Parliament for approval. If a proposal is not accepted by the Environmental Protection Committee, the committee has the right to block it.

Instead of its own environmental protection agency, the Latvian government has an adviser on problems concerning nature protection and environmental law. It appears that the adviser is used as a sort of intermediary, mediating between the government and the Parliament. In this way, potential conflicts over different political issues can be resolved.

It is still too early to judge whether the Latvian model of environmental administration will work. In March 1991, the new authorities were still organising themselves. Latvian officials point out that there is a general consensus on environmental policy at the moment, since Latvia needs to be united in its negotiations with the Soviet Union about control of natural resources on Latvian territory. However, there is an obvious risk that the government will find it difficult to work with an independent environmental committee outside its control. Sooner or later, conflicts between economic and environmental priorities will arise. If the economic crisis heightens, the government may have to force through decisions in the Parliament. If this happens, the committee will lose much of its credibility, which in turn may have a negative influence on the enforcement of environmental control throughout the country.

Problems of this kind are already visible in *Lithuania* which has chosen a model for environmental management similar to that of Latvia. The Lithuanian Environmental Commission has more than 600 employees and has a significantly larger organisation than its counterparts in Estonia and Latvia. Despite this, progress with environmental management in Lithuania has been somewhat slower than in the other two Baltic republics. One sign of this is that the introduction of taxes on natural resources and pollution has been delayed.

There are indications that the commission, the government and the parliamentary committee have difficulties cooperating. Despite the fact that the commission is formally the organisation responsible for environmental policy-making in Lithuania, the government is now creating its own structure of environmental experts. Reporting by the environmental commission and the government to the environmental protection committee at the Parliament is not working well. Given the strained political situation in Lithuania, communication problems between different authorities involved in environmental management are quite understandable. However, they are at the same time the result of differing opinions between the commission and the ministries in the government.

D. Conclusions

Compared with the Soviet Union, where several regions today are facing virtual environmental catastrophe, the Baltic republics are in a stronger position to address their environmental problems. Estonia, Latvia and Lithuania are smaller and more sparsely populated than most European countries. This makes them simpler to administrate. Their location on the shore of the Baltic makes it easier for them to cooperate with foreign countries than is the case of most other parts of the Soviet Union.

Politicians and governmental officials in the Baltic republics are well aware of the environmental problems in their countries. They have a clear picture of what has to be done to stop the ecological degradation. There is a lively debate in the Baltic governments, Parliaments and among the general public on the means and measures to achieve an improvement of the situation. However, to really improve the environment in Estonia, Latvia and Lithuania, some key issues must be tackled.

The major problem for the Baltic republics is their relation to the Soviet Union. Most of the major polluters in the three republics are all-union enterprises or power plants still under the control of central ministries in Moscow. Before some kind of general agreement is achieved with the Soviet Union regulating the status of these enterprises it will be difficult to stop the pollution by them.

There is a wide consensus in the Baltic republics on the need to improve environmental protection. Revised laws on environmental protection, taxes for the use of natural resources and higher charges for pollution are being introduced in all three republics. Awareness and concern about the environment is well developed among the population. However, despite broad political support, it will not be easy to implement radically new environmental policies. With urgent economic problems and minimal financial resources, the Baltic governments will have to make decisions that may conflict with environmental priorities. It will be difficult to close down old and polluting industrial plants, or even reduce their output, if production is vital for other sectors of the economy. Conflicts of this kind are already retarding the progress of environmental management and will continue to do so in the near future.

Environmental controls will be easier to implement when enterprises and other polluters of the environment become responsible for their economic decisions. If an enterprise is forced to cover its expenses including pollution costs, it will obviously take some action to reduce polluting activity. It is also important to enhance the role of environmental inspection. The main question in this respect is not whether this is done at local, regional or republican level but that it should be made clear to everybody that there is a body which has the right and power to charge polluting enterprises or even to stop their production.

There is some evidence that enterprises in the Baltic republics have been more actively trying to solve their pollution problems since the new environmental protection agencies began their work. Earlier, they knew that the local and republican authorities had little power to control their activity. Another factor is increasing public pressure. In fact, environmental protest has already terminated industrial projects in all three republics. It is equally important to stimulate enterprises to reduce the intensity of energy and material use. The most evident way to do this is to introduce realistic prices for raw materials. Some pollution abatement technology must be imported. To purchase such equipment, financial assistance will be required from outside the Soviet Union.

The Baltic republics themselves regard their most urgent problems to be the low standard of waste water treatment and air pollution. The latter problem is concentrated in a few large stationary sources. These priorities are also in line with priorities set by international agreements concerning the state of the Baltic Sea and transboundary air pollution in Europe. On the Baltic Sea, Narva, Kohtla-Järve and to some extent Tallinn in Estonia, as well as Riga and Liepaja in Latvia, must get effective sewage treatment facilities. The same is true for the Lithuanian towns Palanga and Klaipeda and Sovetsk and Neman in the Kaliningrad area.

To reduce air pollution, the two thermal power plants in Narva, the oil-shale processing plant in Kohtla-Järve, the thermal power plants in Riga, the oil refinery in Mazeikiai, and the power plant at Elektrenai must be provided with desulphurisation equipment. The oil-shale industry in Kohtla-Järve may even have to close down, since it is questionable whether it will be economically viable. In Lithuania, air pollution must also be reduced from the cement industry in Akmene and the plant producing fertilisers in Jonava.

The most complex problems arise in the oil-shale region in northeastern Estonia, which together with Tallinn encompasses about two-thirds of Estonia's population and most of its industrial activity. This is the most polluted part of the Baltic countries with several serious problems such as water pollution, groundwater contamination, air pollution, forest damage and land degradation. Today, there are still no concrete plans to solve the environmental problems of this region.

Education and training in environmental management must be promoted on a large scale. It is especially important to raise the competence of environmental protection staff at the local level, in municipalities and towns. To achieve this foreign assistance will be needed, since the Baltic republics lack most of the needed infrastructure and knowledge.

Air and water pollution does not stop at borders. The effects from polluting emissions can be felt far away from their original sources. Today, virtually all European countries agree that an improvement of the environment calls for international cooperation. Western countries and international organisations like the World Bank have offered to help the countries of Eastern Europe to solve their environmental problems. Aid programmes and financial assistance have already been mobilised, most notably in Poland. In 1990, the Nordic countries (Denmark, Finland, Iceland, Norway and Sweden) decided to commit funds for investment in environmental protection in the Baltic republics. At the beginning of 1991, about US$ 100 million in bilateral and multilateral credits were earmarked for such investments. More money is likely to be made available in 1992, when the action plan for the Baltic Sea is presented by the member countries of the Helsinki Convention.

There is, however, a risk that the help now being offered to the Baltic region will be delayed because of the unresolved status of the Baltic republics in the Helsinki Convention (as well as in other multilateral organisations).

Soviet, Russian, and Baltic authorities are all interested in environmental credits from the West. St. Petersburg, the largest city on the Baltic Sea with almost six million inhabitants, and the Kaliningrad area are two of the largest polluters of the Baltic Sea. Unless solutions are found that satisfy all the interested parties, it will not be easy to deliver foreign assistance to the Baltic region.

11 Industry

A. Introduction

Industry is the single most important economic sector in the Baltic states, employing about a third of the labour force and providing around half of national income, as officially measured. Baltic industry is also quite diverse. Engineering produces a vast array of products, which are supplied all over the Soviet Union. The Baltic food and textile industries produce goods which find a ready market. There are also significant chemical and wood industries as well as a number of other industrial branches.

Though an important industrial tradition existed before 1940, it is the period from 1950 that has marked the sector's accelerated development. Extensive investments have 'over-industrialised' the region, it is often said, meaning that the Soviet command system has brought in an industrial sector which is too heavy and too dependent on a non-Baltic labour force and on serving the Soviet economy. Left to themselves, the Baltic republics would have developed a lighter, less-polluting, more knowledge- and service-intensive and more outward-looking industrial sector.

It is possible that such an industry really would have developed. It is in any case the direction in which Estonians, Latvians and Lithuanians would like to see their industries develop now. Things are starting to change. Cooperatives, joint-stock companies and joint ventures are developing fast, creating a new, dynamic group of entrepreneurs. There is also considerable managerial competence among the existing state-owned firms which have come to act on a much more independent basis. As the economic policy environment changes, there is potential for reorientation, diversification and innovation.

Many of the issues related to enterprise reform have been discussed in Chapter 8 and will not be repeated in this chapter. However, one general point is worth making. While Baltic industrial enterprises have a number of the resources required for successful performance by international competitive standards, the inherited endowment is quite unbalanced because of the nature of the Soviet system.

Engineering skills are well developed. Some equipment is advanced and many of the needed supporting services are available. While there are problems with infrastructure (for example weak telecommunications, poorly organised transport), much of the basic capital stock (for example roads, rail and power) is in place. The scientific community (for example the academies of science) has high levels of professional competence in specialised areas.

However, there are a number of gaps. The tasks assigned to an industrial enterprise under the planned economy led to an emphasis of production geared to achieving physical targets. Economic calculation — accounting and costing — to minimise costs and maximise returns were little developed. In a supply-constrained shortage economy, marketing and design skills were underemphasised. And in the production line sophisticated state-of-the-art technology operates side by side with out-of-date and makeshift methods.

Industrial restructuring will require the shifting of existing skills to new tasks, the quick development of new skills to fill gaps and a widespread reorganisation and selective retooling of industrial capacity.

While it is possible to identify the elements on which a new pattern of industrial development could be based, it is not possible to specify what will be the structure of a new pattern of industrial activity. There are a number of reasons for this.

The industrial sector was the part of the economy which was most strongly integrated into the Soviet planned economy. This meant that Baltic firms produced not only end products for the Soviet market, but in many cases produced intermediate products which formed one link in a complex chain of activity stretching throughout the Soviet Union.

This model of industrial development has produced a large number of oligopolies and oligopsonies. In the Soviet system one factory often specialises in producing a particular product or component; for example, all the tuners for television sets produced in the Soviet Union are made in the Banga factory in Lithuania. This has resulted in a larger average size of industrial enterprise than would be the case in the OECD economies. For example, industry in Lithuania has an average of 850 employees per enterprise. This compares with an average of 163 employees per enterprise in the countries of the European Community. The reasons for this difference include: the lower level of productivity of workers in the Soviet Union, the choice of technology, the enterprise tendency to hoard labour, the integrated nature of enterprises, the administrative convenience for central planners of dealing with few, large units as well as the relative absence of small and medium-sized firms. In the Soviet Union as a whole, 60 per cent of industrial enterprises have more than 500 employees compared to 7 per cent in the EC. This absence of a small-scale industrial sector is unfortunate as this would be the sector best placed to take advantage of some of the dynamic opportunities which will emerge in the coming period. At the policy level, while considerable attention is being addressed to the large enterprises and particularly to their privatisation, inadequate attention is being given to the need to encourage the development of small-scale businesses.

Enterprises tend to be both horizontally and vertically integrated as well as sometimes engaging in activities seemingly unrelated to their main function. Enterprises often have their own construction and transport branches as well as almost no reliance on outside design, management, financial or other specialists. Endless problems with input supply have forced enterprises to develop this all-inclusive nature. Though this has given the large enterprises a degree of autonomy, it has led to inefficiency and also limited technical change. By contrast, the large corporations of the West consist of autonomous divisions and subsidiaries, and make widespread use of subcontractors, providing greater flexibility. Restructuring of enterprises, along with commercialisation and privatisation, will be crucial components of a programme for industrial reform. The break-up of the over-integrated enterprises could create greater competition and provide opportunities for small-scale entrepreneurs.

The twin set of forces bringing change to the Baltic economies, increasing economic autonomy and the shift to a market economy, will profoundly affect Baltic industry. At the moment, the crisis in the Soviet economy seems likely to engender a deepening decline in industrial production. The medium-term future will depend on how that crisis is resolved and on what terms the Baltic firms continue to trade with the rest of the Soviet Union. For example, if the Soviet Union moves to a realistic pricing system, to what extent would firms in the Soviet Union find Baltic suppliers a satisfactory source of supply as compared with sources outside the Soviet Union? With the achievement of Baltic independence, what trading relationships will be agreed with the Soviet Union? Many of the issues related to the future pattern of trade were discussed in Chapter 7, but eventual outcomes will be influenced by the terms of settlement with the Soviet Union. The outcome would be very different if the Baltic republics remain part of the Soviet common market than if trade barriers are established.

In the longer term there is a more fundamental source of uncertainty. The pattern of industrial production which will emerge from a response by entrepreneurs, foreign and national, to market opportunities will differ profoundly from the existing structure. Many industries will decline and new industries will appear. However, new industries will result from the initiatives of entrepreneurs and will succeed and fail according to their profitability — they will not be the result of the plan. If the Baltic economies shift to operate on market principles, the pattern of future industrial activity will not be something that can be predicted by government planners. The industrial sector, producing tradeable commodities, will be particularly responsive to opening up to the influence of trade with the rest of the world. The Baltic economies are small. The emergence of a few successful industrial enterprises producing for export will have a great impact on the economy. What these firms will be is impossible to guess.

A further source of uncertainty relates to the military-industrial sector. This sector has claimed a disproportionate share of available technical capacity. Compared with the rest of Soviet industry it has reached a high technical level, although, as with defence industries in the West, this has often been with little regard for economic cost. To what extent and effect resources will be released from the military-industrial sector to undertake civilian industrial tasks is unclear but is likely to be quite substantial.

It is possible to get an idea of the relative importance of military production in the Baltic republics from some 1985 employment data by industrial branch published by the Soviet Union. These data are not reproduced here; they are, however, consistent with those provided in Table 11.1. Specialists interpret a residual in these statistics as almost certainly indicating employment in enterprises subordinate to ministries that report to the Soviet Military-Industrial Commission (VPK).

In the Soviet Union as a whole, the percentage of industrial employment in the VPK sector in 1985 was 21.3. For Estonia it was 5.0, for Latvia 15.2 and for Lithuania 12.5. Thus the importance of the VPK sector is in general rather less than in the Soviet Union.

Casual information about military-related production in the Baltic republics suggest that much of it is concentrated in the electronics sector and in shipbuilding. In general, it does not seem to include final-stage assembly of weapon systems. As with VPK production in general (and even before the current 'conversion' campaign), much of it will be civilian products (television sets, refrigerators and radios are typical).

The adaptability of the VPK sector is considerable. Directors of VPK categories have in many cases been active in pursuing joint-venture deals and 'nomenklatura privatisation'. This is easier, moreover, in the kind of VPK production that predominates in the Baltic republics, than, say, in munitions production. On the other hand, the political uncertainties specific to the Baltic republics may inhibit such developments.

So, while this chapter offers an overview of the existing industrial structure, which provides the starting point of future development, it should be recognised that the past pattern can tell little about the direction of future development.

This chapter will first give some basic information on industrial structure by employment, output and branch and by type of firm. It will review the pressures on the old system and how this has given way to crisis phenomena such as barter trade. It will also look at the new emerging economic actors, cooperatives and joint-stock companies. Finally, it will take up some issues in the reform process and comment on the industrial sector's role and potential.

B. Employment and output by industrial branch

An overview of the present industrial structure is given in Tables 11.1 and 11.2, showing industrial employment and value of industrial production by republic and by industrial branch. (It should be noted that mining, power production and fishing are not included in the industrial sector as referred to in this chapter.)

Given the extreme valuation problems that the Soviet pricing system presents, it is appropriate to look at the employment situation first. It can be seen that industrial employment as a share of total employment ranges from 24 per cent in Estonia to 42 per cent in Latvia, with Lithuania at 32 per cent, which is also the regional average. Engineering industry dominates in all three republics, employing close to 40 per cent of the total Baltic industrial workforce. The second largest sector is the labour-intensive textile industry, with 20 per cent of the workforce. Food and wood industries come third and fourth, each employing around 10 per cent of the workforce.

Table 11.2 on the value of industrial production shows total turnover generated by all industrial firms rather than net value added (the usual Western statistic). This does not give an adequate picture of the real importance of each sector. The double-counting that results from adding firms' gross sales is reflected in the difference between the total as given and the total industrial sector contribution to national income (NMP). The latter is

Table 11.1 Industrial employment in the Baltic republics, 1989 (thousands employed)

	Estonia	%	Latvia	%	Lithuania	%	Total %	Sector share of all Baltic industry %
Basic metals	0	0	4	1	2	0.5	6	1
Chemicals	16	8	23	7	22	4	61	6
Engineering	58	30	147	42	209	40	414	39
Wood	28	14	34	10	45	9	107	10
Building materials	14	7	18	5	39	8	71	7
Textiles	43	22	70	20	101	20	214	20
Food	19	10	23	7	52	10	94	9
Other industry	14	7	25	7	47	9	86	8
Total	194	100	344	100	517	100	1,054	100
Total working population	811		813		1,586		3,211	—
Industrial employment as share of total employment (%)	24		42		33		33	—

Note: In these figures the industrial sector does not include mining, power production and fishing.

Source: Official statistics; compilation taken from Grahm and Königsson, 1991.

regrettably not available by industrial branch. It should again be noted that the price system seriously distorts the picture, making any comparisons very difficult between, or even within, branches.

Branch distribution of turnover as indicated by the figures confirms that the engineering sector, with 28 per cent of the total is the most important element of the industrial sector. The textile and food industries each have about another quarter of industrial output. The chemical and wood industry come next with 7 per cent. Together these five branches generate 90 per cent of all industrial output (mining and energy not included).

The profiles by republic are quite similar. The most striking difference is the relatively lower importance of the engineering industry in Estonia which is counterbalanced by its significantly higher shares of the textile, wood and chemical industries. It might also be noted that Lithuania has only small shares of basic metal and chemical industries.

C. All-union and republican firms

The Soviet industrial structure, as it existed, had three kinds of firms, all-union, republican and so-called union–republican firms, which formally were under both Soviet and republican authority. The present transfer of control over the industrial firms from the Soviet authorities to the republics is ending the relevance of this earlier categorisation.

All-union industry was closely integrated in the Soviet economic system.

Table 11.2 Total turnover by industrial firms in the Baltic republics, 1989 (millions of roubles)

Sector	Estonia	%	Latvia	%	Lithuania	%	Total	All Baltic industry %
Basic metals	63	1.3	137	1.8	67	0.5	267	1
Chemicals	518	11	617	8	583	5	1,718	7
Engineering	814	17	2,397	32	3,506	30	6,718	28
Wood	514	11	472	6	718	6	1,705	7
Building materials	203	4	252	3	676	6	1,131	5
Textiles	1,494	31	1,629	21	2,836	24	5,960	24
Food (excl. fish)	959	20	1,698	22	3,012	25	5,669	23
Other industry	214	4	374	5	516	4	1,104	5
Total gross value of industrial production	4,780	99	7,578	99	11,915	100	24,272	100
Total value of industrial contribution to national income (NMP)	1,957		3,437		—		—	
Industrial share of NMP %	43		45		ca 55			ca 50

Note: See Table 11.1.

Source: See Table 11.1.

It comprised practically all of the most important industries, the energy system and most other parts of infrastructure. The all-union firms were controlled by some 20 all-union branch ministries in Moscow. These giant entities attempted to control thousands of firms over the Soviet Union. The all-union industry provided the bulk of Soviet industrial production. Subjected to planning directives from Gosplan, they received their material supplies from Gossnab and were financed by Gosbank. Practically all of the engineering industry, the chemical and basic metal industry and many other sectors were under all-union jurisdiction. It has been said that the purpose of the rest of the Soviet economy was to provide the workers of the all-union industries with food and clothing.

A significant part of the all-union industry is included in the military–industrial complex. These are high-priority industries, considered to be of particular strategic importance. They produce military equipment or components necessary to the defence industry. However, their production is not confined to weaponry and related goods but also includes a significant civilian element, mainly electronics. This civilian part of the military controlled all-union industry is strongly represented in the Baltic republics. The large, high-technology firms of Latvia and Lithuania producing radios, television sets, telecommunications equipment, electronic components etc. are the most important examples.

In Lithuania, 40 per cent of all enterprises were all-union in 1989, whereas 50 per cent were union–republican and 10 per cent republican. Latvia has a similar structure, while in Estonia, where there is less heavy industry, 20

Table 11.3 Output by type of firm, Latvia (%)

	1980	1987	1990
All-union	37	40	37
Union–republican	46	50	21
Republican	17	10	42

Source: Latvian Statistical Committee, 1990.

per cent of all enterprises were all-union in 1988, 60 per cent were union–republican and 20 per cent republican.

The union–republican firms were formally under both union ministry and republican government authority. Obviously, this led to an unclear situation as regards responsibility. Though earlier most of the union–republican firms were controlled by Moscow authorities, this is now changing, with a greater part falling under republican authority. As a majority of firms were in this category, the outcome of these changes is therefore of great significance. While union–republican firms in the infrastructure field (for example power plants, power distribution, post and telephone communications) may to a large extent remain technically dependent on central Moscow authority, other branches, such as wood and construction industries, may more easily be transferred to republican control.

The conflict between the Baltic republics and the Soviet Union over who should own and control the all-union sector and the union–republican firms has been one of the most serious issues at stake between the Union and the republics. All three republics have claimed ownership over all property on their territory. While agreements were reached in 1989 between the Union authorities and the Baltic republics and lists made up for the transfer to republican authority of specific all-union and union–republic firms, the issue has not recently been the topic of much formal negotiation.

The changes are reflected in Table 11.3 showing output figures in Latvia. While output from all-union firms remains roughly constant, there is a significant shift from union–republican to republican-firm output between 1987 and 1990.

Lack of resolution of differences between the union and republic authorities, combined with the rapid decay of the central command structure results in a very unclear structure of authority in the industrial sector. Some firms remain strictly under Moscow authority; many others drift into a situation in which in practice the chain of command is broken, giving great leeway to their managers. In some cases, it might be said, the manager decides whether the company operates as an all-union or republican firm.

With new legislation being adopted in the republics, in particular regarding taxation, environmental regulation and social provisions, many all-union companies will be forced to choose their masters. Many have chosen to obey republican laws and directives. However, most companies are dependent on maintaining links with Soviet companies and so continue to work to the extent possible with the Soviet industrial system as it currently operates.

Though the desire to take control over the firms is strong, it is not all that obvious that republican ownership would always be advantageous for the republics. On balance, many all-union industries are liable not to be much of an asset, either economically or politically. For those firms which can hardly hope for a successful transition or, at best, are likely to face financial crisis, the republics could well be seeking ownership for a liability rather than an asset. Moreover, the republic governments might wish to avoid responsibility for the unemployment that could result from any closures. An example of a plant which could well be a dubious inheritance is the Ignalina nuclear-power station in Lithuania which has a limited life and will require considerable decommissioning costs.

While it is understandable that ownership of most of the all-union sector should be transferred to the republics as a consequence of the move to independence, there is no reason in principle why Soviet or Russian trans-national enterprises should not continue to operate alongside other foreign ventures to some agreed extent in independent Baltic states.

Republican enterprises have not been independent of the Soviet economy system and Moscow's directives. Many are dependent on imports for inputs, for example grain from the Ukraine and cotton from Uzbekistan. However, having a larger share of domestic inputs and having an output which is in high demand both at home and in the Soviet Union, many of these enterprises have come further in developing an autonomous standing.

Industry under clear republic control will be readily commercialised and privatised by republic initiatives. Those enterprises remaining under all-union control will be affected by the pace and directions of reforms at the Union level.

D. Branches of industry*

a. Engineering

The engineering industry, meaning mainly metal-based manufacturing and electronics, is, as already mentioned, the single largest branch in Latvia and Lithuania but comes only third in Estonia. In practice, it is exclusively under all-union control, the most important firms being part of the military–industrial complex. If turnover is measured, Lithuania has over half (52 per cent) of the engineering industry in the Baltics and Latvia more than a third (35 per cent). Estonia has far less (12 per cent). Other comparisons of the republics' shares of the branch have suggested that the Latvian engineering industry is at least as large as the Lithuanian.

The Lithuanian electronics industry is larger and more modern than that in the other two republics. It is closely tied to the military–industrial complex, but much of its production is civilian. Among the major electronic industrial firms with connections to the defence industry are Vilma (tape recorders, electronic components), Volna (military electronics, television)

---

* This section draws heavily on Sandström, 1991.

and Elektronas (antennae), all in Vilnius. In Kaunas and Šiauliai there are a number of television factories belonging to the Banga concern. Other similar firms are Elektronika in Kaunas and Ekranas in Panevežys. There is also a computer firm, Nukleonas, in Šiauliai.

Latvia's electronics industry is concentrated in four of the republic's largest firms, all located in Riga. They are VEF (radio and telecommunication equipment), Radiotehnika (radio equipment), Alfa (computers, integrated circuits) and Komutators (military electronics). VEF is perhaps Latvia's most well-known firm. Already a successful exporter in the 1920s, it has come to symbolise Baltic high-tech potential. Despite having been part of the Soviet military–industrial complex, it now seems clearly oriented towards being part of a republican-led economy, a sentiment not shared by some of the other large firms, such as non-Latvian dominated Alfa.

The much smaller Estonian electronics industry is nevertheless also quite advanced by Soviet standards. RET and H. Pöögelmann in Tallinn produce radio equipment. Baltijets, a large Narva-based firm, produces electronic control equipment. Dvigatel, a large machine-building firm in Tallinn is also a part of the military–industrial complex. The manager of Dvigatel was one of the main leaders of the opposition to Estonian independence. On more than one occasion he organised political protest strikes among the largely non-Estonian Dvigatel workforce of well over 10,000.

The metal-based engineering industry in the Baltic republics is for the most part civilian in character and organisation. This industry has a number of major firms of which most have fallen under all-union ministry authority. In Tallinn these include Volta (electrical motors), Eesti Kaabel (cables), Elektrotehnika (transformers), Tööstusaparaat (measuring instruments), Tallinna Masinatehas (oil-industry equipment), Ilmarine (control equipment for boilers) and Talleks (excavators). In Tartu, the second Estonian city, there is Aparaaditehas (process-control instruments) and Võit (agricultural machinery) and in Pärnu there is Pärnu Masinatehas (food-processing machinery). There are also a number of important shipyards which are mainly engaged in repairs.

In Latvia, the civilian manufacturing industry includes a number of heavy metal-based firms: RAF in Jelgava (minibuses), Rigas elektromasinu rupnica (electrical motors, traction equipment, washing machines), Rigas dizelu rupnica (diesel engines, generators), Rigas vagonu rupnica (tramcars, diesel and electric trains), Kompresors (coolers) and Sarkana Zvaigzne (mopeds). Agricultural machinery is produced in a number of places, among them Riga, Liepaja and Jelgava. In Daugavpils, the Baltic railroads have their main repair workshops. There is also the Milgravis shipyard outside Riga, the largest in the Baltic region.

While Latvia's manufacturing industry is orientated towards heavy machine building, Lithuania's is orientated mainly towards three lighter areas: consumer durables, machine tools and computers. The last is covered by Lithuania's largest concern, Sigma (mainly minicomputers). Altogether, it has around 20,000 employees in a number of plants. Machine tools are made in Zalgiris and Komunaras in Vilnius and at the Dzerzhinsky works in Kaunas. Consumer durables are made in many firms, for example Elfa (tape recorders, small electric motors), Vilnius elektrosvar (welding units, vacuum cleaners) in Vilnius, and Vairas (bicycles, moped motors) in Šiauliai. In Alytus, refrigerators are produced. Mention should also be made of the castings works in Kaunas, the cable works in Panevežys and the three shipyards in Klaipeda.

b. Chemical industry

The chemical industry accounts for 6–7 per cent of overall industrial employment and output. Like the engineering industry, it has mainly been under all-union jurisdiction.

The chemical industry is of greatest relative importance to Estonia. Slant-sechim is the largest plant. There are at least eight plants with a thousand or more employees. The Estonian chemical industry produces plastics, shale-extracted oil, fertilisers, chemical substances, rubber etc. There is also a pharmaceutical factory in Tallinn.

Latvia has a major synthetic-fibre factory in Daugavpils, Kimiska Skiedra. Glass fibre is produced in Valmiera, pharmaceuticals at Olaine, fertiliser at Ventspils and rubber, varnish and paint in Riga.

The major output of the Lithuanian chemical industry is fertiliser, which is produced at Jonava, Lithuania's largest chemical plant, Kaunas and Kedainiai. Synthetic fibres, rubber and plastics are also produced in Kaunas.

Of the relatively insignificant basic metal industries only the Latvian scrap-based steel plant Sarkanais Metalurgs in Liepaja should be mentioned. Its output may exceed 500,000 tons a year.

c. Light industry

Light industry, the production of textiles, clothing, leather goods, shoes etc. is significant in all three Baltic republics, employing about 20 per cent of the industrial workforce. In Estonia, light industry accounts for about 30 per cent of the total industrial output. In Latvia and Lithuania the share is about 20–25 per cent. The Baltic republics export a considerable amount of light-industry consumer goods to other parts of the Soviet Union.

In Estonia light industry comprises about 47 enterprises. Cotton textiles have been produced at Kreenholmi Manufaktuur in Narva since 1857. Cotton fabrics are also produced at Balti Manufaktuur in Tallinn, while linen and wool are woven in the Pärnu area. In Tallinn there is also a significant clothing and shoe industry in companies such as Marat, Klementi, Lembitu and Kommunaar.

Light industry in Latvia comprises about 73 enterprises. Rigas Manufaktura produces cotton fabric, Riga Textils woollen material and the Jelgava-based Latvijas Lini, linen. Riga has a number of clothing factories, among them Rigas Apgerbs, Latvija and the stocking firm Aurora.

Lithuania has over 100 light-industry enterprises. Cotton fabrics are produced in Vilnius, wool and silk fabric in Kaunas and linen in a large plant at Panevežys. The clothing industry comprises a number of firms, among them Geguzes Pirmoji in Kaunas and Sparta and Lelija in Vilnius.

d. Food industry

Baltic agriculture is heavily oriented towards animal husbandry which is reflected in the food industry. Meat and dairy products are by far the most important, but the fish industry is also quite developed.

The Baltic food industry is highly productive and delivers a substantial amount for consumption in the Soviet Union. Official figures show that the Baltic industries' share of milk, cheese, butter, meat and sausage production is in the range of 5–10 per cent of Soviet output. As in the case of light industry, this is 2–3 times the Baltic republics' share of population.

The food-processing industry is described more closely in Chapter 12.

e. Wood and building materials

Forest-based industry has a long tradition in the Baltic republics. The production of pulp has, however, hardly increased since the pre-war period with lack of raw material given as a cause. Many forests are not in good shape, and the paper industry now imports a significant amount of raw material, perhaps around 20 per cent. The branch share of over-all industrial employment (10 per cent) is also larger than share of output (7 per cent), suggesting a low level of productivity. It could, however, be a sector with some potential, at least in the medium term. At present, it supplies 6–7 per cent of the Soviet Union's paper and furniture consumption.

The industry is of largest relative importance to Estonia, where two pulp and paper mills in Tallinn and Kehra provide most of the output. Latvia's major pulp and paper mill is at Sloka. There are also five plants producing paper from imported pulp. In Lithuania, there is only one pulp and paper mill (in Klaipeda) and a couple of paper mills using imported raw material.

The Baltic furniture industry may have export potential. Estonian furniture is already exported to foreign countries. The Estonian furniture manufacturers employ a total of 10,000 people, the two main firms being Standard and Tallinna Vineerija Mööblikombinaat. The number of firms has been small, about ten, but industrial restructuring is creating new and smaller firms. Latvia and Lithuania reportedly have 15 firms each.

Local mineral resources of fairly high quality are the basis for the Baltic building-materials industry. There are a few major cement factories, under all-union jurisdiction, notably at Naujoji Akmene in Lithuania and at Kunda in Estonia. Brick factories, sand and gravel supplies etc. are under republican jurisdiction.

E. Strains on the old system and the emergence of new actors

As the centrally planned Soviet economy is deteriorating, enterprises are forced to take more independent action. This, of course, also applies in the Baltics, where the republican branches of Gosplan and Gossnab have been replaced by ministries of economy and ministries of material resources, respectively. These authorities have, despite current attempts at restructuring, taken over some of the old centralised planning functions, notably the issuing of state orders. These are compulsory, but they also guarantee the supplies needed for production. Although planning directives are no longer issued, the material balances still being set up and the state orders they result in ensure the continued existence of most traditional links between firms.

However, with the widespread crisis in Soviet industry, firms can no longer solely rely on the old links and on state orders to maintain output. Many seek to develop supply networks of their own. Direct exchange of goods between firms are often negotiated as barter trade. Roubles are hardly used for calculation or payments. Clearly, this is a costly form of business. It is not easy to identify suitable exchanges. Firms producing specialised and intermediate goods may find it difficult to find partners willing to engage in barter. Many of the Baltic industries with consumer goods as final output (television sets, radios, other consumer durables, processed foods, textiles and clothes etc.) are in a better position.

While in some ways representing nascent market-economy exchanges, these developments are typical of a period in which the central command economy has broken down and a fully functioning market economy has not emerged to take its place. As well as practical problems in administering and implementing such a complex web of interlocking and possibly conflicting agreements, there is potential for conflict between the direct exchanges and the inter-republic agreements. The latter are an interim measure to ensure the continuation of supplies but they may be used to defend a continuing role for state management, or interference, in these areas. The enterprise-enterprise deals are nascent market exchanges while the republic–republic agreements are a legacy of the planning system, and it is the former which should be allowed to develop further.

Managers in industry now typically spend a lot of time organising supplies and arranging barter deals. With unclear authority and old links no longer to be taken for granted, the role of management has increased. One should not underestimate the importance of managers during the 'period of stagnation', as considerable initiative was needed to secure continued activity of the enterprises. In the present situation their responsibilities are further increasing. The new links now created undermine the old system, and managers emerge as an important group of actors in the economy.

Quite unrelated, but at least as interesting with regard to the emergence of new economic actors; is the appearance of cooperatives, until now the most important form of incipient private enterprise in the Soviet economy. Their rapid growth in number and output is particularly clear in the Baltic republics.

The number of cooperatives has grown very quickly, from a handful in 1987, to several thousand in each republic in 1990. The cooperatives' share of overall republican output and employment is rising fast. These shares vary between the republics but were in the range of 1.6–5.6 per cent in 1989. The cooperative sector is more developed in Estonia and Latvia than in Lithuania but is increasingly important in all three republics. In Lithuania, the cooperative as a special enterprise form has disappeared, a development which may be followed later in Estonia and Latvia.

Table 11.4 Cooperatives: number, employment, turnover, share of overall turnover

	Number of cooperatives	Employment	Turnover (million roubles previous year/ half year)	Share of republican turnover
Estonia				
1 January 1988	256	4,500	8	—
1 January 1989	969	21,500	102	0.9
1 January 1990	2,087	42,100	385	3.3
1 July 1990	2,421	47,100	344	na
Latvia				
1 January 1988	246	5,200	10	—
1 January 1989	1,190	28,700	190	1.0
1 January 1990	4,086	134,800	1,079	5.6
1 July 1990	4,797	158,600	796	na
Lithuania				
1 January 1988	503	5,900	13	—
1 January 1989	1,569	25,500	118	0.5
1 January 1990	4,495	81,400	652	1.6
1 July 1990	4,605	77,900	462	na

Source: Goskomstat, Moscow, 1990.

As shown by Table 11.4, Latvia has the largest cooperative sector. A separate set of Latvian statistics gives a more detailed picture of the cooperatives (see Table 11.5).

The Latvian cooperatives account for a significant part of the national income. In 1989 the share according to these figures was 6.4 per cent. This is very likely to have increased for two reasons. First, the number of cooperatives keeps growing and was, according to the same source, 3,336 in 1990. Second, the scale of the cooperatives seems to be increasing. While the number of cooperatives increased by a factor of four, output increased almost eight-fold. If the 3,336 cooperatives of 1990 produced as much on average as those in 1989 with national income unchanged, the cooperative sector would have contributed almost 10 per cent of national income.

Industry and construction are the largest cooperative activities accounting for 53 and 31 per cent, respectively, net value added, and both branches have very high growth rates. However, the relative importance of other sectors, such as information technology, is particularly interesting to note.

Though cooperatives are important today, they cannot become a dominant future form of enterprise. The cooperative, effectively an embryonic form of private enterprise, is suitable for the quick emergence of new entrepreneurs but for larger production units joint-stock companies will be needed. Some of the first legal projects of the new Baltic governments in 1990 were to establish the legal framework for joint-stock companies.

Table 11.5 Latvian cooperatives: number and output

	1988	1989	Rate of change
Number of cooperatives	531	2,250	4.2 times
Turnover, roubles (m)	88	824	9.4 times
Net production, roubles (m)	62	486	7.8 times
Share of total republican turnover (%)	0.5	4.3	—
Share of total republican national income (NMP) (%)	0.9	6.4	—

Source: Latvian Statistical Committee, 1990.

Table 11.6 Latvian cooperatives: output per branch, 1989

	Measured by turnover			Measured by net value added		
	Roubles (m)	Share of republ. total (%)	Growth from 1989 (times)	Roubles (m)	Share of republ. total (%)	Growth from 1989 (times)
Industry	501	4.3	11.4	259	7.5	9.8
Construction	212	13.9	14.8	151	20.3	13.5
Agriculture	17	0.4	2.0	10	0.5	1.2
Retail trade, restaurants etc.	24	3.9	3.6	19	3.9	3.8
Wholesale trade etc.	21	31.5	2.4	15	27.1	2.3
Information technology	33	37.6	—	20	35.2	—
Others	15	13.6	2.2	13	16.6	2.6
Total production	824	4.3	9.1	486	6.4	7.6

Source: Latvian Statistical Committee, 1990.

When Soviet authorities allowed the creation of joint ventures in 1988, some of the first were set up in the Baltic republics. Their number has expanded quickly, particularly in Estonia. As can be seen from Table 11.7, the expansion is still continuing. However, the Baltic authorities have not given any special support to the joint ventures. Instead they wish to create opportunities for all joint-stock companies to have foreign owners and business relations with foreign companies. In Lithuania, the creation of new joint ventures has not been encouraged.

Estonia has the largest number of joint ventures, mainly owing to the development of foreign economic relations, particularly with Finland and Sweden, in the late 1980s. While Estonia is now developing its own foreign-

Box 11.1 A Latvian cooperative: seeking new opportunities

Fifty kilometres east of Riga, on the banks of the Daugava, a cooperative is exploring the new business opportunities that are appearing in Latvia. Its range of activity, its progress and problems will give a brief illustration of how cooperatives can work.

Under the leadership of the dynamic manager, the chairman of the cooperative, a quite large and very diverse enterprise has been created. The basis is a house, rented from the local authorities, which step-by-step is being turned into a country resort hotel. That was the main business idea.

In the meantime, however, the cooperative is engaging in a very wide range of activities. The cooperative repairs agricultural machinery. Bargain broken-down equipment is brought from kolkhozes, state firms or the military and given new life. The metalwork shop fixes most things. One employee has specialised in wrought-iron fences. Most workers are paid wages tied to productivity, but this smith has an arrangement more like a subcontractor. In the basement, where the swimming pool is going to be, simple furniture is put together from a batch of second-rate fibre board, obtained at cut rate from a state board factory. On the top floor, in the dining-room-to-be, twenty seamstresses are sewing cotton and linen clothing. One of them is also a nurse, who is ready to treat work accidents in a specially furnished room. In another bedroom-to-be, a woman sews fur hats, also more or less on a subcontractor basis. In yet another room, there is a pile of cases with shampoo, received as part of a barter deal, now being sold off.

One major output used to be gloves. However, after the major price rises on food items in January 1991, demand has fallen, and the cooperative is now planning to switch into other markets, mainly food-processing. The cooperative has close relations with a nearby sovkhoz, from where it would be able to buy grain and other produce. Many of the sovkhozes and the kolkhozes are expected to be reorganised and turned into joint-stock companies. These changes are welcomed by the manager, as they will bring new business opportunities.

The new system of Latvian taxes has significantly raised labour costs for the cooperative. Especially the 'social tax', set at 37 per cent of the wage bill, is seen as too heavy. The cooperative has petitioned the government to reduce the tax burden. In order to reduce the wage bill, but also in order to concentrate on the most profitable business activities, the cooperative is planning to reduce the labour force of 600 by at least half.

This cooperative also proposes to engage in a joint venture with a firm in Denmark, exporting wood and wood products and bringing in wood-working machines. In another trade 'chain', the cooperative sells Russian wood in Moldavia, in exchange for high-quality Moldavian brandy which is sold in Riga.

Table 11.7 Joint ventures (thousands of valuta roubles)

	1 January 1990				1 July 1990			
	No. of joint ventures	Exp.	Imp.	Sales (Soviet market)	No. of joint ventures	Exp.	Imp.	Sales (Soviet market)
Estonia	91	3,285	7,947	4,097	105	2,861	3,967	2,748
Latvia	30	1,122	4,706	1,528	47	2,884	1,234	498
Lithuania	13	989	2,204	991	18	541	3,057	2,627

Source: Goskomstat Moscow, 1990.

Table 11.8 Major sources of foreign capital in Estonian joint ventures, April 1991

Country	No. of enterprises	Country	Foreign capital (US$ m)
Finland	137	Sweden	24.1
Sweden	39	Finland	21.8
Soviet Union	35	Yugoslavia	10.6
Germany	17	United States	1.7
United States	12	Austria	1.0
Canada	6	Germany	0.9
Austria	6	Soviet Union	15.5 (roubles)

Source: Estonian State Department for Foreign Economic Relations, 1991.

Table 11.9 Source countries for foreign capital in Estonian joint-stock companies, April 1991

Country	No. of enterprises	Country	Total capital (million roubles)	Share of foreign capital (%)
Finland	136	Sweden	23.9	62.1
Soviet Union	49	Soviet Union	7.1	20.9
Sweden	95	Finland	3.2	9.4
United States	14	Latvia	0.9	2.6
Germany	9	Gibraltar	0.5	1.5
Canada	6	United States	0.3	0.9
Norway	6	Canada	0.2	0.5

Source: Estonian State Department for Foreign Economic Relations, 1991.

investment legislation, most foreign investment has been regulated by the Soviet joint-venture law of January 1987.

A pointer to the possible future role of foreign capital in industrial restructuring is given by the active promotion of foreign investment in Estonia. The

State Department for Foreign Economic Relations distinguishes two organisational forms involving foreign partners: foreign joint ventures and joint-stock companies with foreign participation. It collects extensive data on both. These show that the rate of investment was maintained in spite of the deepening economic problems of 1990. Of the 267 joint ventures established in Estonia by April 1991, about half had been established in 1987–9. There are three kinds of capital involved in joint ventures: domestic Estonian, Soviet (plus Latvian and Lithuanian) and foreign. These firms had a total capital of 153.5 million roubles, of which the Soviet–Latvian–Lithuanian share was 15.5 million roubles (10.1 per cent) and the other foreign share was 61.7 million roubles or US$ 66 m. (40.2 per cent). Foreign partners came from thirty-two countries, with the top seven based on number and value of capital illustrated in Table 11.8.

There were 327 corporations with foreign capital registered by April 1991. These were said to have a total capital of 69.2 million roubles, of which the Soviet–Latvian–Lithuanian share was 8 million roubles and the other foreign share was 25.7 million roubles or US$ 48.2 m. Of the Estonian share, 23 per cent was held by private individuals. There was participation from 23 foreign countries, the seven most important are shown in Table 11.9.

Box 11.2 Laiks and Larossa: gateway enterprising in Riga

Two Riga-based joint ventures illustrate well the business idea that many Latvians cherish, that of being a trade link between East and West.

Founded in 1988, Laiks was the first Latvian joint venture. It was created by a group of mathematicians and other scientists from the Academy of Sciences. The idea of joining Western computer hardware with local software proved very successful. Laiks sells its services for hard currency to firms all over the Soviet Union. As much as 40 per cent of output consists of exports to the West, mainly specialised Soviet-produced materials, components and instruments. Laiks recently chose to change its foreign partner — as with many joint ventures it found the first partner not living up to expectations. It would like to shed its character of joint venture altogether and become a joint-stock company. In practice, it is already a holding company, with 'subsidiaries' in St. Petersburg, Erevan, Odessa, Krasnoyarsk and Novosibirsk. When economic reform gets seriously under way, Laiks is confident of having good business prospects.

Larossa is another joint venture that intends to exploit Riga's position as a gateway for Western business links with the Soviet Union. Using the large state-owned resources of Riga harbour, Latvian shipping, Baltic railways and civil aviation with American and Korean capital, the idea is to organise special transport services for those Western companies wishing to engage in Soviet trade. Specifically, it sees the potential of linking the West, through Riga, by air or rail with

Vladivostok and the Pacific region. To the management of Larossa, Latvian political and economic sovereignty, which it has clearly supported, is not a contradiction to its aim of having close business relations with the Soviet Union. Obviously, the prospects for Larossa depend to a great degree on successful developments in the Soviet Union. Its prospects are also particularly dependent on the Soviet Union, since its strategy is based on using key parts of the infrastructure presently under Union control.

Laiks and Larossa both exemplify the pragmatism of new entrepreneurship in the Baltic republics. As traders with both East and West they are obviously dependent on orderly political and economic relations developing between the emerging independent republics and the Soviet Union, and between the Soviet Union and the West.

Box 11.3 Swedish business links with Estonia

Swedish business has shown a remarkable interest in the Baltic republics and especially in Estonia. Virtually no links existed before the summer of 1988. Now, contacts have developed in all sectors, including banking, insurance and branch organisations.

The reason for the strong interest in Estonia is partly historical and partly owing to the strong community in Sweden of Estonian descent. Estonia's proximity to Finland and the earlier economic reform experiments in Estonia contributed in exposing Estonia to international business practices and has given it an edge over Latvia and Lithuania. No doubt access to Tallinn by the Nordic mobile telephone system is an important asset.

In order to channel business information, a joint Swedish–Estonian Business Council was set up in June 1989. To meet the demand of Swedish industry, the Swedish Trade Council opened an office in Tallinn in May 1990.

The import potential of Estonia is very limited. Thus, the office is often engaged in arranging longer-term deals, involving the mutual exchange of goods and services. The office also believes there is a good potential in subcontracting to Estonian firms component production for Swedish companies. Sectors with considerable potential seem to be forestry, wood working and furniture, light mechanical industry, textiles and infrastructure.

According to the Swedish Trade Council, interest in Estonia has surpassed all expectations, although actual business deals still mean very little to Swedish industry. Most Swedish companies seeking contacts with Estonia are small and medium-sized firms, which lack earlier experience in the Eastern European market. The larger corporations have been more hesitant, partly because of the small size of the Estonian market but also because of the links many of them still have to the Soviet foreign-trade organisations.

A major impediment to business is the unclear legal and institutional setting. Another obvious problem is financing and the handling of foreign exchange, though much ingenuity goes into circumventing official regulations. The most frequent complaints from Swedish businessmen regard situations where the Estonian partner is perceived as not living up to its responsibilities in timing, quality or simply in correspondence.

Nevertheless, the number of deals has grown. April 1991 estimates from the Estonian Department of Foreign Economic Relations indicate that Sweden has become Estonia's most important business partner by share of foreign capital invested.

F. Future industrial strategy

In considering future industrial strategy the Baltic governments will have to seek out a balance between handling the problems of industrial enterprises, as they exist today, and creating the conditions necessary for the creation of a transformed industrial sector.

In the introduction to this chapter, it was emphasised that as the Baltic economies opened up to international trade and shifted to a decentralised market system, detailed decisions affecting the future of industry such as investments in new capacity would shift from the central planning mechanism to the enterprise.

In time, industrial ventures would succeed or fail depending on their flexibility in responding to market opportunities. The task of government in relation to industrial strategy would correspondingly shift, from detailed programming of the industrial sector, to the adjustment of policy instruments which would indirectly influence industrial enterprises by their effect on the incentive system. Thus the government's attention should shift to tax and tariff policies, provision of services, development of credit facilities and related interest policies, and promotional activities; the old notion that investment in industry could be programmed centrally to achieve future outputs targets derived from the plan must be discarded.

However, while this should be maintained as a vision of the future role of government, for a considerable time a large part of the existing state sector is likely to remain in the public sector, so that for some time to come the government will continue to find itself in the role of the owner of significant segments of the industrial sector. Moreover, despite the intention to shift to a market economy, in the transitional period, for reasons which have been spelt out throughout this volume, chaotic conditions in the Soviet Union are likely to require the republican authorities to continue substantial direct interventions and administrative allocations.

The balance to be struck is between the need to continue to operate some of the elements of the old central planning system and the need to implement steps to dismantle it. Even if the state succeeds in reducing its direct involvement in the industrial sector there will remain a challenging set of tasks to improve the infrastructure necessary for the efficient operation of the sector.

To guide policy in this period, it may be advantageous to define an industrial strategy, in the sense of clearly identifying the goals of industrial policy and the instruments for pursuing them, rather than defining quantitative targets. The broad goals of industrial policy are likely to be to create an industrial sector which can contribute to the growth of a high-income economy, with an increasing degree of autonomy from the Soviet Union, capable of repaying maximum benefits from participation in international trade while avoiding environmental degradation.

How can these goals be pursued? The possibilities can be addressed at two levels: the organisation of industry and the future structure of output.

a. The organisation of industry

The analysis throughout this volume has suggested that the typical Soviet (and therefore Baltic) industrial enterprise is too large and too little specialised, in the sense that within the enterprise many activities are undertaken which, in a more sophisticated and flexible structure, would be subcontracted.

Because of uncertanties and absence of effective incentives, materials and workers are hoarded. The lack of specialisation in terms of industrial processes is combined with a high degree of specialisation in final output at each enterprise, according to the demands of the central plan.

The diagnosis suggests the cure. Enterprises initially need to become smaller and leaner. Many subsidiary service activities need to be shed. There needs to be a shake-out, reducing labour and inventories, the selling off of unneeded plants and equipment. And firms need to have the freedom to adjust their product line to take advantage of new market opportunities. At the same time, the most important part of the market, for the medium term, will continue to be the Soviet market, so that there will be an ongoing need to relate to that market through whatever mix of state negotiated deals and barter transactions that proves workable, given the Soviet developments.

The basic requirements for organisation in the transitional period involve four steps:

1. the re-organisation of the government apparatus with the dissolution of ministries responsible for industrial branches having powers of detailed control over enterprises and replacement by a ministry of industry with broad controls over industrial policy;
2. the creation of intermediaries between the new ministry and enterprises which would be responsible for exercising the ownership rights over publicly owned industrial enterprises (for example through holding companies) to which enterprise managers would be answerable for performance and who would supervise capital budgeting;
3. the delegation to the enterprise management considerable initiative in the day-to-day running of enterprises, industry freedom to hire and fire, set prices and adjust inputs and outputs — subject to performance against clearly defined criteria set out by the holding company; and

4. subjecting enterprises to a hard-budget constraint by tightening the credit system and implementing macroeconomic policies to tighten market demand.

At the same time government policies should continue to encourage private business and, in particular, to push the public sector to make use of and provide opportunities for private firms where these make economic sense.

In other words, the basic tactic should be to promote widespread piecemeal improvements and structural change at the enterprise level, so that there will be a steady increase in the efficiency and flexibility of the industrial enterprise.

b. The future structure of output

While it is important to emphasise that any efficient pattern of industrial activity will emerge from decisions made at the enterprise level and is inherently unpredictable at the centre, some of the likely prospects are discernible and will have implications for a number of aspects of government policy.

Given the lack of basic raw materials, including energy supplies, the excessive levels of existing industrial pollution and limited labour supply, the future comparative advantage of the Baltic republics is not likely to lie in the direction of material-intensive, high-energy using industry nor labour-intensive mass production.

If there are a number of negative factors working against certain types of industrial specialisation, there are other positive factors which suggest future lines of development. The earlier description in this chapter indicated that the Baltic republics already have relatively highly developed skill-intensive industries (for example electronics).

Also, if the Soviet Union opens up to world trade, the Baltic economies have a potential locational advantage as a gateway between the Soviet Union and the rest of the world. Although the Baltics have a weak natural resource base, there are some subsectors in which existing primary industries provide a basis for increasing value added in industry — notably food-processing (particularly livestock products) and woodworking.

The vision of an industrial future as a high-tech, high valued-added economy, geared partly to production for world markets and partly acting as an intermediary between the Soviet Union and the rest of the world, is being developed throughout the Baltics as a guide to an industrial strategy.

It has a number of implications for policy. If the industrial future of the Baltic economies is to be based on highly skilled lighter industry, policies are needed to maximise the mobilisation of available skills. This will involve skilled manpower transferring to new tasks, both by enterprises shifting their focus, and innovative professionals setting up new ventures, which may require new institutions to provide venture capital.

It will also be necessary to take action to improve the pool of available skilled manpower. There is some danger that the repeated comparisons which are made between the sophistication of the Baltic labour force and the rest of the Soviet Union could lead to a certain complacency. If the Baltic economies are to achieve the niche being sought in the international economy, and even maintain their positions in the Soviet market if it opens up, then the comparison with the Soviet Union will become increasingly irrelevant. The Baltic economies will have to compete with the low-cost producers in international markets — in electronics, for example, design and engineering skills will have to match those of east and south Asia.

Engineering, scientific and business professional education will need to aim at a high level, and the current generation of technologists, designers and businessmen will need to be exposed much more to international conditions than has so far been possible.

In relation to the future of Baltic industry as an intermediary between the Soviet Union and the rest of the world, negotiation of a political settlement should seek to provide access by Baltic industry to Soviet markets but increasingly on terms reflecting international market prices. Independent Baltic economies could aim to play a similar economic role in relation to their powerful Soviet neighbour as the Benelux countries have in relation to their powerful German neighbour. If other political tensions do not preclude the possibility of rational economic negotiations, future exchanges between Baltic and Soviet industry could be a 'positive sum game', beneficial to both sides.

Probably the most difficult aspects of future industrial policy relate not so much to promoting new growth sectors but rather to the phasing out of redundant activities. In particular, under conditions of crisis numerous decisions may need to be made as to whether enterprises should be helped to survive immediate difficulties, because long-term prospects are positive, or allowed to go bankrupt, with any available resources being used to ameliorate the lot of redundant workers.

Some estimates of possible unemployment are recorded in Chapter 9. There is no way of knowing how realistic such estimates are. All that can be said at this stage is that industrial restructuring will require very substantial shifts in labour. There will be no virtue in disguising the need for or postponing restructuring by subsidising workers in jobs with no future.

G. Policies in the outside world

The uncertainties about economic and political developments in the Soviet Union and in the Baltic states have made short-term prospects for foreign commercial investment poor. However, even in the present situation there are some opportunities for business development that go beyond arbitrage for quick profits.

Business people active in the Baltic republics have found they can operate around the political complications. There are impressive examples (though only a few) of joint ventures in both transport and research-intensive export production in which ethnic Russians work alongside Latvians and Estonians and operate with business partners in other republics.

The opportunities for freight-transport business, possibly including Scandinavia–Central Europe traffic as well as East–West and West–East, are considerable. The joint-venture in Riga mentioned in Box 11.3 shows that it is possible to develop a successful science-based export product, combining skills located in Latvia with production facilities in several other parts of the Soviet Union. The main restriction seems to be that the production should not require either large production areas or large primary-resource inputs.

Such possibilities could well expand as Moscow withdraws military-related production from the region. This is especially true for Latvia. Both skills and production capacity should become more readily available, alongside the scattering of research excellence that already exist in the civilian sector — mainly in the academies of sciences.

It would be open to Western governments, Chambers of Commerce and trade associations to contribute to this sort of development by cooperating with the new firms and Chambers of Commerce in the Baltic republics to publicise opportunities of this kind.

Other forms of technical assistance (by Western governments) that look particularly appropriate include: provision of professional training in law, accounting and economics, as well as management training; the organised diffusion of best-practice know-how in public-sector assistance to small-business development; and the sponsoring of short courses and seminars that bring together specialists, officials and business people from all the Baltic republics; and courses, seminars and visits in which Hungarian and Polish experience, for example, are communicated.

In general, in Western government assistance programmes, it should be possible to cultivate direct links with Baltic organisations and organise training and other projects with them, without going through the central Soviet authorities. There is a strong case for doing this with respect to grass-roots and republic-level activities in the Soviet Union, as a general principle and not only a policy targetted at the Baltic republics.

Short of explicit recognition of the Baltic republics, this approach seems feasible with respect to Western government and multilateral programmes of technical assistance and project aid. It obviously cannot be applied to general balance-of-payments credits to the Soviet Union.

12 Agriculture, forestry and fishing

A. Background

Agriculture is sure to remain a vital sector in the economies of all three Baltic republics, accounting for a significant share of production and trade. The future of agriculture will be strongly affected by the answer to three questions. First, how can farmers cope with the sharp curtailment in material inputs, reflecting the general Soviet supply crisis? Second, what kinds of systemic changes are likely to occur related to land tenure and agricultural organisation? Third, to what extent will the Soviet Union continue to represent the principal market for agricultural exports? Before addressing these questions, however, the historical background and the underlying factors conditioning agricultural potential are discussed.

Before World War I, all three republics had large landed estates. In Latvia and Estonia the landlords were mainly German 'Baltic barons'. With independence came land reform and the dominance of peasant proprietors. By the standards of the time, agriculture performed well and much food, especially meat and butter, was exported to Great Britain and to Germany.

When the Soviets first occupied the Baltic states in 1939–40 and after their return in 1944–5, they promised to respect the rights and interests of peasant smallholders. (The same line was followed in Czechoslovakia, Hungary and elsewhere.) However, in 1949–50 these promises were broken, and collectivisation was imposed. Direct resistance was strongest in Lithuania, where the 'forest brothers' endured until Stalin's death. But there, as in Latvia and Estonia, deportations, arrests and threats compelled the acceptance of the inevitable.

From 1950 until the most recent years agriculture was organised on standard Soviet lines. There were three categories of producers, distinguished by their property relations: kolkhozes (collective farms, nominally a cooperative with an elected management), sovkhozes (state farms, with an appointed management), plus the household plots and private livestock in the possession of rural and suburban families. Members of these families normally also worked for kolkhozes and sovkhozes. The size of the plots and numbers of private animals were, until recently, strictly limited (for example one cow, one sow, no horse).

In practice, the kolkhoz manager ('chairman') was a party nominee, and the farm had to fulfil plans, as did the state farm. It is now accepted even by the official Soviet media that the kolkhozes were pseudo-cooperatives. Until the late sixties the peasant members (unlike the state-employed sovkhoz workers) had no guaranteed minimum income, their pay depending on what was left over after all other financial and delivery obligations had been met. First priority was given to the delivery of a quota of produce to the state, at prices which were for many years far below production costs.

After Stalin's death, policy changed. Procurement prices were increased several times, much more was invested in agriculture and in industries serving agriculture. Performance improved but at quite a disproportionate cost. Inefficiency could no longer be blamed on low prices and neglect. (In Stalin's time the aim was to extract resources from agriculture for the benefit of heavy industry; but from at least the early seventies higher procurement prices, with unchanged retail food prices, plus much higher state investment, led to the emergence of ever-higher net subsidies to agriculture.) What were the basic defects of the system which could not be remedied by throwing money at them?

First, the negative attitude of the peasantry within very large farms. Alienated from the soil, ordered about by officials, treated as day labourers, with little visible connection between effort and result, it proved all but impossible to devise effective labour incentives. As a Soviet observer remarked: in the old days the peasants reasoned, 'why should we work, we will not be paid'. Now they reason, 'why should we work, we will be paid anyway'. Quite different was their attitude to work on the household plot.

Kolkhozes and sovkhozes traditionally have suffered from the poor quality of machinery and equipment, the frequent non-availability of machines which relate to the special needs of the region and a chronic shortage of spare parts. (A prominent editor of a party journal referred to 'painted scrap-iron proudly misnamed "agricultural machinery"'.) While much more fertiliser came to be available, it was often of the wrong kind. In all these respects agriculture was the victim of the failure of industry to respond to demand.

Another notorious deficiency has been infrastructure. Insufficient storage space and packaging materials, refrigeration, specialised transport and so on. There has also been severe criticism of social infrastructure: lack of amenities, poor schools and deficient housing caused the energetic to migrate to town.

Finally much damage has been done by bureaucratic interference. Farms have received orders about what to grow, when to sow, what animals to keep. They have been ordered to build huge uneconomic livestock complexes. Various service agencies (for example for repairs, supplies, 'chemicalisation', drainage) tried to fulfil their own plans in roubles instead of serving the needs of farms. To overcome this deficiency, in 1982 a new agro–industrial hierarchy was created. Though modified in 1985, Agroprom proved to be a clumsy and bureaucratic coordinating agency and was finally eliminated in 1989. Jokes circulated in Moscow to the effect that it was the creation of the CIA!

All the above weaknesses and defects have been known for decades and freely criticised in the official press. Remedies included the encouragement of small-group contracts and (after 1987) of family leases. Many farms undertook joint-processing activities or set up construction brigades. Limitations on numbers of private animals were relaxed. But change was slow, and kolkhozes and sovkhozes were able to retain the bulk of cultivatable land, despite pressures to allow family farms to develop.

Within this unpromising institutional environment, the Baltic republics did

Table 12.1 Grain harvest (centners per hectare)

	1981–5	1987
Soviet Union	14.9	18.3
Estonia	26.1	32.3
Latvia	21.5	29.9
Lithuania	23.6	31.7

Source: Goskomstat.

Table 12.2 Milk yields, 1987 (litres per cow)

Soviet Union average	2,682
Estonia	4,103
Latvia	3,525
Lithuania	3,632

Source: Goskomstat.

Table 12.3 Collective farm workers' pay, 1988 (roubles per month)

Soviet Union	161.8
Estonia	304.9
Latvia	243.1
Lithuania	223.9

Source: Goskomstat.

better than most. Recovering from the damage done by compulsory and brutal collectivisation, already in the seventies they (especially Estonia) outperformed all the other republics. The same was true in the eighties (with the exception, for grain, in 1988, when the weather was very unfavourable). This is indicated by grain harvest figures as shown in Table 12.1.

The same picture emerges for milk yields per cow as may be seen in Table 12.2.

Peasants, especially collective farm workers, were much better paid, again especially in Estonia. The 1988 figures given in Table 12.3 are typical.

The question arises: why did the Baltic republics do better? The answer appears to be as follows: first, the peasant spirit survived since they were collectivised in 1950, not 1930. Also most continued to live in farmsteads, despite orders from Moscow that they should move to compact village settlements. Compared to Russia, fewer young people abandoned the countryside. Commitment to honest work survived.

Second, the local party chiefs, especially in Estonia, were able to protect the farms from an excessive number of orders and delivery plans. After all, agricultural successes could help careers in the party hierarchy (or there could have been genuine commitment to minimise damage to fellow-countrymen). The Estonian party leader persuaded Moscow to allocate more material inputs to that republic, since it was frequently visited by Finns and other Baltic foreigners and therefore should be a showpiece; the former Latvian party secretary was much less helpful.

Finally, success was both cause and effect of the much higher-than-average rates of pay. In Estonia, kolkhoz peasants earned much more than the average industrial worker, and this excluded income from family plots.

B. Basic conditions for agriculture

In the Baltics, the climate is maritime with 170–200 days of vegetation and 600–800 millimetres of precipitation annually, the least precipitation falling in the eastern districts.

Relatively good soils are found in Estonia, with the best agricultural district in the central parts, and the least fertile soils in the southeast. In the northern and western parts, the soils are stony and the soilbed thin.

Soils in Latvia are generally less fertile, often sandy or loamy podzols. East and west of the Gulf of Riga soils are light and acid. The most fertile region with carbonatic soils stretches south from Riga down to Lithuania.

Lithuania can be divided into three agricultural regions: the western, central and southeastern regions. In the western region there are light soils close to the Baltic Sea and a lot of acid podzol soils. Typical crops are grain, potatoes and flax. In the central flat region the soils are carbonatic and more fertile. Common crops are sugar beet and flax. The eastern region is hilly and the soils are diverse but generally poorer. Potatoes, fodder crops and rye predominate. In Lithuania in 1990 63 per cent of the agricultural land had been drained over the past thirty years. Melioration has been less intensive in Latvia and in Estonia.

Agriculture in the Baltic republics is by tradition and also owing to Soviet division of labour focused on livestock production. Even by international standards livestock production per capita is very high.

The structure of animal production is similar in the three republics. The main exception is that pork production in Latvia and Lithuania more often takes place in large specialised units, while in Estonia pork is produced in ordinary state and collective farms. In Latvia and Lithuania there are several pork production complexes that produce more than 5,000 tons live weight annually. In all three republics poultry and egg production is concentrated in large and mechanised units. In Estonia more than 50 per cent of the cows are in herds of more than 400 on state and collective farms. Rapidly developing private farming will probably alter this structure considerably. For example, by 1990 almost one-third of the cows in Latvia were in private ownership.

Statistics on livestock herds and main animal products are presented in Tables 12.5–8. By Soviet standards productivity is good, but it is modest by Western standards. Though fodder conversion ratios are much better than in other parts of the Soviet Union, there is scope for improvement. The slightly higher productivity in Estonia is probably owing to better feed rations and a genetically better herd of cattle and pigs. As many as 98 per cent of the cows and heifers are artificially inseminated in this republic. Productivity in Latvia lags slightly behind the two other republics. For the whole region, live cattle and pigs are an important export to other Soviet republics.

Relative to the rest of the Soviet Union, basic conditions for animal production are good. Competent management and a high sanitary level leaves the Baltics without serious diseases such as tuberculosis and brucellosis that are found further east and south. Veterinary preparates are imported via Moscow, but are now becoming more and more difficult to find.

Livestock production is presently facing serious difficulties, the gravest being shortage of fodder. Over the years, at least 30–40 per cent of the grain and most of the protein concentrates used in the republics has been from other regions. A serious problem today is that deliveries are being reduced. Production and herds decreased a few per cent in 1990 and are likely to decrease more sharply in 1991. There are estimates that pork production will be reduced by 20 per cent and milk by more than 10 per cent in Estonia in 1991. Priority is now being given to the largest and most efficient pork, breeding-stock and poultry production units. In the longer run, the lower amounts of feed grain and protein are likely to lead to a reorientation from pigs to cattle.

Even before the present feed problems, the protein content of the fodder was too low. With a higher protein concentration, animal productivity would increase considerably. One obvious way to improve the protein situation would be to start cultivation of rapeseed.

Plant production is used mainly for feed. While perennial and annual grasses and barley are the dominant crops, rye and potatoes are the most important crops for human consumption.

Shortage of feed grain and protein concentrates is an acute problem. All republics plan to increase grain production. In Estonia the plan is to increase the acreage devoted to grain to 50–60 per cent of arable land, while in Latvia the aim is to intensify production rather than increase acreage. Rapeseed cultivation would increase protein supply and would also be a source of vegetable oil, which is not produced in the region. At present there are no oil-extraction facilities to make use of the rapeseed oil for human consumption. Another problem is lack of adapted cultivars.

Sugarbeet is an important crop in Latvia and especially in Lithuania, but it is not cultivated in Estonia. In Lithuania there are plans to increase beet production significantly. Flax production is also important but like beet cultivation, it faces problems with mechanisation.

A large proportion of all fruit, berries, potatoes and vegetables is produced on private plots. Flower production is more prominent in Latvia and Estonia than in other Soviet republics.

Yield levels are found in Tables 12.5–7. Though these levels are acceptable from a Soviet perspective, there is ample room for improvement. Modern fungicides would probably markedly increase grain output, but at present their use is even decreasing.

Owing to the intensive animal production a large part of total nutrients comes from manure. More than twelve tons of organic matter per hectare of arable land is applied annually. In spite of this, the main soil nutrition problem is that too little phosphorus is applied to the predominantly low-phosphorus soils.

One particular problem is the low-quality Soviet machinery, which is holding back yield improvement. The most striking example is that the combines leave more than 20 per cent of the grain harvests on the fields.

The most serious environmental problem caused by agriculture is the leakage of nutrients from badly handled manure. Particularly serious is the situation at the huge pork production complexes.

Agricultural research in each republic is concentrated in institutes (2 in Estonia, 4 in Latvia and 7 in Lithuania) subordinated to the Ministries of Agriculture. Several state farms are attached to the institutes. Some research also takes place at the Agricultural Academies in Tartu (Estonia), Jelgava (Latvia) and Kaunas (Lithuania) where all agricultural specialists get their education. In Kaunas there is also a Veterinary Academy. Middle-level specialists are taught in technical colleges.

There is some cooperation developing between the Baltic republics on agricultural research. For example, plant breeding is coordinated.

Tractor drivers, milking personnel and other agricultural workers are taught in secondary schools in most of the districts. Some of these schools have started to reform their curriculum, but the experience is of course limited. A particular problem is the lack of proper education for individual farmers.

C. Organisation and privatisation of agricultural production

The ministries of agriculture are responsible for food supply and agricultural production at the republican level. In Estonia and Lithuania there are agricultural offices run by local administrative bodies. In Latvia the ministry has district offices. These offices supervise the district's deliveries of agricultural produce and the distribution of centrally allocated inputs. At the district level there is usually a producers' union, representing the interests of state and collective farms, and a district organisation of the farmers' union which take part in discussions and negotiations.

Statistics on state and collective farms are given in Table 12.8. State and collective farms are larger in Estonia and Latvia than in Lithuania.

Owing to comparatively high prices of animal products, state and collective farms have often had good financial results. Debts are small. The present price increases of farm inputs will, however, present difficulties for the agricultural producers. Newly introduced land and payroll taxes will also add to their costs. Some kinds of production will no longer be profitable. In 1991 many state and collective farms in the region will face difficulties in meeting their wage bills. Investments are decreasing dramatically. Consequently, there is strong pressure on the governments to increase procurement prices even more and to reduce the taxes.

State and collective farms have developed a small-scale industry of their own. In Lithuania 10 per cent of their profits are from non-food production. As a consequence of the expected privatisation of land, the farms now intensify investment into food-processing and other industrial activities.

A visit to a collective farm near Riga showed the still high degree of dependence on the government, now mostly the Latvian government. Procurement prices are fixed by the Latvian ministry, as are the quantities of grain, milk and meat deliveries. This farm keeps large numbers of fur-bearing animals, which are also subject to a delivery quota from the state at prices well below market prices. (The farm uses over-quota furs to barter with the Ukraine for grain, and exports some via the all-union fur trust.)

Private plots of state and collective farm workers are an important source of agricultural products such as fruit, potatoes, vegetables, milk and meat. Private production is most developed in Lithuania where 30 per cent of the meat and more than 40 per cent of the milk is produced in the private sector. In Estonia 10–15 per cent of the milk and meat is currently produced in the private sector. However, the worsening feed-supply situation has a negative effect on production. Until the beginning of 1991 private animal production was stimulated by state and collective farms, which had an incentive to deliver feed, organise transport, insemination etc. to private owners as they could profit from price differences by reselling the output at bonus prices.

Privatisation of state and collective farms is presently the subject of intense discussions and law-making in the republics. Most of the land may soon be divided among private farmers and groups of farmers. Privatisation of other agricultural production facilities is also under consideration.

In Estonia a law on land to be discussed in Parliament in 1991 may give the people the opportunity to own land with the restriction that it has to be farmed for five to ten years before it can be sold and then only to the state. Not more than 10 per cent of the agricultural land is envisaged to be farmed by state farms in the future. Latvia has acted more promptly. A land reform has already been launched and before 20 June 1991 would-be land users are supposed to have applied for land. Lithuania is seeking to establish a legal basis that will swiftly reintroduce private ownership of land. All republics give first priority to those who previously owned land.

The restoration of private farming has been launched in all three republics. Thus in Estonia there are now well over 4,000 farmsteads, averaging 26 hectares, while in 1989 there were only 1,053. In Latvia the number exceeds 7,500, with holdings of 150,000 hectares. In January 1991 there were 4,000 private farms in Lithuania with 65,000 hectares of agricultural land. But all this is but a fraction of cultivated land. Thus, Latvia for example, had 120,000 farmsteads in 1939. Most of the new private farmers are heirs of former private farmers.

The Lithuanian situation sheds some light on the privatisation process. The new law on land reform expected to be adopted in spring 1991 may differ from the Estonian and Latvian laws. First, most of the land will be made private property immediately and second, pre-war landowners who choose not to reclaim land will be compensated. Earlier owners and their heirs have first priority to reclaim land, but as in the other republics, they have to farm the land acquired. Second priority is given to those now working on state and collective farms, while others can apply for the remaining land. Both these groups apparently will have to pay for the land.

Land commissions have been set up to determine who should get what land, a process complicated by claims from former owners, some of whom have no intention of undertaking serious farming. Some of the claimants may have part-time 'hobby' farming in mind. There is a concern that holdings may be too small to be economic under modern conditions. The biggest private farm in Estonia supposedly covers 182 hectares, of which 86 hectares is cultivated (the rest is forest, meadow, etc), but this is quite exceptional.

The reorganisation of agriculture seems to have slowed down in recent months because of serious shortages: of credit, of building materials and of suitable machinery and equipment.

To set up as a private farmer, even if one has an actual homestead to work from, requires considerable initial expenditure, and the republican budget and banks cannot quickly provide the large sums that are needed. But more frustrating still is the fact that money, even if obtained, cannot buy what is needed.

There is also a mixed reaction on the part of the peasants themselves. Some certainly wish to undertake the hard work and accept the risks of family farming. But many have been earning quite well in collective or state farms and have no great desire to change — the more so because of uncertainty about supplies and prices of inputs, of access to markets (see below) and basic political uncertainty. Clearly, in the immediate future the bulk of output will still originate in the collective and state sectors. But here the management operates under great uncertainty: at any time some of their land could be taken for private farming, the farms themselves could be divided, perhaps turned into joint-stock companies. What sort of forward planning can a manager attempt under such conditions?

It is important to realise that the family farms introduced in the Baltic states so far are of greater importance as a cultural and national manifestation than as a means for improving productivity. It will take some years yet before the private farms will make a real contribution to agricultural production. Production facilities are generally of a very low standard, which is a drawback for the farmer no matter how energetic, enthusiastic or stubborn he may be. Of the registered 4,000 farms in Estonia, only about 1,000 are actually producing so far. A structural problem is that new farms are still very small. Many of these small farms will never provide full-time work for the farmer.

Privatisation of larger units for animal and other agricultural production is also underway, though the legal basis for this process is yet to be adopted. The main subject for debate is whether workers' collectives will have to pay for the means of production.

A particular dimension of the privatisation problem is that the state and collective farms have had a social responsibility in relation to their workers. Apartments, roads, kindergartens, schools, sports and cultural buildings, extra pensions are more often than not financed by the farms.

It is too early to say much about the efficiency of the new private farms.

Preliminary results from Lithuania not surprisingly reveal that production costs for livestock production are less than half in the private farms. This is mainly a reflection of low investment and overhead costs in the primitive private farms and a lower evaluation of labour inputs.

In the past couple of years new agricultural organisations have emerged. In all three republics Farmers' Unions have been formed, the Estonian Farmers' Union being perhaps the most independent of these. Representatives of state and collective farms have united to protect the 'interests of the countryside'. These organisations are influential as they represent vital production facilities, and they maintain close ties with the Ministries of Agriculture. In Lithuania there is also a politically active Association of Former Land Owners. There are also some rudimentary political parties and fractions claiming to be peasants' parties, but none of them have as yet any real political significance.

D. Farm inputs

Almost all farm inputs are in short supply, not only the obvious agricultural inputs but also building materials, tools, fuel etc. People have tried to adapt to this situation after decades of similar problems. Materials and equipment are hoarded on the farms (which partly explains the relatively small effect the blockade of Lithuania in spring 1990 had on agricultural production).

The distribution and allocation of farm inputs are still centralised in all three republics. The following example is taken from Estonia. Based on orders from state, collective and private farms, the association Agrisupplies (Agrosnab), closely related to the Ministry of Agriculture orders building material, pesticides, fertilisers, machines, tractors, spare parts, metal, fuel and other supplies for agriculture (except seed and feed concentrates) and allocates the deliveries to district offices of Agricultural Machinery Supplies. These offices are state owned but independent of the ministry. The district offices not only trade but also deal with land melioration, repairs of machinery, transport etc. They also have production facilities for some machines and spare parts. As a rule, the orders from the farms are not fulfilled completely. Allocation to the old farm system and private farms is decided centrally. Tractors are, for example, divided fifty-fifty in Estonia. The district farmers' union participates in the allocation among farmers. A total number of 3,000 factories, 95 per cent of which are from other republics, deliver the inputs distributed by Agrisupplies.

A similar system is also found in Latvia and in Lithuania, the difference being that inputs and machinery for the food industry are also distributed via the same organisation, while pesticides and fertilisers are sold and distributed by another organisation. The allocation of farm inputs to state and collective farms is supposedly not connected with fulfillment of state orders, but if a state or collective farm does not deliver as planned to the state, deliveries of inputs may be reduced.

It is becoming increasingly difficult to obtain deliveries that have earlier been allocated by Moscow. Most factories demand certain deliveries, of

Table 12.4 Reduced prospects for meat production in Estonia (thousands of tons)

	1989	1990	1991
State procurements	182.7	169.4	133.6
Marketed internally	123.8	126.5	101
Exports to Soviet republics	59	39.5	30

Source: Ekonomika Estonii v 1991 godu, Tallinn, 1990.

meat for example, before they honour their obligations. Although Moscow has agreed to deliver the same level of inputs in 1991 as in 1990, the chaotic economic situation will almost certainly lead to cuts in deliveries.

Grain deliveries to Estonia are being drastically cut, the most probable reason being the inability of the centre to procure sufficient grain for intra-republican distribution. Estonia relies on imports for half of its feed grain. Pesticides, herbicides and certain kinds of fertiliser have also been imported from the rest of the Soviet Union. Supplies have become scarce and their price has multiplied. Grain deliveries were already severely curtailed in 1990 and worse is expected in 1991. The result is expected to be a sharp fall in agricultural output, especially of livestock products, and even the need to slaughter many cows and pigs that cannot be fed. This is reflected in Table 12.4.

The story is the same for dairy produce. Supplies to farms of all categories are still mainly in the hands of Agrisupplies, through which purchase requests (*zayavki*) are channelled from kolkhozes, sovkhozes, farmers' unions to Moscow. Thus the head of Agrosnab in Riga has to leave for Moscow to 'vybivat' fondy', which can be rendered as 'to battle for allocations' — of equipment, materials, etc. But this remnant of the old system is becoming ineffective. Apart from cuts in allocations, the designated suppliers may refuse to supply or may set barter-like conditions.

The cost of farm inputs is increasing rapidly. In 1990 Estonian Agrisupplies sold supplies for 380 million roubles. The same volume is estimated to cost 580 million roubles in 1991. At these higher prices demand may well fall. As the central allocation system disintegrates, a more or less free trade develops. State and collective farms as well as private farmers trade actively. Both barter and rouble deals can be closed, though the prices are of course very high in the latter case.

Fertilisers are among the few things that can be bought relatively freely. It is difficult, however, to buy enough phosphorus fertilisers and poor quality is a general problem.

Use of mineral fertilisers has decreased considerably over the last years in Estonia. In 1987, 265,000 tons active substance (N, P_2O_5, K_2O) was used while the same figure for 1990 was 215,000 tons. The obvious reason is higher prices. (Some of the decrease may also be due to a 'green' profile for some farms.) In the beginning of 1991, the price of fertilisers at least doubled, and their expected use in Estonia 1991 is 188,000 tons. In Latvia and Lithuania use of fertilisers has not yet decreased markedly.

Superphosphate and nitrogenous fertilisers are produced in Estonia with imported raw material. At an all-union plant in Maardu 90–100,000 tons superphosphate (P_2O_5) is produced annually from Kola apatite. About a third is used in Estonia. In Kohtla-Järve 100,000 tons of nitrogenous fertilisers are produced. Of this about 20 per cent is used in Estonia. Large deposits of phosphorite in Rakvere could serve as raw material for extensive production of phosphorous fertilisers in Estonia, but the massive opposition by environmental protection groups has stopped all-union ministries from starting exploitation.

In Ventspils, Latvia, liquid nitrogen and phosphorous fertilisers are produced, of which 50 per cent is used within the republic. In Lithuania there are two all-union factories producing mineral fertilisers (nitrogenous in Jonava and phosphorous in Kedainiai). Annual production is 6–800,000 tons of active substance. The nitrogen and phosphorus consumption of the republic is covered by this production, and a large part is delivered to other regions. Natural gas and apatite for the production come from other regions of the Soviet Union.

One-third of the agricultural land in Estonia, mostly in the south, is in need of regular liming. Sixty thousand hectares are limed annually with ashes from the combustion of oil-shale. The reserves of these ashes are practically inexhaustible and are also used for liming in Russia. In Lithuania slightly less than one-third of the acreage has a low pH. Annually more than 200,000 hectares is limed in Lithuania and another 200,000 hectares in Latvia.

Pesticides have been imported from the West. However, considering the decline in hard-currency allocations from Moscow for this purpose, drastic change is about to take place. For 1991 there may still be some remaining reserves, but for 1992 this problem has no obvious solution.

Distribution of feed concentrates is regulated directly via a department of the ministry. The supply of feedstuffs is getting more and more problematic with rapidly increasing prices seriously affecting production. Fishmeal, and in Lithuania the production of a fodder yeast factory, are the only internal sources of concentrated fodder protein.

The region is currently almost completely dependent on Soviet agricultural machinery. A few all-union factories (one each in Estonia and Lithuania and four in Latvia) produce a very limited assortment of agricultural machinery for the whole of the Soviet Union. There are also production facilities connected with Agrisupplies in Estonia and its equivalents engaged in producing spare parts but also some simple machinery. Some machines were earlier also imported from Eastern Europe.

At present supplies of virtually all farm equipment are inadequate, especially those required for the new family farms. Particularly serious for the farmers is the shortage of small tractors and trucks. Some products such as small cooling tanks for milk and grain driers for family-size farms are simply not produced in the Soviet Union at all.

There are some attempts to cooperate with foreign capital to produce modern agricultural machinery. In Estonia drillers are produced in cooperation with a Finnish company and harrows with a Swedish company.

The region is relatively self-sufficient in seed material. Some of the seed-

Table 12.5 Basic facts of Estonian agriculture (official statistics for 1989, if not stated otherwise)

Agricultural land: 1.3 million ha
Including arable land: 0.9 million ha

Crop production (all farms)

Main crops	% of sown acreage	yield (ton/ha)	total production (thousand tons)
Grain, total	43	2.4	967
Winter wheat	2	2.7	38
Winter rye	7	2.5	162
Barley	31	2.4	683
Potatoes	6	17	864
Flax (fibres)	0.3	0.3	1
Vegetables	1	22	144
Fodder crops, total	50		
Fodder root crops	2	45	648
Silage crops			
Annual grasses			
Perennial grasses	43		

Number of animals (thousands, 1 January 1991)

	total	private
Cattle	758	112
including milk cows	281	45
Pigs	960	58
Sheep and goats	140	135
Poultry	6,536	1,170

Animal production
meat   219,000 tons (slaughter weight)
milk 1,208,000 tons
eggs   546 million

Milk productivity: 4,170 kg/cow annually

Source: Unpublished statistical abstracts provided by the Estonian government.

producing state and collective farms are equipped with drying equipment and storage facilities. Some vegetable seed is even delivered to other parts of the Soviet Union. Some foreign elite-seed was imported and paid for by central Moscow hard-currency funds.

Estonia and Lithuania have over the years received a good share of imported pedigree bulls, heifers and insemination material via Moscow. Other than these deliveries, which are not likely to continue, the republics produce their own breeding stocks.

Storage is a major problem though grain-storage facilities in the region are much better than in the rest of the Soviet Union. Poor storage has led to heavy production losses of potatoes and vegetables.

Transport presents a problem, but not to the same extent as in Russia. Roads are much better in the Baltic republics than in the rest of the Soviet Union.

Table 12.6 Basic facts of Latvian agriculture (official statistics for 1990, if not
stated otherwise)

Agricultural land: 2.5 million ha
Including arable land: 1.7 million ha

Crop production (all farms)

Main crops	% of sown acreage	yield (ton/ha)	total production (thousand tons)
Grain, total	41	2.4	1,621
Winter wheat	7.2	2.6	370
Winter rye	8.0	2.5	324
Barley	20	2.3	693
Potatoes	5.2	13	1,016
Flax (fibres)	0.8	0.25	3
Sugar beet	0.8	30	439
Vegetables	0.7	14	151
Fodder crops, total	50		
Fodder root crops	2.2	39	1,351
Silage crops	3.4		
Annual grasses	4.8		
Perennial grasses	39		

Number of animals (thousands, 1 January 1991)

	total	private
Cattle	1,472	304
including milk cows	544	146
Pigs	1,545	175
Sheep and goats	164	129
Poultry	11,244	887

Animal production
meat   331,000 tons (slaughter weight)
milk 1,977,000 tons
eggs   890 million

Milk productivity: 3,637 kg/cow annually

Source: Statistics provided by the Latvian government.

The harbour at Munga outside Tallinn is a very modern port for grain imports serving the entire region. It can handle five million tons annually. The port used to be all-union property and handled grain strictly according to orders from Moscow. In Latvia and Lithuania the major ports were also under all-union jurisdiction and all have grain-handling facilities.

E. The food-processing industry

The state of the food industry is one of the major obstacles to a reasonable food supply. Capacity is too low and almost all of the industries have worn-out equipment. To some extent this is owing to the low profitability of the food industry throughout the Soviet Union.

Table 12.7 Basic facts of Lithuanian agriculture (official statistics for 1990, if not stated otherwise)

Agricultural land: 3.4 million ha
Including arable land: 2.3 million ha

Crop production (all farms)

Main crops	% of sown acreage	yield (ton/ha)	total production (thousand tons)
Grain, total	48	3.0	3,265
Winter wheat	15	3.2	1,176
Winter rye	7.4	2.8	470
Barley	18	3.0	1,191
Potatoes	5.0	14	1,573
Flax (fibres)	1.0	0.4	10
Sugar beet	1.4	28	912
Vegetables	0.7	17	276
Fodder crops, total	41		
Fodder root crops	2.4	49	2,679
Silage crops	7.0		
Annual grasses	4.7		
Perennial grasses	27		

Number of animals (thousands, 1 January 1991)

	total	private
Cattle	2,318	551
including milk cows	841	335
Pigs	2,424	469
Sheep and goats	62	50
Poultry	11,044	c. 6,000

Animal production
meat   694,463 tons (slaughter weight)
milk 2,887,152 tons
eggs   851.9 million

Milk productivity: 3,537 kg/cow annually

Source: Statistics provided by the Lithuanian government.

Collective and state farms have been trying to develop their own means of processing products, but the restricting factor is again lack of equipment. The farmers' unions and big farm organisations are discussing the necessity for developing cooperative slaughterhouses etc.

One problem is that the food industry has relied on imports made by all-union organisations. Raw sugar, cacao, coffee, sausage skins, packaging materials, machinery and spare parts, which have had to be imported for convertible currency, are only a few of the key inputs the absence of which could paralyse important parts of the food industry in the immediate future.

Almost all meat and milk is processed at large milk and livestock complexes. In the region there are 21 meat complexes and 35 dairies. The largest plants are found in Lithuania. Until the recent decrease in animal production, slaughter houses and dairies were seasonally overloaded. Only a small per centage of the meat and almost no milk is processed at the state and collective farms.

With very few exceptions, the technical standard of the plants is very low. The capacity for cold-storage and freezing is quite inadequate, and equipment for packaging and processing is often not available. Hides and animal fat are exported in order to finance imports of some equipment and spare parts.

The main product of the dairies is butter, and the remaining buttermilk is returned to the state and collective farms as an important animal feed.

Feed processing is concentrated in a few plants, while production capacity on farms is low. In Estonia six plants have the capacity to produce one million tons of fodder and meal annually. In Lithuania fifteen plants produce 3.5 million tons of fodder and additional meal, macaroni, etc.

In 1989, three sugar-refining factories in Latvia and four in Lithuania produced 248,000 and 329,000 tons of sugar, respectively. Most of the sugar is produced from Cuban raw sugar, especially in Latvia. All factories are old and in need of new equipment.

The Lithuanian consumption of 170–180,000 tons of sugar is not covered by its own beet production. Owing to lack of refining capacity, 30 per cent of the beet production is even sold to other republics. In order to be self-sufficient, a 30 per cent increase in beet production and a doubling of refining capacity would be needed. Production of canned meat, vegetables etc. adds up to more than 400,000 tons in the three republics.

Margarine production is projected to start in a couple of years in Estonia. A smaller vegetable-oil extraction plant is planned in Lithuania, but existing extraction plants in the region can only produce oil for industrial use.

Vodka, champagne, beer, mineral water and soft drinks are produced in all three republics. However, the shortage of bottles presents a problem.

F. Food trade

In 1991 the system of state orders is still functioning in all three republics. In order to get necessary inputs such as feed, tractors, fuel etc. the state and collective farms have to deliver the major part of production to the state at fixed procurement prices. For example, in Estonia about 80 per cent of agricultural production of state and collective farms must still be delivered to the state system. The Ministry of Agriculture agrees on quotas with the agricultural district office, which in turn reaches a negotiated agreement on them with the state and collective farms. Presently, state and collective farms hesitate to sign agreements because of the low procurement prices.

Retail trade in food is regulated at the ministerial level where available quantities of milk, meat, meal etc. are allocated among the districts. The state retail-trade system operates in the cities, while in the countryside retail trade is in the hands of so-called consumer cooperatives. The actual difference between the two systems is marginal.

Agricultural purchase prices are fixed by the republics as are retail prices. Policies in the republics differ as Lithuania was slower in adjusting and

Table 12.8 Structure of agricultural production in the Baltic states

	Estonia	Latvia	Lithuania
State farms (1989):			
Number	126	248	275
Mean acreage			
Agricultural land (ha)	4,115	4,300	3,007
Mean no. of cattle	2,135	2,111	1,685
Including cows	776	743	488
Mean no. of pigs	3,085	2,490	1,379
Collective farms (1989):			
Number	200	320	835
Mean acreage			
Agricultural land (ha)	4,140	3,900	2,693
Mean no. of cattle	2,181	2,085	1,637
Including cows	784	711	458
Mean no. of pigs	3,000	2,490	1,745
Private farms (1 January 1991):			
Number	4,119	7,518	3,982
Mean acreage			
Agricultural land (ha)	26	21	16
Number of workers in the agricultural sector (1987, including non-agricultural workers of state and collective farms)	143,000	264,000	365,000

Source: Statistics provided by government authorities.

continues a somewhat higher subsidy level. There are legal free (kolkhoz) markets in the towns. Sales outside each republic, including by private peasants, require a licence.

The kolkhoz market is so far the only unregulated source of food. This is where the increase in prices has been most obvious over the last couple of years. In Latvia and Estonia increased state retail prices and better availability of meat have had some effect in stabilising free-market prices. But the higher quality still ensures that prices are higher than in the state shops.

Naturally, the question of agricultural prices is a subject for controversy as is also the case in Western Europe. Totally free prices are seldom found in the real world, West or East.

Estonia was the first Soviet republic to increase retail food prices. On 15 October 1990 some prices were increased two to three times in order to get rid of subsidies, and the retail price level rose by about 60 per cent. In January 1991 an even sharper price rise took place in Latvia. In Estonia it was felt to be politically too dangerous to put retail prices up so soon after the huge increase of last October and so, as in Latvia, the subsidies for butter have continued. In March 1991 Lithuania also raised food prices. The effect of the new prices on total food consumption has so far been slight.

Table 12.9 Trade of feed grain, feed protein, meat and milk products between the Baltic republics and the Soviet Union, 1989–91 (thousand tons)

	1989	1990	1991*
Estonia			
Import:			
Feed grain	661	479	384
Protein concentrates	70	113	136
Export:			
Meat	55	40	30
Milk products**	431	370	350
Latvia			
Import:			
Feed grain	n/a	n/a	560
Protein concentrates	n/a	n/a	200
Export:			
Meat	76	50	50
Milk products	612	500	500
Lithuania			
Import:			
Feed grain	1,113	756	980
Protein concentrates	380	289	280
Export:			
Meat	196	148	140
Milk products**	1,325	1,150	1,085
All three republics			
Import:			
Feed grain	n/a	n/a	1,924
Protein concentrates	n/a	n/a	616
Export:			
Meat	131	238	220
Milk products	2,368	2,020	1,935

* According to agreements.
** Calculated as whole milk.

Source: Statistics provided by government authorities.

In October 1990–January 1991 procurement prices were increased in all three republics to levels similar to those in Russia. Prices of different products differ among the republics. With a few exceptions, agricultural products are not subsidised in Estonia. In Lithuania subsidies have increased. As in the rest of the Soviet Union, prices of fruits and vegetables are not regulated.

Owing to increased costs of production, procurement prices will probably be increased again in all republics. Since the political situation will probably not allow for even higher retail prices on food in Estonia and Latvia, the level of subsidies will again increase.

In all three republics there are restrictions on retail trade. Attempts have been made to restrict sales to those with proof of residence. In February 1991 grain products, sugar and vodka were rationed in the whole region. In Lithuania even butter and meat are rationed in some places.

The Baltic states are heavily dependent on the all-union deliveries of feed concentrates (see Table 12.9). For 1991 imports of more than two million tons of grain have been agreed on, which is about one million tons less than the average in the 1980s. The decrease will have a considerable impact on livestock production, especially as feed deliveries in 1991 have been even lower than those agreed upon. In consequence, less milk and meat are being delivered to St. Petersburg and Moscow. Much of the grain and protein concentrates from the all-union funds are still imported from the United States and other countries.

In order to diminish the dependence on the Soviet Union, Lithuania and Latvia are investigating the possibilities of buying grain from the West. State and collective farms are also developing trade with counterparts in the Ukraine and Kazakhstan.

Most of the wheat for bread and macaroni is also delivered from other parts of the Soviet Union. For all three republics the quantity amounts to 400–500,000 tons.

Between 20–30 per cent of meat production and 30–40 per cent of milk production have annually been delivered to other parts of the Soviet Union. Lithuania delivers the highest relative amounts and Latvia the lowest. The products from Estonia and Latvia are mainly delivered to St. Petersburg, while some cheese and butter end up in Moscow. Lithuanian production is directed to Moscow, with the exception of some meat for St. Petersburg. Presently the volume of livestock products traded for feed from other parts of the Soviet Union is decreasing. The prices of meat and milk relative to grain have been reduced considerably. The agreement with the former Soviet Union Gosplan provided for 1990-level deliveries in 1991 for agriculture of diesel oil, cars, machinery etc. This agreement is said by Baltic represen- tatives to be the first real agreement, instead of another dictate.

Because of procurement price differences among the republics and various parts of the Soviet Union, it is often more profitable for the farms to export their production. Moreover, kolkhoz market prices may be double or more in cities like Moscow or Pskov than those in Vilnius or Riga. Additional inter-republican deliveries of agricultural products, beyond those provided for in the central agreements with Moscow, require a licence. But this rule can hardly be enforced, and it is probable that unrecorded dealings between republics are considerable. In Estonia private farmers can get a licence more easily than state and collective farms, and much of their meat ends up outside Estonia.

Pedigree cattle and pigs are exported to other Soviet republics. More than 50,000 heads of cattle and even more pigs were delivered last year. These animals are now traded in inter-republican direct barter in exchange for grain and protein concentrates.

A common problem for Baltic agriculture is the necessity to earn hard currency for the import of inputs unavailable in the Soviet Union. There is a great need for pesticides, agricultural machinery, machinery for food industry, spare parts etc. At least some minimal amounts were allocated from all-union central funds earlier, but these supplies seem to have been reduced in 1991.

Traditionally, exports of food products outside the Soviet Union (primarily to other socialist countries) were handled via all-union foreign-trade organisations. This business is now largely history, but producers in the agricultural sector want to sell products such as meat, hides, peat, forest products etc. on the international market to earn convertible currency. Owing to licencing rules and banking problems the development of such trade is slow. The most important export products of the agricultural sector are peat in Estonia, wood-pulp in Latvia and wild game meat in Lithuania.

G. Some future issues

In any successful scenario of economic transformation of Estonia, Latvia and Lithuania, agriculture will remain a crucial sector.

Baltic agriculture is facing major reform for the third time this century. The first time was the land reform in the independent countries after World War I, and the second time was in connection with Soviet collectivisation. The main problem now is what organisational shape the sector should have in the future.

An increased role for individual smallholdings is foreseen in all republics, but how should this restructuring take place? There is a risk that production capacity will be drastically reduced in connection with privatisation. While privatisation must proceed, it is important that the process cause only minimum disruption to the remaining state and collective farms, which will continue to be responsible for the bulk of farm output in the next few years.

Resources to invest in new production facilities will be extremely limited. It is doubtful whether these should be used to develop private farms which in any case are likely to prove too small. However, the optimal size of the future individual farm is impossible to predict and should not be overestimated.

In view of the importance of the state and collective farms, a strategy for the more efficient of them may well be needed. Perhaps efficient farms should be kept in being, especially if their comparatively well-paid workers prefer this. Some of the excessively large kolkhozy and sovkhozy could be sub-divided into smaller and genuine cooperatives. There are also ideas to keep the existing collective or state farms' workshops and machinery and make them available to farms on hire. Also, one may recall that farmers in the independence years often formed cooperatives, for example for process-ing meat and dairy produce. Such cooperatives statified in 1949–50 and may be revived.

In practice, the agrarian system which is likely to emerge will involve a mixture of smallholdings, commercial farms and reformed versions of the state and collective farms. The policy need is to allow the system to adjust so that it moves towards a more efficient structure by a process of ongoing reform. Of course, the large political context — notably the impetus to restore property to previous owners — provides a considerable impetus for rapid tenure reform. At the same time, there is inertia in the structure, in that managers and workers in some farms are at home with and benefit from the existing structure. Continuance of larger units may in some instances make good economic sense. It is important that efficiency should be the basis for any strategy of agricultural organisational reform.

A second large issue facing Baltic agricultural reform is the uncertainty of future markets. As independent states, all three republics exported food and some raw materials to the West, first and foremost to Germany and Great Britain. Now Baltic export would have to compete with the subsidy-induced over-production and protectionism of the EC Common Agricultural Policy. This is an important, unresolved issue which the Baltic republics face jointly with the rest of the reforming Eastern Europe.

Another unknown is whether even the present agricultural trade with the Soviet Union can be upheld. The Soviet Union is close, is accessible, needs more meat and dairy produce, which indeed the Baltic republics have been specialising in. The grain crops sown were predominantly feed grains, notably barley, but Russia and the Ukraine supplied a large part of the feed grain and concentrates, as well as grain for human consumption. However, the three states now risk becoming the victims of the breakdown of the Soviet command structure, without it being replaced by either a market or by a rouble with real power to purchase.

Already in the short term, the high degree of dependence on the Soviet Union as a supplier of inputs forces the continuance of administered rationing of increasingly scarce inputs. This in turn is one factor inhibiting a swifter development of private farming as well as of productive capacity generally.

In the longer term, it is clearly possible to increase agricultural productivity. With well-educated farmers, modern farm machinery, pesticides and new plant varieties, it should be possible to almost double yield levels. Animal production may also increase its productivity considerably if for example protein concentrations in the feed were increased.

Horticulture production has a potential to develop significantly because of old traditions and the development of private farming. Fruit, berries and especially flowers could become a significant export product, both east and west of Estonia, Latvia and Lithuania.

H. Forestry

An account of the forest resources in the Baltic region is given in Table 12.10. Latvia is the most prominent in resources and production which is also reflected in more advanced research and production methods. Most of the forests are administered by republican forest organisations ('state forests'). The larger part of the non-state forest in the region is in the hands of state and collective farms.

Since World War II acreage and volume of Baltic forests have increased. One reason is the afforestation of abandoned agricultural land. In Estonia

Table 12.10 Forest resources and production in the Baltic republics

	Estonia (1989)	Latvia (1989)	Lithuania (1990)
Forest-covered land, thousand ha	1,814	2,594	1,823
including highly protected forests, %	36	52	41
State forest land, thousand ha	1,469	2,149	1,209
Coniferous forests, %	63	60–70	59
Total growing stock, million m³	259	426	297
Average growing stock, per ha m³	143	136	163
Current growth, cbm per year	4.2	4.5	4
Annual cuttings in state forests, thousand m³	2,339	3,000	2,625
Volume from thinnings in state forests of total, %	40	35–40	41
Total annual cuttings including state and collective farms	3,112	4,166	3,000

Source: Statistics provided by government authorities.

acreage and volume has more than doubled and in Latvia acreage of forest has increased by 800,000 hectares, while changes are less dramatic in Lithuania.

The republics have been able to maintain a high percentage of coniferous forests in contrast to adjacent regions in the Russian Federation. Forests of the state and collective farms are, however, not as well kept as the state forests.

In all three republics forest organisations on the district level are in charge of forestry — reforestation, fire control, some inspection measures, thinnings etc. — under the supervision of the Ministries of Forestry and other central organs. District forest organisations, subordinate to republican production associations, carry out the cuttings in the state forests of Estonia and Latvia.

Not all of the allowed cuttings are in fact carried through. Nor do state and collective farms harvest all they can. The reason may be that the areas are difficult to exploit or that the species growing there are not attractive. In Estonia experiments started in 1990 to auction cutting rights to cooperatives. Prices turned out to be at least ten times higher than the state cutting fee. This experiment will continue on a broader scale in 1991 and has already resulted in formation of some small private forestry companies. In Latvia and Lithuania prices of roundwood are fixed, while partly deregulated prices have been introduced in Estonia in 1991.

A new legal basis for forestry is under preparation in the republics. Private forests will be recognised but will probably not become a common feature. There is less readiness to accept private forests than private agricultural land. Forests which had been farmers' forests in 1940 and also afforested agricultural land might be privatised to begin with. Private forest land could add up to 600–700,000 hectares in Estonia.

In Tartu, Jelgava and Kaunas there are faculties of forestry at the Academies of Agriculture. Forestry research institutes are located in Tartu and Kaunas. Silava in Latvia is a research and production association engaged in development and production of forestry machinery.

Unlike agriculture and fisheries, forestry is largely independent of all-union influence. This will even more be the case since the Soviet Ministry of Forest Industry (Minlesprom) is being disbanded. The All-Union State Committee for Forests (Goskomles) seems to have no real influence in the region.

Production statistics are found in Table 12.10. Relative volumes from thinnings are exceptionally high in comparison with the Soviet Union (an indication of better forestry) but could certainly be increased even more if birch and other hardwood species were better utilised.

The forests of the region have over the years been 'over-protected'. Though acreage and volume have increased, exploitation has not increased very much. In Estonia cuttings are more or less on the same level as fifty years ago. This is partly a consequence of the Soviet forest policy with an extreme division between productive and protected forests. The bulk of Soviet production has always been in the 'inexhaustible' forests of Russia, and for the republics there has been no incentive to harvest more forest than ordered. Distribution of wood products was in the hands of all-union ministries anyway.

The situation is now changing. Imports of roundwood from other regions of the Soviet Union are being drastically reduced. Even though new national parks are being founded, all republics plan to increase cuttings. Lithuania intends to increase the cuttings by almost one million cubic metres, which is close to the volume which was earlier delivered from the Soviet Union. Plans to increase cuttings in 20 years to 4–5 million m^3 in Estonia and 6–7 million m^3 in Latvia are discussed.

Development of family farming should lead to increased cuttings. In Latvia 300–400,000 m^3 or even more will be made available to new farmers in 1991 for cutting, in order to help them with the supply of building materials.

Much of the forest acreage of Estonia and Latvia is bogland which can only be harvested in the wintertime, especially since Soviet machinery is very heavy and can be used without serious damage to the soil only in cold winters. Inadequate supply of machinery and machinery of poor quality are also factors restricting cutting. In Latvia this problem has been partly solved through the use of imported Scandinavian harvesters and forwarders.

Most of the harvested forest is processed in the region in an industry of a very low standard. In Estonia almost 2 million m^3 of the harvested volume are sawn and used for wood products, 0.5–1 million m^3 is used as firewood while more than 0.5 million m^3 is used by the pulp and paper industry. In Latvia 1.8 million m^3 is used as firewood and more than 1 million m^3 is sawn. In Lithuania 2 million m^3 are sawn and otherwise used for wood products, half a million m^3 is used for firewood and the rest in pulp and paper industry. These figures are very approximate.

A serious problem is that industry is not adapted to the use of much of the hardwood — particularly birch. In projections for future higher harvest levels there are obvious opportunities to increase pulpwood production. But, with the exception of some minor quantities, hardwood cannot be used in the pulp industry. Presently a few hundred thousand m³ of pulpwood, mostly birch, is exported to Finland and Sweden. The intentions are to increase these volumes.

I. Fishing

On the governmental level questions on fisheries are handled by ministries of agriculture in Estonia and Lithuania. In Latvia there is a ministry of fisheries. Their influence has, however, been marginal since most of the important issues had been determined in Moscow. In all three republics there are two production organisations: the fishery collective farms and the high-sea fleets.

In Estonia, starting with 116 collectives after collectivisation in 1950, the number has diminished over the years to 10 huge collectives with more than 20,000 workers and 700 boats altogether. In Latvia there are eleven collectives with 16,000 workers and more than 300 boats and in Lithuania only one with 1,300 workers. Most of the fishing activities are in the Baltic Sea, but some boats operate in the oceans. The collectives are represented by republican associations, which are members of a similar all-union organisation. At the moment the collectives are in the process of being reorganised into different types of companies.

The high-sea fishing fleets had been subordinated to the Ministry of Fisheries in Moscow (Minrybkhoz) and work mostly in the Atlantic and the Pacific. Estrybprom, as the Estonian Ministry of Fisheries used to be called by its Russian acronym, is based in Tallinn. The collective of about 8,000 people has leased the means of production from the Ministry of Fisheries in Moscow. Latrybprom, its Latvian counterpart, has two fleets — one in Riga and one in Liepaja. Litrybprom is based in Klaipeda. The workers in the high-sea fleets are often Russians and may not even live in the Baltic republics. The fleets of Est-, Lat-, and Litrybprom consist of forty-eight, 100 and 150 boats, respectively.

Lake fisheries and aquaculture are most developed in Lithuania where 8–9,000 tons are caught and produced by specialised agricultural collective farms annually.

Most issues, such as catch quotas, deliveries of inputs etc. had been determined in Moscow. There were quite a few disputes with Minrybkhoz on various matters. The main problem as seen by the Estonian fishing industry is that they have been allowed to catch only one-third of the fish caught on the Estonian coast in spite of the processing industry being short of raw material. This was as a result of the Soviet Union redistributing quotas to St. Petersburg and Latvia. There are attempts to settle distribution of quotas between the Baltic republics, St. Petersburg and Kaliningrad without involving all-union organs.

The Estonian fishery collectives annually catch 60–65,000 tons in the Baltic Sea, while Latvian and Lithuanian boats catch 70,000 and 15,000 tons, respectively. More than 70 per cent is herring and sprat.

Estonian and Latvian collectives working in the oceans are estimated to catch about 100,000 tons in total in 1991, but increasing costs make profits marginal. At its peak the Estonian fleet alone caught as much as 133,000 tons.

The fleets of Est-, Lat- and Litrybprom in 1990 caught 250,000, 350,000 and 325,000 tons, respectively. The quantities are impressive, though catches have been decreasing over the last years. Much of it is, however, low-quality fish for fishmeal production. In the last couple of years Baltic fishermen have started to land cod in Denmark in order to earn convertible currency. One of the main problems is the age of the fishing fleet. Boats adapted for fishing in the Baltic Sea are produced in small numbers and only in Russia.

While the quantity of fish is large, the quality of the fish for consumption is poor. The on-board facilities for freezing etc. are not sufficient. The fish processing industry also has problems, but so far there are no difficulties in selling the products in the Soviet market. Approximately 300,000 tons of fish products are produced in Latvia, 250,000 tons in Estonia and 220,000 tons in Lithuania.

The fishery collectives and the high-sea fleets all have their own processing industry. Estrybprom has a fish-processing plant in Pärnu; Latrybprom and Litrybprom each have five plants. Annually, about 200,000 tons of preserved-fish products are produced in the three republics.

About half of the raw material used by the fish-processing industry of Estonian collectives was delivered from the oceans by other organisations, but the quantities are now dwindling which is a major concern for the Estonian collectives.

Two-thirds of the production is delivered to other parts of the Soviet Union at state prices. These are the present conditions to get necessary inputs such as fuel, new boats etc.

In Latvia there are still subsidies on fish products and since meat prices are high, all fish is easily sold. Quite the opposite is true in Lithuania, where meat is still subsidised but fish is not.

13 Transport and communication

A. Operations of the transport sector

a. Role and modal distribution of transport

The transport sector can be subdivided into four main segments: (1) domestic (intra-republic) cargo and passenger traffic, (2) inter-republic traffic to other parts of the Soviet Union, (3) international traffic and (4) transit cargo traffic via the ports on the Baltic coast to the rest of the union and to the Far and Middle East. Basic data are given in Tables 13.1–3.

Domestic cargo transport is dominated by road traffic, natural-gas pipelines and, in Estonia, coastal shipping. Inland water transport and railways are of less importance for cargo. Domestic passenger transport consists primarily of scheduled bus service, whereas rail transport only plays a significant role in mass passenger transit around the main urban centres: Tallinn, Riga and Vilnius–Kaunas. The number of privately owned cars is limited and thus passenger car transport plays a relatively insignificant role. Domestic air traffic is negligible.

Inter-republic cargo traffic is vast on account of the extreme level of specialisation within Soviet production. The predominant transport modes are rail, pipeline and road in order of importance, while air cargo and sea transport is little developed. Most inter-republic passenger traffic is by air and bus, whereas rail transport is of limited importance, largely owing to a rather low level of services.

International cargo from the Baltic republics is transported by road and sea, but rail transport is of little importance, owing to lack of direct connections to the European railways (apart from a railway–ferry link between Klaipeda and Mukran in former East Germany) and the difference in gauge between the railways in the Soviet Union and Europe. International passenger traffic is modest. The traffic is dominated by air transport, except for Estonia, where the passenger ferries connecting Tallinn with Helsinki and Stockholm are important. In Lithuania, the road traffic to Poland is limited by a single common border crossing. A passenger ferry between Sweden and Latvia was inaugurated in October 1990 but was suspended after two voyages. It is planned to open again. Furthermore a new link between Klaipeda and Karlskrona in south Sweden is being planned.

Soviet trade via the Baltic ports accounts for most transit cargo traffic: exports of oil products, chemicals, minerals, cars and equipment, and imports of bulk foodstuff and general cargo in break bulk. A small but expanding transit traffic through the Soviet Union to Japan and the Middle East is based on block trains carrying containers from ports on the Baltic sea.

Otherwise, container traffic and combined transports are little developed within the Soviet Union, owing partly to lack of intermediary organisers

Table 13.1 Transit and import/export transport volumes in the three Baltic republics, 1989–90

	Passenger traffic		Cargo traffic		Share of transport work (%)	
	Passengers (millions)	Passenger-kilometres (billions)	Tons (millions)	Ton-kilometres (billions)	Passenger	Cargo
Sea	1.6	0.2	39.6	105.7	1	55
Road	112.3	2.7	2.9	1.6	18	1
Rail	5.8	5.4	149.0	73.8	37	38
Air	2.3	6.4	0.0	0.0	43	0
River	0.0	0.0	0.0	0.0	0	0
Oil pipeline			28.0	11.8		6
Total	122.0	14.7	219.5	192.9	100	100

Note: Inclusive of traffic between the three Baltic republics.

Source: Government statistical abstracts, latest editions.

Table 13.2 Domestic transport volumes in the three Baltic republics, 1989–90

	Passenger traffic		Cargo traffic		Share of transport work (%)	
	Passengers (millions)	Passenger-kilometres (billions)	Tons (millions)	Ton-kilometres (billions)	Passenger	Cargo
Sea	30.1	1.1	5.0	0.3	5	1
Road	2,134.1	15.3	734.1	14.1	68	42
Rail	188.1	5.4	149.0	18.5	24	55
Air	0.2	0.6	0.0	0.0	2	0
River	5.0	0.0	6.8	0.5	0	1
Oil pipeline			0.0	0.0		0
Total	2,357.0	22.4	894.8	33.4	100	100

Source: Government statistical abstracts, latest edition.

such as forwarders and partly to lack of adequate transhipment facilities.

b. Traffic development

Until 1988, the ports, the railways and the pipelines were fully utilised, while the road network (but not the road transport operators) had significant excess capacity. Since 1988, overall traffic levels have decreased by 20–30 per cent, primarily owing to the general economic decline in the Soviet Union but also to the reduced trade with Eastern Europe. As a result, the transport sector today has a substantial capacity reserve.

The union-wide price reform in the spring of 1991 is expected to lead to

Table 13.3 Cargo turnover at the main commercial sea ports in the Baltic republics (million tons, selected years)

Commodity	Tallinn Old port 1990	New port 1990	Riga 1990	Ventspils 1988	Klaipeda 1989
Grain		4.5	3.0	0.6	
Oil products				31.1[1]	15.0[2]
Other bulk	2.0	0.2	2.1	2.5	15.0[2]
Break bulk	1.4		0.9	1.4	15.0[2]
Reefer cargo		0.5	0.1		
Containers (gross)	0.2		1.2		
RO/RO and rail	0.0	0.8			3.1[3]
Total	3.6[4]	6.0	7.3	35.6	n/a

Notes: [1] In 1990, oil-products turnover is estimated at 23–4 million tons. [2] Port turnover in 1986, the last year before operation of the ferry line to Mukran began. [3] Of which 3 million tons on the Mukran ferry line. For 1991, the ferry traffic is expected to reach 1.5 million tons. [4] In addition, 3.3 million tons coastal trade.

Source: Information gathered from the ministries of transport in the three republics and the port authorities.

an increase in transport prices of 200–300 per cent which in turn is expected to lead to an initial decline in traffic by at least 40 per cent. (When a unilateral price reform was introduced in Latvia, in January, 1991, there was an immediate 25 per cent decrease in intra-republic air travel to Riga, attributed locally to hoarders avoiding Latvia on account of the price level. The supply situation in Latvia reportedly improved significantly following the price increase.) In the longer-term perspective, the price reform is expected to reduce overall transport demand by as much as one-third as compared with today's level.

In the very long term, cargo transport is likely to decline because of the likely transformation of Soviet production from today's transport-intensive system based on production in few but large units towards a more decentralised structure. However, passenger transport, which today is comparatively modest, is likely to develop, in particular if private income rises to a level where increased car ownership and demands for better housing standards combine to induce the development of dispersed suburbs.

c. Organisational structure of the transport sector

The transport sector is controlled by specialised state monopolies affiliated with sector ministries which, in turn, are specialised by mode, for example the ministry of railways, the ministry for merchant marine etc. There are three distinct types of state companies within the transport sector:

1. all-union companies operating as the executive branches of their respective union ministries, for example the railways, Aeroflot and the oil industry transport;
2. all-union companies affiliated with union ministries but operating at regional or republican level, encompassing the shipping companies and the natural-gas distribution companies; and
3. a large number of republican road transport companies affiliated to the republican governments.

Within the last years, the state sector in the three Baltic republics has been supplemented by a large number of cooperative and even private transport ventures. Most of the new companies are in road transport, forwarding and repair services which require little capital for establishment. A few companies, however, operate with significant assets, including:

1. two or three Estonian shipping companies with coasters;
2. the Swedish–Estonian joint-venture Estline with a large car and passenger ferry between Tallinn and Stockholm;
3. the Latvian state cooperative Invertia with three jet liners in international air-cargo traffic on charter basis and major aviation repair and training facilities in Riga airport; and
4. about ten road-haulage companies with 100–200 trucks each and a major road-haulage forwarding company which were all established by carving up a single Estonian state company into smaller, independent ventures.

In terms of cargo moved, the new cooperative and private sector is small compared with the state sector. It is, however, developing fast with active encouragement from the republican governments. The private sector dominates taxi service, with approximately 65 per cent of all registered taxis.

Road transport is controlled by republican state monopolies, in the larger towns organised by type of transport (city bus, inter-city bus, distribution, transport of construction materials, international road haulage etc.) and elsewhere organised as general transport companies monopolising a certain geographic area, typically a group of municipalities.

The road transport companies are subject to tight price regulation by the republican Ministries of Transport, except for the urban bus companies where the municipalities determine the tariff. Otherwise, the companies are gradually being given increasing degrees of operational freedom, with plans to privatise the sector within a few years, except for the urban bus services which are expected to be taken over by the municipalities.

The main obstacle to privatisation in the road transport sector is that most of the companies are unwilling to be broken up into smaller units. Since the republican governments reject the privatisation of effective monopolies, only limited progress has been recorded up to date.

The railways operate under complete union control, although the republics have the right to set tariffs on mass passenger transport lines in the larger town areas. In the Soviet Union, the railways are organised into 32 railway companies. The three Baltic republics and Kaliningrad have together formed one railway district with headquarters in Riga.

The individual railway companies control all aspects of operations within their district and 'own' all fixed infrastructure (rails, signals, communications, buildings, etc.) as well as locomotives and passenger wagons. In principle, these operate only within the districts to which they belong, whereas the freight wagons, which are not assigned to depots, operate throughout the union.

Republican attempts to take over the railways have hitherto been unsuccessful, with the Union ministry of railways ignoring the republics. The Baltic republics have not agreed on the future organisation of an independent railway, for example whether the railways should be split into republican units or made into an inter-republican organisation.

Commercial air traffic is under the union-wide monopoly Aeroflot which operates all commercial airplanes, airports and the civilian air-traffic control system. Similarly to the railways, Aeroflot is internally organised into a number of fairly autonomous districts — one in each of the three Baltic republics. Currently, Aeroflot is under internal restructuring, whereby the airline, the airports and the traffic control system are being separated. Apparently, the intention is to turn the airports over to the republics, to divide the ownership of the proposed republican-based airline between the union and the individual republics and to retain the air-traffic control system under union control.

Sea transport is handled by large, republic-based all-union shipping companies. Until 1 January 1991, the shipping companies incorporated the shipping lines, the ports, the shipyards and all port services. Today, the secondary elements have been made into independent companies, of which some are all-union, whereas others, in particular the secondary ports, have been turned over to the republics. Republican aspirations are to take over all ports and to establish some kind of shared republican and union ownership of the shipping lines. Operationally, the union ministry of merchant marine's central controls over the shipping lines appear to have ceased completely.

d. Transport infrastructure

Transport infrastructure is well developed in the Baltic states, incorporating extensive road and railway networks, five large commercial ports, three international and eleven domestic airports, pipelines for oil, oil products and natural gas and a well-developed natural-gas distribution network (see Table 13.4 and Figures 13.1 and 2). Common traffic services such as repair shops, petrol stations, hotels etc. are, however, scarce and apart from the ports, transhipment points are inadequate.

The basic network of roads, railways and ports was developed before World War II and has not been extended since — apart from the construction of a large export terminal for oil products in Ventspils, in 1961, and the ongoing construction, since 1987, of a second port in Tallinn which has been partly operational since 1989.

Table 13.4 Basic infrastructure, 1989

			Estonia	Latvia	Lithuania
Roads	State roads	km	14,800	20,600	20,900
	Other roads	km	15,000	29,600	28,000
	Bridges	no.	900	980	n/a
Railway lines		km	1,026	2,397	2,000
Commercial airports		no.	6	5	3
Ports	National	no.	2	2	1
	Local	no.	26	20	n/a
Inland waterways		km	520	347	628
Main pipelines (oil and gas)		km	n/a	1,542	n/a

Source: Statistical abstracts, latest editions and government sources.

From a union point of view, the roads and railways primarily serve the transit cargo transport between the Baltic ports and the major production and population centres in the European parts of the Soviet Union, including the centres in the Baltic republics. Consequently, the East–West links, the large international ports and the infrastructure serving the major Baltic towns have been continuously maintained and upgraded, whereas maintenance of the secondary transport infrastructure, such as local ports and secondary roads and railway lines, has been largely neglected. The result is that, for example:

1. the total length of roads in the three republics has decreased by approximately one-third since before 1940 because local roads have been neglected;
2. most of the smaller ports have deteriorated and require extensive rehabilitation; and
3. certain parts of the railway system, for example the north–south connections and the inter-city connections within the Baltic republics have deteriorated and are now in a very poor state of repair.

On the other hand, the average standard of the remaining roads is high, most of the railways and the large ports are well developed and new transport infrastructure such as airports and pipelines has been established. This leaves the three republics with a highly developed primary transport network facing east, but with major gaps in the infrastructure serving local needs and the north–south traffic between the Baltic republics and to Finland and Poland.

In the past, all ports, airports, railways and main pipelines were constructed and operated by union authorities, while the construction and operation of gas distribution networks and roads was executed by the republican authorities, albeit with extensive funding, and under supervision, from the union government. Union investment financing is, however, drying up fast. Thus, there is an increased reliance on republican funds as, for example, for completion of the new port in Tallinn and construction of the

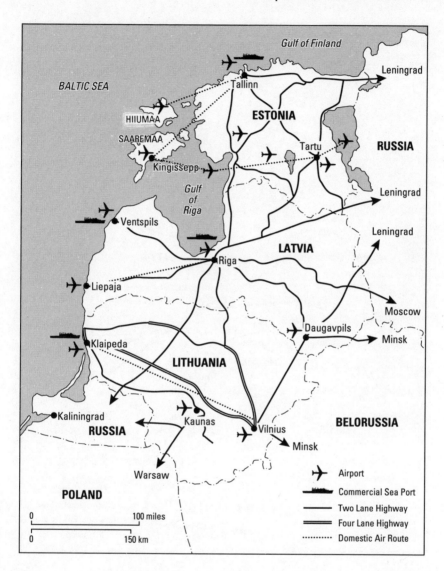

Figure 13.1 Transport infrastructure: roads, ports and airports

new international airport passenger facilities in the republics. Investments
have come to a virtual stop for railways, which remain under union control.
The all-union shipping companies rely entirely on their own investment
funds.

The maintenance level on the primary routes is high and if the current
maintenance level is maintained, the network can easily accommodate the
projected traffic levels for the next decade without deterioration of the

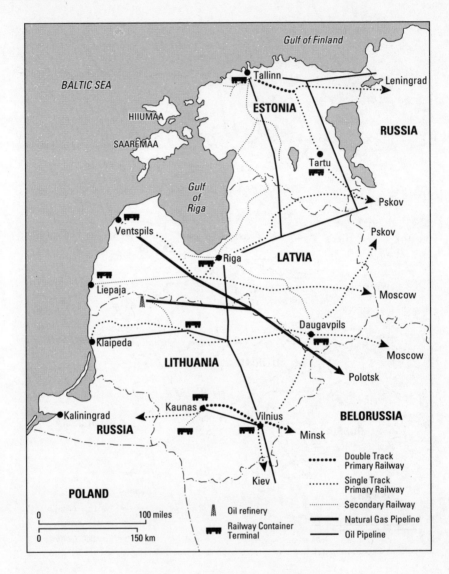

Figure 13.2 Transport infrastructure: railways and pipelines

infrastructure. There are, however, increasing problems with maintenance because of shortage of certain construction materials, in particular rails and bitumen, as well as certain types of maintenance equipment such as rail-grinding machines and road pavers. Funds have up till now been sufficient but budget constraints are expected to become more pressing with the growing economic problems within the union. This will, in combination with the extension of the transport infrastructure, put severe strains on the republican finances.

Table 13.5 Stock of transport equipment, 1989

		Estonia	Latvia	Lithuania
Road traffic	State trucks	n/a	40,394	n/a
	Private trucks	n/a	199	n/a
	State cars	n/a	5,874	n/a
	Private cars	n/a	254,000	n/a
Railway	Locomotives	n/a	n/a	218
	Passenger carriages	300	n/a	354
Air traffic	Airplanes	28	42	33
Shipping	Vessels	82	105	43
	Tonnage million tons dead weight	0.4	1.2	0.3

Source: Statistical abstracts, latest editions and government sources.

Freight transport equipment is abundant whereas means for public passenger transport are more restricted. Private passenger cars are relatively scarce by Western standards, but more abundant than in other parts of the Soviet Union (see Table 13.5).

The bulk of equipment is rather old and the average age is increasing because official allocations of new equipment have dwindled in the last few years. Thus, in January 1991, the allocation of Soviet-manufactured trucks was less than 10 per cent of the 1988 level whereas supply of East European transport equipment, notably Ikarus buses and electric passenger trains, has ceased completely on account of the need for payment in foreign currency.

Road transport equipment consists primarily of trucks and buses whereas passenger cars and vans are scarce. The average age of the fleet is high, probably more than ten years. Despite their privileged access to allocations in the past, even state companies have usually kept their vehicles in operation for 15–17 years (the official norm is 8–10 years) as a result of insufficient allocations for replacement.

The railways are primarily equipped for freight transport, particularly of bulk commodities carried in specialised wagons. Most rolling stock is from the 1970s, but equipment from the 1950s is still in operation. The current rate of replacement is very low, in the region of 1 per cent per year.

Each of the Aeroflot districts in the three republics operates 20–25 passenger jets (80–160 seats), 5–10 turbo prop passenger planes (typically 50 seats) and a few small cargo planes with a capacity of about 4 tons each. The airplanes are typically 15–20 years old.

The three shipping lines operate a combined fleet of about 200 vessels with a total tonnage of nearly 2 million tons dead weight. The bulk of the fleet consists of product tankers, reefer (that is refrigerated) vessels, bulk and timber carriers and RO/RO vessels. Most of the vessels are from the 1970s, but a few were built in the mid-1960s. The most recent vessels are three rail ferries built between 1986 and 1989 for the Klaipeda–Mukran ferry link. Provision of new vessels through the central allocation system has ceased completely.

The individual transport companies operate extensive maintenance facilities for their own transport equipment. Maintenance levels appear to be rather high, given the high average age of the equipment. Insufficient allocation of spares, in particular tyres and engine parts, is an increasing problem.

As a result of the insufficient supplies through the official allocation system, the state transport companies try to obtain equipment and spare parts through informal channels:

1. purchase of spare parts produced or reconditioned within the private sector;
2. barter deals, either directly between individual companies or organised bilaterally between the republican governments such as a trucking company trading meat for spare parts from a truck manufacturer at a rate of exchange of ten roubles' worth of meat for one rouble's worth of spare parts and further agreeing to lend some of its skilled labourers to work for the manufacturer in exchange for supplies of spares;
3. domestic trading in convertible currency; and
4. direct trading abroad (without the participation of central institutions) such as the shipping companies ordering new tonnage abroad, financed internationally on commercial terms and backed by the shipping companies' currency earnings in international traffic; or, on a smaller scale, the extensive import of spare parts and second-hand vehicles from Europe, financed from export proceeds and by seamen in international traffic.

Apart from the current supply problems, the transport sector faces a major problem with the apparent obsolescence of most of its transport equipment, particularly in relation to fuel efficiency and environmental standards.

The low fuel efficiency is bound to lead to extensive cost increases in the domestic transport sector when the expected internationalisation of Soviet fuel prices takes place over the next few years. In turn, this will translate into substantial increases in domestic production cost throughout the economy. To some extent, technical measures and investment in more efficient equipment can reduce the problem of cost increase, but the main problem is that the organisation of production results in excessive use of transport.

International transporters are less vulnerable to increasing fuel costs as they have long been exposed to international prices. They face, however, a major need for re-investment because much of their current equipment, in particular trucks and airplanes, do not live up to contemporary environmental standards in the West and will be barred from operating in Europe within a few years on grounds of excessive emission and noise levels.

e. Pricing, efficiency and cost of production

Transport within the Soviet Union is very cheap even by Soviet standards. The low domestic transport prices reflect a degree of direct subsidising, but are primarily related to the low cost of inputs:

1. cheap fuels, for example 40 kopeks for a litre of petrol or diesel, 7 kopeks for a cubic-metre of natural gas (which is widely used in trucks) and 171 roubles for a ton of jet fuel (the prices are from March 1991 in Lithuania and are equivalent to US$ .07, US$ .01 and US$ 30 respectively at the official tourist exchange rate, while unofficial rates would have been about a fifth of those values;
2. low wages, typically 350 roubles per month plus social expenses (virtually free housing, access to cheap or otherwise unobtainable consumer goods etc.);
3. hitherto inexpensive capital equipment.

International transport, like domestic, benefits from low labour and capital costs and from low fuel costs to the degree that refuelling abroad is avoided. Internationally marketed transport services are priced competitively, usually 10–20 per cent below comparable international prices. This pricing practice makes international traffic highly attractive for the Soviet transport companies because the international prices are at least 5–6 times higher than comparable domestic prices.

Domestic transport, on the other hand, is faced with price controls which usually allow little or no profit margins for the transport companies. Most companies engaged in domestic transport claim to break even, although many, upon closer examination, turn out to do so in terms of direct cost, that is prior to personnel and overhead expenses.

Efficiency in the transport sector is considered by most managers within that sector to be low. The validity of this perception is, however, difficult to evaluate as cost figures comparable to Western figures are difficult to establish, partly owing to differences in definitions and partly because fleet utilisation differs substantially from that in the West.

As an example, monthly returns for January 1991 indicate that average full-cost prices in four city bus companies in Lithuania are 12–27 kopeks per trip (equivalent to US$ .02–.05) which is quite low and hence indicates a high efficiency even when taking the low cost of inputs into account. But the capacity ratings of the buses appear higher than in the West and the services are limited to a degree where average utilisation of offered capacity (seated as well as standing) is 90 per cent or higher which is well above the 60–70 per cent considered the maximum obtainable in the West.

Within the freight transport sector capacity utilisation is manifestly low, primarily owing to the basic organisation of the Soviet transport system which is characterised by:

1. lack of intermediate storage capacity at transhipment points which ties down capacity waiting for pick-up or delivery of cargo;
2. extensive pre-allocation of transport which leaves capacity idle (at no or negligible cost to the transport buyer) whenever demand is delayed; and
3. lack of unitised transport systems and efficient transport coordination which leads to excessive empty return traffic.

f. Internal structure of the transport companies

Compared with most Western transport organisations, the Soviet state transport companies (and even many cooperative and private companies) exhibit a high degree of vertical integration, incorporating within their own organisation most or all of the technical support infrastructure required for primary operations. A striking example is Aeroflot which operates all commercial airplanes and related repair facilities as well as all commercial airports and the civilian air traffic-control system. A result of this high degree of vertical integration is that common support facilities such as independent repair shops and even petrol stations are rare.

Three developments have had a major impact on the operations of the transport industry: a general decline in Soviet economic activity since 1988, a break-down of major parts of the central allocation system and the adoption of new republican legislation covering the all-union companies, often in conflict with existing union legislation.

The state companies' external relations were, until recently, largely confined to communications with their parent ministry at either republican or union level which provided all resources and handled all client relations as part of the central planning system. As a result, most state companies have little, if any, internal capacity for handling commercial customer and supplier relations, the exceptions being a few companies with long standing direct business relations with the West, primarily the shipping companies and Aeroflot.

The weakening of the centralised allocation system and the general decline in overall economic activity have forced the transport companies to change their mode of operation from passive execution of orders into active adaptation to changing economic conditions. Among the new tasks facing company management are:

1. development of new, external relations in order to obtain physical inputs, typically by participating in bilateral barter deals between companies or between republics;
2. ensuring self-financing, in particular with regard to foreign-currency earnings which, often, are necessary for acquisition of capital equipment even when purchased within the Soviet Union (an example is that Soviet truck manufacturers now price their products in a mix of foreign currency and roubles, for example DM 200,000 plus 60,000 roubles for a twenty-ton truck with trailer);
3. developing market relations in order to secure employment and revenues in a declining market (for example the shipping companies offering excess tonnage on time charter in the world market);
4. cost reduction in order to ensure profitability (for example the current rapid reduction in crew size aboard Soviet vessels).

The main challenge facing management within the freight transport sector is the reduction of the apparent excess capacity, in particular as the expected price reforms will lead to increased fuel prices which cannot be passed on to the customers without a sharp decrease in demand. Most company managers find it difficult to lay off their employees. They thus concentrate on efforts to cut non-wage costs, for example application of technical means for decreasing fuel consumption and delayed re-investment in new transport equipment, or they strive after revenue-generating business ventures outside the companies' normal scope of operations (such as a distribution company transporting goods to Poland as part of what would appear to be a somewhat shady business transaction).

The emergence of republican legislation covering, in principle, the all-union as well as the republican companies, has placed the republican-based all-union transport companies in a difficult position where they must choose whether to obey union or republican legislation. In the case of corporate taxation most all-union companies have chosen to follow republican rules on the grounds that republican taxation is lower than the comparable union taxes (approximately 35 per cent and 45 per cent respectively, both taxed in principle on net profits). In the case of foreign currency, however, most companies follow union regulations which typically require all-union transport companies to sell 40 per cent of gross foreign-currency earnings to the union government at the official exchange rate.

B. Government policy

a. Issues and policies

The general economic and political transition process in the Baltic states has a number of implications for the transport sector. In particular, transport is affected by:

1. abolition of government control over production, investment and input allocation, commercialisation and de-monopolisation of the state companies and deregulation of prices;
2. transfer of control over taxation and foreign-currency holdings from union to republican level, transfer of control and ownership of all-union companies to the republics (for example the shipping companies, the gas distribution companies and the international road transport companies) and breaking-up of the union-wide monopolies (for example the railways and Aeroflot) into republican enterprises;
3. privatisation, including the return of nationalised property to the former owners or their descendants; and
4. the nationality issue, in light of the fact that most all-union transport companies tend to employ very high proportions of non-Baltic nationals, typically more than 90 per cent of the workforce.

On matters of common interest for the republics (like the handling of all-union property and the transfer of legal powers from the union to the republics) policies have been coordinated into a common stance for the three republics, encompassing:

1. replacement of the specialised transport sector ministries on republican level with a unified ministry of transport charged with regulating the industry rather than detailed management of the individual companies;
2. establishment of republican legislation encompassing republican as well as the all-union companies as a first step towards establishing republican supremacy over the all-union companies;
3. republican take-over of activities spinning off from all-union companies, for example the secondary ports and the expected takeover of airport operations and merchant marine and aviation training centres;
4. active encouragement of the development of alternatives to the all-union transport companies, for example establishment of private or cooperative transport companies and operations by foreign companies; and
5. establishment of republican ships and airplane registers and establishment of republican control for air, sea and rail traffic.

Besides the legal proposals, the three republics have defined a number of strategic development projects designed to establish a capability to receive supplies, in particular oil products, from outside the Soviet Union and to enhance connections with Europe:

1. establishment of strategic oil import facilities in the oil ports in Ventspils and Klaipeda which are currently equipped for export only and in Tallinn;
2. a proposed construction of a pipeline from the oil refinery in Mazeikiai to Ventspils in order to import oil from places other than the Soviet Union;
3. the ongoing development of international passenger facilities in the airports and in Tallinn and Riga ports and the related drive towards establishment of international air and ferry connections; and
4. development of 'Via Baltica', which is a concept for establishment of a well-serviced transport corridor from Helsinki via Tallinn, Riga and Kaunas to Warsaw, where it would connect with the proposed 'East European Highway' from Gdansk to Istanbul.

b. Liberalisation and commercialisation

The republican governments have realised that liberalisation of the transport sector involves three consecutive steps: commercialisation of the individual companies, de-monopolisation and, only then, full deregulation of prices.

The first step, commercialisation of the companies, is in progress following the abolition of the traditional sector ministries within the Baltic governments and the widespread collapse of the central allocation system on union level. As a result of this, the bulk of traditional ministry control over the individual companies has been effectively dismantled, except for the railways and the pipeline operators.

The process is however hampered by a severe lack of proper markets for the companies to operate in and by the current price structure which renders many companies commercially unviable. The republican transport ministries quite sensibly maintain tight controls over prices and conditions of carriage in order to avoid monopoly pricing and to ensure transport to areas which would otherwise not be served. Whether the expected price reform will make the transport companies economically viable remains to be seen. If that is not the case, commercialisation of the sector is likely to grind to a halt.

The second step: de-monopolisation is being actively pursued by the Baltic governments but only limited results have been achieved so far:

1. the spin-off of secondary activities such as ports and agency services from the shipping lines;
2. partitioning of a few monopoly trucking companies into smaller, competing companies; and
3. the emergence of new private transport companies which, however, in most cases are very small and thus have little impact if any on the monopoly position of their large, state-owned competitors.

The main problem appears to be the price system, which leads to extensive cross-subsidising within the individual companies and thus prevents a sensible partitioning because some of the new companies would not be self-sustaining.

The last step, deregulation of prices, is not contemplated yet given the limited progress of de-monopolisation.

c. Transfer of ownership and legislative powers over all-union companies

The process of transforming ownership of the republican-based all-union companies to the republics would, after independence, seem to be a relatively straightforward business. However, negotiations and legal issues may well make the process a protracted one. In addition there are the interests of management and employees in securing their current positions and even claiming shared ownership.

In relation to the conflict between union and republic law, it appears that management of the republican-based all-union transport companies in general has chosen to adopt a neutral position between the union and the republics, while utilising their newly acquired freedom of action to choose which set of rules to follow based on their own company interests.

Transfer of ownership of the union-wide transport monopolies — the railways, Aeroflot and the pipeline operators — requires two steps: first partitioning the companies into republican units, possibly after segregating certain functions which are to be retained under the union, such as the civilian air-traffic control system under Aeroflot, followed by transformation into joint-stock companies as described above.

The three republican governments actively seek to break up the union-wide companies into republican units. However, this earlier met with little apparent success in the case of the railways, though there was some promise in the case of civil aviation where, as a first step, segregation of the airfields from Aeroflot and subsequent republican takeover seems imminent. The break-up and republican takeover of the airline operations is also expected.

d. Privatisation

Management within the transport industry expresses rather mixed feelings towards privatisation. A few managers consider privatisation an opportunity for commercial development, either in terms of market openings or better conditions for implementation of internal restructuring, particularly lay-offs. Most managers view the issue with caution, however, especially in light of the potential conflicts with the labour force and favour solutions where ownership is dominated by government and the companies' own employees.

With regard to the all-union transport companies which are of apparent strategic interest to the union in general, the standard model for privatisation advocated by the three Baltic transport ministries was before independence equal share-holding by the union government, the republican government and the general public. The position with regard to non-strategic all-union companies and the republican state companies is less clear cut but leans towards a mixture of employee and general public ownership.

The political desire within the republics to return property to former owners is in the transport sector only relevant to shipping, which is the only mode with significant private capital during the independence period. Management at the shipping companies consider it likely that actual ships will be returned to the former owners. Within the ministries of transport this solution is seen as a short-cut to a competitive shipping market. It is quite possible that management favours the idea too as an opportunity to off-load excess tonnage in a situation where their main market, Soviet international trade, is in decline.

e. The nationality issue

The nationality issue is particularly relevant for the all-union companies, which are all staffed primarily by non-Baltic nationalities. The problem has two aspects:

1. the possible future position of non-Baltic nationals within the Baltic republics which does not seem to concern the non-Baltic managers at the all-union companies;
2. future limitations in the access to non-Baltic labour which seems to be a major concern, in particular at the ports.

The problem with access to non-Baltic labour is acute, in particular in Estonia and Latvia where there has been a major shortage of labour. Difficult, hard and unrewarding jobs, such as working as a docker, seem only to be able to be filled with temporary immigrants who accept the jobs on account of the ministry of merchant marine providing them, for instance, with housing in their home towns upon satisfactory completion of their contracts. The break-down of the central allocation system which facilitated the award system and the new Baltic restrictions on immigration have combined to create a situation where such positions can no longer be filled. Presumably, the situation is temporary and will be resolved when redundant workers start being laid-off as part of the process of streamlining the Baltic economies.

C. Commercial prospects and limitations facing the transport sector

a. Development strategies

Apart from the general drive towards commercialisation and republicanisation of the economies, a number of specific policies are being pursued by the three governments:

1. establishment of new transit routes supplementing the dwindling freight transit traffic via the Baltic ports to the rest of the Soviet Union;
2. expansion of the traffic links with the West while maintaining the traditional traffic links to other republics within the union, thereby establishing the Baltic republics as a gateway for international trade with the Soviet Union bolstered by their knowledge of the Soviet economic system;
3. development of new import and export relations as means of general economic development but also as a strategic means of reducing the dependence on union markets; and
4. restructuring domestic transport in order to develop an efficient and cost effective utility capable of servicing small- and large-scale industry and the population's general needs.

Some elements of transport strategy are coordinated among the three republics, incorporating practical cooperation in terms of common development projects such as the 'Via Baltica' concept and the formation of common stands *vis-à-vis* the union government. Firm plans for establishment of common transport companies, such as a common airline and a common railway, do not exist, even though the benefits associated with scale of operations in air transport and the conservation of a harmonious railway network are generally appreciated.

b. Transit traffic

Cargo transit traffic via the Baltic ports to the Soviet Union has traditionally dominated the Baltic transport sector and, thus, the requirements of the transit traffic determined the development of transport infrastructure within the republics.

The transit traffic to the union is declining as a result of the general deterioration of the Soviet economy but development of new forms of cargo transit traffic can compensate for some of the losses in transit volume and have the potential to generate substantial currency revenues:

1. container transit traffic via the Soviet Union to the Far East and the Middle East which is already developing fast, constrained only by the capacity of the Transsiberian railway connection and cumbersome

operational procedures within the Soviet railway system;

2. transit traffic from Finland via the Baltic republics to Poland and hence to Central Europe could be an attractive alternative to the current ferry connections between Helsinki and Germany; and
3. in the longer perspective, transit traffic might develop from Finland and Sweden, via the Baltic republics and Belorussia to the Middle East, the Balkans and Italy, in response to the growing traffic congestion in Central Europe.

The main constraints to the development of alternative freight transit traffic for the railways are: the differences in gauge between the Soviet and the European railways (apart from Finland), poorly maintained north–south links and the lack of a railway crossing into Poland. For road traffic, the lack of public road traffic services (such as repair facilities for Western trucks, petrol stations and proper restaurant and over night facilities etc.) within the Baltic republics in particular, and the union in general, and cumbersome border-crossing procedures between the Soviet Union and East Europe and internally between the Eastern European countries are the major difficulties.

Currently, development of new freight transit traffic is concentrated on the rail-based container traffic to the Far East, which is being developed by a number of international container shipping lines, and development of the 'Via Baltica' project. The development of 'Via Baltica' includes:

1. Tallink, a ferry and RO/RO link between Helsinki and Tallinn operating as an Estonian–Finnish joint venture with the Estonian Shipping Company as the local partner and the development of new ferry terminals in Tallinn City Port;
2. establishment of road services which are being developed partly with foreign capital, for example the Finnish investments in new filling stations in Estonia and British investments in motels in Lithuania;
3. upgrading of certain road sections, in particular in Lithuania where a road bridge across the Nemunas River is under construction as part of a by-pass of Kaunas, and the road from Kaunas to Marijampole (towards the Polish border) is being upgraded to four-lane standard; and
4. a proposed upgrading of the customs facilities on the border to Poland.

Development of a railway transit corridor between Finland and Poland is not envisaged for the time being, but the prospect of establishing a railway connection to Europe and a by-pass of St. Petersburg (which currently is a major bottleneck for Finnish railway traffic to the Soviet Union and beyond) could be interesting from a Finnish point of view. Development would, however, require extensive capital investment to establish a railway–ferry link between Helsinki and Tallinn, extensive track rehabilitation on the Tallinn–Riga–Daugavpils line and establishment of a railway connection into Poland (from Marijampole to Trakiszki) equipped with facilities to re-axle.

In addition to transit by rail and road, Latvia is seeking to develop air cargo traffic between Europe and the Far and Middle East via Riga. It would also like to establish republican supremacy over the air-traffic control system which generates substantial air passage revenues, since Riga is on the international air route between Northern Europe and the Far East.

c. International traffic

International traffic connections are expanding fast, and currently encompass:

1. RO/RO and container services to Finland, Sweden, Denmark, Germany, the Netherlands, Belgium and France; ferry links to and from Tallinn to Helsinki and Stockholm, a ferry link from Riga to Norrköping under establishment and proposals for establishment of further ferry connections from Riga, Ventspils and Klaipeda to Sweden and Denmark;
2. expanding international road haulage to Scandinavia and Central Europe, encouraged actively by the Baltic governments and facilitated by the transformation of former state companies into more or less privatised road hauliers, as well as road transport forwarding companies operating as alternatives to the union-wide monopolies which traditionally dominated Soviet international trade;
3. expanding international scheduled air traffic, notably the services by Finnair, SAS and Aeroflot from Tallinn to Helsinki and Stockholm and from Riga to Copenhagen and Stockholm; and
4. a growing charter traffic by Aeroflot and other East and West European airlines which in 1990 reached a combined 2–3 weekly departures, primarily to Warsaw and Hamburg but also to more distant destinations such as for example regular charters to Tel Aviv which were planned to commence from Riga by February but were delayed by the outbreak of the Gulf War.

The current surge in international traffic is partly dictated by the need for the Baltic transport companies to earn foreign currency in order to obtain spares and replacement equipment, illustrated by a long-term time charter of five jet liners from the Lithuanian Aeroflot to Colombia, and partly by the growing direct business relations between the Baltic states and Western Europe outside the scope of the centralised all-union trade channels.

In spite of the current high level of activity, the international road and air traffic sector faces serious problems because most trucks and air planes are old, fuel-inefficient and sub-grade in terms of international environmental standards and therefore will be banned from operations in Europe within a few years. Replacement is a major problem as most equipment will have to be bought in convertible currency even from Soviet sources. Since adequate domestic funds are unlikely to be available, future development will have to rely on external financing, either credits, long-term leasing arrangements or capital infusion through merger with Western companies.

Table 13.6 Basic features of the telecommunications system, 1989

		Estonia	Latvia	Lithuania
Telephone lines	thousands	354	709	840
Of which private	thousands	214	464	n/a
Telex lines International	no.	200	n/a	200
Union	no.	2,500	n/a	3,000
Telephones/100 inhabitants	lines	22	22	28
Switching type				
Electro-mechanical	%	94	95	95
Digital	%	6	5	5
International calls	millions	n/a	0.2	n/a
Inter urban calls	millions	27.6	45.3	86.2
Total number of calls	millions	n/a	n/a	790.0

Source: Statistical abstracts, latest editions and government sources.

d. Domestic traffic

Domestic traffic is shrinking rapidly in pace with the general decline of the economy. Furthermore, the domestic transport sector is affected by lack of spare parts and fuel which has particularly hurt the emerging cooperative and private road transporters. These are outside the official allocation system and must rely on high-priced black-market supplies. The large republican state companies are also experiencing rising operational costs, following the break-down of the central allocation system and furthermore are still subject to price controls.

Streamlining operations and reduction of capacity to conform with actual demand becomes evermore critical within the state sector. However, lay-offs are difficult to implement, and proposals for break-up of the companies into smaller units, of which the majority are likely to fail within a short period of time, are easily resisted. As a result, the restructuring of the road transport sector is stalled. Many businesses may in the end have to await bankruptcy, which, however is not yet a legal option.

D. Telecommunications and mail services

In all three Baltic states, public telecommunications and mail services are organised within the framework of a republican ministry of communications. Separate communications systems are maintained by the railways, the ministry of energy, the police and other government agencies, operated in most cases by the relevant union ministries. The basic features of the telecommunications system are given in Table 13.6.

By Soviet standards, telecommunications have been well developed in the three Baltic republics; but in comparison to Europe they lag behind with regard to public access to telephones, quality of services and, in particular, the waiting time for private lines (around 10 years).

Table 13.7 Mail traffic, 1989 (millions)

	Estonia	Latvia	Lithuania
Letters	73	113	103
Newspapers etc.	386	628	748
Money orders	5	9	10
Telegrams	3	3	3
Parcels	1	2	n/a

Source: Statistical abstracts, latest edition and government sources.

Subscriber charges are low, about 2–3 roubles per month for private subscribers, and 6–8 roubles per month for business subscribers. Local calls are not charged but trunk calls are, the lowest rate being 20 kopeks per minute for intra-republic calls. Telephones are provided as part of the subscription whereas other equipment, such as telefax, is sold by the communications ministries for foreign currency. Except for Latvia, where the telephone tariff recently was increased to full-cost level, subscribers' charges cover approximately 80 per cent of the operational expenses. The rest is covered by the government.

Direct dialling and direct trunk dialling is available within the Soviet Union but all international traffic is handled via operator at the international exchange in Moscow, which serves the entire union and provides the three Baltic republics with some 20–25 international lines each. Data links are not provided but modem traffic and telefax is generally supported. Telex is divided into two systems: an international telex system and a union system, the latter without access to the international network.

Mobile cellular telephones (NMT 450) are being introduced in Estonia and Latvia, hooked-up to the Finnish NMT network and established primarily as an alternative to the international lines going through Moscow. Introduction of the NMT system is under consideration in Lithuania, but alternative international telecommunications are already established there by means of a satellite connection to France. Furthermore, establishment of an independent international switch with a capacity of 1,200–1,400 lines, connected by fibre optic cable to Warsaw, is being negotiated.

All cables and handsets, and most microwave systems and all switches are of Soviet or East European manufacture. The loss of supplies from Eastern Europe is felt seriously in certain areas such as handsets and components for switch manufacturing. Most switching equipment (90–5 per cent) is electro-mechanical, the latest model is, however, enhanced with microprocessor-based traffic control. Optical fibre cables do not exist in the republics.

Apart from establishment of independent international telecommunications which is considered strategically important by the republican governments, the most pressing issue is the general undersupply of subscriber lines, in particular to businesses. The main constraint to expansion of the telephone network is local area cabling (that is the cable between the switch and the subscriber) which is caused by a severe shortage of cable within the Soviet

Union, but subscriber and trunk switches are also strained and lack of funds hampers extension of the switching capacity. The trunk network is generally considered to have substantial excess capacity.

The postal system primarily handles ordinary mail and parcels. Figures on the mail traffic appear in Table 13.7. Postal payments are not very developed and postal bank services are unknown. Domestic mail is delivered within two days. International mail has gone through Moscow except for direct mail to Denmark, Sweden and Poland and usually takes two weeks to reach the receiver. Mail sorting is generally manual although a Soviet optical sorting system has been developed. In Lithuania, an automated sorting centre equipped with German sorting equipment is under establishment.

All three Baltic states have started to issue their own stamps and have asked for recognition of the stamps in international mail traffic.

14 Energy

A. Introduction

In a world of dwindling non-renewable energy resources and growing ecological concern, the energy supply–demand balance has everywhere appeared high on the economic policy agenda. As small economies heavily dependent on imported fuel, the Baltic republics are no exception. Special characteristics of the Baltic situation include the current links with the broader Soviet energy grid and the impact of Soviet central planning on the pattern of energy use.

Quite apart from energy issues arising from the redefinition of their relationship with the Soviet Union, the Baltic governments would be challenged to ensure current supplies to requisite energy needs at a time when the Soviet economy, and in particular the energy sector, is suffering a steady decline in production. Looking to the future, Baltic energy specialists find it exceedingly difficult to plan given the uncertain political relationship with the Soviet Union. The Lithuanian blockade of March 1990 stresses the severity with which a sudden disturbance in Soviet energy supplies could disrupt the Baltic economies.

Although it is natural to be preoccupied with short-term considerations of securing supply, it is also evident that the long-term prosperity of the Baltic economies depends critically on a more efficient use of energy in industry, agriculture, transport and private use. The relatively poor endowment of indigenous primary energy supplies means that attention must be concentrated on the demand side of the energy equation. Systemic changes are required including the introduction of a market price for energy. In addition, massive investments in energy-saving capital equipment, including substantial import requirements, will be called for.

Although indigenous oil-shale deposits have made Estonia less dependent on imported energy, its dwindling supply, high production costs and contribution to pollution make further development increasingly difficult.

While the implications of heavy dependence on Soviet energy cannot be denied, it should also be emphasised that in certain respects the dependence is mutual. For example, Lithuania is a large net exporter of electricity and refined oil products, and houses a port in Klaipeda through which petroleum exports are shipped. Such mutual dependence provides the basis for successful future Baltic–Soviet negotiation on energy issues.

B. Demand

Primary energy consumption in the Baltic republics increased steadily in the 1970s and 1980s. In 1989–90, the three republics together used

Table 14.1 Primary energy consumption

	Estonia		Latvia		Lithuania		Sweden
	1985	1990	1985	1990	1985	1989	1988
Total in PJ	328	342	280	300	618	648	2,355
Total in TWh	91	95	78	83	172	180	652
Per capita (GJ)	205	214	214	111	167	175	280

Excluding electricity exports from Estonia and Lithuania. Preliminary figures for Estonia and Latvia in 1990.

Source: Calculated out of material provided by the ministries of energy in Estonia, Latvia and Lithuania. Figures for Sweden taken from *OECD in figures* (June/July, 1990).

approximately 1,290 petajoules (PJ) or 359 terawatthours (TWh). Of this, Estonia consumed 342 PJ (95 TWh), Latvia 300 PJ (83 TWh), and Lithuania 648 PJ (180 TWh). Per capita consumption varies considerably between the republics. In Estonia per capita demand of primary energy was about 214 gigajoules (GJ) in 1990. This was well above the average in the Soviet Union (195 GJ), but lower than in Sweden (289 GJ). Lithuania's per capita consumption was 175 GJ in 1989 which is comparable with that of Czechoslovakia (182 GJ). Latvia has the lowest per capita consumption of the Baltic republics. In 1990, it used about 128 GJ per person, forty per cent less than per capita consumption in Estonia (see Table 14.1).

The major part of the used energy is converted to electricity and heat. A smaller amount is used directly as motor fuels for vehicles or as raw material in industrial production. It is difficult to establish the distribution of energy consumption for electricity and heat production since only approximative figures are available. In Latvia and Lithuania, roughly 50 per cent of the primary energy sources are converted to heat (including steam and hot water), 20–25 per cent converted to electricity, and 20–30 per cent used as motor fuels and raw material. In Estonia, 46 per cent was used for electricity generation in 1988, 40 per cent for heat production and 11 per cent for transport.

Because of incomplete statistical data, distribution of final energy use in the Baltic republics can only be roughly estimated. Figures are available from Latvia and Lithuania for the year 1985. Industry was the major energy consumer and accounted for 58 per cent of total final consumption in Latvia and 44 per cent in Lithuania. In Latvia, the residential and service sector consumed 16 per cent the same year, while the corresponding figure for Lithuania was 27 per cent. Transport and agriculture production accounted for 23 per cent in Latvia, and 26 per cent in Lithuania (see Table 14.2).

The final-demand pattern in the Baltic republics reflects a structure of energy use typical of centrally planned economies. Calculated on a per capita basis, energy use for industrial and agricultural production is larger than in most developed market economies, consumption for freight is about the

Table 14.2 Final energy use in Latvia and Lithuania, by sector, 1985 (%)

	Latvia	Lithuania
Industry[1]	57.6	44.5
Agriculture	11.5	7.5
Households and service	16.1	26.7
Transport	11.5	18.6
Others	3.3	2.7[2]

Notes: [1] Including own needs of power plants. [2] Construction.

Source: Energeticheskaya programma Latvii, Fiziko-energeticheskiy Institut Akademii Nauk Latvii, Riga, 1990; Lithuanian Ministry of Energy.

Table 14.3 Electricity consumption (excluding own needs of power plants and grid losses)

	Estonia		Latvia		Lithuania	
	1985	1990	1985	1990	1985	1990
Total consumption (TWh)	6.6	7.0	7.9	8.7*	11.7	12.7*
Per capita (MWh)	4.2	4.4	2.9	3.2*	3.2	3.3*

* Preliminary figures.

Source: Energetika respublik Pribaltiki, Belorussii i Severo-zapada RSFSR, Tallinn, 1990; Estonian Ministry of Industry; Lithuanian Ministry of Energy.

same, while consumption for homes, services and travel is smaller than that in Western countries.

Gross consumption of electricity increased by 2–3 per cent annually in the late 1980s in Estonia and Latvia and by 4–5 per cent in Lithuania. This trend was broken in 1990, when electricity consumption fell by 1.5 per cent in Estonia, 5.5 per cent in Latvia and 3.5 per cent in Lithuania. The reason for the decreased electricity demand was the decline in industrial production.

Total and per capita electricity consumption is shown in Table 14.3. Electricity consumption in Estonia and Latvia was about 7.0 and 8.7 TWh in 1990 respectively and in Lithuania, 16.4 TWh. Per capita consumption was 4,400 kWh in Estonia which was well above the per capita level in Latvia (3,200 kWh) and Lithuania (3,300 kWh). Per capita electricity consumption in the Baltic countries is comparable with that of the East European countries but lower than that of developed market economies.

In all three republics, industry is the largest electricity consumer. According to official figures, it accounts for 40–50 per cent of total consumption. The residential and service sector uses 20–35 per cent, agriculture 15–25 per cent, and transport 2–5 per cent. These figures may be somewhat misleading it is unclear whether residential use at the countryside is included in agricultural demand or not. Notwithstanding these reservations, it is clear

Table 14.4 Electricity consumption by sector, 1985 (TWh)

	Estonia*	Latvia	Lithuania*
Gross consumption:	9.4	9.5	14.7
Used at power plants	1.7	0.3	1.4
Grid losses	1.1	1.2	1.6
Net consumption:	6.6	7.9	11.7
of which (in %),			
Industry	50.6	42.7	49.2
Agriculture	24.0	15.1	19.6
Residential & service	21.3	36.2	26.8
Transport	2.6	5.0	2.1
Construction	1.5	0.8	2.2

* Excluding electricity exports.

Source: Jørgen Fenhann (ed.): *Energy and Environment in Estonia, Latvia and Lithuania* (Risø, 1991).

that the consumption pattern in the Baltic republics is different from that in developed market economies. In the latter countries, households and services use up to half the total electricity supply. The relatively small residential consumption in the Baltic republics is explained by a general housing shortage and a limited use of electric household appliances in Baltic homes (see Table 14.4).

C. Supply

a. Background

With the exception of oil-shale, which is exploited in Estonia, the Baltic republics have very limited domestic energy resources. Latvia and Lithuania have a small potential hydro power. Peat has traditionally been used for fuel in all three republics and is still being exploited in Estonia and Latvia. Wood fuel is mainly used in the countryside but is only of marginal importance in the picture of overall energy consumption.

The Baltic republics satisfy their energy demand almost exclusively through using fossil fuels. In Estonia, oil-shale accounts for 45 per cent of primary energy consumption, followed by oil (34 per cent), and natural gas (14 per cent). Coal, peat and wood make up the remaining 7 per cent. In Latvia, natural gas accounted for about 35 per cent of the total energy supply in 1985, oil for about 25 per cent and coal for about 10 per cent. Domestic sources such as peat, hydro power and firewood contributed 27 per cent. Lithuania gets the lion's share, 56 per cent, of its energy supply from oil, 28 per cent from natural gas, 6 per cent from coal, 6 per cent from nuclear power and 5 per cent from other sources, mainly hydro power and firewood (see Table 14.5).

The Baltic republics are highly dependent on energy imports from the Soviet Union. This dependence is most significant in Lithuania, which

Table 14.5 Energy supply by source (in per cent)

	Estonia[1] 1990	Latvia 1985	Lithuania[1] 1989
Oil-shale	44.5	—[2]	—
Oil	34.4	23.6	55.7
Natural gas	14.2	33.6	27.6
Coal	1.8	10.0	5.8
Nuclear power	—	—[2]	6.1[3]
Indigenous sources (peat, wood, hydro power)	5.0	27.1	4.8
Total (PJ)	342	280	648

[1] Excluding exported electricity.
[2] The remaining 5.7 per cent were provided by imported electricity (produced by oil-shale and nuclear power).
[3] Calculated as coal equivalents demanded for conventional thermal electricity production.

Source: Calculated from information provided by the Ministries of Energy in Estonia, Latvia and Lithuania.

imports more than 90 per cent of its primary energy supplies. Thanks to its oil-shale resources, Estonia imports roughly half of the energy it uses.

Electricity production capacity is dispensed unevenly among the Baltic republics. Power plants for electricity generation have been located and constructed according to Soviet plans for a much larger region. Estonia, Latvia and Lithuania are parts of the 'unified electric energy system' (*edinaya energeticheskaya sistema*). Together with the Kola peninsula, Karelia, the Leningrad and Pskov administrative areas (*oblasti*), Belorussia, and the Kaliningrad area, they are incorporated in the electricity grid of the northwestern Soviet Union. The main office of this network (*glavnoye dispetcherskoye upravleniye*) is in Riga. From here all electricity production in the northwest of the Soviet Union is coordinated and allocated to different parts of the region. The grid consists of several 330 kilovolt (kV) lines, connecting the main parts of the northwestern region with each other, and one 750-kV line from St. Petersburg to Moscow. There are also two 330-kV connections to Finland, and one 220-kV line from Belorussia to Poland. Altogether, the network has access to a total installed capacity of 36,000 megawatt, a third more than the total capacity in Poland.

Soviet energy planning for the northwestern region has been influenced by a number of factors such as fuel availability, load demands and technological preferences. Because of oil-shale deposits in northeastern Estonia, this was a natural place to build thermal-power plants. These plants not only serve Estonia but also supply Latvia, Leningrad and the Pskov region with electricity.

There are three nuclear power plants in the northwestern region, one of them situated in Ignalina in the northeastern part of Lithuania. This plant is an important supplier of electricity to Lithuania and Belorussia.

In the 1970s and 1980s, Soviet energy planners aimed at developing nuclear power as the main means of meeting basic-load demand in the northwestern region, while peak-load demand was to be satisfied by building new pumped storage and hydro-power facilities. Beside the Ignalina plant, original plans called for two new nuclear-power stations in Karelia and Belorussia respectively. Also, construction works were started on a pumped storage/hydro-power station in Kaišiadoris in Lithuania.

After the Chernobyl accident in 1986, this strategy was confronted with a series of difficulties. As a result of growing public concern and local protest, as well as technical problems and shortage of funds in the nuclear-power industry, the construction of the Karelian and Belorussian nuclear-power plants have been cancelled. At the Ignalina station, only two reactor blocs out of four have been completed, and further expansion of the plant is not envisaged. Since the second block at Ignalina was taken into production in 1987, new capacity for electricity production has not been developed for the grid of the northwestern region.

In contrast to other grids in the Soviet Union, the northwestern power grid on average generates a surplus, which is transmitted to neighbouring grids. According to Soviet experts, the grid will operate at a deficit by the mid-1990s if electricity demand in the northwestern region continues to grow at the same rate as in the late 1980s. At present, minimum load is 22,000 MW and maximum load 36,000 MW. This means that the northwestern grid has to work at its full capacity during peak load, when it is unable to transmit electricity to other regions of the Soviet Union. The lack of reserve capacity in the Soviet Union is a serious problem. The Soviet government has several times been forced to reduce industrial production in parts of the union on cold winter days to avoid overloading the electricity system.

b. Estonia

Estonia is the only Baltic republic with sizeable indigenous energy resources. Domestic oil-shale, and some peat and wood, satisfy about half of Estonia's primary energy demand. The rest is provided by imported fuels from Russia and Belorussia, mainly oil and natural gas.

Oil-shale is exploited in the northeastern part of the country in the region between the cities Kohtla–Järve and Narva. Only the shale with highest content of organic material is used. This kukersite, or brown oil-shale, has an energy content of 8.4–9.6 megajoules per kilogramme (MJ/kg), almost three times lower than that of hard coal. The mining of shale occupies 7.5 per cent of Estonia's surface area. The oil-shale basin stretches over the border into the Leningrad administrative area. Total production from the basin reached a peak of 36.5 million tons in 1980. It decreased in the 1980s and was down to 28 million tons in 1989. Usable resources are estimated at 1.7 billion tons. An additional 1.2 billion tons is regarded as technologically possible to exploit.

In 1989, 23.3 million tons of oil-shale was extracted in Estonia by the all-union enterprise Estonslanets (the Estonian name is Eesti Põlevkivi). In the same year, about 5 million tons of shale was produced at the Leningrad deposit, and roughly half of it was exported to Estonia. Estonslanets mines about 50 per cent of the shale from four open-pit quarries and the rest from six underground mines. It produces shale in two qualities; either coarse (diameter 25–125 millimetres) or crushed (up to 25 millimetres). Coarse oil-shale is processed into shale oil, which is used as raw material in the chemical industry and as fuel for different purposes. About 2.5 million tons of coarse oil-shale is used in this way every year. Crushed oil-shale is combusted for electricity production. Since 1988, an annual amount of 22–23 million tons has been utilised for electricity production. The residual ashes from the combustion process are stored, some being used for building materials, and some are also used in agriculture for liming acid soils since the ashes have a high lime content.

Oil-shale is the primary source for electricity production in Estonia. Production is concentrated at two thermal-power stations in Narva: the Estonian (1,610 MW$_e$, that is megawatt electricity output) and the Baltic (1,435 MW$_e$) power stations. They use about eleven million tons of oil-shale each, annually. There are also three smaller power stations fuelled with oil-shale which together have a total capacity of 70 MW$_e$. In addition, there is the Iru power plant in Tallinn with a capacity of 190 MW$_e$, run on heavy fuel oil. The three smaller oil-shale power plants are all forty years or older and will be taken out of production in the next few years. The Baltic thermal-power plant was built in 1959–65 and is in need of reconstruction. The Estonian power plant was built in 1969–73 and the Iru power plant in Tallinn was completed in 1978.

Estonian electricity output reached a peak of 19.2 TWh in 1979. Before the Ignalina nuclear-power plant in Lithuania was commissioned, Estonia was the largest electricity producer in the Baltic region. In the early 1980s Estonian electricity output decreased somewhat, and stabilised around 17.5–18 TWh annually after the mid-1980s. In 1990 production fell to 17.0 TWh (see Table 14.6).

Of the total production in 1990, 1.7 TWh was required for the maintenance of the power plants, 1.3 TWh was lost in transmission, 7.0 TWh was exported and the remaining 10 TWh used for domestic consumption. Exports went to Latvia (3.4 TWh) and the neighbouring Leningrad (1.0 TWh) and Pskov (2.6 TWh) areas. The Estonian network is linked to the northwestern grid via seven 330-kV lines; three between Narva and the Leningrad area, two connecting with the Pskov area and two with Latvia. For domestic distribution, 330-, 220- and 110-kV transmission lines are used. There is also a 35-kV submarine cable supplying the islands with electricity. Figure 14.1 shows the 330-kV electrical network and the connection to the northwestern power system.

The all-union enterprise Estonenergo (Eesti Energia) has a monopoly on electricity distribution in Estonia. Electricity is transmitted by five regional network companies to about 600,000 households and 50,000 other subscribers, of which about 1,500 use more than 750 MWh per year. Industry is the largest consumer; in 1989 it required 52 per cent of the total electricity output (including the power plants' own needs), followed by households and service (23 per cent) and agriculture (22 per cent). The

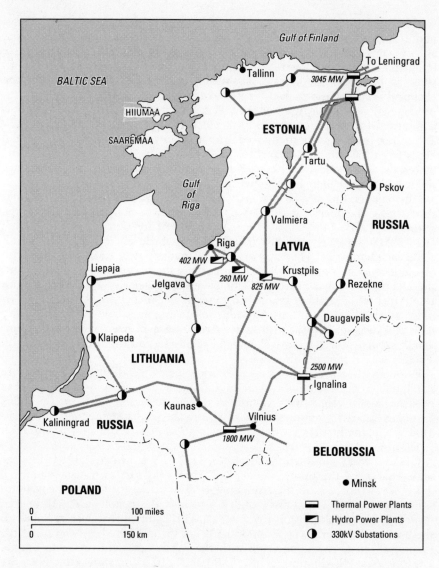

Figure 14.1 Electrical network

Source: Energy in Estonia, Latvia and Lithuania, published jointly by the three ministries of energy, Tallinn, Riga and Vilnius, 1991.

oil-shale-mining and processing industry is by far the largest industrial consumer. Together with the chemical industry based on oil-shale, it accounts for almost a quarter of all electricity used by industry.

The future of the oil-shale mining and electricity production complex in the northeast is a key issue for the development of Estonia's economy. Two possible solutions are being discussed. The first is to continue the production of oil-shale and electricity at the present level while maintaining electricity exports. The second would be a decrease of the oil-shale production, thus reducing or even stopping the export of electricity. A lower production level, 15.5 million tons for electricity generation and 2.2 million tons for chemical production, has been suggested as a possible way to satisfy domestic electricity demand until 2005.

There are several factors supporting the second option. The quality of the extracted oil-shale is decreasing each year, making it increasingly difficult to maintain electricity output without expanding the input of shale at the thermal-power plants. According to estimates made by the Estonian Academy of Sciences, maintaining oil-shale production at the present level would require the opening of new mines with a total annual capacity of five to six million tons sometime in the mid-1990s. The Academy also points out that the shale could be exploited in a more effective way; up to 50 per cent of the shale in the mines remains unexploited or is lost during the different stages of processing. Moreover, the equipment used at the pits and mines is old and worn out. New equipment must be purchased from the Soviet Union or abroad.

It seems obvious that even a somewhat lower production of oil-shale will be difficult to maintain in the future. Oil-shale mining puts severe strains on the environment. Every year, about 350 hectares of land is lost as a result of expanding pits and mines. About 350 million cubic metres of water, partly polluted by salts and metals, are pumped out of the mines each year and released into the Baltic Sea. Residuals from the combustion of oil-shale is another serious problem. The two thermal-power plants in Narva produce about ten million tons of ash each year. Only 40 per cent of this is used, the remaining 60 per cent is deposited in large storage fields. Leaking water from these deposits contains pollutants such as heavy metals and phenols.

The power plants in Narva account for about 70 per cent of the sulphur dioxide and 50 per cent of the nitric oxides emitted in Estonia. According to the international convention on transboundary air pollution, which was signed by the Soviet Union, emissions of sulphur dioxide are to be reduced by 30 per cent from the 1980 level by 1993. The Soviet Union has signed another agreement with Finland to reduce emissions into the air from Estonia and other areas near Finland by 50 per cent by 1995. These agreements have put increased pressure on Estonia to reduce the emissions from its electricity production. If desulphurisation equipment is not installed, electricity output will have to be decreased to 12.7 TWh in 1995. Such equipment must be purchased, and at least partly financed, from abroad.

Heat is produced by approximately 4,000 central boilers, of which 2,000 are used for industrial heating. Besides these boilers, there are also numerous small boilers used in private houses in the countryside. About 80 per cent of households in apartment blocks are supplied with central heating, and about 70 per cent with hot water. In 1985, fuel supply for heat production was based on heavy fuel oil (43 per cent), natural gas (25 per cent) and oil-shale (21 per cent). Total heat production amounted to 23 TWh. Estonenergo accounts for 40 per cent of the total heat production. It supplies

approximately 50 per cent of the households in the four largest cities —
Tallinn, Tartu, Narva and Kohtla-Järve. In 1990, Estonenergo had an
installed capacity for heat production of 3,200 megawatts. All thermal-
power plants are used for co-generation, although the two in Narva can use
a smaller part of their capacity to produce heat. An overview of heat production in the Baltic Republics is provided in Table 14.7.

Industry is the largest consumer of heat: in 1985 it used 56 per cent of
total demand. The residential and sevice sector accounted for 28 per cent,
agriculture production for 9 per cent and transport for 3 per cent.

c. Latvia

Latvia satisfies about 25 per cent of its energy demand from domestic
sources. Natural gas provides about 35 per cent of total supply and is
imported via pipelines from western Siberia. One pipeline connects Riga with
Novopolotsk in Belorussia, and another goes through Lithuania into the
south of Latvia. Latvia has a natural underground storage space for natural
gas. The site is located northeast of Riga and has a total capacity of 2.1
billion cubic metres, the only one of that size in the Baltic region. Heavy fuel
oil (called *mazut* in Russian) accounts for about 25 per cent of total fuel
consumption. It is delivered from oil refineries in Russia and Belorussia and
the Lithuanian refinery in Mazeikiai. Latvia also gets petrol and diesel fuel
from these refineries. About 10 per cent of Latvia's energy supply is coal.
Two-thirds of it is brought from the Donetsk Basin (the Ukraine) and
Kuznetsk (Russia). A third is Silesian coal brought through Belorussia to
Latvia.

Latvia is an important transit area for Soviet oil exports. The Latvian port
Ventspils southwest of Riga is the largest export harbour for Soviet oil to
Western Europe. Between 1978 and 1988 about thirty million tons of oil
was exported via Ventspils each year. In 1988, exports reached a maximum
of thirty-two million tons of oil products, 50 per cent crude oil, 30 per cent
diesel fuel and 20 per cent petrol. These shipments were made in spite of the
fact that the port only has a capacity of twenty-four million tons. The oil
is piped to Ventspils via Belorussia and Latvia; about half of the diesel fuel
is transported by a separate pipeline, and the remaining oil products are
transported by railroad to the port.

As a result of environmental protests and technical considerations, parts
of the port's oil-loading facilities are under reconstruction. Consequently, oil
exports from Ventspils dropped in 1989 and 1990. The reconstruction has
been delayed, probably because the port turned out to be in a worse state
than was expected. In 1990 oil exports were down to 17.2 million tons
(plans for the same year called for 25.2 million tons).

The distribution of revenues from the oil shipped out from Ventspils is an
issue for negotiation between the Latvian and Soviet governments. Until
1989, Latvia did not receive any reimbursements from Moscow for the oil
transported through Ventspils. For the years 1990 and 1991, the Soviet
government has agreed to transfer 0.5 per cent of its revenues from this
export to Latvia. This share is in turn divided between the Latvian state (50

per cent) on one hand and the oil shipping company and local authorities in Ventspils on the other. For after 1991, the Latvian government has suggested a transit fee from Moscow of US$ 5.50 for each ton of oil products exported through its territory. (According to this plan, a total transit of 24 million tons would give Latvia an income of US$ 13.2 million.)

The port of Riga has an export capacity for 200,000 tons of liquified petrol gas (LPG). The gas is transported to Riga by rail. However, as a result of production problems in Russia, no LPG has been exported since 1989.

Latvia is dependent on the neighbouring republics for most of its electricity supply. In 1990, imports amounted to 3.7 TWh, almost 40 per cent of Latvia's total demand. About two-thirds of the electricity imports came from Estonia. The same year, domestic production was 6.5 TWh, an increase of 15 per cent compared with 1989 and the highest annual output recorded so far. (The increase was probably a result of favourable climatic conditions for hydro power, since no new capacity has been installed for many years.) About two-thirds of domestic electricity production are provided by three hydro-power stations located along the Daugava River. They have a total capacity of 1,487 MW and generated 4.5 TWh in 1990. Two thermal power plants in Riga produced 2.0 TWh. They are mainly fuelled with natural gas and have a total generating capacity of 512 MW (see Table 14.6).

According to earlier plans, additional hydro-power capacity of 460 MW was to be constructed near the town of Daugavpils in eastern Latvia. However, the project had to be cancelled after strong opposition from the local population and Latvian environmentalists. Since imports from Estonia are likely to diminish in the next few years, the Latvian government is now discussing possible solutions to make up for the future shortage of electricity supply. At present, the construction of hydro-power stations in Daugavpils and Jekabpils is being discussed. New thermal-power capacity is also discussed: either one new block in Riga or two smaller stations in Daugavpils and Liepaja (on the Baltic coast), respectively.

Electricity production is controlled by the all-union enterprise Latvenergo which supervises the hydro- and thermal-power stations and distributes electricity in Latvia. Of the 10.2 TWh used in 1990, 1.6 TWh was required by the power plants or lost in transmission. Of the remaining 8.6 TWh, 45 per cent was used by industry, 30 per cent by the residential and service sector, 20 per cent by agriculture production, and 5 per cent was used for transport and other purposes.

Fifty-seven per cent of all Latvian households in cities are supplied with central heating. There are approximately 8,000 boilers in the country, of which 5,000 are of the smaller size used in the countryside. All kind of fuels are used for heat production; in 1985 a third of the fuel consumption was natural gas and heavy fuel oil. In 1990, 38 TWh of heat was produced. About 40 per cent of total production was provided by the republican organisation Latvijas Siltums, which supervises boilers in cities and communities all over Latvia. Latvenergo accounted for 23 per cent, mainly through co-generation from its thermal-power plants, and the remaining 37 per cent came from industrial and agricultural enterprises (see Table 14.7).

Consumption is more or less evenly divided between industry and the

Table 14.6 Electricity balances (TWh)

	Estonia			Latvia		Lithuania		
	1980	1985	1990	1985	1990	1980	1985	1990
Gross production:	18.9	17.8	17.0	5.0	6.5	11.7	21.0	28.2
Thermal:	18.9[1]	17.8[1]	17.0[1]	2.0	2.0	11.2	11.1	10.8
Nuclear:	—	—	—	—	—	—	9.5	17.0
Hydro power:	—	—	—	3.0	4.5	0.5	0.4	0.4
Gross consumption:	8.2	9.4	10.0	9.5	10.2	11.6	14.7	16.4
a) Own needs of power plants:	1.8	1.7	1.7	0.3	—	0.7	1.4	2.1[2]
b) Network losses:	1.0	1.1	1.3	1.2	1.6[5]	1.4	1.6	1.6[2]
Transferred net to/from:								
Latvia:	10.7[3]	8.4[3]	3.4	—	—	− 1.6	− 1.2	− 0.4[2]
Belorussia:	—	—	—	4.5[4]	3.6[4]	0.2	5.3	9.9[2]
Kaliningrad:	—	—	—	—	—	1.6	2.1	2.5[2]
Pskov:	—	—	2.6	—	—	—	—	—
Leningrad:	—	—	1.0	—	—	—	—	—

[1] About 95% from power plants fuelled with oil-shale
[2] Preliminary figures
[3] To Latvia, Pskov and Leningrad areas
[4] From Estonia and Belorussia
[5] Own needs and losses

Source: Material provided by Estonenergo, Latvenergo and Litovenergo as well as the ministries of energy in the Baltic republics.

residential and service sector, which account for about 45 per cent each of total consumption. Less than 3 per cent is required for agricultural production.

d. Lithuania

Almost all of Lithuania's primary energy sources are imported (including uran for nuclear power). In 1989, Lithuania imported 5.1 billion cubic metres of natural gas, 4.7 million tons of heavy fuel oil and 1.5 million tons of coal. As in the case of Latvia, Lithuania gets its imported fuels from Siberia (gas, coal), Belorussia (heavy fuel oil), and the Ukraine (coal). Coal has also been delivered from Poland through Belorussia.

Lithuania has some domestic oil resources. About one million tonnes per year is estimated to be recoverable. Besides the import of heavy fuel oil for domestic consumption, in 1989 about thirteen million tons of crude oil was piped to the refinery in Mazeikiai in northwestern Lithuania. About eight million tons of heavy fuel oil was exported from the port of Klaipeda on the Baltic coast. The oil is transported by rail from Mazeikiai and refineries in Belorussia for export to Western Europe.

The Mazeikiai refinery was completed in the early 1980s and is the largest industrial complex in Lithuania. It produces all kinds of refined-oil products, mainly heavy fuel oil, diesel fuel and petrol. In 1989, output was 12.8 million tons of oil products. In 1990, partly as a result of the Soviet blockade, total production fell to 9.6 million tons. About half of the production is exported. Heavy fuel oil and diesel is shipped abroad via Klaipeda. Mazeikiai also provides the Baltic republics and the Soviet Union with refined products, mainly motor fuels.

Klaipeda is one of the largest Baltic ports. It has a total capacity of fifteen million tons. Like Ventspils, Klaipeda was used well above its capacity during the 1980s. The oil harbour in Klaipeda was built in 1959 and partly renovated in 1964. It was originally planned to handle 4.5 million tons of oil per year. From 1982 and onwards, oil exports grew rapidly and amounted to 11.2 million tons in 1988, 2.5 times more than planned. The Lithuanian government is negotiating with the Soviet Union about the future distribution of revenues from the port. There are plans to modernise the oil harbour and equip it for oil imports as well.

Lithuania is the largest electricity producer among the Baltic republics. From 1985, two blocks with a total capacity of 2,500 MW_e were taken into production at the nuclear-power plant in Ignalina. As a result of this, total electricity generation jumped from 11.7 TWh in 1980 to 21 TWh in 1985 and 29.2 TWh in 1989. More than half of the production in 1989, 16.4 TWh, was exported. The following year, total output decreased to 28.2 TWh and exports fell to 12 TWh. Most of the exported electricity goes to Belorussia, and about 20 per cent to the Kaliningrad area (see Table 14.6).

Of the total production in 1990, Ignalina provided 17.0 TWh. About 8 TWh was supplied by the Lithuanian power plant at Elektrenai between Vilnius and Kaunas. This power plant has a capacity of 1,800 MW_e and is fueled by natural gas (60 per cent) in 1990 and heavy fuel oil (40 per cent). The remaining 3 TWh was produced by thermal-power plants in Vilnius (capacity 384 MW_e), Kaunas (190 MW_e) and Mazeikiai (210 MW_e). A hydro-power station outside Kaunas which has a generating capacity of 101 MW_e provided 0.4 TWh.

In 1979, construction work started on a pumped storage and hydro-power station at Kaišiadoris near Kaunas. This station was designed to use surplus electricity, mainly from Ignalina during periods of minimum load, to pump up and store water. The water could then be used to generate hydro power during peak load. Original plans called for a total installed capacity of 1,600 MW_e provided by eight 200-MW turbines. However, because of technical problems and public protests, the construction has been delayed and it is not clear whether the whole project will be realised or not. According to the latest schedule, the two first turbines will be ready for regular generation at the earliest by the end of 1991.

The nuclear-power plant at Ignalina is controlled by the Soviet Ministry of Nuclear Power Industry, Minatomenergoprom. The administration of the Ignalina plant is dominated by Russians. During the Soviet blockade of Lithuania in 1990, the management of Ignalina threatened to close down production which led to a serious conflict with the Lithuanian Ministry of

Energy. This action was eventually stopped on direct orders from the Soviet government.

Ignalina was planned to have four reactors. The first block was taken into production in 1985 and the second in 1987. After the Chernobyl accident in 1986, strong environmental protests led to the decision in 1988 to cancel plans for a fourth reactor. The protests were based on the fact that the reactors at Ignalina are of the same type as in Chernobyl. Protesters were also concerned with possible negative effects of cooling water from the plant on a nearby lake. In 1989, construction on the third reactor was also stopped.

The energy enterprise in Lithuania, Litovenergo, is organised in the same way as Estonenergo and Latvenergo. It has about 14,000 employees and is one of the largest enterprises in Lithuania. In contrast to Estonenergo and Latvenergo, which still have strong ties to all-union authorities, Litovenergo is virtually working as a republican enterprise. It runs all the thermal- and hydro-power plants in the republics with the exception of the nuclear-power plant at Ignalina. In 1990, it produced 11.2 TWh of electricity and 21 TWh of heat. Litovenergo supplies 40 per cent of the total electricity production in Lithuania, distributes electricity to all consumers in the republic and provides about half of the heat production.

In 1990, industry accounted for 52 per cent of total electricity consumption in Lithuania, households and service 26 per cent and agricultural production used 22 per cent. The largest industrial consumers during the same year were the machine-building, chemical, and building-material industries.

Total heat production in Lithuania was about 40 TWh in 1990. Almost a third of the produced heat is provided by combined heat and power plants. There are more than 8,000 boilers in Lithuania used for heat production. Roughly half of the heat supply is provided by Litovenergo, which in turn gets nearly half of its produced heat from its thermal-power plants. Of the total heat production 38 per cent comes from industrial boilers, 6 per cent from other boilers and 4 per cent from heat pumps. Industry is the major heat consumer. It uses about half of the total consumption, households and service consume 28 per cent, agriculture 8 per cent and other sectors 7 per cent (see Table 14.7).

D. Energy management in transition

Until recently, the energy distribution system in the Baltic republics was almost completely under Soviet control, supervised by the all-union ministry for electricity and energy, Minenergo. Most of the previous links between all-union and republican organisations still exist but are changing their relevance for the energy management in the republics. Simultaneously, the Baltic governments are establishing their own energy ministries.

There are two major explanations for the current situation. One involves the increasing difficulty the Soviet Union is experiencing in maintaining energy production at previous levels. The other is the Baltic republics' ambition to control their own energy supply and use. The first signs of change

Table 14.7 Heat production and consumption

	Estonia	Latvia		Lithuania	
	1985	1985	1990[1]	1985	1990[1]
Produced heat (TWh)	23.2	35.9	37.8	40.3	40.0
By producers Eston/Latv/Litov-					
energo (%)	36.9	24.9	23.4	54.4	52.6
Industry	63.1	—	37	38.2	37.2
Other	—	75.1[3]	40	7.5	10.2
Disribution losses[2]					
(TWh)	0.6	0.9	0.8	1.4	1.4
(%)	2.6	2.5	2.1	3.5	3.5
Gross consumption[2]					
(TWh)	22.6	35.0	37.0	38.9	38.6
By consumer (%)					
Industry	56	44.7	44.3	57.2	51.8
Residential and					
service	28	46.4	46.2	28.8	28.1
Agriculture	9	2.3	2.5	7.6	8.4
Transport	3	1.3	1.3	2.1	2.7
Construction	4	0.7	0.9	4.3	4.5
Other	—	4.6	4.8	—	4.5

[1] Preliminary figures.
[2] There are no exact figures for total losses by heat distribution. These figures are obviously too low. Baltic energy researchers estimate the total losses as at least 20 per cent.
[3] Including industry.

Source: Sirje Pädam, *Energy and Environment in Estonia*, Stockholm, 1990; *Energeticheskaya programma Latvii*, Riga, 1990; Lithuanian Ministry of Energy.

came in 1988 when republican committees for fuel and energy were created in the Baltic republics. This was in accordance with the Soviet economic policy of that time to increase energy efficiency by devolving some of Minenergos's responsibilities to the republican level. However, as the economic situation in the Soviet Union deteriorated further, it became increasingly obvious that decentralisation alone could not solve the difficult energy-supply problem.

The worsening conditions in the Soviet Union compelled the Baltic governments to reinforce the role of the republican energy management. After the parliamentary elections and the independence declarations in the spring of 1990, the new governments in Estonia, Latvia and Lithuania decided to abolish the committees and create their own energy ministries. (In Estonia, the Ministry of Industry has a department of energy headed by a deputy minister.) The intention is to establish energy ministries working more or less in the same way as their counterparts in Western countries, that is mainly making policy and implementing regulating measures.

So far, the Baltic energy ministries' main occupation has been supervising the production and distribution of electricity and heat as well as securing the supply of fuels to the republics. Basically, they have taken over the functions previously executed by all-union ministries on their territory.

In Lithuania, the major enterprise Litovenergo is now operating independently from Moscow, it pays taxes to Lithuania and is formally subordinated to the Lithuanian Ministry of Energy. The Lithuanian government has announced that it is preparing to make Litovenergo self-financing, cutting subsidies to it later in 1991. The ministry has very limited influence over the nuclear-power plant in Ignalina. The refinery in Mazeikiai is formally subordinated to the ministry, following its directives regarding deliveries of refined products and price levels but is still influenced by Moscow.

In Latvia, the former all-union enterprise Latvenergo is paying its taxes to Latvia, although its relation to the Latvian Ministry of Energy is not quite clear. The management of the enterprise have expressed their willingness to cooperate with the ministry but are keeping the contacts with the all-union Minenergo in order to secure deliveries of certain equipment.

The Estonian Department of Energy seems to be the weakest of the Baltic energy authorities. It has good relations with Estonenergo, the largest electricity producer in the Baltic region, but is still too weak to manage an enterprise of that size. Estonenergo, in its turn, has been forced to maintain strong links with Minenergo, since the management of the thermal-power plants in Narva is mainly in the hands of Russians opposed to the government in Tallinn.

Thus, at present, one major concern of the energy ministries in the Baltic republics is to establish clear relations with the former all-union energy enterprises on their territory in order to ensure effective energy production. Another problem for the ministries is to secure the supply of fuels for power plants, enterprises, petrol stations and so on. Previously, supply lines were organised through all-union ministries. Enterprises used to get specific annual quotas of oil, natural gas, coal and other fuels, on the basis of which they could plan their production. Now, because of Moscow's declining influence over energy supply in the Soviet Union, the Baltic governments must help enterprises get their energy inputs. There is simply nobody else doing it for them.

One of the first economic measures introduced by the new Baltic energy ministries was to adjust energy prices. Until 1989, energy prices were controlled by the Soviet government and were more or less the same in all parts of the Soviet Union. Since 1990, price control has gradually loosened as individual regions and enterprises in different parts of the union have developed barter agreements with each other, resulting in fuel price increases. The unstable price situation in the Soviet Union has forced the Baltic governments to increase energy prices.

On 1 January 1991, Estonia increased the price of electricity from 1 kopek to an average of 5 kopeks per kWh for enterprises and 4 kopeks for other users. At the same time, the average price for heat rose from 10 roubles to 23–6 roubles per Gigacalory (Gcal) for enterprises, and from 3.9 to 7.0

roubles/Gcal for private users. The new price of electricity is roughly equal to costs as of January 1991, while the actual cost for producing heat is estimated at 20 roubles/Gcal.

The price of electricity exported from Estonia to Leningrad and Pskov areas is subject to dispute between the Estonian and Soviet governments. The Soviet side, essentially represented by Minenergo, has refused to pay the higher price of five kopeks demanded by the Estonians, thus resulting in substantial losses on Estonian exports of electricity to Russia. Estonenergo claims that even a price of 5 kopeks would be too low to cover actual production cost. Higher prices for raw materials and increasing wage costs make electricity production more and more expensive. On 1 January 1991, the Estonian government increased the price for oil-shale by more than 300 per cent to 16.7 roubles per ton.

Latvia also increased prices of electricity and heat on 1 January 1991. The average price of electricity rose from 2.4 to 6.4 kopeks per kilowatt-hour, whereas the price of heat jumped from 3.3 to 35–40 roubles/Gcal. In Lithuania the electricity price has been 5.0 kopeks since the beginning of 1991. Prices of fuels have risen by several hundred per cent. For instance, the price of coal increased by up to 500 per cent.

Another reason for the substantial price increases for energy in Estonia, Latvia and Lithuania is the Baltic governments' intention to make energy use more efficient. Although no exact figures are available, rough estimates suggest that energy intensity (energy used per output) is up to three times higher than in developed market economies. Huge losses of energy occur in heat distribution. For instance, residential buildings in Estonia use about four times more heat per square metre than those in Sweden or Finland (which have a climate similar to that of Estonia).

E. Conclusions

The possibilities for the Baltic states to improve their energy situation in the next few years are limited. Energy supply from the Soviet Union is becoming increasingly unreliable. The former centrally supervised supply system is virtually not working any more. Oil and coal production is likely to fall by up to 20 per cent in 1991, and output of natural gas will be difficult to increase. Soviet energy producers at local levels have started to trade directly with different parts of the union. The energy ministries in Estonia, Latvia and Lithuania must negotiate continuously with different ministries in Moscow as well as energy producers all over the Soviet Union to secure deliveries of different energy products. In the spring of 1991, the situation was not yet critical. Power plants and boilers for central heating were getting the supply they needed; petrol was available although rationed. However, in spite of the efforts of the Baltic governments to secure an energy supply for the rest of the year, there is no guarantee that deliveries will be sufficient to cover the needs in the three republics.

Obviously, a crucial factor in the future energy situation in Estonia, Latvia and Lithuania will be their relations with the Soviet Union until some kind of general agreement on the economic–political relations between the Baltic republics and the Soviet Union is reached, the room for manoeuvre of the republics is strictly limited. At present, both administrations and enterprises in the three republics seem to be awaiting new initiatives from Moscow. This state of 'wait and see' is paralysing much of the work needed to change the energy policy in the Baltic countries.

Occupied with daily concerns to secure energy supply, the Baltic energy administrations have had little time to develop and implement a long-term energy supply strategy. In spite of these difficulties, energy programmes for the period until 1995 have been worked out in all three republics. Estonia has already approved its programme, while draft versions are being discussed in Latvia and Lithuania. Basically, the programmes have similar contents. They state the need to reduce dependence on energy imports from the Soviet Union, to develop domestic resources, to stimulate energy conservation throughout the economy by higher energy prices and new technology and to establish an infrastructure for future energy imports from other parts of the world. They also point out the need to reduce air pollution from power plants in accordance with the international agreements signed by the Soviet Union concerning the period until 1995. The programmes elaborate different scenarios for future energy consumption and give detailed suggestions for investments in new capacity and technology as well as modernisation of existing power plants and distribution networks.

Despite the awareness in the Baltic republics of their serious energy situation, few steps have so far been taken to change the economic conditions influencing energy use. It is still too early to judge whether the price increases for energy products introduced at the beginning of this year will have any effect. Most probably, energy consumption will decrease in 1991, but as a result of supply shortages and falling industrial production rather than a more effective energy use. Enterprises are still working in a supply-constrained market and are faced with soft budget constraints. This makes them more or less indifferent to price increases for energy. To this could be added the influence of 'the social factor'; governments are reluctant to close down energy-wasting or unprofitable enterprises, since they fear the effects of unemployment. Furthermore, even if an enterprise wanted to decrease its energy consumption, it is dependent on equipment and investments that are allocated from the organisation or ministry to which it is subordinated.

A major problem for the energy sector is that in technical terms the energy production and distribution system is worn out and highly inefficient. Moreover, the resources needed for energy conservation are missing or in short supply — such as insulation material and metres or regulators for electricity and heat consumption. Information and training on how to use energy more efficiently are virtually non-existent. The infrastructure and strategies needed for a better energy economy have yet to be developed. Both the demand for new capacity and equipment and the need to develop a new approach to energy conservation will require large investments over a considerable period of years. Considerable effort must also be made in order to improve the quality of energy statistics. Without reliable data on energy use, it will be difficult to improve efficiency.

These general difficulties are the same for all the Baltic states. However, there are also geographical and technical differences between the three republics which may influence them when considering possible ways of restructuring their energy system.

In the short term, Estonia seems to be in the best position to manage its energy situation. By world standards, oil-shale energy is costly and thus would probably be uneconomic at world prices for inputs and outputs. Nevertheless, thanks to its domestic resources of oil-shale, Estonia can cover its electricity demand and part of its heat production through its own means.

From a longer-term perspective, Estonia's energy situation does not look too positive. First, Estonia must import all motor fuel and most of the fuel for heat production. Researchers at the Estonian Academy of Sciences have estimated that, calculated in actual world market prices, the net Estonian energy imports in 1989 would have cost approximately US$ 500 million.

The power plants at Narva are based on old technology and some of their blocks are already worn out. The quality of the oil-shale is decreasing, making it more expensive to maintain electricity production. Moreover, mining costs are increasing each year. Closely linked to this problem are the ecological consequences of oil-shale use. The northeastern part of Estonia where the oil-shale is mined is the most polluted area in the Baltic republics. The water balance of this area is seriously threatened by the expansion of pits and mines for oil-shale. An even more acute problem is air pollution from the thermal-power plants. To satisfy international requirements on emission reductions, Estonia will probably have to decrease its output of electricity.

The need for new equipment and deteriorating environmental conditions will require large investments in the next few years. Even if such investments were to be secured, the oil-shale industry will hardly be economically sustainable for more than 10–15 years. After the turn of the century, the importance of oil-shale for the energy balance of Estonia is likely to diminish quickly.

The restructuring of the oil-shale industry in Estonia might turn out to be a difficult process. The oil-shale provides the single base for energy and the petrochemical industry. In 1989, these two industrial branches accounted for 17 per cent of all industrial production, 32 per cent of fixed industrial assets and 15 per cent of industrial employment. Most of the workers engaged in oil-shale production are Russians.

Latvia has the most acute energy situation of the Baltic republics because of its dependence on fuel *and* electricity imports. Converted to world market prices, Latvia's total energy imports are estimated as at least US$ 1,000 million per year. Electricity from Estonia may not be available in the future, maybe as soon as 1992, and it is not clear whether this loss can be compensated for by imports from Lithuania. The constrained electricity supply calls for new generation capacity in Latvia which in turn requires investment and imported equipment.

In terms of future negotiations with the Soviet Union on energy supply, Latvia has a bargaining counter in the port of Ventspils, through which substantial Soviet oil exports flow. A first step could be that the Soviet

Union guarantees Latvia energy products in exchange for the oil transit via Ventspils. Similar agreements already exist for Soviet gas exports to the West through Czechoslovakia. At present, the Soviet government seems unwilling to conclude such agreements. However, in the long term, it could pay for both the Soviet and Latvian side if the management of the Ventspils port was made independent and self-financing. For example, the port could charge the Soviet oil exporter for its services and then pay taxes to the Latvian budget. The Latvian government would then guarantee the maintenance of the pipelines and railways through its territory.

Over a longer term, Lithuania may have the most favourable position of the Baltic republics. It produces a large surplus of electricity, it has the only refinery in the Baltic region on its territory and it has access to one of the best ports on the Baltic Sea. Moreover, all transport of energy products to Kaliningrad goes through Lithuania.

Notwithstanding these advantages, Lithuania has some key issues to solve in the immediate future. In the short term, the most complicated issue for Lithuania is the nuclear-power plant in Ignalina. The electricity export from it is of crucial importance for Belorussia. Because of this, the Soviet Union does not wish to lose its control over Ignalina. However, Ignalina provides Lithuania with about 40 per cent of its electricity consumption. Without doubt, both the Soviet and Lithuanian sides are interested in maintaining the production at Ignalina. However, since the reactors at the plant are of the same type as those at Chernobyl, they will hardly be able to be used after the turn of the century without being reconstructed.

Much like the Ventspils port in Latvia, the refinery in Mazeikiai and the port of Klaipeda are likely to be the subject of negotiations between Lithuania and the Soviet government. The Soviet Union has a shortage of refining capacity and is interested in certain products from Mazeikiai, mainly fuel for airplanes. On the other hand, the Soviet Union could also stop the supply of crude oil to the refinery in case of an economic or political conflict. Since Mazeikiai also provides the Baltic states with motor fuels and other refined products, disturbances in Soviet deliveries of crude oil to the Lithuanian refinery would seriously affect Baltic fuel supply.One option is to use the port in Klaipeda (or the Latvian port of Ventspils) for oil imports, so Mazeikiai could buy crude oil from the world market. However, such a project would require investments and equipment from abroad.

Bibliography

There is a striking lack of international literature on the Baltic states. That is reflected in this bibliography, which mainly contains statistical publications in Estonian, Latvian, Lithuanian and Russian. Most of the information related in this book is taken from these publications and from other material gathered in interviews. The governments of the Baltic states and international financial institutions are at present compiling new data on the economic situation. That work will provide a significantly better database than was available at the time of research for the present book.

On the Baltic economies, Philip Hanson's review for the Economist's Intelligence Unit was particularly helpful, as was the manuscript of Per Sandström's book in Swedish, *Baltiskt dilemma*, which was generously shared with the team. For historical reference, the main sources were the books by von Rauch, mainly on the pre-war period, and by Misiunas and Taagepera.

Two general studies on the Soviet economy were used as references: one by the IMF, the World Bank, the EBRD and the OECD, and one by the Commission of the European Communities, both conducted in late 1990.

Apkartejas vides aizsardziba un dabas resursu racionala izmantosana Latvija. (Riga: Latvijas republikas valsts statistikas komiteja, 1990).
Argumenty i Fakty, no. 50, 1989.
Asilis, C. and Brown, S., 'Efficiency and Stability of Decentralized versus Centrally Arbitrated Regional Reform in the Soviet Union: the Non-Interventionist Case'. Department of Economics, Georgetown University, Working Paper no 90-22, 1990.
Balodis, A., *Lettlands och det lettiska folkets historia.* (Stockholm: Lettiska nationella fonden, 1990).
Baltic Council on Cooperation Commission. *On Work in the Baltic Council on Cooperation.* (Tallinn, Riga and Vilnius, December 1990).
Brown, S. and Belkindas, M., 'Who's Feeding Whom? A Balance of Payments Approach to Soviet Interrepublic Relations'. Manuscript, Department of Economics, Georgetown University, 1991.
Byulleten' IME. (Tallinn: Institute for Economic Development. Various issues, 1989–90).
Cepenas, P., *Naujuju laiku Lietuvos istorija, I-II.* (Chicago: Isleido Dr. Kazio Griniaus Fondas, 1977, 1986).
Commission of the European Communities. *Stabilization, Liberalization and Devolution. Assessment of the Economic Situation and Reform Process in the Soviet Union.* (Brussels: European Economy No. 75, 1990).
Darbo statistikos matrastis. (Department of Statistics, Vilnius: 1990).
Demograficheskiy ezhegodnik SSSR 1990. (Moscow: Finansy i statistika, 1990).
Dokumenty o mnogostoronnem i dvustoronnem sotrudnichestve Estonskoi Respubliki. (Tallinn, 1991).
Eesti NSV rahva-majandus. Statistika aastaraamat 1988. (Tallinn: Olion, 1989).
Eesti statistika aastaraamat 1990. (Tallinn: Olion, 1991).

342   *Sectoral issues*

Ekonomicheskoe i sotsial'noe razvitie soyuznykh respublik. (Moscow: Finansy i statistika, 1990).

Ekonomika Estonii v 1991 godu (prognoz i iskhodnye polozheniya deyatel'nosti pravitel'stva). (Unpublished material. Estonian Ministry of Economics, November 1990).

Energetika respublik Pribaltiki, Belorussii i severo-zapada RSFSR. (Tallinn: Institut termofiziki i elektrofiziki AN, 1990).

Energy in Estonia, Latvia and Lithuania. Energy Efficiency and Technology Transfer. Ministry of Industry and Energetics, Estonia; Ministry of Energy, Latvia; and Ministry of Energy, Lithuania. (Tallinn, Riga and Vilnius, 1991).

Environment '89. (Tallinn: Estonian Nature Management Scientific Information Centre, 1990).

Fenhann, Jørgen (ed.): Energy and environment in Estonia, Latvia and Lithuania. (Risø, 1991).

Finansu statistikos metrastis. (Vilnius: Statistikos departamentas prie Lietuvos respublikos vyriausybes, 1990).

Gamtonauda ir gamtosauga Lietuvoje (1989 m. pagrindiniai rodikliai). (Vilnius: Lietuvos valstybinis gamtos apsaugos komitetas, 1990).

Goldenberg, L., 'Otdel'nye voprosy razrabotki i analiza pokazateli vvoza i vyvoza produktsiy po dannim mezhotraslego balansa'. (Manuscript. Goskomstat, Soviet Union, 1990).

Grahm, L. and Königsson, L., 'Baltic Industry'. (Manuscript. Göteborg, 1991).

Greimas A. and Zukas, S., 'Les Pays baltes: la Lithuanie'. Manuscript. To be published in a French encyclopedia.

Hanson, P., 'Property Rights in the New Phase of Reforms'. *Soviet Economy.* (6, no. 2 (1990), pp. 95–125).

Hanson, P., 'The Baltic States. The economic and political implications of the secession of Estonia, Latvia and Lithuania from the USSR'. *The Economist Intelligence Unit Briefing, Special Report No 2033.* (London: 1990).

Hanson, P., 'External economic relations of the Baltic states'. (Manuscript to an article to be published in the *Economic Bulletin for Europe*, No. 43, November 1991, United Nations Economic Commission for Europe, New York.

Horm, P., 'Some notes on the Estonian economy'. (Unpublished paper, 1990).

Iedzivotaju dabiska kustiba un migracija Latvijas republika 1989. gada, statistikas biletens. (Riga: Latvijas republikas valsts statistikas komiteja, 1990).

IMF, World Bank, OECD and EBRD. *A Study of the Soviet Economy.* (Paris, 1991).

Kapital'noe stroitel'stvo SSSR. Statisticheskiy sbornik. (Moscow: Finansy i statistika, 1988).

Kukk, Kalev, 'Polmilliarda v dolg'. *Vecherniy Tallinn.* (13 January 1988).

Latvian Republic Economic and Demographic Information. (Unpublished material. Latvian Ministry of Economics, 1990).

Latvija citu valstu saime. (Riga: Zinatne, 1990) (Reprint of *Ibid.*, Riga: Armijas spiestuve, 1939).

Latvijas PSR tautas saimnieciba, 1988. gada, statistikas gadagramata. (Riga: Avots, 1989).

Latvija skaitlos 1989. gada. (Riga: Latvijas republikas valsts statistikas komiteja, 1990).

Latvija sodien, socialekonomisku aprakstu krajums. (Riga: Latvijas PSR valsts statistikas komiteja, 1990).

Latvijas tautas saimnieciba, statistikas gadagramata '89. (Riga: Avots, 1990).

Lietuviskoji enciklopedja XV. (Chicago: 1968).

Lietuvos gyventojai, statistikos rinkinys. (Vilnius: Statistikos departamentas prie Lietuvos respublikos vyriausybes, 1990).
Lietuvos socialine ir ekonomine raida 1990 metais. (Vilnius: Statistikos departamentas prie Lietuvos respublikos vyriausybes, 1991).
Lietuvos statistikos metrastis, 1989 metai. (Vilnius: Lietuvos statistikos departamentas, 1990).
Lietuvos TSR mokymo istaigos, Statistikos rinkinys. (Vilnius: Lietuvos TSR valstybinis statistikos komitetas, 1990).
Lithuanian Review (The English-language newspaper of Lithuania, 1990, I-VII; 1991, I).
Material'no-tekhnicheskoe obespechenie narodnogo khozyaystva SSSR. (Moscow: Finansy i statistika, 1988).
Miljöteknik i Baltikum samt Leningrad- och Kalinigradområdena. (Stockholm: Sveriges Tekniska Attacheer, Utlandsrapporter, 1990).
Misiunas, R. and Taagepera, R., *The Baltic States. Years of Dependence 1940–1980.* (Berkeley and Los Angeles: University of California Press, 1983).
Mokamos paslaugos gyventojams Lietuvos Respublikoje, 1989 metai, statistinis rinkinys. (Vilnius: Statistikos departamentas prie Lietuvos respublikos vyriausybes, 1990).
Narodnoe khozyaistvo Latvii. (Riga: Avots, 1988).
Narodnoe khozyaistvo SSSR. (Moscow: Finansy i statistika, various years).
Okhrana zdorov'ya v SSSR. (Moscow: Finansy i statistika, 1990).
O korennoy perestroyke upravleniya ekonomikoy. Sbornik dokumentov. (Moscow: Politizdat, 1987).
Otsason, R., Sillaste, Yu. and Truve, E., *Khozyaystvennyi mekhanizm v sfere bytovogo obsuzhivaniya. Opyt Estonskoy SSR.* (Moscow: Ekonomika, 1988).
Oxenstierna, S., *From Labour Shortage to Unemployment?* (Stockholm: Almqvist & Wiksell International, 1990).
Perekhod k rynku. Chast' I. Kontseptsiya i programma. (Moscow: Arkhangel'skoe, 1990).
Politika razvitiya narodnogo khozyaistva Latviskoi respubliki i prognoz na 1991 god. (Unpublished material. Latvian Council of Ministers, November 1990).
Problemy ekonomicheskogo razvitiya sel'skogo khozyaystva Estonskoy SSR. (Tallinn: Valgus, 1980).
Problemy sovershenstvovaniye ekonomicheskikh soyuzi Litovskoy respubliki. (Vilnius: Institute of Economics, Ministry of Economics, 1990).
Purins, V. (ed.), *Latvijas PSR Geografija.* (Riga: Zinatne, 1975).
Pädam, Sirje, *Energy and Environment in Estonia.* (Stockholm: Statens Energiverk, 1990).
Rajasalu, T. *Estonian Economy and its Development Problems.* (Tallinn: Estonian Academy of Sciences, Institute of Economics, Preprint 26, 1990).
Sandström, P., *Baltiskt Dilemma.* (Stockholm: SNS, 1991).
Sotsial'noe razvitie Litvy v 1989 godu. (Vilnius, 1990).
Sotsial'noe razvitie SSSR. (Moscow: Finansy i statistika, 1989 and 1990).
Statisticheskii ezhegodnik Estonii 1990. (Tallinn: Department of Statistics, 1990).
Statisticheskii ezhegodnik Litvy 1989. (Vilnius: Department of Statistics, 1990).
Sveikatos apsauga Lietuvos, statistikos rinkinys. (Vilnius: Statistikos departamentas prie Lietuvos respublikos vyriausybes, 1990).
Trud v SSSR. (Moscow: Finansy i statistika, 1988).
Vestnik statistiki, nos 3 and 4, 1990. (Moscow).
Von Rauch, G., *The Baltic States. The Years of Independence. Estonia, Latvia, Lithuania, 1917–1940.* (London: C. Hurst & Co. Ltd., 1974).

Raun, T., *Estonia and the Estonians*. (Stanford, California: Hoover Institution Press, 1987).

Zinojums par Latvijas republikas tautas saimniecibas attistibu 1990. gada. (Riga: Latvijas valsts statistikas komiteja, 1991).

IV Tallinskoe soveshchanie glav i predstaviteley pravitel'stv. Dokumenty zasedaniya 14–15 fevralya 1991 goda, g. Tallinn. (Tallinn: Konsul'tativniy komitet pravitel'stv, 1991).

NMLFF

We hope you enjoy this book. Please return or renew it by the due date.

You can renew it at www.norfolk.gov.uk/libraries or by using our free library app.

Otherwise you can phone 0344 800 8020 - please have your library card and PIN ready.

You can sign up for email reminders too.

22/7